D1374002

THE CITY OF LONDON

By the same author

Covent Garden (Abelard-Schuman)
The British Hotel Through the Ages (Lutterworth)
Two Villages – The Story of Chelsea and Kensington (W. H. Allen)
The Years of Grandeur – The Story of Mayfair (W. H. Allen)
Hampstead and Highgate – The Story of Two Hilltop Villages (W. H. Allen)
Background to Archaeology (Pelham)
Willingly to School – A History of Women's Education (Lutterworth)

THE
CITY OF LONDON
A HISTORY

Mary Cathcart Borer

David McKay Company, Inc.
New York

Contents

Acknowledgements

I am most grateful to the superintendents of Smithfield, Billingsgate and Spitalfields markets for their generous help in the preparation of the chapter on The City Food Markets and to Mr Derek Walker of the Baltic Exchange, Mr Richard Keene of Lloyd's, Mr Stanley Jones of the Corn Exchange, Mrs D. Mayne of the Tea Brokers' Association of London, Mr Ivan Robinson and Mr Eric Foote of Brooke-Bond's and Mr Kenyon of the British Fur Trade Association for their kindness and help in the writing of the chapter on The Commodity Markets.

M.C.B.

Illustrations

Frontispiece: Ludgate Hill – a block in the street. Gustave Doré, 1872

I

The Roman City

The City of London has existed for nearly 2,000 years. Beneath its modern pavements lie the relics of its eighteenth-century counting houses and exchanges, warehouses and coffee houses, remains of the London which was devastated by the Great Fire of 1666, of Tudor London, the London of the Plantagenets and Normans, the Angles and Saxons, and beneath them all, some fifteen or twenty feet below the present ground level, the scattered remnants of its founders, the Romans, and the Celtic inhabitants of Britain whom they conquered.

It was only some 7,000 or 8,000 years before the arrival of the Romans that the British Isles became separated from the mainland of Europe, as the land level of the north-western part of the continent slowly sank and the waters flowed in to form the North Sea and the English Channel. From this time the river Thames was no longer a tributary of the Rhine but a waterway winding deep into the heart of the southern part of the newly-formed Britain, a country of dense forests and woodland, desolate heaths and moors and miles of marshland, through which roamed a population of perhaps some 10,000 souls, a primitive, hunting people living in a stone age of culture.

Very slowly, over the centuries, small numbers of immigrants from the mainland of Europe faced the hazards of the Channel crossing and arrived in their frail craft on the shores of Britain, some to explore, some to settle, bringing with them the developing skills and cultures which were evolving in western Asia and eastern Europe and slowly infiltrating westwards. Yet life moved with infinite slowness, for the connection with Europe was tenuous and these mist-shrouded islands on the distant edge of the known world remained a region of mystery, wide tracts of them still unexplored and un-inhabited.

By about 4,000 B.C. the people of Britain had acquired the arts and crafts of the New Stone Age. They had become farmers, having learnt the skills of agriculture and domesticated the farmyard animals, but their tools were still of stone and wood and their drinking and cooking vessels of hand-made baked clay. Another 2,000 years passed before a new wave of immigrants

brought the art of metal working. These newcomers, descended from a
mixed strain of Nordic tribes and people from the Iberian peninsula, were a
race of farmers and stock-breeders. They were the builders of Stonehenge
and Avebury and they found the tin and copper resources of Britain to make
their bronze tools and weapons.

The Bronze Age in Britain, beginning about 2,000 B.C., lasted for some 1,500
years, during which time the population of Europe gradually increased. By
about 900 to 800 B.C. more immigrants arrived in Britain, the Celts, who had
wandered from the east through Europe to Gaul. They came first in small
family groups and then in ever-increasing numbers, until whole tribes were
arriving. From Holland and Belgium they landed in eastern and north-eastern
Britain, from northern France they reached the south and south-east of the
country.

They were belligerent, dominant barbarians, with a tribal organisation, and
having acquired a knowledge of the use of iron, they were quickly able, by
virtue of their superior weapons and agricultural implements, to establish
themselves as a British aristocracy. They rode horses and introduced the use
of the wheel, which they had adapted from the Etruscans. Carts and chariots
were seen for the first time in Britain and eventually the potter's wheel.

The population of the country rose to perhaps a quarter of a million during
these years of the Celtic occupation, and it has been estimated that by now
about one-sixth of the country was inhabited, although the deep forests of the
midlands were still hardly penetrated.

The Celts were artists and their gold and silver jewellery and bronze armour,
helmets and shields were beautifully wrought, often inlaid with brilliantly
coloured enamels and incised with strange, curvilinear patterns, but their
religion was savage and brutal, little more than a highly developed animism.
They made human sacrifices to the gods of springs and rivers, mountains and
forests. Their priests were the Druids, who used the existing Bronze Age temples for their own purposes and wielded a harsh and terrible power, performing
sacrificial massacres in the secrecy of their sacred groves, hidden away in the
depths of the forests.

The wealth and strength of the Celts depended on trade and there was a
ready market in Europe for iron from the Forest of Dean and tin from Cornwall. They were ready to do battle for them, fighting not only the indigenous
people of Britain but any of their own tribes who seemed to be acquiring an
unfairly large proportion of the spoils. They went naked into battle, painting
themselves blue with the dye from the yellow woad flower, and prisoners of
war were made slaves in the households of their captors or offered as sacrificial
victims to the Druids.

The 500 years before the birth of Christ were a time of turbulence throughout the whole of Europe, but the Celts of Britain maintained a desultory but valuable trade, sending metals, furs, salt and slaves to the Mediterranean countries in exchange for fine pottery, bronze wine vessels and quantities of Mediterranean wine, for which they seem to have had an inordinate thirst, and it was during these years of the British Iron Age that Britain was first mentioned by the contemporary classical historians.

As early as 325 B.C. the Greek explorer Pytheas wrote of Britain. Herodotus referred to 'the islands where the tin comes from' and in the first century B.C. Diodorus described the skill and organisation of the Cornish tin miners. The miners, he said, prepared the tin, cast it into cubes and carried it in carts at low tide to St Michael's Mount, where the Gaulish traders bought it, transported it to Gaul and 'finally, travelling through Gaul on foot, in about thirty days' brought 'their burdens to the mouth of the Rhone'.

With the passing years and the development of more effective and murderous weapons, the Celts on the mainland of Europe grew increasingly aggressive. They invaded northern Italy and threatened Rome before they were driven back. About 75 B.C. there were fresh Celtic invasions of south-eastern Britain from Gaul of the most advanced of their tribes, the Belgae, who fought with swords and spears from wheeled chariots and no longer painted themselves with woad.

Other Celtic tribes in Britain at this time were the Trinovantes, sworn enemies of the Belgae, who were entrenched in Essex and eastern Hertfordshire, the Iceni in Norfolk, the Dobunni in the Cotswolds, the Domnonii in Cornwall, the Ordovices and the Silures in Wales and the Marches, the Parisii and the Brigantes in Yorkshire, all politically independent of each other: and the Belgae established themselves in Kent and the western part of Hertfordshire.

In 59 B.C. Julius Caesar, whose armies were now masters of the Mediterranean and southern Gaul, determined to subdue the rest of Gaul and rout the troublesome Belgae. As Caesar's conquering armies advanced, the defeated Belgae fled across the Channel to join their kinsmen in Kent. Caesar prepared to follow them. He assembled a fleet of more than a hundred ships and an army of 10,000 legionaries and cavalry, and in August, 55 B.C. the Roman armada set sail from Portus Itius (Boulogne) for the Kentish coast. They had difficulty in finding a suitable landing place. A sudden storm blew up, so that the cavalry transports were delayed in Boulogne for a few days. The army eventually landed and the cavalry set sail, but another violent storm arose and they were forced to return to harbour, while the Roman transport ships, riding at anchor or beached on the Kentish coast near Deal, were battered and broken by the wind and waves.

'A number of ships were shattered, and the rest, having lost their cables, anchors and the remainder of their tackle, were unusable, which naturally threw the whole army into great consternation,' recorded Caesar.

Hastily the craft were repaired and after a few minor skirmishes with the Celts, Caesar ordered a retreat to Gaul, in order to prepare for a second landing the following year. The campaign of 54 B.C. was more successful, although by no means decisive. The Roman armies captured the Belgic encampment near Canterbury, but the Belgae retreated across the Thames to join Cassivellaunus, chief of the Hertfordshire Belgae. Caesar, with the help of the Trinovantes, discovered and captured his camp near Wheathampstead, a wide stretch of flat land surrounded by forests and marsh and fortified by a rampart and ditch, but during this operation the Romans came dangerously near to being cut off by the Kentish Belgae, who attacked their coastal base. However, Caesar saved the situation and within a few weeks had come to terms with the Belgae, optimistically exacting an annual tribute and forbidding them to extend their territory, neither of which agreements were the Belgae to keep for long. Thereupon Caesar departed from Britain to finish his work in Gaul.

In Britain the struggle for supremacy amongst the Celtic tribal chieftains continued. The enmity between the Belgae and the Trinovantes was bitter and when the Atrebates arrived from Gaul and settled to the west of the Belgic territory, the Belgae watched them jealously and built a fortress where the city of Winchester was later to arise, as an outpost from which to keep the advance of the newcomers in check.

For the next 50 years the three regions of the southern part of Britain, the countries of the Atrebates, the Belgae and the Trinovantes, lived in rivalry, but their people cultivated the land and gradually cleared the forests, while trade with the countries of the Roman Empire continued and slowly developed. Strabo, writing towards the end of the first century B.C., said that Britain 'produces corn, cattle, gold, silver, iron. All these are exported, together with hides, slaves and dogs useful for hunting . . . there are four crossings in common use between the island and the continent, namely from the mouths of the Rhine, the Seine, the Loire and the Garonne. Those who cross from the Rhineland do not start out from the river estuary but from . . . Portus Itius [Boulogne] which Caesar used as a naval base. . . .'

In A.D. 10 Cunobelin – Shakespeare's Cymbeline – the great-grandson of Cassivellaunus, was chief of the Belgae, ruling from his stronghold which was to become the Roman city of Verulamium and later St Albans. He invaded the country of the Trinovantes and captured their encampment at the mouth of the river Colne, where the city of Colchester was to arise. This was a collection of widely scattered huts stretching over an area of several hundred

acres and protected by a defensive system of dykes. The chief of the Trinovantes was forced to flee with his family and eventually reached Rome, where
he sought the protection of the Emperor Augustus. Cymbeline now controlled
a kingdom which stretched from Kent to the frontier of the Iceni in East
Anglia. northwards to include Hertfordshire, Northamptonshire and Oxford-
shire, and as far west as the frontier of the Atrebates. He chose Colchester as
his capital, from which, by way of the Colne, he was able to conduct his
expanding trade, receiving now glass and delicate jewellery as well as red-
glazed pottery and jars of southern wine, in exchange for British corn, cattle,
hides, gold, iron, silver and slaves. At the height of his power and wealth he
turned westwards to attack the Atrebates and marched victoriously through
Sussex, Hampshire and Dorset, capturing Maiden Castle, the ancient iron-age
hill fortress which had been built on the site of a Neolithic barrow.

Cymbeline ruled his large kingdom with a strong hand, but when he died
in A.D. 40, the organisation collapsed. He had been on friendly terms with the
Romans, but his son Caratacus, who succeeded him, hated them and the
country fell into a state of anarchy, as the uncontrolled Belgae marauded
murderously through the countryside. The ruling family of the Atrebates,
like the Trinovantes before them, fled to Rome. The Emperor Claudius had
succeeded Augustus. He listened to their story and decided that the time had
come to conquer the turbulent Britons and bring the country, with its valuable and as yet hardly tapped resources, to order within the Empire

In A.D. 43, with Aulus Plautius in command, a Roman army, some 40,000
strong, including men from many countries of the Empire, who were also
engineers and craftsmen, set sail from Portus Itius for the Kentish coast, many
of them fearful of what they might encounter in this distant island, of which
even yet so little was known beyond its southern shores.

Their first objective was Colchester. They marched inland to the Medway
crossing, where the defending Belgae were routed and retreated to the Thames.
They crossed the river by a ford where, said Caius Dio, 'it empties into the
ocean and at floodtime forms a lake'. This is the first recorded mention of the
Pool of London. The fleeing Belgae retired towards Colchester. The Romans
crossed to the north bank of the Thames, mostly by a hastily contrived bridge
of rafts, although the German contingent of the army swam across. Here they
paused for a while to await the arrival of the Emperor Claudius with reinforcements. In taking stock of their surroundings, they found that just above the
ford, the little Walbrook stream, flowing from the north, emptied into the
Thames. To the east of the Walbrook valley the river bank was some 30 feet
higher than further downstream, forming a gravel plateau which was the
first rising ground above the marshy estuary. West of the Walbrook, the ground

rose even a few feet higher before sinking to the valley of the Fleet river, which
ran where Farringdon Street now lies.

It was probably during this brief respite in their conquest that the Romans
built the first London Bridge, over which Claudius and his corps of elephants
may well have crossed, in order to lead the triumphal march into Colchester,
although by this time Caratacus had fled to the Silures in South Wales. During
his sixteen days' stay in Britain Claudius received the homage of eleven British
chieftains in the south-east of the country and at the bridge-head on the north
bank of the Thames, by the Celtic ford, a Roman supply base was established,
the beginning of Londinium – the Roman London.

Little is known of this first little bridge-head settlement which grew up round
the banks of the Walbrook, on the eastern hill which today is known as Cornhill, nor is it clear how it received its name. For many years it was assumed
that there was a Celtic settlement on the site, called by the Celts 'Llyn-Din' –
the Hill by the Pool – yet no archaeological remains have been discovered to
suggest that there was a human settlement of any significance here before
Roman times. All that has been conceded, on the evidence of a few pieces of
pre-Claudian imported Italian pottery, found here and in Southwark, is that
'a few prospectors from the Roman world . . . may have built a wharf and a
warehouse somewhere near the site of London Bridge a decade or so before
the legions arrived.'[1]

Colchester was the most important native settlement in south-eastern
Britain, but very soon after their arrival, the Romans seem to have realised
the strategic advantages of the site of London. It was almost at the limit of
tidal waters, which made for the easier handling of heavily laden boats, it
was the first rising ground above the malarial Essex marshes, it could be easily
reached by trading ships from Europe, but was far enough inland to be safe
from marauding sea raiders, and it was on a waterway leading into the heart of
the country.

The first buildings of London were of brick or wattle and daub, the materials
for which were on the spot. The nearest supply of stone was in Kent and the
only stone building known to have been undertaken here in the first years
of the conquest, probably used as an administrative centre, was of Kentish
rag-stone, which was brought to the city by way of the Medway and the
Thames in flat-bottomed barges. It was built along the line of an east–west
Roman road, which today is approximately followed by Lombard Street.

London Wall was not to be built for another two centuries but the settlement may have been surrounded early in its history with an earth rampart
and ditch which have long since disappeared, for the ground level of London

1 Sir Mortimer Wheeler, *Royal Commission on Historical Monuments*, 1928.

was at least fifteen to twenty feet lower during the first century than it is today and was still gradually sinking, causing a great deal of serious flooding in the process, while the Thames was considerably wider, its northern shores being about where the southern side of today's Thames Street now runs.

The first inhabitants of this newly created Roman settlement seem to have been immigrant traders, business men and moneylenders, with their wives and families. They were surrounded by marsh and heath and there was no food supply readily at hand, most of it coming from the farmlands a few miles up-river, but this obvious inconvenience was offset by London's geographical position and its accessibility both by river and sea.

With Colchester and most of south-eastern Britain in their hands, the Romans turned westwards to conquer the rest of the country. By A.D. 47, after a savage struggle, Maiden Castle had fallen. In the face of a barrage of iron-tipped arrows hurled from a *ballista*, the Romans had forced their way up to the huts built outside the eastern gate and set them on fire. Under cover of the smoke they forced their way into the camp and massacred most of the inhabitants, leaving the survivors to bury their dead.

Within three or four years the Romans were in control of all the land south of the Humber and east of the Severn, although in the hills of Yorkshire and Wales they met with stiffer resistance: and while the little city of London gradually developed into a Roman trading centre and storage depot, the engineers set about developing the road system through the forests and across the moors which was essential for the conquest and proper control of the country. Although in remoter parts of the country, some of the roads followed the ancient tracks of the Stone and Iron Age Britons, the most important of them radiated from London and were as straight as the contours of the countryside allowed.

Ermine Street ran almost due north from London to Lincoln and then on to York and the North. Watling Street ran from Dover and the Channel ports to London and from London north-westwards through the Midlands, with branches to Chester in the west and Newcastle and Carlisle to the north. A group of roads served Colchester and the eastern counties and another ran westwards to Silchester and then, by a number of branches, to South Wales.

The Fosse Way, not touching London, ran across the country from north-east to south-west, joining Lincolnshire and Leicestershire with Cirencester, Bath and Exeter, while Akeman Street, running over part of the ancient British track, the Icknield Way, was another road from St Albans, over the Cotswolds to Bath.

Ostorius Scapula, succeeding Plautius as military governor, pursued Caratacus to the Silures' stronghold in South Wales. Caratacus escaped again, fleeing this time to Yorkshire, but here he was betrayed by the Queen of the Brigantes and taken in shackles to Rome.

Ten years later, in A.D. 60, Paulinus was governor. He undertook a campaign in the west to subdue the Silures and then marched north, to rout the remaining Druids, who were making a last stand in the island of Anglesey. As he was about to return to London news reached him that East Anglia was in revolt. Prasatagus, Chief of the Iceni, had recently died and Roman officials had moved into his encampment, probably with the intention of appropriating the land for a Roman settlement, but some brutish Roman soldiers had seized his possessions, flogged his wife Boudicca and raped her daughters. The outraged Iceni tribesmen had rallied to avenge the insult and the neighbouring Trinovantes, smouldering with resentment that some of their land, like that of the Iceni, had been sequestered for the endowment of retired Roman officers, joined forces with them. Together they marched on Colchester and then St Albans and London, burning and destroying each in turn, for while the campaign was being launched against the west and Anglesey, these cities had been left only lightly guarded.

The rebels were merciless – butchering, hanging and crucifying – and they took no prisoners. All that has survived of the first Roman London, discovered by archaeologists deep below the later Roman buildings, are a few charred remains of wattle and daub walls, fragments of tiles and stone walling, scraps of Gaulish pottery and traces of the main east–west road. The destruction must have been almost complete and skulls found in and around the bed of the Walbrook stream may well have been some of the decapitated heads of the victims.

Paulinus took swift revenge. Marching rapidly eastwards, he encountered the rebels somewhere between London and St Albans. Boudicca took poison rather than submit to capture and Paulinus continued to exact such savage punishment on her people that the Emperor Nero, hardly renowned for his humanity, recalled him to Rome, and it was his successor who, adopting more conciliatory methods, gradually restored south-eastern Britain to order again.

During his term of office from A.D. 75–84 Agricola reached as far north as the Scottish highlands, but then turned back, finding neither the country nor the warlike, wild Picts to his liking and seeing in them no interest or profit for Rome.

The official capital of the country was still Colchester, but all the evidence suggests that it was about this time that London, already the focus of the road system, became the centre of the financial administration of the province as well: and as the second Roman London was built it acquired the dignity of the capital city of Britain. Yet we know little of what it was like, for about the year

A.D. 120 London was partially destroyed by a second fire, which was probably accidental, and there are indications that there was also disastrous flooding about this time, when the bed of the Walbrook silted up and overflowed its banks.

In A.D. 122, when the Emperor Hadrian was visiting Britain, he ordered the building of Hadrian's Wall, to mark the northern limit of Roman occupation and hold back the turbulent Picts.

About the same time, or a few years earlier, a large stone fort, covering eleven acres, was built in the north-western corner of the city of London, where later the Cripplegate was to arise, the fort serving as a permanent garrison and also as an accommodation for troops in transit. The walls of the fort were four to five feet thick and it was protected by a bank and ditch eleven feet wide. The main gate opened on to a courtyard with administration offices and officers' quarters and beyond them, neatly aligned along a net-work of streets crossing each other precisely at right angles, were the barracks, granaries, workshops and a hospital.

In the heart of the city the great basilica was built, a vast hall, 500 feet long, which served as a law court and meeting place of the Senate. Its site was across the northern part of Gracechurch Street, where it meets Cornhill, and it stretched from about St Michael's Alley in the middle of Cornhill to the west and as far east as the site of Leadenhall market and Whittington Avenue. Side aisles were separated from the main body of the hall by colonnades and there was a raised recess at one end – the tribune – where the magistrate sat during court hearings.

The remains are, of course, only fragmentary, and there are signs that this basilica may have replaced a smaller one which had been destroyed during the fire of A.D. 120

A few years later the forum was built, attached to the south side of the basilica, a large, open courtyard reaching down to Lombard Street, which served as a market place and exchange and became the heart of the business life of the city, while a street where Gracechurch Street now runs joined the forum to the bridge-head and the riverside docks.

The Roman Britain of which London was the capital was divided into twelve cantons, their capitals being the sites of the old tribal centres. Silchester, for example, was built on the old encampment of the Atrebates. These cities varied in size from as little as thirteen acres to Cirencester's 240 acres, but London, with the gardens of its more luxurious houses, had soon spread over 350 acres and its population by about the end of the second century has been estimated at between 30,000 and 35,000.

In addition to the cantonal capitals, which were the administrative centres

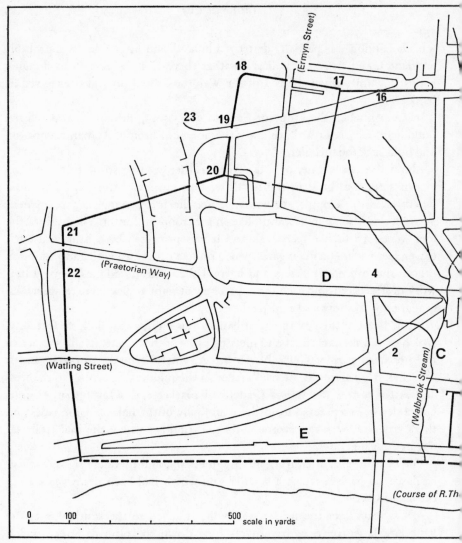

(Ermyn Street)

18

23   19   17

16

20

(Praetorian Way)   D   4

21

22

(Watling Street)   2   C

(Walbrook Stream)

E

(Course of R.Th

0   100   500
scale in yards

ROMAN REMAINS

A Forum and Basilica
B Governor's Palace
C Site of the Temple of
   Mithras on east bank of
   Walbrook Stream
D Site of Roman Baths in
   Cheapside
E Public baths in Huggin
   Hill, Upper Thames Street

1 London Stone
2 Reassembled Temple of
   Mithras in Temple Ct,
   11 Queen Victoria St

3 Geometric mosaics found
   on site of Bank of England
4 3rd-century mosaics found
   in Ironmonger Lane
5 Red tessellated floor, crypt
   of All Hallow's Church
6 Roman house with at-
   tached bath
7 Roman wall, near White
   Tower
8 Roman wall, north side of
   Tower Hill
9 Roman wall, Tower Hill
   Underground Station
10 Roman wall, Trinity Square

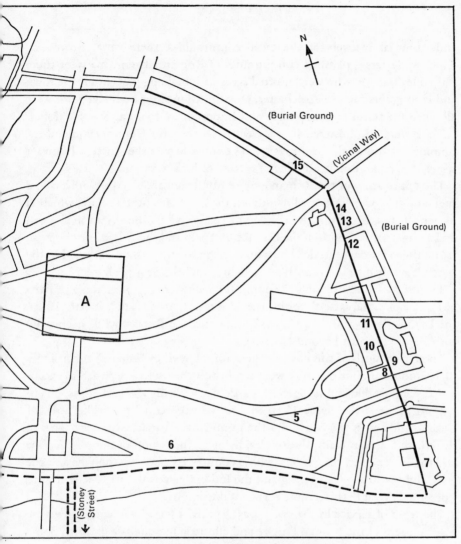

and principal markets of the tribal communities, there were also *coloniae*, which were large, planned communities of Roman citizens, many of them retired legionaries, who were allotted areas with building plots inside the town and land grants outside. Colchester, Lincoln, Gloucester and later York were all given the status of *coloniae* and most important of them all was London.

They were administered by an elected senate who from their members, nominally a hundred, chose magistrates to preside over the senate, administer justice, supervise public building and control local taxation.

The entire army of the Roman empire numbered about 500,000 officers and men and they were stationed mainly on the frontiers of the Empire, which at its zenith stretched from the borders of Persia and the Black Sea in the east and across Europe, south of the Danube, to Spain and the Atlantic in the west. Its southern border included the whole of the North African coast and in the north it reached to the mouth of the Rhine and the Scottish border.

The officers were Roman citizens but the men were recruited from all parts of the Empire, Italy, Gaul, Spain, the Rhineland, Switzerland, North Africa, the Danube lands and Asia Minor, Thrace and also Britain, while eventually barbarians from just beyond the frontiers were also enlisted.

About one-tenth of this cosmopolitan force served in Britain, a surprisingly high proportion, but not only were the British themselves regarded as exceptionally intractable and belligerent, particularly during the early days, but to the north were the fierce Picts, to the west the equally warlike Scots of Ireland, and across the North Sea the primitive, barbarian Germanic tribes of the North German plain, the Angles, living in the region of the middle Elbe and the Weser river, the Saxons, whose country lay between the Elbe and the Ems, and the Jutes of Schleswig and the Jutland peninsula, all of whom were a potential threat to this remote corner of the Empire.

The term of service in the army was 25 years, after which legionaries were made citizens of the Roman Empire and allotted an estate as a gratuity. Some returned to their native lands, but others remained in Britain and married British women. The wealthy built large villas on their country estates, parts of which were cultivated by their slaves and the rest rented to British farmers.

Early in the third century, Britain was divided, for administrative purposes, into two parts, York becoming the capital of the northern province, Britannia Inferior, while London remained the capital of Britannia Superior. During the fourth century the country was further divided into four parts, with Cirencester the capital of Britannia Prima, Lincoln the capital of Flavia Caesariensis, York the capital of Britannia Secunda and London the capital city of Maxima Caesariensis, and some years later a fifth province was added, probably carved from Britannia Secunda, with Carlisle created its capital city.

Though for the most part the British remained farmers and craftsmen, succeeding generations, during the 400 years of the Roman occupation, assimilated the new civilisation of Rome, as in the past they had benefited by the cultures of earlier refugees and invaders. Some, especially in the towns, learnt to read and write Latin. The wealthy built country villas and their way of life was similar to that of the Romans, many of whom, with the passing years, were as racially mixed as themselves. For the peasants, however, life changed little. They still lived in their isolated hamlets of small, round huts, while in the remote west country many had not yet taken to the agricultural innovations of the Belgae, introduced hundreds of years earlier.

Roman London was cosmopolitan, with an upper class comprising people of Italian and Gaulish descent, Spaniards, North Africans, Danubians and Britons. Among the merchants there was a strong Greek element. The smaller tradesmen were mainly British and Gaulish and the slaves mostly British, although as the fighting died down and the country entered a period of relative peace the number of British slaves diminished and others were brought in from Europe, some of whom were highly skilled and treated with due respect.

Although Latin was spoken by relatively few people in the country districts it was the common language of the official and commercial circles of London. The toga, of fine white wool, was the formal dress of the principal Roman citizens and their wives, but most people wore a short tunic and hooded cloak, with open leather sandals. Their jewellery included bronze brooches inlaid with coloured enamels, torques, bracelets, armlets and finger rings of bronze, silver, gold and jet; and their weapons were spears, javelins, daggers, swords, arrows and shields.

The two main streets running from east to west through the City were Cheapside and Cannon Street. The houses of the wealthy were soundly built of ragstone and roofed with overlapping tiles. They had mosaic floors and hypocaust heating, and occasionally glass windows, although more often they were fitted only with shutters. Some of the largest houses were equipped with their own baths, while for the less prosperous there were a number of public bath houses, remains of which have been found, for example, in Lower Thames Street, on the site of the old Coal Exchange, in Upper Thames Street, Threadneedle Street, Cannon Street, Lime Street, Mark Lane and on the north side of Cheapside.

The houses and shops of the artisans were of clay and timber framework, with thatched roofs and wooden shutters, earth floors and plaster walls, which were sometimes painted. Where there was no hypocaust heating, they kept warm with braziers, and although they had candlesticks they mainly used small, terracotta oil lamps for lighting.

They had bronze kettles, jugs and frying pans and bronze and pewter table-ware, although the glossy red Gaulish pottery was cheaper for most people, while the very rich ate from silver plate and drank from glass drinking vessels.

There was a plentiful supply of water in the city, drawn from the wells in leather buckets which are almost indistinguishable from the firemen's buckets which were being used more than 1,500 years later, and the Roman ladder which is on view in the Museum of London in the Barbican looks startlingly modern and ready for use.

Druidism was almost exterminated from Roman Britain and the pagan gods of the Romans, more benevolent than those of the Celts, rejecting human sacrifice but propitiating the gods with the first fruits of the harvest, became associated with the gentler Celtic spirits of the woods and streams.

In the early days of the Roman Empire the official religion was the worship of Jupiter, Juno and Minerva but by the time of the conquest of Britain, in an attempt to unify the Empire, with its enormous variety of peoples and religious beliefs, the State cult had been introduced, in which the guardian spirit of the Emperor was worshipped during his lifetime, and after his death he joined the gods. Although they were deeply suspicious of Christianity for so many years and persecuted the Christians so relentlessly, the Romans were tolerant of most other cults, if they had no political implications. Jupiter, Juno and Minerva were still worshipped after the introduction of the State cult, as well as dozens of lesser gods, and at the root of most of this paganism was the cult of the mother goddess. Scores of religious emblems have been found in the foundations of Roman London – amuletic representations of the mother goddess to help in childbirth, little clay figures of Diana, Mercury, Apollo and Jupiter from household shrines, goddesses of springs and streams, phallic emblems to avert the Evil Eye, votive offerings of models of animals or human heads. In time, however, coins were substituted for sacrifices, particularly in the foundation deposits of new buildings, and these have proved a boon to archaeologists to establish approximate dates.

The cult of Isis and Osiris and their son Horus was established early in Roman London and also that of Cybele, the Great Mother Goddess of Asia Minor, whose lover Attis, a youth depicted in a Phrygian cap, was a god of vegetation who died and was resurrected each year. This was an orgiastic religion, in which the priests were castrated.

These pagan shrines and temples were mostly very small, for they were not built for corporate worship: people came privately and alone to pray to their gods and offer their sacrifices. Near St Nicholas Lane have been found relics of a temple to the emperor, a manifestation of the State cult. A group dedicated to the mother goddess has been discovered in Seething Lane, and on the site of the Goldsmiths' Hall an altar carved in relief with a representation of Diana, while remains of two more pagan temples have been found in Gracechurch Street.

The temple of Mithras, remains of which were found by the bank of the Walbrook, was different from these far smaller temples, for it was a meeting place or basilica, where men worshipped together. Their numbers were very small, however, and there was room for probably no more than twelve worshippers at a time.

Evidence of the worship of Mithras has been found as early as the fourteenth century B.C. throughout the Middle East, but it developed most strongly in Persia. The supreme god of Mithraism was Aeon, conceived as 'boundless time'. Below him in the hierarchy of the gods were the beneficent god of light and the evil god of darkness. Mithras was associated with the god of light, manifested in the sun, the moon and the stars. A god himself, he was the mediator between the gods and men and he developed into the god of fertility, of victory in battle, of truth and the inviolability of the pledged word. It was during the first century B.C. that the cult reached Rome, by way of Asia Minor, where the god had been depicted wearing the Phrygian cap. The central mystery of the Mithraic legend was the sacrifice of the Great Bull. Before the creation of earthly life, Mithras was ordered by the messenger of the sun to capture and kill the primeval bull. With his face raised to heaven, in pity for the suffering he was imposing on the creature, Mithras dragged it to a cave and stabbed it to death. From its blood sprang life-giving vegetation and from its semen all animal life and the essence of goodness, to oppose human evil.

By the third century A.D. the cult was established in Britain. The remains of three *mithraea* have been found near Hadrian's Wall, another at Carnarvon and the fifth in London.

The London temple of Mithras was partly below ground, for the original worship had been conducted in a cave and all the *mithraea* are small and secret places. It was entered from an eastern vestibule, from which a double door led to a flight of wooden steps leading down to the nave, some two and a half feet below. Aisles on either side, at a slightly higher level than the nave, and serving as benches for the worshippers, were separated from it by colonnades of seven pillars supporting the roof, the pillars representing the seven grades of initiation. The sanctuary was at the western end, its reredos a sculptured stone slab depicting the legend, with Mithras plunging his dagger into the bull's throat, while the dog, the snake and the scorpion, symbols of evil, are trying to poison its life-giving blood.

At the opposite end of the temple was a small, screened recess, with a hearth where incense was burned and a coffin-like pit in which the initiate, at one stage in the ritual of his initiation, had to lie in darkness for a time.

The Mithraic cult, with its emphasis on the sacredness of the plighted word, was widespread yet had only a limited following. No women were admitted and it appealed in particular to senior army officers, who had given their oath of allegiance to the Emperor, and to men of business who depended on the good faith of verbal contracts.

Although Mithraism was associated with many elements of paganism at its most primitive, and in some of the sanctuary scenes depicting the complicated legend of the god were added the signs of the zodiac, the four winds, the four seasons, Oceanus and Saturn and similar pagan gods, it contained a core of spiritual idealism commanding a respect as sincere as that granted centuries later to the City of London merchants and brokers whose word was accepted unquestioningly as their bond.

While the Mithraic cult was spreading through the Empire during the second and third centuries, so, in secret, and in the face of dire persecution, was Christianity. Some of the arrivals at the little port of London must have been secret converts, for gradually, as people of different races and creeds met and married, the multitude of pagan gods and goddesses worshipped throughout the Roman world were coming to be regarded as manifestations of the same, all-embracing deity, and paganism was moving inevitably towards monotheism.

It is not possible to describe London as it developed, stage by stage, during the four centuries of Roman rule, for as new buildings arose on the foundations of older ones little was left from which the archaeologist can draw a clear picture. To add to the difficulties, the city was troubled by more flooding from the Walbrook stream and the ground level had to be artificially raised from time to time by shovelling layers of earth along its banks, which inevitably upset the archaeological layers which can sometimes be found in undisturbed sites. The evidence of coins and potsherds suggests that this oldest part of the settlement along the banks of the Walbrook was a market place, covered not with permanent dwellings but with booths and stalls, while the splendid mosaics which have been found at Bucklersbury and on the site of the Bank of England indicate that the finest and most luxurious houses were built in this quarter.

The wall enclosing the city was probably built towards the end of the second century or early in the third century, but the precise date is uncertain. It was a protective measure taken after the first signs of danger to the Empire had appeared. It was built on a sandstone plinth, the wall being of Kentish ragstone with a core of mortared flint rubble and bonding courses of tiles at about three feet intervals. The ragstone was eight feet thick just above the plinth and tapered to about seven feet at a level of some six feet above it. The full height of the wall is not known but fragments rising to fourteen and a half feet have been recorded and it was probably some twenty feet high above the plinth when it was completed: and beyond it was an earth bank 100 feet wide. The wall encircled the city from just west of where the Tower of London was to be built, in a great arc which reached to the Ludgate in the west and extended down to the river. In its north-west corner it incorporated the north and west walls of the fortress, which were thickened at this time to match the width of the new defensive wall. Along the riverside, embankments and retaining walls were built and rebuilt throughout the years of occupation, but it is doubtful whether the defensive wall itself continued along the water-front. Nevertheless, on the landward side the wall extended for more than two and a half miles, forming an approximate semi-circle based on the Thames and bisected by the Walbrook. Today it can be traced from Tower Hill almost due north to Aldgate, north-westwards to Bishopsgate, westwards to the fort at Cripplegate and then almost due south to Aldersgate, westwards to Newgate and south to Ludgate and the river, but when the wall was first built there were only two gates, one near the site of the later Newgate, through which went Watling Street, leading to the north-west and Chester, and the other a little to the east of Bishopsgate, through which Ermine Street ran north-eastwards to Norfolk and Suffolk and the Vicinal Way led to Essex.

This Roman city covered about half a square mile and the vast amount of stone for the building of the wall was transported from quarries near Maidstone by barges along the Medway and the Thames.

To east and west of the city were stretches of undrained marsh and to the north, beyond a few miles of desolate, uncultivated heath, rose the northern heights of the dense Middlesex forest. Unlike most cities, therefore, which were built in the midst of farmlands, London's main food supply still came from up-river by barge and there was little building outside its immediate environs, Southwark, at the southern end of the bridge, being the only true suburb. However, with the acceptance of Christianity and the concept of immortality, the practice of cremation gave way to that of burial, and burials had, by law, to be outside the city walls. Cemeteries have been found in Whitechapel, in Bishopsgate and Fleet Street. Remains of a Roman building have been found in Fleet Street and as well as the settlement at Southwark one was beginning on a patch of dry ground rising from the marshy heath which was to become Westminster, where there was a river crossing and another burial ground.

By the time the wall was completed the enemies of Rome were gathering strength. As early as A.D. 180 the barbarian Picts whom Agricola, a century before, had left to their own devices, were making incursions into Britain. Hadrian's wall was strengthened and rebuilt in places, but the raids increased in violence and the defence of this northern frontier grew costlier every year.

In A.D. 193 there was dissension and near anarchy within the Empire. Commodus, the Emperor, had died, and amongst the claimants for the succession was Clodius Albinus, the governor of Britain. Though he failed and Severus was proclaimed Emperor, Albinus secured his own following and also announced himself as Emperor. Severus marched westwards to Gaul where he met Albinus in battle. Albinus was defeated and killed in A.D. 197 and it was probably about this time, with the Picts taking advantage of the diversion to overrun Hadrian's Wall again, that plans were made for the building of the London wall, but the building did not begin until at least the time of Caracalla, the successor to Severus.

Towards the end of the third century there was more trouble for Rome. A humbly-born Dutchman, Carausius, who had risen in the Roman navy to become a commander of the Channel fleet, had been given the task of suppressing the Frankish and Saxon pirates who were preying on the North Sea and Channel shipping with increasing frequency, and there was a strong suspicion that he was in league with them and sharing the booty. The Emperor Maximian ordered his arrest, whereupon Carausius retired to Britain with his fleet and arrived in London, declaring himself Emperor of Britain. Maximian sent an army to attack him, but Carausius was too well dug in to be shifted and he reinforced the city walls with great circular bastions. For the next six years he ruled from London, as Emperor of Britain, and although he was a usurper and a rogue he had some likeable traits and undoubted ability. He did well for Britain and established the first official mint in London.

However, in A.D. 293 he was murdered by his finance minister, Allectus, who declared himself Emperor of Britain in his place for the next three years, although he was by no means as successful or acceptable as Carausius and was said to have been a hard and brutal taskmaster.

In A.D. 296 Constantius Chlorus landed in Britain to recover the country for Rome. Allectus and his hastily recruited army marched to meet him but were defeated and Allectus was killed. His followers returned to London, intent on looting and plundering the city, but Constantius and his army, sailing round the Kent coast and up the Thames, surprised and routed them and London was saved.

Constantius fought a long and indecisive campaign against the Picts and strengthened the northern frontier defences yet again, but now a fresh danger loomed with the arrival of the Scots from Ireland, fierce tribes probably descended from Celts who had fled from Britain 300 years earlier. They settled in western Caledonia and began a series of incursive raids into Britain on their own account.

Constantius died at York in 306 and his son Constantine was proclaimed Emperor to succeed him: and although Constantine was not baptised into the Christian Church until he lay on his death-bed, it was during his reign that Christianity became the religion of the Empire.

Although Christian emblems and the *Chi-Ro* symbol of Christ have been found on the sites of many Roman towns in Britain, including London, there are hardly any remains of Roman Christian churches, and in London none at all have yet come to light, but this may partly be because, being in the highest archaeological Roman levels, they would have been the first to disappear when later medieval churches were built. There is no doubt that Christianity was established in London early in the fourth century for in 314 London sent a bishop to the synod at Arles.

As the faith gained strength hundreds of pagan gods were carefully buried by their priests, in order to save them from destruction, for those who had sincerely believed in them are not likely to have forsaken them without a pang of regret, not to mention a real fear that they might suffer some dire retribution for their perfidy. The Christians and the followers of Mithras were particularly antagonistic, for the two faiths had many details of ceremonial in common, including baptism by water and the taking of the sacred meal, and Christians regarded Mithraism as a travesty of their holy rites. By the end of the fourth century the *mithraea* in Rome were being systematically destroyed and those on Hadrian's Wall were also deliberately wrecked, but at the Walbrook the pagan sculptures were carefully buried by the priests underneath the floor and the *mithraeum* itself continued in use, presumably as a place of worship. It has been suggested that it became a Christian church, but there is no evidence for this and the discovery of a marble group of Bacchus and his companions implies that the temple may have been used for secret pagan worship after Christianity had been proclaimed as the religion of the Empire.

Constantine moved his capital eastwards to the ancient Greek city of Byzantium, where he created the Christian city of Constantinople, leaving Rome in a secondary position, as the capital city of the western part of the Empire, with its own governor and ultimately its own emperor.

In 367 there was a concerted attack on Britain. Picts raided from the north. The west coast was threatened by the Scots. Germanic tribes – Saxons and Franks – raided the south-east and landed. The commander of the coastal defences, known as the Count of the Saxon shore, and the commander-in-chief of the inland forces, who bore the title of the Duke of Britain, were both defeated and killed. London was protected by her wall but was in a state of siege, while the neighbouring countryside which supplied her food was ravaged by the invaders. The Emperor sent Theodosius to relieve the situation, and with an army in which there were a large number of German mercenaries, he landed at Richborough and marched on London. He met the invaders, laden with booty and driving chained prisoners and cattle before them, on their way back to their boats. Theodosius freed the prisoners, saved the cattle, routed the marauders and then marched on to the relief of London. He made the city his headquarters that winter and the following year moved north to restore order along the Scottish border.

It was at this time that for a short period the name of London was changed to Augusta, but the reason for it is obscure and it was soon to be known as London again.

After his successful campaign in Britain, Theodosius departed for Rome. One of the officers he left behind in Britain was a Spaniard called Maximum, who, like Albinus before him, made a bid to become ruler of the Western Empire. In 383 he declared himself Emperor of Britain. Then, unwisely, in order to swell the ranks of his army, he withdrew troops from the northern frontier and crossed the Channel to make himself master of both Gaul and Spain. No sooner had he set sail than inevitably the Picts swarmed over Hadrian's Wall again. Maximum, notwithstanding, marched through Europe towards the frontier of Italy where, in 388 he was met by Theodosius, vanquished and put to death.

One more attempt was made on the part of Rome to restore order again to Britain and drive out the northern barbarians, but Rome herself was by this time seriously threatened and her strength was dissipated. In Central Asia there had been a period of prolonged drought so severe that the horse-riding nomadic Mongols had been driven eastwards towards the great wall of China. The Chinese had withstood them and driven them westwards. By 375 they had crossed the Volga and the rivers that flow into the Black Sea. They met the Germanic Goths and the Goths in their turn were pressed westwards towards the borders of the Roman Empire.

In 376 the Emperor gave permission for some of them to cross the Danube and take refuge in Thrace, but soon they were swarming over in hordes and gradually taking possession of the country.

Britain suffered more raids and appealed to Rome for help, but Rome was no longer able to send reinforcements. Very soon she was recalling her legions to help defend the crumbling empire, in the war against the Goths of 401 and 402.

In Britain the remaining forces set up the usurper Marcus to command the country, but he was very soon murdered, as was his successor, the usurper Gratian. Then a general known as Constantine III was appointed. He made a valiant effort to save the situation and was acknowledged by the Emperor Honorius, not as a usurper but as a man who was trying to save Britain for the Empire. He crossed to Gaul in an attempt to defend the Rhine frontier from the Franks, but straightway the barbarians from Scotland began their invasions again into northern Britain. Constantine III appealed to Honorius for help, but by this time it was too late. The Goths were fast closing in on Rome. In 410 the British defenders were told to 'see to their own defences', for in this year Alaric and the Visigoths entered and plundered Rome.

For Rome it was not yet the final catastrophe, but from this time Roman rule in Britain was at an end.

2

After the Romans

During the fifth century the whole of Europe was in turmoil as the barbarians swarmed in from the north and east to occupy the countries of the fast disintegrating Roman Empire. The history of London and the whole of Britain during these years is obscure. When Honorius had bidden Britain to see to her own defences there had been a hint that Rome's withdrawal was to be only temporary, and for the next 50 years or so the Romano–British civilisation made a valiant but fast-weakening struggle for survival, but the incursions of the Picts and the Anglo-Saxons grew steadily fiercer and stronger. In the *Anglo-Saxon Chronicle*, Gildas recorded that in 443 'the Britons sent over the sea to Rome, and begged for help against the Picts; but they had none, because they themselves were warring against Attila, the King of the Huns'.

There was no centralised government left in Britain. The country dissolved into independent groups, ruled by local governors and tribal leaders. They fought the invaders to the best of their ability but it was a losing battle. One of their number, Vortigern, who had risen to considerable power, sought help from Jutish mercenaries, led by Hengist and Horsa, who had served with the Roman armies on the Rhine.

King Vortigern gave them land in the south-east of this country on condition that they should fight against the Picts, and had the victory wheresoever they came. Then they sent to the Angles, desired a larger force to be sent, and caused them to be told the worthlessness of the Britons and the excellence of the land. Then they soon sent thither a larger force in aid of the others. At that time came men from three tribes in Germany – from the Old Saxons, from the Angles, and from the Jutes.

Six years later, Hengist and Horsa, having turned treacherously against the Britons, were fighting King Vortigern at the battle of Aylesford. Horsa was killed but Hengist and his son fought on and by 457 the British had forsaken Kent and 'in great terror fled to London'.

Elsewhere in Europe the Goths were conquering and settling in Greece,

Italy and Spain, the Vandals in North Africa, the Burgundians in south-eastern France and the Franks in the rest of the country. In 450 Attila, the Scourge of God, had led his Huns across Europe, finally settling in the plains of Hungary. Rome was sacked again in 455 and in 476 a German chieftain entered the city and expelled the last of the Roman emperors, after which Italy became a Gothic kingdom, although the Pope remained, exerting something of the authority of the late emperor.

In Britain the battle was long and terrible. Bede, writing 300 years later, said:

Public as well as private structures were overturned; the priests were every-where slain before the altars; the prelates and the people, without any respect of persons, were destroyed with fire and sword; nor was there any to bury those who had been cruelly slaughtered. Some of the miserable remainder, being taken in the mountains, were butchered in heaps. Others, spent with hunger, came forth and submitted themselves to the enemy for food, being destined to undergo perpetual servitude if they were not to be killed upon the spot.

The little cities of Roman Britain were all gutted and destroyed. The villas with their mosaic floors and painted walls, their gardens and colonnaded walks, the farm-houses, the inns, shops and market places, the basilicas and temples and the newly dedicated Christian churches were all forsaken and then pillaged, after which they were either deliberately destroyed or abandoned once more, until they crumbled away into ruin and desolation. The halls of the British chieftains were left 'without fire, without light, without song'.

By 450 large parts of Essex, Kent and Sussex were in Saxon hands, but inland and further west British leaders, including perhaps King Arthur, managed to hold them for a time. There was a respite for some years, but by the middle of the sixth century the Angles and Saxons renewed their advance and the Britons were slowly pressed back to the peninsula of Devon and Cornwall, to the Lake District or the south-western part of Scotland, only a scattering of descendants of the primitive Celtic peasants who had lingered on from the pre-Roman days being left in the heart of the country, where they survived in the forests of the Chilterns, on the Pennine moors, in the Cotswolds and in the lonely marshes of the Fen district.

By the end of the century the East Saxons were established in Essex, the South Saxons in Sussex and the West Saxons on Salisbury plain. The Jutes were in Kent and the Isle of Wight, the Angles in Norfolk and Suffolk, and their kinsfolk were soon to form the kingdom of Mercia in the heart of the country, while farther north another group of Angles, intermarrying with

B

the British tribes living between the Humber and the Forth, formed the
kingdom of Northumbria.

Yet these separated kingdoms were all very sparsely inhabited and widely
separated by large stretches of forest, woodland or swamp.

In Europe, after the first savage onslaughts of the barbarians, much of
Roman civilisation remained and was preserved, for many of the invaders,
coming from the fringes of the empire, had already absorbed some of its culture. In Gaul, for example, the conquering Franks assimilated the high degree
of civilisation they found there, including the religion of Christianity and the
Roman legal system, and the Roman tradition continued almost unbroken.

In Britain, which was now to become known as England, it was a different
story. The Angles, Saxons and Jutes were all more primitive people, still in an
iron age of culture. They were solitaries, a farming people who disliked living
in towns, and had changed little since Tacitus had described their ancestors
centuries earlier. 'None of the Germanic people dwell in cities, and they do not
tolerate houses which are built in rows,' he said. 'They dwell apart, and at a
distance from one another, according to the preference which they may have
for the stream, the plain or the grove. . . . They do not make use of stone cut
from the quarry, or of tiles; for every kind of building they make use of un-
shapely wood, which falls short of beauty or attractiveness.'

In those days each man was a law unto himself, a free and landed man who
had never bowed to any master, but with the passing years social classes had
emerged. The head of the tribe became a war leader and king, who in time was
vested with godlike attributes. Beneath him were the various degrees of freemen, the highest being the nobility of earls or thanes, who were advisers
to the king and who in return for their services were given tracts of land to
govern which, in England, became the English shires. Below them were the
common freemen or churls, most of whom owned a small plot of land sufficient to maintain a single household: and at the bottom of the social order
were the slaves, whose numbers were maintained by conquest, poverty or
their own crimes.

Having no taste for towns, the English, on their new lands acquired from
the dispossessed British, built their solitary homesteads, the head of the family
in his large wooden hall, his sons and their families in small households close
by, near the farm buildings and the slave huts. These isolated homesteads,
with fields and grazing grounds outside the fence and ditch boundaries, became
the sites of most of the English villages which exist to this day. The English
made a certain amount of use of the Roman roads, but did not extend them
nor in fact do anything to maintain them, preferring to penetrate and explore
new country by way of the rivers.

The pagan gods of the English were terrible and ever hungry for propitiation by the sacrifice of horses, oxen, sheep and men. Woden, the god of war, and Thor, the god of thunder, storm and rain, were stark contrasts to the Christian faith, which was gaining strength in Europe and still survived in western parts of the British Isles. For the English there was no greater honour than to die in battle and be chosen by the Valkyries, the virgin attendants of Woden, to join him in his celestial Valhalla: and their folk stories were the savage sagas of Beowulf and the monster Grendel.

What happened to London during the first years of the English invasion no one can say for certain. The import and export trade on which the city had thrived during the Roman days disappeared, for the country was cut off from Europe. The merchants were ruined and the slaves and artisans had no work. There was no one left to bring in the vital food supplies from Essex and the farmlands of the southern counties.

No great battle of London has been recorded, in which the invaders sacked the city and killed the inhabitants. The people seem just to have drifted away from a dying city, although this slow desertion is a very different story from the terrible slaughter and destruction recorded by Gildas throughout the rest of the country.

In a moving narrative, an unnamed 'Chronicler of London' has left his version of what happened:

When the East Saxons and the Angles occupied the east country, and the South Saxons the south, trade was lost with all this region. Then the gate of the Vicinal Way and that of the Bridge were closed. Also the navigation of the Lower Thames became full of danger. And the prosperity of Augusta daily declined. Still there stood open the great highway which led to the middle of Britannia and the north, and the river afforded a safe way for barges and for boats to the west. But the time came when these avenues were closed. For the Saxons stretched out envious hands from their seaboard settlements, and presently the whole of this rich country where yet lived so many great and wealthy families, was exposed to all the miseries of war. The towns were destroyed, the farms ruined, the cattle driven away. . . . Nothing was brought to the port for export; the roads were closed; the river was closed; there was nothing, in fact, to send; nay, there were no more households to buy the things we formerly sent them. They lived now by the shore and in the recesses of the forest, who once lived in great villas, lay on silken pillows and drank the wine of Gaul and Spain.

Then we of the city saw plainly that our end was come; for not only was there no more trade, but there was no more food. The supplies had long been scanty, and food was dear; therefore those who could no longer buy food left the town; and sallied forth westward, hoping to find a place of safety, but many perished of cold, of hunger, and by sword of the enemy . . . our slaves deserted us; the wharves stood desolate; a few ships without cargo or crew lay moored beside our quays; our churches were empty; silence reigned in the streets. Now had the enemy attacked the City there would have been no resistance, but no enemy appeared. We were left alone, perhaps forgotten. The marshes and moors which surrounded the City on all sides became our protection. Augusta, to the invader, was invisible. And she was silent. Her enmity could do no harm, and her friendship could do no good. She was full of rich and precious things; the Basilica and the Forum, with the columns and the statues, stood in the midst; the houses contained pictures, books, baths, costly hangings; yet the Saxon wanted none of these things. The City contained no soldiers, and therefore he passed it by, or even forgot its existence.

There came the day when no more provisions were left. Then those who were left, a scanty band, gathered in the Basilica, and it was resolved that we should leave the place since we could no longer live in it. . . . I, with my wife and children, and others who agreed to accompany me, took what we could of food and of weapons, leaving behind us the houses where our lives had been so soft and happy, and went out by the western gate, and taking refuge where we could in the forest, we began our escape. . . Every year our people are driven westward more and more. . . . My sons have fallen in battle; my daughters have lost their husbands; my grandchildren are taught to look for nothing but continual war. And of Augusta have I learned nothing for many years. Wherefore am I sure that it remains desolate and deserted to this day.[1]

A handful of slaves and a few artisans may have remained in the stricken city, living secretly by the riverside, subsisting on fish and such food as they could find in the ruined overrun Roman gardens, but for perhaps 50 years or more London seems to have been almost empty. It is inconceivable that a few Saxons did not venture in to explore the place, but they can have found nothing to attract them, and much to fear, in a deserted city of ghosts, already falling into ruin.

By the end of the sixth century the English reigned throughout all eastern, south-eastern and southern England. The flames of British resistance had flickered and died in despair, and the survivors in the west were left in peace for a time, while the new English kings turned upon each other, in their

1 Quoted in Walter Besant, *London*, Chatto and Windus, 1910.

struggle for supreme power. Yet the fertile, pleasant lands of eastern and south-ern England gave an ease and plenty of living which gradually subdued the temper of the English and when the first few traders approached them from Europe – from Scandinavia, the Rhineland, France and the Netherlands – arriving at the deserted London wharves with small cargoes of pottery, glass and wine to offer in exchange for English metals and English wool, which had been famous for its fineness since the days of the Romans, word of their coming soon reached the countryside and slowly a small foreign trade with the Continent was re-established.

Overcoming their dislike of walled cities, a few Saxons, the first English merchants, moved into the deserted city, because they needed the Thames as a commercial highway. They renovated the quays and began to build a primi-tive wooden settlement within the massive stone walls. No one knows the ultimate fate of the Roman buildings. The frailer ones must have fallen into ruin by this time but the rest may have been deliberately destroyed now or have collapsed during the many fires which were to ravage the city in the years to come.

Both commercial and diplomatic relations developed between England and northern Europe. Foreign goods began to arrive at other south-eastern ports – Southampton, Ipswich and Norwich – as well as London and King Ethelbert of Kent married Bertha, the Christian daughter of the Frankish King of Paris.

It was in 589 that the Roman abbot Augustine and his band of monks were sent from Rome by Pope Gregory to visit Queen Bertha and begin the conver-sion of the English to Christianity. In 601 the Pope sent more missionaries, including Mellitus, who was intended to be Bishop of London, and Paulinus who was destined for York, the two capitals of the ancient Roman provinces. By 604 London seemed to have been converted and Mellitus was duly installed as London's first Bishop, in the first little wooden cathedral church of St Paul founded by King Ethelbert, but his stay was short, for after the death of Ethel-bert, in 616, many of the lesser kings of south-eastern England, over whom Ethelbert had exerted a strong influence, had second thoughts about Christi-anity and reverted to paganism. Mellitus was expelled and had to take refuge in Canterbury, where Augustine had remained for many years, and here Mellitus ultimately became Archbishop of Canterbury. And despite protests from later Bishops of London that London should be the see of the Primate, it has remained ever since at Canterbury.

It was Theodore of Tarsus, Archbishop of Canterbury from 668 to 690, who reorganised and strengthened the Christian Church in England. He restored the cathedral of St Paul and established the see of London, which lay on the frontier of the East Saxons, and although the population of London was still very small, its trade became increasingly significant, for England was once more part of a great cultural empire based on Rome.

Bede, writing early in the eighth century, described the city as 'the mart of many people, coming by land and sea'.

During these years monasteries were founded throughout the country and pilgrimages to Rome were made by clerics, kings and princes, who faced the perils of the long journey through France and Switzerland, but few, if any, ventured on to the Holy Land yet, for it was in the hands of the Moslems. Mohammed had died in 632 and in the eastern Mediterranean his followers were battling westwards. They had conquered Arabia, Syria and Egypt, advanced along the North African coast of the old Roman Empire, and early in the eighth century invaded and conquered Spain, so that for many years the sea route through the Mediterranean from Europe to Constantinople was effectively blocked.

We know little of the appearance of Saxon London for hardly anything has survived. The first St Paul's Cathedral was destroyed by fire in 961 and the second in 1084, while the entire city was devastated by the fire of 1135, but it is fair to assume that the houses were mostly of wattle and clay, that the more important ones were timber-framed with only shutters or lattices for light and ventilation and no glass windows, and that the churches were very small, most of them built of wood.

For years very little was known about the Anglo-Saxon way of life or of its art, apart from a few superbly illustrated manuscripts which have survived in cathedral museums and treasuries, and during the Reformation Henry VIII's commissioners removed and dispersed countless treasures from the cathedrals and churches, but gradually more archaeological remains are coming to light.

In 1956 the remains of an eleventh-century Saxon hut were discovered on the site of the *Financial Times'* building near St Paul's. It was about ten feet square and the walls were formed by split tree trunks. In 1962, beneath the foundations of the Tudor palace on which Number 10 Downing Street was built, the remains of a great Saxon hall of the eighth or ninth century were found, which may have had some connection with St Peter's Abbey of Westminster.

Two City churches which still exist, All Hallows By-The-Tower and St Bride's, Fleet Street, were built on the foundations of Saxon churches. Even before Saxon times there was building on the site of All Hallows, for at the bottom of the stairs leading from the west end of the church to the undercroft a piece of the floor is tessellated pavement belonging to the house of some wealthy Roman, living here in the early years of the occupation, during the reign of the Emperor Claudius, and the wall surrounding it is part of the

Saxon church. With the bombing of 1940, fragments of two Saxon crosses came to light and seven feet below the surface of the present church have been found the ashes of the first Roman London burned by Queen Boudicca in A.D. 61.

St Bride's also suffered mortally from the 1940 bombing and it was during the excavations for the rebuilding of the church that the foundations of the sixth-century Saxon church, dedicated to St Bridget, were discovered, as well as the relics of a Roman building which once occupied the site.

On the shores of Scandinavia and the islands of the Baltic lived men who wrested a living from a meagre soil and stormy, wind-swept seas. They were descended from the ancestors of the English, a branch of the family who were still sea-wolves. These Danes and Norwegians were the pirates of the North Sea – the Vikings. They began small-scale raids on England's eastern shores and then made full-scale descents. The Norwegian Vikings sailed eastwards to the Shetlands. One group turned down the west coast of Scotland and crossed to Ireland, where they settled for the next two hundred years. Others skirted the east coast of Scotland until they reached Northumbria. The Danish Vikings attacked the south-eastern shores of England and in 851 350 ships, each carrying 80 to 100 warriors, sailed up the Thames and burnt London. They were as savage as their forefathers who had sacked Roman London and as pagan.

During the next twenty years the Vikings overran Northumbria, Mercia and East Anglia, destroying, pillaging and murdering. In 871, as they were advancing on Wessex, Ethelbert, the Saxon king of Wessex, died and the throne passed to his youngest brother Alfred, who regrouped his forces and fought back. It was the first serious resistance the Vikings had met. The battle was ferocious and long, but Alfred succeeded in driving them from his territory for a time and they retired eastwards with their plunder and settled for the winter in London, which for several years was their base.

During this respite Alfred increased the strength of his navy, building war galleys some of which were twice the size of the Viking ships: and at the same time he reorganised his army and created 25 fortified strongholds throughout the country – towns or boroughs – which would serve as centres of resistance against further invasions. Some of these, including Rochester, Exeter, Chichester and Winchester, were built on the sites of Roman cities, but others, such as Oxford and Shaftesbury, were newly created.

Every district had to support its town and every local thane was obliged to build a house in it and either live there himself or maintain a fighting man to defend it, and so he became a burgher of the earliest planned towns of Saxon England. A few of these new towns did not last but those which survived became market towns as well as administrative centres.

Buying and selling were from earliest times strictly controlled and a market could be held only with the King's permission, his reeve or sheriff being present to collect the royal tax on all trade transactions. In return the burgesses received privileges and freedoms in the management of their affairs. In particular they had their own courts of justice, which saved them long journeys to the shire courts, although the sheriffs, when they collected their rents and dues for the King, also took a proportion of the profits from their courts. The burghers were free men and the boroughs became associated with freedom so that, in the years to come, a peasant who managed to escape from his feudal lord and live for a year and a day in a town unchallenged, was also allowed to consider himself a free man.

Ethelred, the King of Mercia, married King Alfred's daughter and Alfred helped him to regain control of his kingdom. In 886 Alfred occupied London and established Ethelred as lord of the City. The *Anglo-Saxon Chronicle* records that he entrusted the borough to Ealdorman Ethelred, at a ceremony in which 'all the English people that were not under subjection to the Danes submitted to him'.

This is the first recorded use of the word 'Ealdorman' or 'Alderman', which at the time meant the chief official of a shire, who acted as magistrate and administrator of the King's justice. The Danes called their earls ealdormen but in later years the word was used to describe men of lesser rank.

London was part of the kingdom of Mercia for the next few years, as was the little county of Middlesex, once the country of the Middle Saxons, which had been depleted by successive conquests and encroachments of the East Saxons of Essex and the South Saxons of Surrey and Sussex.

At this time the walls of the city were repaired and reinforced and the ruinous wharves rebuilt, the most important of which was Billingsgate, just below the bridge. Billing was probably an English alderman but the legend of Billingsgate is that it was named after Belin, a Celtic king who was living in about 400 B.C. and built the first wooden quay there, with a water gate. When he died his body was cremated and 'the ashes set over the gate in a vessel of brass, upon a high pinnacle of stone'.

The Danish Vikings, unlike their predecessors, began gradually to assimilate the civilisation of the people they had invaded and partly conquered. They adopted the Christian faith and, being excellent farmers, colonised much of the eastern Midlands, East Anglia and north-eastern England: and for all their piracy and violence they were great traders and sailors. Not only did they discover and settle in Iceland and eventually reach the coast of Labrador, but their travellers and merchants made the overland contact with Constantinople. Early in the tenth century they established Novgorod as a trading centre in Russia and from here made astonishing journeys to the Caspian and Black Sea. They used the rivers as much as possible – the Dnieper, the Volga and the Don – and where this was not practical they carried their shallow boats with their brilliantly striped sails overland. They carried amber, furs, slaves, wax and honey and exchanged them with the traders of Constantinople and the Islamic Empire for silk, gold and silver jewellery and vessels, and also the exotic produce of the distant East – pepper and spices, ivory, rare perfumes and rich brocades, which had come by the ancient camel caravan routes from China and India to Damascus: and many of these luxuries they now brought to England, most of the new trade coming through London, for by this time the Vikings were as much at home in London as the English. In their English domains they created the trading towns of York, Leicester, Lincoln, Nottingham, Derby and Stamford, places which had been the headquarters of their armies, while London was soon restored to the important port it had been in Roman times. For a few years the whole of south-eastern England became comparatively peaceful and London prospered and grew as a centre of international trade.

From its quays went English wool, corn, animal skins and honey and in return came wine and fish from Rouen, timber and pitch from Scandinavia. The Far Eastern produce eventually came by Arab dhows across the Indian Ocean and then by camel caravan over the desert to the ports of the Levant and thence from Venice across Germany to Antwerp and the Thames. Elephant ivory came from Africa and walrus ivory from Greenland. London thrived again and its tolls, collected by the royal port-reeve, swelled the king's treasury at Winchester.

London became cosmopolitan. On its wharves the wine-merchants of Rouen traded and settled in the Vintry. Cloth merchants from Flanders and Cologne lived around Dowgate, where the Walbrook joined the Thames. In the market place of East Cheap lived the goldsmiths from Ghent and Ponthieu.

'I go overseas,' wrote one of these traders, 'and buy purple and silk, precious gems and gold, many coloured garments and dyes, wine and oil, ivory and brass, copper and tin, sulphur and glass.'

Every encouragement was given to this overseas trade and a man who travelled three times as far as the Mediterranean in his own ship was given the status of a thegn or friend and servant of the king, a member of the new nobility from whom the earls, bishops and judges were chosen.

In essentials, England was of course self-supporting and was to be so for centuries to come, the vast majority of Englishmen living by their own labours in the villages where they were born, but this luxury trade, fraught with so many dangers, though only relatively small and for the few who could afford to pay for it, brought great wealth to London. There were eight mints in the city and strict rules were established for testing weights and measures. The details of the government of the city at this stage are not clear. A folk-moot – the ancient assembly and court – was held each week in the open space beside St Paul's and here points of policy and law concerning the city were heard and discussed before a magistrate, but the office of mayor had not yet been created nor had the city yet been divided into wards.

The nation that was evolving from the fusion of conflicting temperaments and ancestry was gradually turning from barbarity. Slavery was slowly disappearing, under pressure from the Church, and by the tenth century the sale of children by their parents was prohibited after the age of seven. Slaves were not allowed to work on Sundays and holy days and then came the time when they were able to buy their freedom. Finally the slave trade was prohibited from English ports, although it continued surreptitiously for many years to come, and by the end of the eleventh century there were still some 25,000 slaves in the country.

Despite the movement to free the slaves, class distinctions became more marked during the ninth and tenth centuries. The kings of the English kingdoms increased in importance, until they acquired an almost sacred significance. They had more power than the bishops, while their courtiers, on whom they bestowed large tracts of land, were socially above the old nobility of earls. The old English freeholders, who had bowed to no man and had accepted only the justice of their own folk, were now tenant farmers, who must conform to the wishes of their overlords. No longer did they have a voice in the government and law-making. The democratic days were over and the English nations, still not united, were each governed by an autocracy, headed by its king.

King Alfred died in 901 and Ethelred kept his trust with London by maintaining the defences and also the docks and wharves, and for many years his name was remembered by one of the most important of them, which was known as Ethelred's Hithe until the time of Henry I, when the name was changed to Queen Hithe.

By 918, when Mercia and Wessex were united, London had become an independent city, treated almost as a shire in itself.

During these years another band of Norsemen was sailing up the Channel to land in France, and after some initial setbacks they founded a settlement in Normandy. They took to themselves the language and culture of the country of their adoption, waxed strong and prosperous, and in 911 the King of France granted their leader the Dukedom of Normandy.

By the end of the tenth century King Alfred's great-grandson, Ethelred II, was King of Wessex and during his reign there were important trading contracts between England and Normandy, for, having been widowed in his mid-thirties, he had taken for his second wife Emma, sister of Richard, Duke of Normandy. Norman traders came to London and the merchants of Rouen, settled in the Vintry, became especially privileged.

But now there were more invasions of Danish Vikings along the shores of England. The *Anglo-Saxon Chronicle* records that in 982 'three ships of Vikings arrived in Dorset and ravaged in Portland. That same year London was burnt down.' It is not clear whether the burning of London on this occasion was an act of God or of the Vikings, but in a subsequent record, for 994, the *Chronicle* says that Olaf of Norway and Swein, King of Denmark, 'came to London on the nativity of St Mary with 94 ships, and they proceeded to attack the city stoutly and wished also to set it on fire; but here they suffered more harm and injury than they ever thought any citizen would do to them'. So the Vikings departed, but Swein continued to lead sporadic raids along the south-east coast and in 1013 he came to stay.

At first he failed to take London, but eventually the City submitted and Ethelred and his family fled to Normandy. Swein died the following year and his son Canute succeeded him, but Ethelred formed an alliance with another Olaf, later to become King of Norway, and together they set out to recapture London. They sailed up the Thames and found that the bridge was strongly fortified against them, and that Southwark, at the southern end, was equally well defended, with ditches and 'walls of wood, stone and turf'.

On the other side of the river there was a great market town called Southwark, and there the Danes had a great host fitted out; they had dug dikes and within they had set up a wall of trees and stone and turf, and they had a great army. King Ethelred made a mighty attack upon it, but the Danes warded it, and King Ethelred won nothing. There was a bridge over the river between the bourg and Southwark, and the bridge was so broad that two wagons could be driven past each other over it. On the bridge there were built strongholds, both castles and bulwarks, down towards the stream as deep as waist-high, but under the bridge there were piles which stood down in the bed of the river.

Whether this was the ancient wooden Roman bridge or a later one built by the Saxons is not certain, and the *Chronicle* makes no mention of what happened next, but according to the early thirteenth-century Norse sagas Olaf had the idea of covering and protecting his boats with wattle and clay from the surrounding houses, so that his men were able to row up the river and under the bridge in safety. Then they tied ropes to the timber piles, waited till the flood-tide and rowed downstream again, bringing the bridge crashing down behind them, so that all the defenders fell into the river, the survivors taking refuge in Southwark.

Unless the bridge was already on the point of collapse, it is an unlikely story, but there was a record of an exceptionally high tide on Michaelmas Eve of 1014, so the bridge may then have collapsed and the disaster been later attributed to the magic skills of Olaf. Whatever the truth of the story, he was later canonised, and in the coming years no less than six churches were dedicated to him, one in Southwark and the rest in the City of London.

Ethelred returned to London for a time and Canute departed to Denmark, only to return shortly afterwards with reinforcements. Edmund Ironside, Ethelred's eldest son, fought against him unsuccessfully and in the spring of 1016 'went to London to his father. And then after Easter, King Canute turned with all his ships towards London. Then it happened that King Ethelred died before the ships arrived.'

He was buried in St Paul's Cathedral and Edmund remained in London, while a large number of representatives of a dissident faction of the country – bishops, abbots and aldermen – went down to Southampton and acknowledged Canute as their king, but 'all the councillors who were in London and the citizens chose Edmund as king, and he stoutly defended his kingdom while his life lasted'.

In the end, however, after battles and intrigues, Edmund and Canute met and divided the country between them, Edmund taking Wessex and Canute Mercia and London. Shortly afterwards Edmund died and Canute reigned supreme, strengthening his position by marrying Ethelred's widow, the much-loved saintly Emma of Normandy. Her son Edward the Confessor was growing up in exile in Normandy and she was to become the mother of his half-brother Harthacanute.

What did London look like to Canute? It was the chief port of England, the centre of communications with the Continent and of the markets of England and north-western Europe: and its citizens played an important part in choosing or acknowledging the King. There had been a disastrous fire in 982, but the defences and the wall had remained intact. Immediately above the eastern bank of the Fleet river rose the only access from the west, the great West Gate, standing a little to the west of the later Newgate, while west of the Fleet river was a wide tidal marsh where the eastern end of Fleet Street was one day to be built. Facing the West Gate was a wide open space, occupied by the butchers' stalls and the shambles. To the south-east was St Paul's, to the east the market place of West Cheap, later to be known as Cheapside, and east again the East Cheap. The king's dwelling, a collection of wooden buildings dignified by the name of palace, was probably in the north-west corner of the City, near the site of the old Roman fort, and farthest east, in the valley of the Walbrook, the London Stone still stood, the Roman milestone from which the Roman roads had been measured, and perhaps other Roman remains which have long since vanished.

Apart from St Paul's there were probably not more than three or four churches and most of the little wooden dwellings were down by the river, around Dowgate, Billingsgate and Ethelred's Hithe for there were still many large open spaces within the City walls, particularly in the east, between East Cheap and Billingsgate.

Canute succeeded in welding the four great provinces of England into one kingdom, over which he ruled wisely and well. It had been the aim of Swein to unite the countries of Scandinavia and England into a Scandinavian empire, of which England should be the head, and while his son Canute aimed to continue this project, the country prospered. It was still a primitive land and large areas were still uncultivated, covered with forests, heaths and moors, while fens nearly 100 miles long separated East Anglia from the rest of the country, but the work of reclamation was gradually forging ahead as people of the countryside drained new land for farming – and in London foreign trade was increasing.

'What do you bring to us?' asked the merchant in an old English masque.

'I bring skins, silks, costly gems and gold,' replied the trader, 'besides various garments, pigment, wine, oil, and ivory, with brass, and copper, and tin, silver and gold, and such like.'

Men from the Rhineland and Normandy moored their vessels along the Thames and on the wharves appeared crates of cloth from the looms of Lombardy, iron-work from Liège, butts of French wine and vinegar, pepper and spices from the East.

Canute died in 1035 and the days of peaceful prosperity were over, for the two sons who succeeded him ruled with brutal violence and were hated and feared. Their reigns were very short, however, for Harald died in 1040 and his half-brother, Harthacanute, son of Emma, in 1042. While attending a wedding feast in Lambeth, 'he collapsed and died, as he drank'.

Godwin, Earl of Wessex, a relative by marriage to Canute, whom Canute had appointed his viceroy when he was out of the country, now arranged for Ethelbert's and Emma's son, half-brother to Harthacanute, the frail and gentle Edward, still living in Normandy, to claim his birthright and return as king. There was no law of primogeniture. It had been the custom for the King to be chosen by the Witan, with the approval of the folk-moots, from the most promising members of the royal family, the Witan being a royal advisory council of earls and bishops who acted with the agreement of representatives of the folk-moots. But these days of democracy were over and as the kingdom had grown the power of the Witan and the folk-moots had passed into an oligarchy of influential officers of the Church and the State, only the citizens of London retaining the democratic power to give their approval or disapproval at the election of a king.

Edward was very much under Godwin's influence for many years of his reign and he married Godwin's daughter Edith, but he was French-speaking and he came to England with a retinue of Normans whom the English resented. The resentment deepened and Godwin, steadily increasing in power and wealth, further united the English, and in particular the people of London, in a common discontent.

For a time Godwin was sent into exile with his family, but when he sailed up the Thames again, with a fleet which threatened to encircle the King's, the citizens of London persuaded Edward to make a peaceful settlement. Godwin was restored to his estates and when he died, in 1053, his son Harold was made Earl of Wessex and under-king, as powerful a man as his father had been before him. Edward accepted the situation but he moved from the City of London and began the rebuilding of the monastery at Westminster. Its site was Thorney Island – the island of thorns – the patch of relatively high ground among the marshy banks of the Thames where the Romans had made a burial ground and where, in the sixth century, Sebert, King of the East Saxons, had built the first church, dedicated to St Peter. Over the next five hundred years it had become a Benedictine monastery, with an endowment for the support of twelve monks, and while it was being rebuilt Edward restored the little wooden palace of Westminster close by, which had been destroyed by fire a few years earlier.

Here, in 1066, only few days after his new Abbey Church had been consecrated, Edward died. He was buried before the high altar of the Abbey and Harold was proclaimed King of the English by the citizens and members of the Witan in London.

However, Duke William of Normandy, illegitimate son of Robert the Magnificent and a nephew of Queen Emma, insisted that Harold, on a visit to Normandy, had promised that his own claim to the English throne should be considered when the time came, and that Edward the Confessor had named him his heir. To challenge what he declared to be Harold's perfidy he landed in England only a few months later.

Harold was killed in the first battle and William began a slow and cautious march on London, leaving a trail of desolation in his wake. London had been described to him as 'a great city, overflowing with froward inhabitants and richer in treasure than the rest of the kingdom. Protected on the left side by walls, on the right side by the river, it neither fears enemies nor dreads being taken by storm', but William was determined on total subjection.

In London the earls of the realm gathered at a meeting of the Witan and elected as King Prince Edgar, the only likely prince of the line of Alfred, a great-nephew of Edward the Confessor, who was only fifteen years old.

William established himself in the palace at Westminster and prepared to besiege London.

He built siege-engines and made moles and three iron horns of battering-rams for the destruction of the city; then he thundered forth menaces and threatened war and vengeance, swearing that, given time, he would destroy the walls, raze the bastions to the ground, and bring down the proud tower in rubble.

In the end, however, William outmanœuvred the plans made by London and the Witan to defend the City, and by diplomacy and promises London surrendered peacefully. Prince Edgar was granted a generous estate and William was crowned in Westminster Abbey on Christmas Day, 1066.

He had a profound respect for London and its wealthy citizens and treated them circumspectly: and soon after his coronation he granted the City his charter.

William king greets William the bishop and Geoffrey the portreeve and all the citizens in London, French and English, in friendly fashion; and I inform you that it is my will that our laws and customs be preserved as they were in King Edward's day, that every son be his father's heir after his father's death; and that I will not that any man do wrong to you. God yield you.

3

Early Medieval London

Although London had accepted William he was well aware that the city had acquired the traditional power to influence the choice of the king and he had a healthy respect for its 'fierce and vast' population. He was anxious to maintain the city's cooperation, but was ready to use force at any sign of insurrection, and after his coronation he retired to Barking for a few weeks, while the first wooden tower of London was built, up against the eastern wall of the city, 'like a padlock in a chain'.

The castle was an essential part of Norman warfare. The cavalry usually fought in the open country, supported by the unmounted archers, but the secret of the Normans' success lay in their skill in building quickly and relatively cheaply castles, which could withstand attack and were established as formidable bases. Where possible they chose a hillock or stretch of rising ground, but if the country were particularly flat they created an artificial mound of earth – the motte – on which they built the main tower of the castle, the keep. The invasion armies had brought the walls and foundations of a wooden castle with them from Normandy, the separate parts packed in huge barrels and stowed away in the ships: and when they landed at Pevensey they reassembled it so quickly that it was ready for use by the evening of the first day.

When William had accepted the crown and was moving towards London for his coronation, he had, says William of Poitiers, 'sent forward to London picked men to build a fortress in the city and to make suitable preparations for the coming of the royal splendour'.

The place chosen was just outside the city boundary, by the eastern end of the Roman wall, down by the river, on the site of an old Roman garrison, so that the wall gave protection to part of the bailey. Close by was the church of All Hallows Barking, a dependency of the Abbey of Barking, founded by Erkenwald, Bishop of London in the seventh century.

William had come to conquer England and not to settle, but of the army of six thousand mercenaries led by Norman, Breton and Flemish noblemen, who had accompanied him on the venture, a large number of the noblemen expected to be rewarded with confiscated English land.

Events moved swiftly and early in 1067 he began to divide the spoils of conquest amongst them, for he regarded every acre of England as his personal property. Such great landowners who had not been killed during the conquest were virtually dispossessed, having to yield most of their land in order to buy the right to remain on what was left. The earldoms of Northumbria, Mercia and Wessex were abolished and sheriffs were appointed by the king for the government of each shire. The division of the shires into the old English hundreds was maintained and each hundred was divided into manors, a term introduced by the Norman clerks which at this time meant any fairly commodious house with a small estate, owned by a man of substance.

The European feudal system which William created in England was a military one and legally different from the old Saxon arrangement of master and vassal. For himself and his family William kept as his personal property about one-quarter of England's land: about one-sixth was bestowed on some 170 of his noble supporters, but of these baronial lands almost half was in the hands of only ten men. This gave them tremendous power, but it was held in check, for every villein had to swear a separate oath of allegiance to the King as well as to his immediate overlord: and although the existing legal system was maintained, in which each hundred had its own court of justice, William decreed that every court should come under the ultimate jurisdiction of the King's Court.

The towns of England, with their complicated laws and privileges were a different matter. Their citizens were undisturbed, and this applied particularly to London, where the population during the early years of the Conquest remained predominantly English, but William's sheriffs collected the royal taxes and he ordered defensive castles to be built in almost every county town throughout the country, while the barons, with the king's permission, built similar castles on their estates.

As well as introducing an alien aristocracy to England, which for at least the first generation was cordially hated, William introduced the reformed European Church, for his invasion had had the especial blessing of the Pope, and William, who always wore a profusion of sacred medals, was deeply influenced by him.

The lands of the English church were left intact and as Norman bishops and clergy replaced the English incumbents their properties were steadily increased, but at the same time they were made an integral part of the feudal system, so that bishops and abbots were expected to send men from their domains to fight for the King when occasion arose.

The wooden motte and bailey castles were in time replaced by permanent stone castles, which at this stage in the development of weapons of warfare were almost impregnable, for the Normans brought with them skilled stone-masons. The motte and ditch at London had been built in a matter of days, and in 1068 William ordered the newly appointed Gundulf, Bishop of Rochester, a Benedictine friar who had visited the East and was renowned for his skill in stone-building, to begin work on the massive White Tower, the first building of the Tower of London.

It is square in section with a flat roof surmounted by four turrets, three of which were square and the fourth, used as a watch-tower, circular. The walls are fifteen feet thick at the base, tapering to twelve feet at the top. It is built partly of Kentish ragstone and partly of Norman limestone imported from Caen, and is four storeys high, comprising the vaults, the main floor, the banqueting floor and the State floor. Each storey has three rooms, a long west room, running north to south along the entire width of the Tower, with a smaller room parallel to it to the east and a cross chamber in the south-east corner, the walls between them being at least ten feet thick: and into the walls were built a number of small, dark and secret chambers.

The entrance was originally on the first floor, through a single, easily de-fensible gateway which has now disappeared. There was no access to the ground floor from the outside and the only light came from loop-holes in the walls, through which filtered little enough daylight but plenty of cold, damp air from the river.

The main rooms of the vault were used for the storage of weapons and food, the cross-chamber, the darkest and dampest of them all, as a dungeon, which was to house many a famous prisoner in the years to come, including Guy Fawkes.

On the first floor the largest room was a guard-room and the cross-chamber was the crypt of St John's Chapel on the floor above, a grim place sometimes used as a prison, although one of the niches built into the thickness of the wall may have been the secret jewel house.

The long room on the floor above was the banqueting hall, the only room in the White Tower to possess a fireplace, and the cross-chamber was the beautiful little chapel of St John, which rises up to the next storey: and on the top floor were the Council Chamber, a smaller hall where the justiciaries sat and the galleries of St John's Chapel, from which a passage led to the royal apartments, for the Tower, although built for the defence of London from attack by sea and river was also intended as a royal palace, yet even by eleventh-century standards it was far from comfortable and William spent very little time there. Gundulf also built the first St Peter's Church on Tower Green, but it was later Norman and Plantagenet kings who added to the great complex of buildings which arose round the White Tower and it was not until the twelfth century that the curtain wall and the moat were built.

At the western end of the city the first Baynard's Castle arose, just below St Paul's on the east bank of the Fleet river, a grim stone fortress built by Ralph Baynard, on whom William had bestowed the barony of Little Dunmow in Essex: and close by the Montfichet family raised their stronghold of Montfichet Castle, using the Fleet river as part of the moat.

St Paul's had been burnt to the ground in 961 and nothing is known of the cathedral which took its place and was destroyed by fire in 1086. Maurice, the Norman Bishop of London, began work on the third cathedral in 1087, the year of the Conqueror's death, but it was another 200 years before it was completed, so although parts of old St Paul's, which was to become one of the most beautiful cathedrals in all Europe, was partly built with rounded Norman arches and heavy pillars, later parts were in the more elaborate, decorated styles of the thirteenth and fourteenth centuries.

William did not stay long in England after his coronation for in February, 1067, leaving two Regents, William FitzOsborn in Winchester, where the royal coffers, jewels and robes of state were kept, and Odo of Bayeux in Kent, he returned to Normandy, bearing quantities of treasure looted from the dispossessed English countryside, although what impressed the Normans most seems to have been the magnificent new clothes in which he now appeared.

However, the conquest of England was by no means over and there was still a constant threat from the Danes. Later that year William had to return, to quell a revolt of Harold's sons. By the summer of 1068 he considered it safe enough to bring his wife to England, to be crowned at Westminster, just before the birth of her fourth son, the future Henry I of England, but for the next three or four years there were constant rebellions, particularly in the eastern counties, where the exiled Hereward was joined by Earl Morcar in the Fens, and in the north, where the English were remorselessly punished and more castles were built to hold them in subjection.

The south-east remained loyal to the new regime, and although during the early years London's foreign trade suffered, with the loss of the Danish market, it soon recovered as business developed with the French merchants who brought wine and fish from Rouen to Dowgate, and men from the Rhineland who, capturing some of the old Viking trade of the East, brought spices, pepper and cumin, luxurious fabrics and beautifully wrought gold and silver vessels from Constantinople, and from their own country wine and coats of mail, with grain at times when the harvest failed in England.

More important still was the trade with Flanders. The Flemings bought

English cheese, cattle, hides, lead and tin, but by far the most valuable trade
was in English wool. Throughout the eleventh and twelfth centuries the
Flemish cities were fast rising to economic power through the manufacture
of woollen cloth, which they sold throughout Europe. The demand was so
great that the Flemish weavers, outrunning supplies of local wool, were soon
becoming increasingly dependent on the supplies of English wool from the
damp, rich pastures of the Yorkshire dales, the Cotswold hills and the Sussex
downs.

William the Conqueror had married a Flemish princess and the bond between
the two countries was close. Centuries earlier a visiting Roman had remarked
on the quality of English wool, saying that 'the wool of Britain is often spun
so fine that it is in a manner comparable with the spider's thread', but in the
eleventh century the spinning and weaving of wool in England were as yet
small cottage industries to supply the wants of the family or perhaps the
village, and it was to be many years before they developed into an export of
any significance. In the meantime the sheep farmers and the entrepreneurs in
London who collected the wool from them prospered from its sale to the
cities of Flanders, in particular Bruges and Ghent, and to Arras.

Throughout England more boroughs were founded by the king and also
by his barons. They were settled by men who were willing to rent plots for
purposes of trade and pay the market dues – weavers, tailors, drapers, grocers,
brewers, shoemakers, bakers, innkeepers, pastry cooks, goldsmiths, blacksmiths, saddlers, pewterers, vintners, butchers, tanners, dyers, glovers, carpenters, bow-makers, tilers and builders – but they still lived a life which was close
to the countryside, and outside the town walls were the unenclosed town
fields, with their strips of cornland, and the common lands where they grazed
their sheep and cattle: and at harvest time they were expected to down tools
and lend a hand.

In Saxon times the earls had maintained a town house in the borough
nearest to their estates, a replica of their primitive, wooden, rush-strewn hall
and bower of the countryside, but the Norman nobles seldom lived in the
provincial towns, although there was an increasing tendency for them to
establish residences in London, for although London was not the capital city,
in the sense of being the seat of the Court, in every other way it was accepted
as such, being the greatest commercial centre, the largest town in the kingdom,
the focus of political and economic power and the city which had acquired
a special rôle in the acceptance of the king.

Its population, compared with some one and a half million for the whole
of the country, was rising to 10,000 and becoming increasingly cosmopolitan.

The new generation of Normans built mansions set in large gardens within the city walls, amidst the smaller houses of the merchants and the cottages of the artisans, and soon building was taking place outside the walls, in the north around Holborn and to the west, along the muddy strand of the river towards Westminster, where one of the earliest suburbs had already come into existence with a colony of Danes, granted land there after their second invasion and peaceful settlement with King Alfred; and there they had built the first little church of St Clement Danes.

King William had, in fact, no capital city in England, for during the last eighteen years of his life only half his time was spent here and during these visits he and his court moved from one castle stronghold to the next, in a constant, wearying circuit, a custom followed by all the Norman kings, which exasperated the unfortunate entourage. Peter de Blois described some of the hazards involved in this peripatetic progress through the primitive early medieval countryside.

Sometimes the king declares he will leave early, then slumbers till noon, while pack-horses droop under their leads, chariots stand ready, couriers fall asleep and everyone grumbles. . . . But when the king changes his mind about a destination – what chaos! Probably only one house can be found there. Then we, after wandering miles through an unknown forest, often in the dark, may find by chance some filthy hovel. Indeed, courtiers often fight for lodgings unfit for dogs.

Each year, however, William held three great meetings in the three important towns of the south, to show himself to his subjects. At Christmas the meeting was held at Gloucester, at Easter time at Winchester, where the royal hoard was still kept, and at Whitsuntide in London, when he stayed at the White Tower, appearing in the great hall in the full and impressive panoply of his crown and robes of majesty.

An important step in the progress of London's power during Norman times was in the gradual concentration of the mint within the City. On his accession William had found that the Saxon method of minting money was efficient and altered it only very gradually. Every borough had its own mint and bullion was carried to it for exchange. It had at least one maker of coins – a moneyer – who was the royal agent, and several cities had more than one. London in 1066 had eight, and every provincial moneyer had to go to London to obtain the dies for his coins.

Throughout early medieval times the universal coin was the silver penny, with the king's image and his name on one side and on the other a cross inscribed in a circle, with the name of the moneyer and the place of the mint, and these coins were distributed throughout the country in sacks or barrels. There was no gold coinage yet, and for halfpennies and farthings halves and quarters were clipped from the penny, the cross being used as a guide, but the smaller denominations of a half and a quarter of a farthing must have been even more of a hazard.

Throughout Norman times the manufacture of the dies remained in the hands of London merchants, who employed highly skilled 'hammer men'. The contents of the coins were regularly tested and the punishment for issuing debased coins was grim. Around Christmas time in 1125 Henry I, on hearing that a group of moneyers had been issuing bad pennies, ordered his Chief Justice to summon them to Winchester, and because they had 'foredone all the land with their great quantity of false money', all 94 of them were punished according to the law. One by one they were castrated and their right hands cut off, the work being completed, it is recorded, by twelfth night.

The metallic content of the coins was stabilised and by 1163 the quality of the silver penny was almost the same as that of today's sterling silver.

In time the mint became concentrated in London, as in borough after borough, the number of moneyers was reduced, but it was a slow business, and although when Henry II succeeded in 1154 London had eighteen moneyers, the King's coins were still being minted in thirty other boroughs. Nevertheless, there was very little money in circulation as yet. Obligations were often fulfilled by personal service, while payments, including rents and fines, were usually made in kind.

The castles and churches which William I built throughout the country cost a great deal of money, a proportion of which came from feudal dues and taxation, which included the money his sheriffs collected from the boroughs – London's share being £500 a year – but although he had a substantial hoard of money at Winchester it was not enough for his building plans and he, as well as his barons and clergy, had to borrow. Christians were forbidden to practise usury and the Normans therefore used the services of the Jews, the first capitalists of Europe, a colony of whom William invited over from Rouen, although there were already a few Jews in England in Saxon times.

By the end of the twelfth century there were small colonies of Jews in most of the larger cities of England but on their arrival, soon after the Conquest, they settled mainly in London, with smaller colonies at Stamford and Oxford. The Jews were not allowed to hold land, they had no rights of citizenship and were outside the common law, but were under the special protection of the King. Like the royal forests, he regarded them as his personal property, and their lives and fortunes depended on him. They lived for the most part in especially designated Jewries and only with royal permission might they settle elsewhere. In London there were two colonies, one in Old Jewry, near the ancient Saxon royal palace, and the other within the liberties of the Tower.

The Jewish moneylenders and pawnbrokers were the only source of capital and they were sorely needed. They charged enormously high interest rates – an average of 40 to 45 per cent but sometimes as much as 60 per cent – which meant that some of them, although by no means all, became enormously rich, but they justified this extortion by declaring that they were sometimes never repaid. Their clients usually hated them and they were certainly anything but prompt payers. Nor, in the early years, did the Jews have any legal protection.

They are said to have been the first people in England to have lived in stone houses, which they built for the practical reason that they were a good deal safer from assault by their enraged debtors than wooden ones. Nevertheless, throughout the reign of William I and William Rufus they prospered. They were allowed to build synagogues and appoint Rabbis. Many were learned men and through their connections with the Spanish Jews and their Arab contacts had acquired a knowledge of medicine far in advance of anything yet known in England, for which many people had reason to be grateful.

Yet they were an alien people with unfamiliar ways which made them feared by the ordinary run of unsophisticated folk who had no need of financial dealings with them, and when they began to convert people to the Jewish doctrine, the Church very quickly sent monks to preach against them.

William Rufus, who spent most of his time on the hunting field and was a great spender, soon exhausted the royal coffers at Winchester and turned to the Jews, to whom he gave special patronage and protection, and with the help of whose money he accomplished his one lasting memorial, the rebuilding in stone of the great hall of the palace of Westminster. At the time of his rather mysterious death, his brother Robert was far away in the Holy Land, fighting the first Crusade, so despite protests from those barons who still had interests in Normandy and were anxious for the two dominions of England and Normandy to be under one rule, it was the Conquerer's fourth son who became Henry I of England.

Henry was well aware that his claim to the throne was not particularly strong and although he kept a firm control, he appeared to make concessions to the more flagrant restrictions of feudal despotism. He courted the City of London, reducing the annual tax or 'farm' from £500 to £300 a year, and he seems at one time to have granted the citizens the right to elect their own sheriff to collect it, but from the rather scanty records that have survived, this promise seems never to have been kept. However, his queen, Matilda of Scotland, presented the City with the foundation of the Priory of the Holy

Trinity, Aldgate, and she also endowed the leper hospital of St Giles-in-the-Fields.

Henry did not spend many years of his reign in England. In 1106 he was fighting his brother Robert in Normandy and seized the Duchy by conquest. It became a dependency of the English Crown, the result for London being a large-scale immigration of Norman craftsmen and merchants, who gave an impetus to her business and foreign trade.

Twice a year Henry would sit with his chief officers round the Exchequer Board, which was a board squared to form a simple counting device: and here he received and audited the money his sheriffs had collected from the counties as well as the taxes paid personally to the King, and the bulk of this money was sent down to Winchester for safe-keeping.

It was towards the end of his reign that feeling against the Jewish money-lenders began to run strong and in 1130 the Jews of London were fined between them £2,000 for 'a sick man whom they had killed'. He was presumably a patient whom a Jewish doctor had been unable to cure, and the entire Jewish community in London had to suffer for it. But this was only the beginning and a few years later, during the reign of Stephen, a systematic persecution began.

Henry I left London for the last time in 1133, the year of yet another disastrous fire in the City, which was thought to have started in the house in Cheapside of the Norman merchant Gilbert à Becket, a sheriff of London: and it destroyed so much of his property that his son Thomas was brought up in comparative poverty.

Two years later Henry died in France, during a long campaign against the ungodly Angevins, who possessed large provinces in central and southern France and were casting covetous eyes on Normandy. The succession had been agreed to his daughter, the Empress Matilda, but when the barons of England and the City of London heard that in order to placate the hated Angevins she had been secretly married to Geoffrey Plantagenet, the Angevin heir, they were aghast and challenged Matilda's right to the throne: and when Stephen of Blois, Henry's nephew and a grandson of William the Conqueror, put forward his claim they did not dispute it. He had been brought up in England and through his wife Matilda, heiress of Boulogne, owned land in Essex and an establishment in London, as well as controlling the merchant ships of Boulogne which carried English wool to Flanders.

He presented himself at the gates of London. No Norman nobles accompanied him but London welcomed him. 'Aldermen and wise folk gathered together at the folkmoot, and these providing at their own will for the good of the realm, unanimously resolved to choose a King.' At the same time it was made clear to Stephen that he should acknowledge the City's right to choose him.

Throughout Europe, particularly in northern France and northern Italy, the larger towns were forming themselves into communes, and it seems probable that during these preliminary negotiations with Stephen he agreed that London should receive its independence in this way, but from the beginning Stephen's reign was a disaster, and with the landing of the Empress Matilda to claim the throne for herself civil war broke out, for she had a strong following. London remained loyal to Stephen and when he was captured it took all the persuasion of the Church to convince the City commune that Stephen was unfit to rule. The Empress and her army then approached the City. A delegation of London citizens came out to meet her, and discuss terms for handing over the City and she was escorted to Westminster to await her coronation.

Then Matilda made several blunders. She granted to Geoffrey de Mandeville, who had recently been made Earl of Essex by Stephen and was already hated by most Londoners, an extension of his rights and lands, including the Tower of London, which he was allowed to fortify: and from the wealthy citizens of London she demanded a large sum of money, treating their protests and newly acquired rights with contempt and a violent outburst of temper.

Before the matter was settled, news came that Stephen's queen was approaching the City. The citizens, disillusioned by the behaviour of the Empress, suddenly broke into revolt, rampaging through the streets 'like swarms from beehives'.

To the astonishment of the Empress, all the bells of the City began ringing.

She, with too much boldness and confidence, was just bent on reclining at a well-cooked feast, but on hearing the frightful noise from the City and getting secret warning from someone about the betrayal on foot against her, she with all her retinue immediately sought safety in flight. They mounted swift horses and their flight had hardly taken them farther than the suburbs when, behold, a mob of citizens, great beyond expression or calculation, entered their abandoned lodgings and found and plundered everywhere all that had been left behind in the speed of their unpremeditated departure.

The Empress retaliated by increasing Geoffrey de Mandeville's control over London and appointing him sheriff. The brief days of the commune were over. but Matilda was never crowned at Westminster. In 1141 Stephen was released from captivity, but to the consternation of the City he reaffirmed de Mandeville's appointment as sheriff of London and Middlesex.

De Mandeville began a campaign of high-handed extortion of London, demanding far in excess of the £300 farm. Only when it became too blatant did Stephen take action. Then he deposed de Mandeville, depriving him of his castles and estates, and shortly afterwards he met a violent death.

Yet the business and social life of the City continued to develop. It was about this time, if not earlier, that London was divided into small administrative districts comparable with the hundreds of the shires. As the population increased and more parts of the city became inhabited the number of these wards increased and by the early part of the twelfth century there were probably already 24, although their identification at this early date is difficult, for each ward was at first named after the alderman at the head of its administration – a man who was considered to have a special knowledge of the law – and for a time the office of alderman seems to have been hereditary, which suggests that at first he was the feudal lord of the district, the inhabitants of which had acquired their freedom. The business of the wards was managed in the ward moots, which were similar to the hundred moots of the countryside, but the complicated legislation of the international trade of the City was conducted at the Court of Hustings, in a small building which was to become the Guildhall. Here every Monday the aldermen gathered, forming a bench of legal experts.

There remained in the City small areas – the liberties – as at St Martin's-le-Grand; and outside the walls, to the north and east, were large areas – the sokes – owned by individuals or by foundations such as that belonging to the Holy Trinity Priory of Aldgate, the tenants of which were free of certain tolls and taxes, but the legislation concerning them is obscure.

It was during these years that the 100 or more little City churches were built, most of them proprietary churches established by wealthy citizens or groups of citizens who maintained them and supported a priest from their own donations. Their parish boundaries seem to have been fairly arbitrary at first and were probably controlled by the property boundaries of the men who had built the church. Sometimes the parish boundaries marched with those of the wards but by no means always, for some of the wards, such as Farringdon, Aldersgate, Cripplegate, Bishopsgate and Portsoken, reached outside the City walls and by 1222 the medieval City had spread to its present boundaries, covering an approximate square mile.

The Church was an integral part of the State and from birth to death the Christian religion was one of the most powerful influences in people's lives. God and the Devil, Jesus, Mary and all the Saints were living realities, and in every street of the City were to be found monasteries and convents, churches, hospitals and priories. With their gardens and courts and chapels they covered a quarter of the entire area of the City and all day long their bells rang out, for festivals and feasts, pageants and processions, births, marriages and funerals and for the many services held throughout the day, from dawn till sunset.

It was in accordance with an agreement made with London in the previous year that Henry II, son of the Empress Matilda and Geoffrey Plantagenet, succeeded to the throne on the death of Stephen in 1154. Early in his reign the new King granted London a new charter, confirming its privileges. No citizen was obliged to attend a court outside the City and the Court of Hustings was to meet once a week. Londoners were freed from certain tolls exacted in other parts of the country and a number of earlier royal taxes, and their hunting rights were confirmed in Middlesex, Hertfordshire, the Chilterns and Kent. Yet the City was not given the independence of a Continental commune, the farm was still collected by the King's sheriff, and throughout his reign he demanded substantial 'gifts' from the City.

Like his grandfather, Henry I, Henry Plantagenet had little time for tradition, but he succeeded in restoring order after the anarchy of Stephen's reign. Outstanding was his system of justice, and the itinerant courts administered by his judges, the soundness of his government and exchequer gave a new prestige to England in Europe. He established the Exchequer Court in West-minster and authorised his chief officers of state to take care of it. After a time he seldom met the sheriffs himself, all questions arising from the payments being settled by the Exchequer Court: and within a year the treasury had been moved from Winchester to Westminster.

For much of his reign he was in France controlling his extensive possessions, for in addition to the Angevin lands he was Duke of Normandy and was married to Eleanor of Aquitaine. He needed a permanent base in England where he could meet and consult with his secular and ecclesiastical lords with as little delay as possible. Westminster became established as the King's Court and London as the meeting place of his councils and assemblies. It therefore became necessary for the lords to maintain households in the City or its sub-urbs, close to the source of power and influence. Fitzstephen, writing during the King's reign, said that 'almost all the bishops, abbots and great men of England, are, in a manner, citizens and freemen of London; as they have magnificent houses there, to which they resort, spending large sums of money, whenever they are summoned thither to councils and assemblies by the king or their metropolitan, or are compelled to go there by their own business.'

During Stephen's reign the Jews had been savagely persecuted. They were accused of ritual murders of young children, with whose blood they anointed their own people, and they were said to raise devils and engage in all the dark practices of medieval sorcery, black magic and witchcraft, but Henry II, needing their money, offered them a measure of protection, though maintaining that, since they followed a profession which was condemned by the Church, their money and possessions were forfeited to the Crown on their death and could be recovered by their heirs only by purchase.

Aaron of Lincoln was one of the richest and most influential Jewish money-lenders during Henry II's reign, financing the building of some of the finest cathedrals and abbeys in the country, including Canterbury and Lincoln Cathedrals and the abbeys of Peterborough and St Albans: and when he died, in 1186, his affairs were found to be so complicated that a special exchequer was set up to trace all his debtors and attempt to collect them for the Crown, but twenty years later many had still not been paid and Aaron's son was still negotiating with the Crown to try and salvage something for himself.

With the fall of Jerusalem to the Saracens in 1187 there was a new enthusiasm for the Crusades and at the same time an increasing hatred and persecution of the Jews. To finance the third Crusade Henry II demanded one-tenth of the property of his Christian subjects and from the Jews one-quarter, which they paid and somehow survived.

An account of London was not included in the 'Domesday Book' and Fitz-stephen's description of the city is the earliest we have. He was a Londoner who became a monk of Canterbury and witnessed the murder of Thomas à Becket in 1170. Shortly afterwards he wrote the life of Thomas, to which he appended his account of London during the reign of Henry II.

'Amongst the noble and celebrated cities of the world, that of London, the capital of the kingdom of England, is one of the most renowned, possessing above all other abundant wealth, extensive commerce, great grandeur and significance,' he began, for he was full of civic pride and unconcerned by the medieval squalor of unpaved, muddy streets, open sewers and piles of rotting refuse.

In addition to St Paul's there were also in London and the suburbs, he said, 'thirteen large conventual churches, besides 136 lesser parochial ones'.

St Paul's was a vast monastic house and its foundation eventually included the Bishop, the Dean, four Archdeacons, the Treasurer, the Precentor, the Chancellor, 30 greater Canons, twelve lesser Canons, some 50 Chantry priests and 30 vicars, as well as the Sacrist, three vergers, the master of the singing school, the master of the grammar school, the almoner and his four vergers, the servitors, the book-binder, the chamberlain, the rent-collector, the baker, the brewer, the singing-men and choir boys, as well as a fraternity of sextons, grave-diggers, bell-ringers, makers and menders of the ecclesiastical robes, painters, carvers and gilders.

Fitzstephen was describing the beautiful Gothic St Paul's, with its magnificent steeple, the highest in Europe, rising to 493 feet, which was built after the fire of 1087 and to which Henry I donated land for the spacious churchyard. This was enclosed by a wall running from the north-east corner of Ave Maria Lane along Paternoster Row to the north end of Old Change in Cheapside and then south to Carter Lane and Creed Lane, and in addition to the great western gate it had five smaller posterns. During Stephen's reign the cathedral had suffered from another fire, but the damage had been repaired. The Bishops's palace was on the north-west corner, the Chapter House on the south side. There was a charnel house with a chapel over it and close beside it a small enclosure called Pardon Churchyard, where Gilbert à Becket, father of the Saint, founded a small chapel. Nearby was the Chapel of Jesus, serving the parish church of St Faith, until it was destroyed by fire, when it was re-established in the crypt of St Paul's. To the east of the churchyard was the large, open green, where the folk-moot met in the open air and Paul's Cross stood at the eastern end of the north transept.

Of the conventual churches St Martin's-le-Grand off Cheapside was a collegiate church which had been founded by a king of Kent in 750 and en-larged only a few years before the Conquest as a college for Augustinian canons. It claimed the privilege of sanctuary and many a prisoner from New-gate tried to escape and reach its safety. It was one of the churches where, as at Bow Church, Cheapside, St Giles's, Cripplegate and All Hallows Barking, the curfew was rung in time of trouble, to warn citizens to stay indoors. St Katharine's by the Tower had been founded in 1148 by Matilda of Boulogne, wife of King Stephen, for the repose of the souls of her son Baldwin and her daughter Matilda, and for the maintenance of a master and thirteen poor brothers and sisters: and after her time it received many more bequests, Queen Philippa bestowing a beautiful new church which stood in a precinct of eleven acres. The foundation became a centre of religion and education for the poor of this corner of East London and the church survived until it was pulled down for the building of St Katharine docks in the nineteenth century.

The priory of St Mary Overies on Bankside had, according to Stow, been first founded as a nunnery long before the Conquest. The legend was that Mary, the daughter of John Overy, a rich old miser who ran a ferry service over the river, was courted by a young man whom she loved dearly, but old Overy refused to countenance the match and kept her secluded in the house. One day, to save the price of his servants' meals, he decided to pretend to be dead for 24 hours, in the fond hope that the men would fast, as a token of mourning. He wrapped himself in a sheet and placed tapers at his head and feet, but to his fury the servants, assuming that he really was dead, were delighted. They raided the store cupboards and gave themselves the best meal of their lives, whereupon the old miser rose from his shroud and bela-boured them furiously. But one of the men, mistaking him for the Devil, hit him over the head and killed him. Mary's lover, hearing that old Overy was dead at last, came riding up to London to claim his bride, but in his eagerness he rode too fast and broke his neck, whereupon Mary, who had inherited all her father's money but was broken-hearted at the loss of her lover, founded the priory which bore her name and retired there for the rest of her life.

In later years the nunnery was refounded by two Norman knights as a house for Augustinian canons, and at the Dissolution the Priory church was bestowed by Henry VIII as the parish church of St Saviour.

Queen Matilda's Priory of the Holy Trinity, Aldgate, received many later gifts and became one of the most wealthy and beautiful in the City, famed for its hospitality and charity to the poor, and the Prior was alderman of the Portsoken ward, but at the Reformation the Priory was demolished and the stones and monuments sold for building material at sixpence the cartload.

The Augustinian Priory of St Bartholomew had been built by Rahere during the reign of Henry I, on the Smooth Field which became known as Smithfield, where a horse fair was held every Friday and also a cattle market, known as the King's market. This was just outside the City wall but within its jurisdic-tion, in the ward of Farringdon Without. The story goes that after Prince William had been drowned in the White Ship, on his way from Normandy to England, King Henry was so grief-stricken that the Court was plunged into a long-lasting mourning. Rahere, a Canon of St Paul's who had been one of the liveliest members of the Court, was so sobered that he went on a pilgri-mage to Rome.

During the journey he fell seriously ill and in his delirium he had a vision of a great beast with the wings and talons of an eagle, which was about to cast him into a bottomless pit. Terrified, Rahere vowed that if he lived he would devote himself to the poor of London. The beast changed to the figure of a man who declared himself to be Bartholomew, the Apostle of Jesus Christ who had come to save him, and Rahere decided that once he was safely home again, he would build a church as well as a hospital.

Henry granted him the site of the Smooth Field, with the valuable tolls of the King's market, and here in 1123 Rahere founded his priory, with the hospital close by. The priory became a place of pilgrimage, particularly during the times of the church festivals. Hucksters, chapmen, and merchants of all kinds always put in an appearance on these occasions, for pilgrimages were usually some-thing of a holiday as well as a holy duty, and they found plenty of customers. The Smooth Field became a fair ground on these days and St Bartholomew's fair was soon established, an important trade fair which, in these early days, dealt largely in woollen cloth. The little streets which survive close to the Church, Cloth Fair and Cloth Court, are reminders of the old fair. The priors of St Bartholomew were the Lords of the Fair, receiving the tolls, and the drapers and cloth merchants kept their wares within the Priory walls for safety.

The weekly horse market was still held, and on other days Smithfield was a place for tournaments and archery contests, but also it was the place for public executions.

St Bartholomew's hospital is, of course, the descendant of Rahere's little hospital, but the Priory has a strange history. At the Reformation, the monastic buildings, the Lady Chapel, the Close and the Cloth Fair were sold to the Rich family, who held them until the nineteenth century, but in Mary Tudor's brief reign, during which at least 200 Protestants were burnt at the stake at Smithfield, the Priory was granted as a home for Dominicans for a few years. With the accession of Edward VI the nave and many other parts of the building were pulled down, leaving only the choir of the old Priory Church, with some of the chapels, including the Lady Chapel, the transepts, part of the south wall of the nave and the lovely west gateway.

The nave was never rebuilt and the burial ground now occupies the site, the thirteenth-century archway leading to it having once been the entrance to the nave. The old choir is now the main body of the church, consisting of the top of the original cross, the north and south transepts and the former chancel.

For years it was neglected. The Lady Chapel behind the east end of the choir, first built by Rahere and rebuilt in the fourteenth century, became a dwelling house after the Dissolution. Then, early in the eighteenth century, it passed into the hands of a printer, one of whose employees was the young American Benjamin Franklin, and in part of the triforium above the south aisle a Nonconformist school was held. In the choir a factory for wool and silk fringes was established early in the nineteenth century, and by 1833 the factory had spread into the Lady Chapel. The north transept was occupied by a blacksmith's forge, the bays of the cloisters were used for stables and the crypt, once a charnel house, became a coal and wine cellar.

Then the preservationists came to realise the havoc that had been wrought. One by one the artisans and the stable-keepers were bought out and in the late nineteenth and early part of the twentieth century the work of repair and restoration was carried out.

It is surprising how much of Rahere's church remains. The entrance path to the west front, which runs alongside the tree-shaded graveyard, has been cut down to the level of the original nave and is where the original south aisle ran. The Norman arches of the church are magnificent in their unpretentious strength – arcades of plain, round pillars rising into rounded arches. beyond which are the side aisles, and above them the triforium.

The original clerestory was pulled down and replaced in 1405, being built in the contemporary perpendicular style. The rounded apse was then replaced by a square one, but during the nineteenth century the earlier form was restored, so that it now looks much as it did in Rahere's day. In the south aisle, above the third arch, is the little oriel window built by Prior Bolton, the last but one Prior of the community before the Dissolution.

Rahere's beautiful canopied tomb, restored to its medieval colour and brilliance, is on the north side of the Sanctuary, close to the High Altar, and the medieval font – one of the very few to have survived in London from before the Reformation – stands in the south aisle.

Fitzstephen described the Friday horsefair at Smithfield to which earls, barons and knights, as well as most of the citizens, flocked, either to look or to buy.

A knight's war horse had to be immensely strong to carry the weight of the rider's mail armour, as well as its own, and was far more expensive than the palfrey he used for ordinary riding or the pack-horse which carried his luggage. All these were to be bought at Smithfield as well as 'the young blood colts, not yet accustomed to the bridle' and the plough and cart horses: and in another part of the field were sold cows, pigs and agricultural implements.

There were often horse races at the fair.

The jockeys, who are boys expert in the management of horses . . . inspired with the love of praise and the hope of victory, clap spurs to their flying horses, lashing them with their whips, and inciting them by their shouts. The horses, too, after their manner, are eager for the race; their limbs tremble, and, impatient of delay, they cannot stand still; upon the signal being given, they stretch out their limbs, hurry over the course, and are borne along with unremitting speed.

Of the other conventual churches of Fitzstephen's time, Queen Matilda's hospital for 40 lepers and the associated conventual buildings, founded 1101–1109, was close to the present church of St Giles-in-the-Fields. This was one of the oldest leper houses in the country and lasted until the Reformation.

The Hospital of St Mary of Bethlehem, in the parish of St Botolph Without, Bishopsgate, was founded after Fitzstephen's time. It was first established in 1247 by Godfrey, bishop of Bethlehem, on land granted by Simon FitzMary, then a sheriff of London.

The magnificent priory of St John of Jerusalem was established in Clerkenwell by Lord Jordan Briset and his wife Muriel in 1144 and for the next 400 years was the London home of the Augustinian order of the Knights of St John. The order had originated a few years earlier when some merchants from Amalfi obtained permission from the Mohammedans to build a refuge for sick and needy Christian pilgrims near the Holy Sepulchre in Jerusalem. During the first Crusade the hospital at Jerusalem was filled with wounded Crusaders, many of whom joined the Order and adopted the black robe and white cross symbolic of John the Baptist's dress in the wilderness: but the Order soon became a military one, sending reinforcements to the Crusaders. Matthew Paris described how, in 1237,

the Hospitallers sent their prior, Theodoric, a German by birth, and a most able knight, with a body of other knights and stipendiary attendants, and a large sum of money to the assistance of the Holy Land. They having made all arrangements, set out from their house at Clerkenwell, and proceeded in good order, with about thirty shields uncovered, with spears raised, and preceded by their banner, through the midst of the City, towards the bridge, that they might obtain the blessing of the spectators, and, bowing their heads with their cowls lowered, commended themselves to the prayer of all.

By this time the knights had adopted a red cassock and white cross for their military dress and their standard was red with a white cross. The Order had begun in poverty but partly through the fruits of early victories and privateering exploits in the Mediterranean, after the capture of Rhodes, but more through the bequests of lands and manors it received, it became immensely rich and in a position to lend money to the Crown.

Not until 1522 was Rhodes lost to Suleiman the Magnificent. The Knights of St John then in Rhodes were offered asylum in Malta, and when, a few years later, Henry VIII dissolved the Priory in Clerkenwell and suppressed the Order, some of the Knights joined their brothers in Malta. The gateway of the Priory survived into the nineteenth century but the Priory itself was destroyed at the Reformation, being blown up with gunpowder. Only the original crypt of the Priory Church survives, below the eighteenth-century St John's church, which was built on the site.

The Knights Templars were a military order founded early in the twelfth century by eight French knights to protect Christian pilgrims on the hazardous journey to Jerusalem, and in 1128 their first London home was established on the south side of Holborn, just outside the bars marking the City boundary.

C

Like the Knights of St John, the order was strict and idealistic in the early days, the Knights wearing the white garments of chastity. 'All scurrility, jests, and idle words' were to be avoided; and after any foolish saying, the repetition of the Lord's Prayer was enjoined: and every Templar was to shun 'feminine kisses, whether from widow, virgin, mother, sister, aunt or any other woman'.

These were the years when the troubadours of Provence were imbuing the ancient European legends of King Arthur with a new spirit of romance and adding the legend of the quest of the Holy Graal and of Sir Galahad, 'sans peur et sans reproche', but Christendom soon learnt that no war is ever holy and its romance a vast illusion. Like the Knights of St John, the Templars soon grew immensely rich. During the reign of Henry II, when Fitzstephen was writing, they moved from Holborn, choosing for their new site the stretch of land between Fleet Street and the river. Here they built their beautiful Temple Church with its circular nave, modelled on the plan of the Church of the Holy Sepulchre, their new monastery, with quarters for the prior, his chaplain, the serving brothers and the knights, a council chamber, a refectory, a range of cloisters and a river terrace for military practice and the exercise of the horses.

The Templars had fought gallantly. In 1146 the whole Brotherhood had joined the second crusade. They saved Jerusalem and stormed the walls of Askelon. They drove Saladin from Gaza and nearly broke through his mameluke guards to capture him near Askelon, but the following year Saladin's armies fought back so ferociously that the entire Order was nearly exterminated.

By 1187 Saladin had captured Jerusalem and it was now, nearly at the end of his reign, that Henry II raised money from his own people and the Jews to finance the third Crusade, on which Richard I embarked immediately after his coronation, with a fresh band of Knights from London. The Templars led Richard's vain attack on Jerusalem and after Richard had abandoned the fight and made his treaty with Saladin, they helped him to escape to the Adriatic, disguised in a Templar's white robe.

The later Crusades were disastrous for the Templars. Hundreds lost their lives and as it grew apparent that their cause was lost the survivors grew cynical and corrupt, though increasingly rich. Sinister stories were told of them and they were accused of a long string of vices, which read like a sorcerer's handbook for the celebration of a Black Mass.

There is no doubt that the scientific knowledge the Crusaders brought back from the East was of inestimable value in helping to lift the fog of superstition and credulity which bemused the people of medieval Europe, but it took many years to infiltrate.

In France many were arrested and burnt at the stake. In England they were
sent to the Tower, accused of blasphemy and heresy, and their lands were
confiscated. Some were brought to St Martin's, Ludgate, to answer the charges
before the papal inquisitors and the Bishops of London and Chichester, others
to All Hallows By-The-Tower. They made public confession and were recon-
ciled to the Church at High Mass at St Paul's Cathedral, although many submitted only after torture: and the order was formally abolished by Pope
Clement V in 1312, its revenues being granted to the Knights of St John at
Clerkenwell.

Of the churches Fitzstephen lists, 99 were within the walls of the City, and
outstanding among them was St Mary-le-Bow in Cheapside, the church where
the Archbishop of Canterbury held his Court of Arches, for ecclesiastical
trials and appointments. It was lost in the fire of 1666, rebuilt by Wren, bombed
again in 1941 and restored in 1964 by Laurence King, but the magnificent Norman
crypt, built some time between 1080 and 1090, is still there, restored, as far as
possible, in its original form, and it is from the Norman arches of the crypt
that it derives its name, for it was said to have been the first Church to be built
in this way on arches or 'bows' of stone and was accordingly first called St
Maria-de-Arcubos. Some Roman brick was incorporated in the building and
the nave of the crypt has aisles separated from the main body of the nave by
pillars of solid stone.

The rest of the building seems not to have been so solid, for there is a record
of a terrible storm during the reign of William Rufus when the wind wrenched
part of the roof off the church into the street below and four of its huge
rafters, each 26 feet long, were driven 22 feet into the ground: and in 1270 its
steeple collapsed and killed several people, but it was soon rebuilt, for it was
from here that the eight o'clock curfew was rung, ordering people to extin-
guish their lights and go to bed.

Another church which Fitzstephen must have known was St Alban, Wood
Street, even older than Bow Church, for it was built in the eighth or ninth
century, perhaps by King Offa of Mercia, who built St Alban's Abbey, or by
King Alfred, after he had driven the Danes from London, and here again there
are said to have been Roman bricks incorporated in the building. The church
was rebuilt after the Great Fire but almost completely destroyed in 1942 and
today only the tower remains.

Most of the churches of the eleventh and twelfth centuries in London, as
in other cities throughout the country, were very small and intimate, though
sufficient for the tiny parishes they served. Some had stone towers and little
wooden turrets, some only turrets. A few had steeples and they all had gilded
vanes, while inside they were bright and gay with wall paintings, painted

altar pieces and stained glass windows in the red, green, blue and gold so beloved of medieval people. More than half the London churches were lost in the Great Fire of 1666 and of these 35 were not rebuilt, although in some cases the churchyards were preserved. Some were rebuilt during the eighteenth century and in 1782 there were 69 churches in the City. The Georgians and Victorians demolished some of Wren's churches, including St Antholin, Watling Street, St Benet Fink, Threadneedle Street, and St Mildred, Poultry, while during the Second World War nearly all the churches were damaged in some way, several being totally destroyed, and of these eleven, including seven of Wren's churches, have not been rebuilt. Yet of the survivors, even after much rebuilding, a few still retain reminders of their medieval past.

Fitzstephen described the defences of the City, the White Tower of great strength, the mortar in its building having been 'tempered with the blood of beasts', while Baynard Castle and Montfichet Castle were both strongly fortified. He speaks now of seven large double gates in the City wall, and although he does not name them, Stow interprets them as the postern gate by the Tower, Aldgate, Bishopsgate, Aldersgate, Newgate, Ludgate and the Bridgegate. Moorgate was built a good deal later, in the fifteenth century.

The postern by the Tower was partly demolished at the end of the twelfth century and the stone used for the enlargement of the White Tower. Aldgate was a free gate, open without toll, built by the Canons of the Priory of the Holy Trinity. No one can say for certain after which bishop Bishopsgate was named, but it may have been Bishop Erkenwald: and it was repaired during the reign of the Conqueror by the Norman Bishop William. By the time of Henry III the Hanseatic[1] merchants, in return for certain tax exemptions, were made responsible for its maintenance, and during the reign of Edward IV they rebuilt it. This was a convenient way out of the City for passengers to the north-east and saved the long journey over Bethnal Green and Cambridge Heath for passengers to the north who previously had left the City by Aldgate.

The postern at Cripplegate, not mentioned by Fitzstephen, was very ancient. Stow says it derived its name from the fact that cripples used to stand there to beg. In 1010, when the Danes were conquering East Anglia, the body of King Edmund the Martyr was brought for safety from Bury St Edmunds to London, by way of the Cripplegate, and as it was carried through the gate several cripples standing there were miraculously cured and able to walk again. However, a less romantic but more likely origin of the name is that it was once the 'crepel' gate – meaning a covered way – into the Roman fortress. A century after Fitzstephen's time, the gate-house had become a debtors' prison.

Aldersgate was built soon after the Conquest and survived until the early

1 See p. 89.

seventeenth century, by which time it had become so dangerous and dilapidated that it was pulled down and rebuilt.

Newgate was opened about the time of Henry I or Stephen, when St Paul's was being rebuilt after the fire of 1086. The streets surrounding the Cathedral were so blocked with building materials that foot passengers could not easily reach Ludgate, so the wall was breached at Newgate as an alternative way out of the City to the west, but as early as King John's time it had become a prison for debtors and felons, a terrible place which in 1218 the King ordered the sheriffs of London to repair 'for the safe keeping of his prisoners', promising that they should be repaid from the Exchequer.

Geoffrey of Monmouth, that most unreliable and credulous of historians, declared that Ludgate was named after the mythical King Lud who built it in 66 B.C., 200 or 300 years before the wall existed, but its original name was probably the Fleet or Floodgate. The date of the first gate is not known but it was rebuilt in the thirteenth century and not long afterwards became a prison like Newgate, when it was decreed that all freemen of the City guilty of debt or trespass should be committed to Ludgate, while prisoners guilty of treason, felonies and other criminal offences should be kept at Newgate.

4

Medieval London — I

Fitzstephen described how 'the artisans of the several crafts, the vendors of the various commodities, and the labourers of every kind, have each their separate stations, which they take every morning'.

These markets were centred on the large West Cheap or Cheapside, originally a large open square to the east of St Paul's churchyard, and the smaller East Cheap, just north of the bridge. The sites of these markets have been preserved in the names of the streets which grew up in and around the square. Originally the food was displayed on open stalls, the vendors living close by, but the craftsmen lived at their workshops. The important point is that the dealers in the various commodities, whether food or crafts, tended to congregate in the same areas.

To the north-west of the West Cheap were the butchers' stalls, where they had been for generations. To the east, at the corner of St Paul's churchyard, was the cornmarket. The fish market was in Friday Street and Old Fish Street until it was moved to a new market closer to the river. North of the West Cheap, in Foster Lane, were the saddlers and harness makers. Then came the markets of Wood Street, Milk Street, Honey Lane, Ironmonger Lane and Coneyhope Lane, where rabbits and poultry were sold. There was a corn market on Cornhill and a wool market close by in Lombard Street, near the church of St Mary Woolnoth. From south of West Cheap ran Bread Street, where the bakers lived, and Cordwainer Street where the shoes were made, and just to the south, down by the river, was the Vintry, an area where the foreign wine merchants lived. Candlewick Street, the home of the soap and candle-makers – now Cannon Street – joined the Walbrook to the East Cheap and Budge Row was the place where budge, a specially dressed lamb's wool, used for lining the long, medieval gowns, was made and sold.

Stow says that the mercers and haberdashers used to trade in West Cheap until they moved to the new London Bridge, which when Fitzstephen was writing, was just being built. The goldsmiths moved to the south side of West Cheap, the pepperers and grocers to Bucklersbury, the drapers of Lombard Street and Cornhill to Candlewick Street and Watling Street, the skinners into Budge Row and Walbrook. The bowyers who, like the fletchers, were by Stow's time practising a dying craft, gradually scattered from Bowyers Row by Ludgate, but 'the brewers for the most part remained near the friendly water of the Thames'.

All these traders and craftsmen had their unions or guilds. The earliest guilds in England were the frith-guilds of Saxon times. The old Saxons who had settled in their solitary homesteads had been bound together by family bonds and held mutual responsibility for each other, but as life become more complex and people tended to move around the country more freely, the family ties were weakened and the freemen of a district, instead of living in isolation, tended to join together in guilds, for the mutual protection of both life and property.

These frith-guilds grew up all over Europe during the ninth and tenth centuries, but while on the Continent they were discouraged and even repressed by the King and the nobility, as a potential danger to established authority, in England they were accepted, both in the country and the towns, as the basis of social order.

They were not yet associations of merchants or craftsmen but the members accepted a mutual responsibility, declaring: 'Let all share the same lot. If any misdo, let all bear it.' They took an oath of fidelity and met once a month for a guild feast, their leader being known as an alderman, the former Alderman or Ealdorman who had been the head of a shire being by now termed an Earl. A guild member could rely on help from other members in time of trouble. If wrongly accused of a crime, they would appear at court to support him. If he died a poor man, they would pay for his burial. On the other hand, if he wronged a fellow member, he was considered to have wronged the guild and faced a fine or even expulsion, in which case he became an outcast, forbidden to follow his trade or craft.

The early guilds had various aims. In London during the tenth century there was a well regulated frith or peace guild formed for the purpose of pursuing thieves: and by the eleventh century, both in England and the Continent, there came into existence dozens of religious guilds, invariably attached to their nearest church, in which members took an oath of admission, paid into a common fund and devoted the proceeds to the bestowing of alms, the saying of masses for the dead and the holding of feasts and processions.

In London by the twelfth century the groups of traders, in their defined localities, meeting day by day as neighbours, began to join together in similar groups of Christian fraternities, gathering in their local church, adopting its saint as their patron, providing masses for the dead, candles for the altar, rich vestments and funeral palls, and the services of a chaplain to give their souls especial guidance and a safe passage in an increasingly difficult world.

The alderman of the guild was assisted by two wardens, whose duties were mainly to summon the guild members to mass and to funerals, the funerals being followed by the inevitable feast, which was usually held in the house of one of the members. These fraternities were small, private religious and social clubs of which few records have survived, for their aims were mainly very limited, although one or two developed a wider purpose, such as the founding of academic colleges as, for example, Corpus Christi, Cambridge, established in 1352. There was a guild of St Lazarus, which seems to have been a leper charity, and the Pilgrims' Guild for people who wanted to go on a pilgrimage, as well as four Bridge Guilds, which undertook to help keep London Bridge in repair.

At the same time, amongst these neighbourhood guilds other types of guilds arose, concerned less with the religious aspect than the interests of their trades and crafts, although religion still played an important part in their organisations and every guild had its patron saint. The fraternities of the Mercers, Drapers and Pewterers were dedicated to the Virgin Mary, the Haberdashers to St Catherine, the Goldsmiths to St Dunstan, the Vintners to St Martin, the Musicians to St Cecilia, the Grocers to St Anthony and the Barber Surgeons to St Cosmo and St Dunstan.

Two types emerged, the merchant guilds and the craft or trade guilds. The merchant guilds had a high entrance fee and were exclusive. They sought control of their trades and most towns had a guild merchant who made the rules concerning the sale of goods, saw to it that quality was maintained, that markets were properly controlled and that no one traded without a licence: and they also had the power to attempt to recover bad debts. London, however, never had a guild merchant and the merchant guilds did not survive beyond the fourteenth or early fifteenth centuries. It was the craft guilds which acquired the power and as early as the thirteenth century they had undermined the power of the guild merchant. They were occupational associations formed by all the artisans of a particular craft or industry and often they included the suppliers of the raw materials and the wholesalers associated with them.

Most were modelled on existing religious guilds, having begun as social and religious fraternities and developed their economic functions later. These guilds, called 'mysteries' in medieval times, comprised a hierarchy of master, journeyman and apprentice, and their policy was in the hands of the alderman, one or two wardens and a council of advisers.

To become a member of a craft guild an apprentice had to serve for seven years, living in his master's house, along with the servants. After that time he became a labourer craftsman or journeyman working for a master, or established himself as a master craftsman, himself taking apprentices. The quality and value of the work done by craftsmen was regularly inspected, hours of work were fixed from daybreak to curfew and there was a fixed minimum wage. Shoddy and careless work was confiscated and anyone disobeying a guild's orders was fined and, on occasion, expelled. Members contributed to the guild funds and the money was used to help them in sickness and old age.

In theory the king's consent was necessary before a guild could lawfully be established and the weavers seem to have been the earliest, having received a charter from Henry I in 1130, while about the same time the saddlers established a guild at St Martin's-le-Grand, where they paid their dues. The bakers received a charter from Henry II and during his reign another eighteen guilds were charged with having formed themselves without permission and were duly fined, adding a useful income to the Crown. Some of these guilds were named only by the alderman at their head and it is not possible to tell which trades they represented, but amongst them were the butchers, the pepperers and the goldsmiths, and the one certain thing about them is that they all enjoyed themselves enormously at their monthly feasts: but it was not until the reign of Edward II that the guilds rose to power and influence and their municipal functions and privileges were firmly established.

As master craftsmen and the employers of labour grew richer, their workers argued and fought for higher wages, and when the Statute of Labourers was issued, after the Black Death, it was directed against the members of the craft guilds as much as the farm labourers, though it met with as little success. But that was two centuries ahead, and in the twelfth century, when Fitzstephen was writing, they were only sketchily organised and the records are scanty.

Fitzstephen described the public eating-house down by the riverside amongst the wine shops, where

> every day, according to the season, may be found viands of all kinds, roast, fried and boiled, fish large and small, coarser meat for the poor, and more delicate for the rich, such as venison, fowls, and small birds. If friends, weary with their journey, should unexpectedly come to a citizen's house, and being hungry, should not like to wait till fresh meat be bought and cooked ... they hasten to the river bank, and there all things desirable are ready to their hand.

The riverside was as busy as Cheapside and East Cheap. The principal wharves were Paul's wharf, just east of Baynard's Castle and close to the large brewery and bakehouse of St Paul's, Queenhithe and Garlickhithe near the Vintry, Dowgate, and to the east of the bridge, Botolph's wharf and Billingsgate, where fish caught in the river and the estuary were landed and a general market had developed.

'Let us now,' said Fitzstephen,

come to the sports and pastimes, seeing it is fit that a city should not only be commodious and serious, but also merry and sportful . . . we may begin with children's sports, seeing that we have all been children . . . annually on the day which is called Shrovetide the boys of the respective schools bring each a fighting cock to the master, and the whole of that forenoon is spent by the boys in seeing their cocks fight in the school-room: after dinner, all the young men of the city go out into the fields to play at the well-known game of foot-ball. The scholars belonging to the several schools have each their ball; and the tradesmen, according to their respective crafts, have theirs. The more aged men, the fathers of the players and the wealthy citizens, come on horseback to see the contests of the young men, with whom, after their manner, they participate, their natural heat seeming to be aroused by the sight of so much agility, and by their participation in the amusement of unrestrained youth. . . .

The lay-sons of the citizens rush out of the gates in crowds, equipped with lances and shields, the younger sort with pikes from which the iron head has been taken off, and there they get up sham fights, and exercise themselves in military combat. When the king happens to be near the city, most of the courtiers attend, and the young men who form the households of the earls and barons, and have not yet attained the honour of knighthood, resort thither for the purpose of trying their skill. The hope of victory animates every one. The spirited horses neigh, their limbs tremble, they champ their bits, and, impatient of delay, cannot endure standing still. When at length . . . the young riders having been divided into companies, some pursue those that go before without being able to overtake them, whilst others throw their companions out of their course, and gallop beyond them.

Fitzstephen is vague about London schools. He mentions that the three principal churches, St Paul's, Holy Trinity and St Martin, 'have famous schools by privilege, and in virtue of their ancient dignity, but through the special favour of one or more of those learned men who are known and eminent in the study of philosophy there are other schools licensed by special grace and permission'.

Sons of noble families were sent to other great households for training and education, mainly in the skills which would fit them to become knights and manage their estates, but they were taught French and Latin by the household priest or a visiting monk. Otherwise education was in the hands of the Church. Boys were taught at the song schools attached to the cathedrals and churches, and abbots and priors often employed secular clergy to run schools for boys who were not intending to enter the order.

During the reign of Stephen, the papal legate, Henry, Bishop of Winchester, ordered the Chapter of St Paul's and the Archdeacon of London to excommunicate any who had presumed to hold a school without the licence of the master of all the city schools, this master having been a Canon of St Paul's who had recently been granted the mastership of St Paul's school, which had been established a few years earlier.

We know hardly anything of these early schools, but the realisation of the need for education was growing. The parish priest sometimes taught Latin, still a living language in which educated people from all over Europe conversed, in which scholars taught, priests conducted their services and merchants and lawyers transacted their business: and a parish priest sometimes taught it to a few boys, holding a small school inside the porch of his church, while Chantry bequests often provided for the priest to hold a small school for boys. The schools at Oxford and Cambridge, which were to develop into the universities, were only just being formed in the mid-twelfth century, while the famous grammar schools were not to be founded for another 200 or 300 years.

Fitzstephen went on to describe the summer sports of London – the water sports and displays, with plenty of people on hand to pull the unlucky ones out of the river. There was also shooting, wrestling, casting the stone, practising their shields, and dancing, the girls joining in the dance 'as long as they can well see'.

In winter they enjoyed winter sports on the frozen marshes of Moorfields with ingeniously devised skates. 'They place certain bones – the leg-bones of animals – under the soles of their feet,' he said, 'by tying them round their ankles, and then, taking a pole shod with iron into their hands, they push themselves forward by striking it against the ice, and are carried on with a velocity equal to the flight of a bird, or a bolt discharged from the cross-bow.'

The only inconveniences of London, he declared, are 'the immoderate drinking of foolish persons, and the frequent fires'.

This was by no means everyone's view, however. Richard of Devizes, a monk of Winchester, wrote of London in his *Chronicle*, late in the twelfth century:

I do not at all like the city. All sorts of men crowd together there from every country under the heavens. Each race brings its own vices and its own customs to the city. No one lives in it without falling into some sort of crime. Every quarter of it abounds in grave obscenities. . . . Whatever evil or malicious thing that can be found in any part of the world, you will find in that one city. Do not associate with the crowds of pimps; do not mingle with the throngs in the eating-houses; avoid dice and gambling, the theatre and the tavern. You will meet with more braggarts there than in all France; the number of parasites is infinite. Actors, jesters, smooth-skinned lads, Moors, flatterers, pretty boys, effeminates, pederasts, singing and dancing girls, quacks, belly-dancers, sorceresses, extortioners, night-wanderers, magicians, mimes, beggars, buffoons: all this tribe will fill your houses. Therefore if you do not want to dwell with evil-doers, do not live in London. I do not speak against learned or religious men, or against Jews: however, because of their living amidst evil people, I believe they are less perfect than elsewhere.[1]

Work on the first stone London Bridge began in 1176, just after Fitzstephen had written his description of the City. Money for the venture was raised by Peter, a priest and chaplain of St Mary Colechurch of Coneyhope Lane, on the north side of Poultry. The City had no funds available but Peter seems to have organised various charities. The Guilds bequeathed funds and the King contributed with the proceeds of a new tax on wool, about which the wool merchants were none too pleased.

The site of the new bridge was a little to the west of the old wooden bridge, which had suffered so many disasters. There is a story that during the dreadful whirlwind of 1090, which tore away the roof of St Mary-le-Bow, nearly 600 houses were blown down, several other churches near the Tower were severely damaged, while the wooden bridge was completely swept away. It was rebuilt but had been totally destroyed by fire in 1135 and the next replacement had become so unsafe that it had been rebuilt in 1160, but was already becoming dangerous again.

The river in Peter of Colebrook's time was a good deal wider than it is today and the transport of the stone for the new bridge was, in itself, an arduous undertaking. The bridge, 926 feet long and 40 feet wide, was composed of nineteen pointed arches and the piers were protected by heavy platforms of elm, which can be seen in old pictures of the bridge, surrounding the bases of the arches at water level. This meant that although the river was about 900 feet wide, the effective waterway through the bridge was reduced to less than 200 feet, and it caused such a sharp fall in the stream that the water rushed through the narrow arches and made navigation extremely difficult. It was not until

1. Richard of Devizes, *Chronicle*, Ed. J. T. Appleby, NMT, 1963, pp 64–7.

the fifteenth or sixteenth centuries that this powerful run of water was put to good use by the creation of a water wheel and effective waterworks, devised by an ingenious Dutch water engineer, so for many years it was nothing but a serious hazard to shipping.

The bridge was curiously irregular, for the width of the arches varied from 10 feet to 32 feet. Over the tenth and longest pier a two-storey chapel was built, the lower chapel being built inside the pier, with stairs leading to the upper chapel, which was on a level with the bridge road, and another flight which made it accessible from the river.

The chapel was dedicated to St Thomas of Canterbury, the newest saint in the Church calendar, for whose death the King had done heavy penance, but he was known for a time as St Thomas of Acon or Acre, his mother having been born in Acre.

The bridge gate and tower were built about 300 yards from the Southwark end and formed the boundary between Southwark and the City, and adjoining it on the Surrey side was the drawbridge, with another tower built on the second pier, almost at the entrance to Southwark.

The bridge took 33 years to build and Peter, who died before it was completed, was buried under the chapel staircase. Despite the fact that on several occasions it appeared to be falling down, which was the reason for the old nursery rhyme, Londoners were fond of their bridge: and with frequent repairs, which were in the hands of various Bridge Trusts, it remained for close on 650 years, until it was finally pulled down in 1832, at which time old Peter's bones were discovered.

Only four years after its completion it was partially damaged by fire. By this time the first houses had been built on it and London merchants and tradesmen, seeing the importance of the site and ignoring the fire hazards, quickly established themselves there. Soon it was completely lined with houses except for two open spaces, one towards the City, known as the Square, and the other at the Southwark end, by the drawbridge. The houses with shops on the ground floors were built up against the parapets and the roadway passed through the centre of the bridge: and by the early thirteenth century there are records of glovers, goldsmiths and bowyers established there.

It was the obstruction of the arches and the heavy platforms surrounding them which caused the river to become ice-bound so often, and in exceptionally severe winters it was sometimes frozen over for several weeks at a time. Nobody seemed to do much work on these occasions and the frozen river was an opportunity for ice fairs and junketings of all kinds, with more winter sports for the schoolboys.

This was the London to which Richard I succeeded in 1189, on the death of his father in Normandy. Richard assumed the Dukedom of Normandy and crossed to England for his coronation, but then, in fulfilment of an earlier vow, set out on the Crusade for which he and his father had long been seeking money. Additional funds for his venture, which involved 8,000 men-at-arms and foot soldiers and a fleet of 100 ships, was raised by his officials through selling charters to more English boroughs. London had already contributed to Henry II's demands, and now, with extra money exacted by Richard, they at last received the right to choose their own sheriffs.

The annual farm which had been raised was reduced again to £300, but this was not so generous as it might appear, for many additional demands for money were made during the next few years by the Crown, in order that the City might maintain this privilege. The boundaries of the wards were more closely defined and by the end of the thirteenth century they had mostly acquired their present names. These were Farringdon in the north-west, stretching far beyond the City wall to the bars at Smithfield, Holborn and the Temple, which marked the limit of the City's jurisdiction, Aldersgate, Cripplegate and Bishopsgate, all of which reached far beyond the wall, the Portsoken ward, which ran outside the eastern wall, and inside the walls, Castle Baynard, Bread Street, Queenhithe, Bassishaw, Cheap, Cordwainer, Vintry, Coleman Street, Walbrook, Dowgate, Broad Street, Cornhill, Langbourn, Candlewick, Bridge, Lime Street, Billingsgate, Aldgate and the Tower.

The large Farringdon ward was divided into Farringdon Within and Farringdon Without in 1394 but not until 1550 did the borough of Southwark, known as Bridge Ward Without, come under the City's jurisdiction.

The freemen from each ward now elected an alderman to sit on the council which was to govern the City, and from these aldermen they also elected each year their sheriff. The organisation evolved slowly. When Richard I set off on his crusade he left William de Longchamp, Bishop of Ely, in control as chancellor and papal legate, head of both the State and the Church, much to the annoyance of his brother Prince John, who was given no specific authority. And Longchamp soon incurred the animosity of the barons as well as John by his autocratic behaviour and his extortions, as well as his ominous strengthening of the Tower. From Nottingham, John proceeded to march towards London in order to seize the City. The citizens met at their guildhall to decide what should be done. Foreseeing the danger of barring the City to him, they compromised. In the meantime, Richard, receiving disturbing reports of Longchamp's behaviour, changed his mind about him and appointed Walter of Coutances, bishop of Rouen, to take his place, sending him forthwith from Sicily to London.

John entered the City one night early in October of 1191 and was welcomed by a procession of citizens bearing lanterns and torches. The following day a concourse of clergy, nobles and citizens crowded into St Paul's to discuss their next move and then Walter of Coutances arrived, to announce his appointment by King Richard. Longchamp, who had taken refuge in the Tower, was deposed, ultimately escaping to France, disguised as a woman, and Coutances took over the office. He and John agreed that the citizens of London should have their commune, while the bishops and secular nobles cannily announced that they would maintain the City's status 'as long as it pleased the king'. In return, the citizens of London swore their loyalty to the Crown and promised that if Richard died without an heir, they would accept John.

King Richard was taken prisoner in Austria on his way home from the Crusade, and it was at this point, in 1193, that there is the first mention of a mayor of London. For Richard, learning that – despite Coutances' removal of Longchamp – he had failed to keep John in check (he now claimed the title of 'supreme governor of the whole realm'), sent Hubert Walter to replace him and find the money for his ransom: and one of the men whom Hubert entrusted with this task was Henry FitzAilwin, described now as mayor of London. The title meant literally 'the chief of the community' and was an important innovation. He held office for the entire remaining twenty years of his life. Little is known about him but he was a man of substance and the son of one of Henry I's sheriffs. He lived near London Stone and held lands in Hertfordshire, Kent and Surrey. With his appointment began the custom of electing two City sheriffs, who should hold office for only one year, although in the early days there were one or two exceptions to this and it was perhaps during FitzAilwin's term of office that the Court of Aldermen was instituted, but this is by no means certain. There had probably been some form of council governing the affairs of the City long before his time, but no details of it have survived, and the Common Council had not yet come into existence.

The most ancient court of the City, the folk-moot, now met only three times a year, at Michaelmas to acknowledge the new sheriffs, at Christmas to discuss the proper policing of the wards and at Midsummer to supervise fire precautions. The more serious business of the City government was transacted at the Court of Hustings. Before the advent of the mayor one of the King's sheriffs had presided at this Court but now his place was taken by the mayor, attended by his two sheriffs. Within a few years, probably still in FitzAilwin's time, the Court of Hustings had disappeared, most of the work being undertaken by the mayor's court.

In order of precedence the Mayor of London ranked equally with a viscount and a mitred abbot, and from the outset was addressed as 'your worship', but at first he was described only intermittently as the Lord Mayor and the title was not used regularly until 1545.

No sooner had Richard returned to England in 1193, after the payment of his ransom, than he had to cross to Normandy to defend it from the invasion of Philip II of France. In 1199 he was killed in battle and John succeeded to the throne of England as well as the Dukedom of Normandy, his mother's kingdom of Aquitaine and the family domains of Anjou, Maine and Touraine.

John crossed to England. The City of London honoured their promise and he was crowned at Westminster by Hubert Walter. Shortly after this King John granted the City a charter formally accepting the new custom of allowing the citizens to appoint their own sheriffs at a farm of £300. These sheriffs were answerable to the Exchequer judges but retained their rights as London citizens: but the City had to pay 3,000 marks for this privilege and no mention was made of the Mayor or the commune.

Philip of France was invading John's territories and he was desperately short of money to launch a campaign for their recovery. He levied heavy taxes not only on the City but throughout the country, including a customs duty of one-fifteenth on goods passing in or out of England, and his popularity began to wane very quickly.

The next few years were a disaster for the reign. When John lost Normandy to Philip it created legal difficulties not only for himself but for the barons who possessed land both in England and Normandy. They were given a choice of allegiance to Philip or John. Most of the barons negotiated with Philip but John who, despite his English grandmother, was more French than English, was determined on an attempt to regain his losses. He took money where he could find it, from the barons and from the Church, but the barons, nearly all of whom had fared well with their private legal arrangements with Philip, resisted his demands and the country was soon on the verge of civil war. The Pope excommunicated him until he had agreed to repay the money he had taken from the Church and accept the Vatican appointment of Stephen Langton as Archbishop of Canterbury. He waged his disastrous campaign on the Continent with foreign mercenaries, since few of the barons would fight for him, and when he returned to England in 1214, after the battle of Bouvines, having lost nearly everything he had ever possessed in France, including Maine, Anjou and Normandy, Archbishop Langton and the barons were waiting for him with the Great Charter.

Leading the barons was Robert Fitzwalter, Lord of Dunmow and of Baynard's Castle. When Ralph Baynard had died during the reign of William Rufus, the castle had been inherited by his grandson Henry, but Henry I sequestered it when Henry Baynard was involved in a traitorous rebellion, and bestowed it, together with the barony of Dunmow, on Robert Fitzgerald: and by the time of King John it had been inherited by Fitzgerald's grandson Robert Fitzwalter. The story goes that King John fell in love with Robert Fitzwalter's beautiful daughter Matilda, but when it became clear that neither Matilda nor her father fancied the match, the King ordered Robert's arrest. Baynard's Castle was conveniently placed for a secret midnight escape by way of the river and Robert managed just in time to flee to France and join King Philip, whereupon the enraged and frustrated John ordered the demolition of Baynard's Castle. The following year King John was fighting in France, but during a truce one of his knights, bored with the inactivity, called across the river, to where a party of French knights was encamped on the opposite bank, and challenged one of them to come across for a joust. Amongst them was Robert Fitzgerald, and disguised by his vizor and ready armoured, he and his horse were ferried across. At the first bout he brought King John's knight to the ground and the King, amazed at the skill of the stranger, exclaimed, 'By God's sooth, he were a king indeed who had such a knight!', whereupon, once Fitzwalter was safely back on the French side of the river, his friends called out his identity. King John thereupon forgave Fitzwalter and recalled him from exile, appointed him governor of the Castle at Hertford and allowed him to rebuild Baynard's Castle. But that was not the end of the story. On his return to England, Fitzwalter found that Matilda was dead, killed, it was said, by an agent of the King who had sprinkled poison on nothing more romantic than a poached egg. Apocryphal as the story was, it was believed by many of the citizens of London while Fitzwalter played his part in the preparation of the Great Charter: and another baron who joined forces with him was the Earl of Gloucester, a descendant of Geoffrey de Mandeville, who was hoping to reassert his family's claim to the Tower of London.

In the meantime the City was preparing its own demands from John, which included the abolition of all 'evil taxes'. The mint was to be restored to the City, foreign merchants should be allowed to come and go freely and responsibility for the river Thames should rest entirely with London.

John at this time confirmed the privileges of the Moneyers' Company and entrusted them with the production of the entire coinage of the country, the Mint being in the Tower of London, where it remained until early in the nineteenth century, when the present Mint was built on Tower Hill. It was Henry III who appointed a Comptroller of the Mint, to send in his accounts separately from those of the Warden and Master, and at this time the first gold coinage was used in England – a gold penny valued at twenty pence. In the following reign circular silver halfpennies and farthings were minted, in place of the square ones which had succeeded the haphazard division of the ancient silver penny.

During the reign of Edward III, as national wealth increased, the gold florin, the groat and the half groat were introduced, the gold florin, valued at six shillings, soon giving way to the gold noble. The bullion came from silver mines in Devonshire and gold and silver mines in Wales. Henry VII originated the gold sovereign, double sovereign and half-sovereign, as well as the silver shilling, Henry VIII the silver crown-piece and Edward VI the half-crown, sixpence and threepenny piece, and by this time the Mint was receiving silver from Peru and gold from Mexico.

With no reference to FitzAilwin's long reign, the City also demanded of King John that a mayor should be elected annually in the old and almost defunct folk-moot. This implied that there had been dissatisfaction with the reign of FitzAilwin, who in some way had favoured the powerful and rich to the detriment of the ordinary citizens and merchants. He had died in 1212, nominating Roger FitzAlan as his successor, thinking he would be in office, like himself, for life, but the mood of London was changing and they were seeking a freer form of election.

Roger FitzAlan lasted for only two years, although why his mayoralty ended no one knows. In the year that John returned to England Serle, the Mercer, was elected Mayor and it was during his time that John granted the City a charter which allowed the citizens to elect a Mayor each year, either re-electing the same man each year or choosing someone different each time. During his first term, Serle served for only a year, but he was re-elected in 1217 and held office for the next five years.

John's quarrel with the Barons was unresolved and London, under the guidance of Serle, the Mercer, sided with the barons against the King. When Robert Fitzwalter, at the head of the barons, marched towards London, they met no resistance. They entered the gates and prepared to fortify the City. With the loss of London, John was forced to agree to the signing of the Great Charter, and when he attempted later to annul it civil war broke out, ending only in the King's sudden death and the acceptance of his small son Henry, only nine years old, as the successor to the throne.

The organisation of London was gradually assuming its present form. King John had stipulated that after the citizens had elected their new Mayor each year, he should be submitted to the King for his approval, which is why the Lord Mayor's procession at the time of his election first took place, but it was not until the fifteenth century that it developed into the elaborate pageant which has lasted until the present day.

During the long reign of Henry III the City was governed by its Mayor, who was often re-elected three, four or five times, his sheriffs and the aldermen, who would summon to their help the leading men of any particular trade where problems had arisen, for there was still no Common Council yet.

The early years of the reign were peaceful and the City flourished with the increasingly valuable wool trade, but when Henry III came of age the political troubles began once more. His interests, like those of his father, were more French than English, and not only did he prepare for an expedition to Poitou, in order to regain some of his family's lost possessions, but he invited scores of his French relatives over to England, so that the Court circles and holders of high office became mostly French.

They spent lavishly and built great town and country houses for themselves. Peter of Savoy, his uncle, whom he created Earl of Richmond, built the Savoy Palace in the Strand, a mile or so outside the City boundary, and here he entertained in regal style, his visitors including dozens of beautiful young French noblewomen, some of whom he claimed to be his wards, and for most of whom he found English husbands.

The king himself, who had a passion for building, rebuilt most of Westminster Abbey, and by 1269 the eastern part of the new Abbey, with the choir and transepts, was completed, a superb example of thirteenth century English Perpendicular, which is one of the country's most precious heritages. But this all cost money and according to Matthew Paris 'the sum of £2,591, due to the widow of one David of Oxford, a Jew, was assigned by him (the King) to that use.'

The Jews had survived the persecution of Stephen's reign but when Richard I embarked on his crusade, the feeling against them rose to violence. At his coronation a crowd of citizens had set up a deputation of Jews who had met in London to discuss the question of a gift to the King. Abuse changed to brickbats and bludgeons and as they fled back to the City a rumour spread among the crowds that the King had ordered their extermination. Some were murdered in the streets. The rest were chased back to their houses in the City, which were burned and pillaged. The rioting spread through the country and in York 2,000 Jews are said to have been slaughtered, including Josce of York, the richest of them all.

The main concern of many of the rioters was to destroy the records of their debts, and for the Jews' future protection special chests with triple locks were provided for the safe-keeping of their bonds, and it was decreed that all loans should be made in the presence of an Exchequer of the Jews, where their affairs could be dealt with in a more orderly manner. In the result, the King had a tighter hold than ever on the Jewish moneylenders.

John extorted money from them and tortured and imprisoned those who did not pay up readily. During the Baron's War they suffered more persecution when the barons destroyed several of their London houses, using the stones to repair and reinforce the City walls. Yet they survived and a few of them were still able to grow rich. Aaron, the son of Josce of York, became one of the richest in his time and besides rebuilding his father's house in York, he opened a house in London, where he lived in great splendour.

During the Regency of Henry III they were left in comparative peace but compelled to wear two white tablets of linen or parchment for identification, but when he acceded to the throne Henry not only seized a third of their possessions but took their synagogue in Old Jewry from them and turned it into a church for the brothers of St Anthony of Vienna. He and his courtiers continued to extract increasingly large sums of money from them, which were now becoming far in excess of their dwindling assets. Aaron of York was forced to pay 4,000 marks of silver and 400 of gold, and when he died, in 1286, he was penniless.

It was early in Henry's reign that the first black friars of St Dominic arrived in England, soon to be followed by the grey friars of St Francis, and they alone seem to have befriended the Jews, apart from a few clergy who tried to convert them to Christianity. Those who joined the Church were welcomed and in the 1230s the King founded a home for Jewish converts in Chancery Lane, on the site of the present Record Office. Converts gave up their property on entering the home, the men receiving 1½d a day from the King and the women 8d a week. But for the rest of his reign the extortions continued and they were taxed mercilessly. Those who resisted or had no money left were burnt at the stake or hanged, so it is not surprising that within a few years there were well over 100 converts in the Chancery Lane house.

With the accession of Edward I came the end. Their days of usefulness were over. Not only had many of them been reduced to poverty but already Christians, overcoming with no great difficulty the old scruples against usury, had begun to enter the moneylending business. One of the first was William Cade, a Flemish cloth merchant and moneylender whose activities ranged over much of northern Europe. As early as the twelfth century he was visiting London, where he had a house, and was lending not only to Henry II but also to the Cistercian monasteries, who were engaged in the early development of the wool trade. William Cade bought their wool, advancing money on the expectation of the clip. He also advanced money to the sheriffs vainly trying to straighten their accounts for the Exchequer Court. But Cade for some unknown reason fell into disgrace, and in the end Henry gave him no better treatment than the Jews, for when he died, in 1166, he seized all his assets in England, including bonds worth £5,000.

Another source of money came from the Knights Templars, for although they did not practise usury, they used their vast store of money to act as international bankers, giving credit and handling bullion: and until the order was disbanded in 1313 the Temple precincts had been used as one of the royal treasuries, more convenient than Winchester, until the royal treasure was concentrated at Westminster.

By the middle of the thirteenth century, however, moneylenders and merchants from Genoa, Lucca, Florence and Venice – the Lombards – had arrived in London, establishing themselves in Lombard Street and acting as bankers and pawnbrokers. They remitted money to Italy by bills of exchange, thereby paying the Pope and the Italian Church the fees and incomes due to them from the English Church: and before long they were lending money to the English government, taking a mortgage on customs dues as security.

With the arrival of the Lombards, Edward I forbade the Jews to practise usury on pain of death, yet a few years later, in order to raise the money for the building of Caernarvon and Conway castles, he extorted money from them. The persecution intensified. On a charge of clipping coins, nearly 300 Jews were put to death and their possessions seized. Then all the Jews in the country were imprisoned one night and not released until they had paid a ransom of £20,000. Finally, in 1290, came their expulsion, when between 15,000 and 16,000 were forced to leave the country. Ships were provided for them and they were allowed to take some of their money, but their houses were confiscated and all outstanding mortgages were forfeited to the Crown. Many were wrecked on their way to France, others robbed and flung overboard. One shipmaster of a 'mighty tall ship', whom a number of still comparatively wealthy Jews had especially hired, set sail with them from just below London Bridge but cast anchor near the estuary with the ebbing tide, so that they were stranded on a sand bank. He invited the Jews to walk with him on the sands for exercise, but then, as the tide turned, he slipped back to his ship and abandoned them. As the incoming waters washed over the sand bank they cried for help, but he shouted back to them that Moses had saved their ancestors from the Red Sea and they must now pray for a new Moses. The helpless Jews were left to drown.

Throughout the thirteenth century the City's guilds were growing steadily in power and it was in 1273, a few years before the expulsion of the Jews, that the Common Council of London was formed, a group of men elected by the whole community, to consult with the Mayor and aldermen on City affairs, consisting in the first place of 25 of 'the more discreet men of the City'.

It was during the reign of Edward I that the first Merchant Adventurers began to export manufactured woollen cloth, although they did not receive their charter of incorporation until the time of Henry VII. Edward I granted charters to the fishmongers and the merchant taylors, the merchant taylors being the first to acquire a hall of their own, when, in 1331, they bought an existing house in Threadneedle Street. Edward II ordered that no person should be admitted to the freedom of the City unless he were a member of one of the trades or mysteries, and in the reign of Edward III the guilds were mainly transformed into companies of crafts or mysteries, the head of the company now being called the Master or Warden, instead of assuming the ancient and confusing title of Alderman. Edward III granted many more charters to the city companies and now for the first time a new rank was established amongst their members, that of the liverymen. These were the upper ranks of the freemen, and only from these men, who alone in the company were entitled to wear a distinctive dress, were the members of the governing body chosen.

In 1347 instead of a free election throughout the City, members of the Common Council were selected representatives from each ward. Then, in 1376, the Common Council members were elected from the livery companies, of which there were now more than fifty, each company nominating from two to six of their members, but this arrangement lasted for only a short time and by 1383 the right of election of members of the Common Council was restored to the inhabitants of the wards, but the election of the Mayor, Sheriffs and other officers has remained in the hands of the livery companies ever since. These officers include the lawyer or Common Serjeant and the town clerk, termed the Common Clerk, both appointments having been created in 1290, but the Remembrancer, in charge of the correspondence of the City, was not appointed until 1570.

5

Medieval London – II

It was shortly after the accession of Henry III that the first friars came to London. Unlike the monks of the established monasteries – the Benedictines, the more austere Cistercians, who had grown wealthy by gifts of land and profitable sheep farming, and the silent order of the Carthusians – they arrived in poverty. For the first few months they had no settled home, denying themselves the comfort and culture of monastic seclusion. They slept at night in the simplest shelter and begged for their sustenance. They regarded themselves as missionaries and made at first for the big towns, particularly London and Oxford, preaching at street corners and in the market places. They were the first revivalists and soon, to the consternation of the parish priests, acquired a strong following and a steady flow of funds.

The black-robed friars of St Dominic of Spain, arriving in England in 1221, soon made their headquarters in a small house in Holborn. In 1224 nine penniless grey friars of the Order of St Francis, of whom only one was a priest, came to England from Italy. They reached Canterbury, where they slept at night in a room which by day was used as a school. After a few days four of them moved on to London, where they were given shelter for a short time at the Dominican priory in Holborn. Then they rented a piece of ground in Cornhill for a few pence and built themselves tiny cells of wattle and clay, set in a herb garden, but by the following year John Ewin, a City mercer who eventually became a lay brother of the Order, presented them with a piece of ground on the north side of Newgate Street, on the corner of Stynking Lane, close to the meat stalls and the shambles.

Here their following grew strong, for people loved the Grey Friars for their sincerity and eloquence, their poverty and their simplicity. Gifts and money flooded in and soon they were able to enlarge their austere chapel. By 1327 they were wealthy enough to rebuild it and it became the most beautiful conventual church in the City, for a mayor of London built the choir, another the nave, while a third built new dormitories for them. Other wealthy citizens gave the chapter-house, vestry house, infirmary and refectory. Queens and noblemen added to its beauties and in 1429 Sir Richard Whittington bequeathed the magnificent library building and most of the books.

The black friars remained in Holborn for the first 50 years of their establishment in London, but in 1276 the Mayor of London granted to the Archbishop of Canterbury the abandoned Montfichet Castle for their new house. The castle was demolished and the Blackfriars monastery and church built on the site, within its walled precinct.

The Carmelites – the White Friars – were another order of mendicant friars which had originated from the hermits who had settled on the slopes of Mount Carmel and was founded by Sir Richard Grey in 1241. When they reached London Edward I granted land for their monastery to the east of the Temple, down by the riverside, and their gardens stretched over the land where Bouverie Street, White Friars Street and Carmelite Street now lie. Their church was rebuilt for them in 1350 by the Earl of Devon and in 1420 a Bishop of Hereford added the steeple.

As at the monastery of the Grey Friars, many famous people were buried there and their house had the right of sanctuary, which lasted until long after the Dissolution and the destruction of most of their beautiful buildings.

As a place of sanctuary, this part of Fleet Street down to the river became the haunt of thieves and murderers and one of the most vicious and depraved slums of London – the notorious Alsatia: and it was not until 1697 that the right of sanctuary was revoked.

The house of the Crutched Friars – the friars of the Holy Cross, who wore a cross of red cloth on their backs and always carried an iron cross – was in Hart Street, just off Mark Lane, opposite St Olave's Church. It was founded at the end of the thirteenth century by two London men who themselves became friars of the Order. As the Crutched Friars saw their security in jeopardy, at the time of the Dissolution, they petitioned the City to take their house under its special protection, but when the agents of Thomas Cromwell came upon their prior in dalliance with his mistress, their hopes of reprieve vanished. The church became a carpenter's yard and tennis court, the friars' hall a glass factory: but the hall was destroyed by fire in 1575.

The Austin or Augustinian friars, formed in 1253, had their church just off Broad Street and the nave survives as the Dutch Protestant church.

The large amounts of money the friars received proved their undoing. As their churches grew larger, their food better, their clothing warmer and their life more comfortable, they employed servants to do the manual work which in the early days they had been proud to do themselves: yet they still subsisted by begging. By the end of the thirteenth century there were more than 100 friaries throughout the country and each one appointed from amongst its members 'limiters' or professional beggars, who sometimes farmed the alms by paying an agreed sum into the friary funds in exchange for the exclusive right to beg in specified districts and pocket what they received. They took burial and confession fees and also, like Chaucer's Friar Hubert, sold absolutions. Yet it would be wrong to condemn them all as decadents. Many continued to do good work, especially in the schools at Oxford and Cambridge, although they deplored the first scientific experiments of Roger Bacon, declaring that he was delving into secrets which should never be revealed.

London's foreign trade during the eleventh and twelfth centuries had been mainly with the Germans, Flemish and French, but by the twelfth century the Germans were predominating in the City, as elsewhere in western Europe. William of Malmesbury, writing around 1125, said that London was full of wealth and merchants 'coming from every land and especially from Germany', for in addition to German wine, metal work and coats of mail, and boatloads of grain at times of poor harvest in England, they were entrepreneurs for the produce of the East and the luxury cloths from Constantinople.

The German merchants, particularly those from Cologne, soon eclipsed the Danes, and by 1225 had taken over their settlement in the parish of St Clement Danes and established themselves in their guild house on the river at Dowgate. Later in the century merchants from Lubeck, Hamburg and other towns of eastern Germany arrived in London. At first there was trouble between them and the men of the Cologne house, but before long they combined, as part of the Hanseatic League, in an association of North German towns and merchants trading abroad, which was now formed for the defence of their trading interests. By 1282 their London house was built, down by the river, on the site of the present Cannon Street station. It had a beautiful hall overlooking the river and a river frontage where the merchants anchored their ships. The warehouses were grouped round a courtyard at the back, opening on to Thames Street. Here the merchants lived a segregated life, governed by a master and council of twelve, who administered German law. It was called the Steelyard – a corruption of *Stapelhof* – meaning a courtyard where samples of merchandise were stored or displayed.

Their hall, said Stow,

is large, built of stone, with three arched gates towards the street, the middlemost whereof is far bigger than the others, and is seldom opened, the other two be secured up. . . . The merchants . . . used to bring hither as well wheat, rye, and other grain, as cables, ropes, masts, pitch, tar, flax, hemp, linen cloth, wainscots, wax, steel and other profitable merchandise.

The Steelyard merchants were exempt from English jurisdiction and many of the restrictions usually imposed on foreign traders. Their customs dues were lighter and they were allowed to engage in retail trade and deal directly with other foreigners. These privileges had been granted them by Henry III and renewed by Edward I, for although they were resented by English traders they were of great value to the English economy at a time when England had not yet sufficient shipping to compensate in the carrying trade. Moreover, like the Jews and the Lombards, the Steelyard merchants provided useful loans to the Crown.

One of their duties, in return for these privileges, had become the maintenance of Bishopsgate, hitherto the responsibility of the Danes, and Stow related a bitter controversy between the City and the Steelyard merchants during the early years of Edward I's reign, when the gate was in a dangerously ruinous state and they refused to honour their obligation until they were summonsed.

With the passing years they provoked increasing resentment from the English merchants, as for example when their large imports of corn undercut English prices, but it was not until the reign of Edward VI, by which time England's mercantile shipping was vastly stronger, that the Merchant Adventurers, now a strong chartered company, made a final, vigorous protest at the unfairness of their trading privileges, and they were revoked. Ambassadors from Hamburg and Lubeck came to intercede for the merchants of the Steelyard, but to no avail, and a few years later, in 1579, Queen Elizabeth ordered their expulsion. Their hall was deserted and gradually became derelict, and in the Great Fire it was totally destroyed.

During the thirteenth and fourteenth centuries the most valuable supplies of wool for the cloth manufacturers of Flanders and Italy came from England. England's commerce and her politics were based on wool. It paid for Richard I's ransom, for the wars of Edward I and II with Scotland and for Edward III's disastrous war with France, which was to drag on intermittently for a hundred years. To this day the Lord Chancellor, when he takes his seat in the House of Lords, sits on the woolsack, the symbol of England's medieval prosperity. By the end of the thirteenth century it was said that 'the wool of England amounts to half the value of the whole land' and the wool tax was one of the principal sources of royal revenue.

Wool was grown on the estates of the great landowners – the earls, bishops and abbeys – as well as on the small manors and by the peasant farmers. In the early days of the boom it was the wool from the large landowners and religious orders which dominated the trade. The Cistercians in particular were wonderful sheep farmers and for Richard I's ransom the whole of their wool production for 1193 had been sequestered.

During these years the flocks, bred for their wool, were steadily increasing. The Nuns of Minchinhampton had 1,700 sheep grazing on the common. Ely Abbey had more than 13,000. There were 20,000 on the lands of the Priory of St Swithin's, Winchester. Peterborough and Crowland Abbeys had between them more than 16,000 while among the lay landowners, the Earl of Lincoln had 13,400.

To dispose of this wool, contracts were made directly with an export merchant, the exporter or his agent riding round the estates to view the crop and make his contract. Most of the wool, particularly from the monastic houses, was sold by advance contract and two medieval lists have survived, one in Flemish and the other in Italian, of the monastic houses in England with wool to sell, together with the probable amounts and the quality.

The monasteries often sold two or three years in advance and sometimes far longer, cases of fifteen or even twenty years having been recorded. The merchants, who had plenty of liquid capital, were prepared to pay large sums in advance, which were really loans on security of the wool, and the producers, who had little capital, were glad of the arrangement, although it often ran them into dire trouble, for some soon fell heavily into debt, from which they found it well nigh impossible to extricate themselves.

For a few years these merchants were Lombards, some of whom, as receivers of papal taxes from the monasteries, accepted wool as payment. Their end came when they began to make loans to the Crown. Edward I, borrowing £11,000 from the Frescobaldi house of Florence, assigned to them the whole Irish revenue for a year as repayment, and Edward II paid them another £6,500 which his father had owed them, but when they had nothing left they were expelled from the country. The Bardi and Peruzzi houses of Florence were bankrupted when Edward III failed to repay them the money he had borrowed for the early campaigns of the Hundred Years War. In a melancholy procession, one after the other of the Italian firms which had acted as Royal bankers failed and left the country, leaving the field clear for the new English bankers.

The nature of the wool trade was changing. The old manorial feudal system was disintegrating. Tenants of large landowners were commuting field service for rents and increasingly the owners of large estates were letting out their lands and living on the rents. In this way the business of sheep-rearing passed into the hands of the small-scale farmers and peasants, while the sale of wool was handled by English merchants, many of them Londoners, who bought in the local markets, either directly or through middlemen. Moreover Edward III, who had married the Flemish princess, Philippa of Hainault, encouraged the weaving industry in England by inviting Flemish weavers to settle, mainly in London or East Anglia, as, for example, John Kemp, whom he asked to come to England to teach his art 'to such of our people as shall be inclined to learn it' and promising protection to himself and his family, his workmen and apprentices. While these weavers were settling in, providing a new market for English wool, the English Wool Staple was established, a place where wool for export was compulsorily collected, taxed and sold, in order that customs dues could be levied, on which the King's finances largely depended.

The Staple towns were fixed in various places, the two places of export being Newcastle and London, but the King wanted a Staple on foreign soil, in order to gather in additional revenue. Despite protests from foreign merchants and growers alike, who preferred a free trade, it was fixed in Antwerp and then Bruges, but finally, with the capture of Calais in 1347, this was considered the most convenient place on foreign soil.

By the end of the century the Company of the Staplers had been established, which had a partial monopoly in the export of wool, and despite the heavy taxes which the King demanded from them, these merchants, operating be-tween London and Calais, and with close connexions with the Cotswolds, from which so much of the best wool was being produced, became wealthy and may be regarded as the first English capitalists. Many of the beautiful stone houses of the Cotswolds were built by them and amongst the London merchants of the Staple who prospered during the early years of the fifteenth century were the Cely family of Mark Lane.

Like most of the substantial City houses, the gateway in the wall protecting it from the street gave on to a courtyard, on either side of which were the store houses and kitchen quarters. The main feature of the Celys' house was the lofty hall, panelled and beamed, with its great stone fireplace. Behind it were the bower and several bedrooms and there were more bedrooms on the first floor.

After the first sheep-shearing in May, Richard Cely, one of the sons, would set off on the two or three days' ride to the Cotswolds to buy the wool.

This same day I depart into Cotswold . . . and there rides with me William, upon Pye your horse; and I have with me my falconer. . . .

wrote Richard to his brother.

The stay in the Cotswolds lasted two or three weeks and then began the long journey of the heavily laden pack-horses back to Mark Lane, where the wool was stored. The wool sacks were then taken to the Customs House close by on the riverside, for weighing and the assessment of Customs dues. The dues were paid and the seal of the Staple affixed to each sack. They were then loaded on to small boats and towed out to the cargo ships, lying at anchor in mid-stream. Some were loaded on to their own boat, the *Margaret Cely*, but the rest was divided between several other cargo ships, for sea travel was hazardous and it was unwise to risk a valuable cargo to only one vessel. Once the wool was stowed aboard, the searchers arrived to check that no wool had been smuggled on to the boats without the customs' mark.

Armed against pirates and stocked with food for at least 24 hours, the ships set sail for the walled city of Calais. George Cely, living in lodgings in the busy little port, was waiting for it, for his brother had already written to him:

My master has shipped his fells at the Port of London, which fells you must receive and pay the freight.

George had to pay freight and port dues before moving the wool to the Staple warehouse attached to the guild hall of the Staplers. Here it was weighed again and sampled for quality, before the Flemish merchants, who came mainly from Bruges and Ghent, arrived to negotiate a price and to buy, taking the wool the long journey home again by pack-horse or pack-mule trains.

All this business was conducted in a chain of credit dealings, but now it was the buyer who was being given credit, not the seller. The Celys and wool dealers like them bought on credit from the Cotswold sheep farmers, never paying more than two-thirds in a down payment. London merchants who, unlike the Celys, did not themselves visit the sheep-farmers, bought on credit from the dealers. The Flemish customers in Calais bought on credit from the Celys and other Staple merchants, who presented their bills some six months later, usually at one of the great trade fairs of the Netherlands. Since they were not importers and did not wish to invest the money in goods, it was transferred to England by arrangement with a mercer or merchant adventurer who was visiting the Netherlands to buy and needed the money to discount his bills. The money was later collected at the London offices of the importers and paid over to the Staple merchants, who were awaiting it in order that they could pay the Cotswold farmers.

The bills carried interest. The longer the credit, the less favourable the rate of exchange to the debtor: and thus the early discount market arose in the City of London.

The cloth trade grew steadily in England, for the weavers had the advantage of a supply of raw wool close at hand: and the industry was further stimulated when Edward III forbade the import of foreign cloth. Raw wool was still England's largest export through the Calais Staple but woollen cloth, the export of which was in the hands of the Merchant Adventurers, gained ground, and by the middle of the fourteenth century was beginning to eclipse the

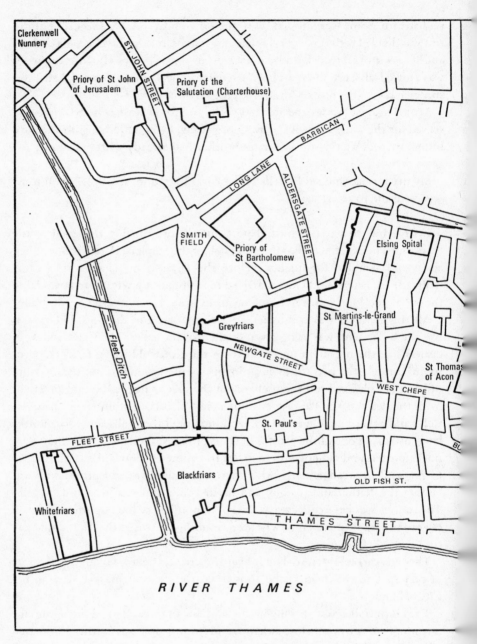

MEDIEVAL LONDON

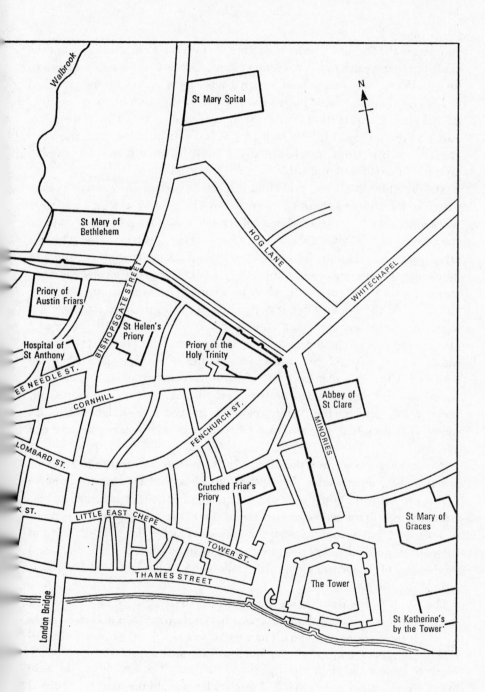

St Mary Spital

N

Walbrook

St Mary of
Bethlehem

HOG LANE

WHITECHAPEL

Priory of
Austin Friars

BISHOPSGATE STREET

St Helen's
Priory

Priory of the
Holy Trinity

Hospital of
St Anthony

EE NEEDLE ST.

CORNHILL

FENCHURCH ST.

Abbey of
St Clare

MINORIES

LOMBARD ST.

Crutched Friar's
Priory

St Mary of
Graces

K ST.

LITTLE EAST CHEPE

TOWER ST.

THAMES STREET

The Tower

London Bridge

St Katherine's
by the Tower

business of the Staplers. The manufacture of cloth was a rural industry but the trade brought wealth to the collecting towns, such as Colchester, and particularly to the City of London from which it was exported. As with the raw wool industry, the entrepreneur played a vital part, for the cloth industry required capital for the organisation of the numerous processes in both the manufacture and the selling of the finished article. It was from these men, the wool staplers and the cloth merchants, that Edward III now turned for capital, after the failure of the Lombards.

And watching it all and taking an important part in affairs was Geoffrey Chaucer. He was born about the year 1340, in Thames Street, where his father was a vintner and his grandfather a collector of customs on wine. He entered the employ of the Duke of Clarence and saw service in France, where he was taken prisoner for a time. In 1360 Edward III paid £18 towards his ransom and by 1367 he had become one of the king's esquires, making several journeys abroad on his behalf, as in 1372, when he went to Genoa to arrange with the citizens the choice of an English port where they should have trading privileges. In 1374 he was appointed comptroller of the Customs of Wools and Skins in the Port of London and it was during these later years that he wrote much of his poetry and gave us his living picture of the begging friar and the pardoner with his wallet 'bret-full of pardons, come from Rome, all hot', the jovial monk and the merry prioress. In fact it was only for the poor parson, the Oxford scholar, the kindly ploughman and the knight with his squire and attendant yeoman that Chaucer seemed to have had any real affection.

He was only a boy when the Black Death made its appearance in London. It was in 1349, shortly after the capture of Calais, that the disaster came to Europe, in the form of a plague so virulent that by the time it had abated an estimated 25 million people – a quarter of the entire population of Europe – had perished. In England the death rate was even higher, for at least a third of the population died in less than two years, including half the labourers, and by the end of Edward III's reign the population of England and Wales was reduced to 2,000,000.

The Black Death was a series of epidemics extending over more than ten years. The worst was the bubonic plague, which is thought to have been brought by sailors from China to Genoa. The survivors of that journey passed the disease to almost every one they met and it spread rapidly through Italy and the south of France and thence to Spain and England. The first outbreaks were in the West Country but soon it had reached London. In the narrow, medieval streets with their open drains and piles of refuse there was no escape. Once it had struck it was a death sentence, for no cure was known. People died in their

Marble depicting the sacrifice of the bull, in the recently discovered Temple of Mithras at Walbrook

Roman coin depicting the
Emperor Claudius, and minted
in London

Roman coin of Carausius who
proclaimed himself Emperor of
Britain in AD 287

Roman tessellated pavement found in the City near Mansion
House

Wooden water pipes from Roman times, found in the City

Remains of a Roman ship found in the City

(*Right above*) Later reconstruction of a map of Saxon London, AD 1000
(*Right below*) Saxon spearheads, 8–9th century, found in the River Thames (*scale 1″*)

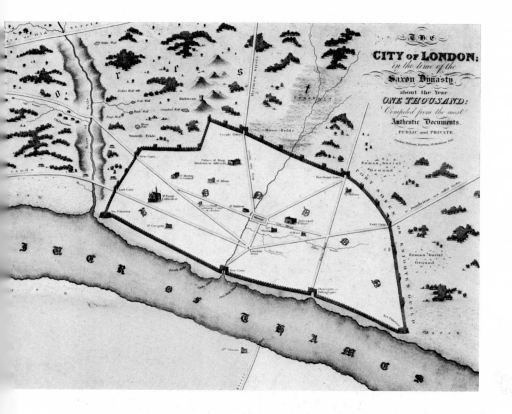

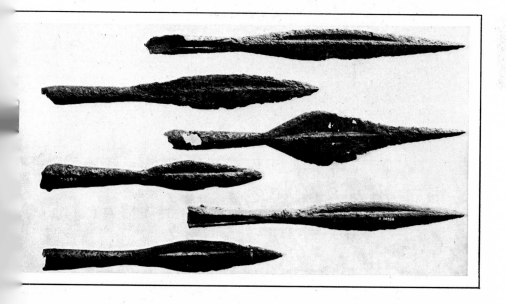

CANUTE THE GREAT.

Verue delin.   Published as the Act directs May 5, 1804 by J. Stratford N° 112 Holborn Hill.   A.W. Warren sculp.

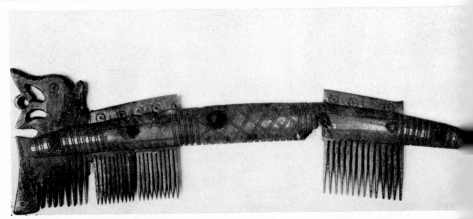

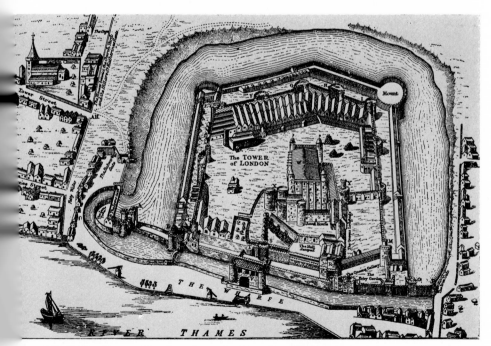

(*Above*) The Tower of London, drawn by Wenceslaus Hollar, 1647
(*Below*) Plan of the Tower of London, 1597, made by W. Haiward and J. Gascoyne

(*Left above*) King Canute. Engraving from an old sculpture
(*Left below*) Viking bone comb 10–11th century, found in the City

Moor gate

Aldgate

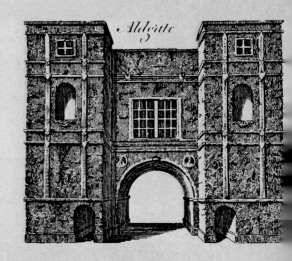

Ludgate

New gate

Bishopsgate

Cripplegate

Aldersgate

Bridge gate

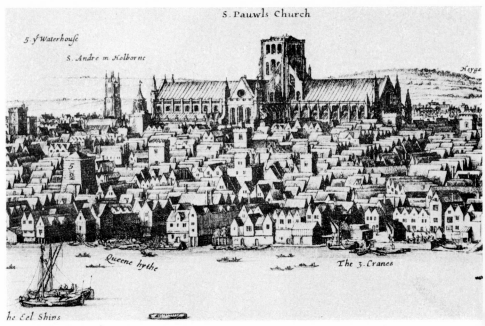

Old St Paul's after the fall of the spire, by Wenceslaus Hollar, 1647

The Chapter House of Old St Paul's, from a view by Hollar

The place of execution in old Smithfield

Wenceslaus Hollar's view of London, showing Fishmongers' Hall, The Old Swan,
St Laurence Poultney and the Royal Exchange, 1547

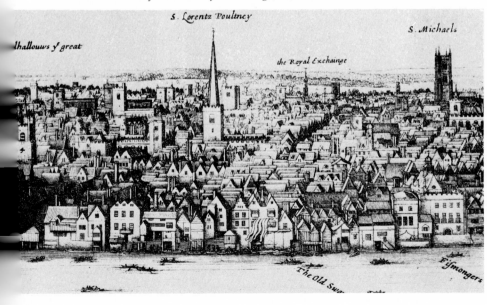

The Steel Yard and neighbourhood, 1540, from Van Wyngard's Plan

Baynard's Castle, 1790

Sir Richard Whittington, Lord Mayor of London. Engraving from an old portrait

Sir Thomas Gresham, founder of the Royal Exchange

London Bridge, 1647, by Wenceslaus Hollar

thousands, their bodies shovelled into burial pits while there were still sufficient able-bodied men to carry them there.

The Bishop of London, appalled at these burials without the blessing of the Church, consecrated three acres of waste ground outside the City walls, near the Church of St John of Jerusalem at Clerkenwell, which he named the Pardon churchyard, and here he built a small chapel where masses were said for the repose of their souls. As the plague raged on in London and the numbers of dead mounted, Sir Walter de Manny bought an adjoining plot of eleven acres from St Bartholomew's hospital, and here, during 1349 alone, more than 50,000 Londoners were buried.

A few years later, in 1371, Sir Walter de Manny bequeathed this land, together with the Pardon churchyard and the chapel, to the Carthusians and here they founded the London Charterhouse.

Despite the ravages of the Black Death the war with France continued and the wool merchants made their fortunes, some of them now turning to the hazards of speculative finance. The earliest and most famous of them was William de la Pole, 'second to no merchant in England'. He and his brother Richard belonged to a flourishing business house in Hull, active both in trade and the royal service. Richard held the post of King's butler and also undertook army contracts and made loans to the Crown, but with the outbreak of the War William suddenly became even more important. Together with a London wool merchant, Reginald de Conduit, he ran the syndicate which handled the requisition of 30,000 sacks of wool for the King at the outset of the French war. The following year he was personally responsible for a loan of £18,000 to the Crown, and in 1339 he became Baron of the Exchequer, handling most of the King's war finance, but after a few months he found himself in prison for a spell, accused of dishonesty, and after that time he remained behind the scenes, although still backing some of the large syndicates which were created at this time to handle the royal finances.

These syndicates had two sources of security. They farmed the customs for £50,000 a year and they were given the right to discount varying amounts of the royal IOUs to the merchants whose wool the King had seized, which enabled them to recover some of the money owing to them from customs dues on future exports.

One of these financiers was Sir John Poultney, a member of the Draper's Company and four times mayor of London, who founded the house of the Earls of Bath, but he was killed by the Black Death in 1349.

Some of these men reached positions of great wealth and power but others fared no better than the Lombards, losing their money as quickly as they made it and suffering bankruptcy, imprisonment and ruin. With the failure of the

D

London Merchant Walter de Cheriton, the brief days of the great medieval financiers were over and when, a few years later, the government tried to float a loan of £60,000 from the wool merchants, for a new expedition to France, a committee replied:

> The merchants fear to raise this loan to our Lord the king or to do anything in this respect whereby any man might hereafter say that any of them had tricked or deceived their said lord, as hath been done on former occasions in the like case, as with Monsire William de la Pole, John Wesenham, John Malwayn, Walter Cheriton and many other great merchants, who for such transactions made with the King in his great need and for a little gain, have since been impeached for this cause and in other collateral ways and in the end some of them utterly destroyed. Wherefore the merchants now in Parliament fear the like impeachment, if they make the said loan and will by no means make it.[1]

After this time, although the wool trade still financed the King through a permanent tax, the tax was controlled through Parliament, and even though merchant princes still made loans to the Crown, they were henceforth on a far smaller scale.

The Black Death caused a serious shortage of labour in England and for a time labourers were able to demand higher wages, despite bitter protest from the landowners: but the peasants' brief triumph ended with the retrogressive Statute of Labourers, which, despite the rising cost of food, pegged their wages to the amount they had received before the plague had tied them to the land of their feudal landlords. The problem affected in particular the new tenant farmers who had leased their land from the great landowners and who had been employing landless labourers. There were strikes and riots and small unions were formed, which were quickly repressed. Resentment grew and by 1381, stirred by the socialist preaching of John Ball and the levying of a poll tax to help pay for the French wars, the peasants rose in revolt and began their march on London.

From Norfolk, Suffolk and Cambridgeshire, from Hertfordshire and the counties of the south they came, pillaging and ravaging as they marched, burning manor houses and monasteries, symbols of the wealth in which they had no share. As they approached the capital their numbers grew into armies tens of thousands strong. The Essex and Kent contingents were led by Wat Tyler, whom the young King Richard, a boy of fifteen, courageously rode out to meet, in the country at Mile End.

1 Quoted in Eileen Power, *The Wool Trade in English Medieval History*, OUP, 1941

From him they demanded their freedom and the King granted it, promising that their feudal duties should be commuted for a rent of 4d a week and that they would be granted a free pardon. The rebellion might have ended here, but while this meeting was taking place another peasant army, admitted to London by some sympathetic aldermen and apprentices, had swarmed over London Bridge and occupied the Tower of London. They murdered the Archbishop of Canterbury and hung his head on London Bridge. They destroyed the palace of the Savoy, now occupied by John of Gaunt, and the new inn of the lawyers, who had moved into the Knights Templars' quarters, and soon the houses of many of the foreign merchants were ablaze. The following morning Wat Tyler and a turbulent mob came by chance upon the King and the Mayor, William Walworth, at Smithfield. In speaking to the King, Tyler placed his hand on Richard's bridle, and William Walworth, fearing for the young King's life, killed Tyler on the spot. It was the signal for action. Froissart describes how the warning spread through the City that the peasants 'were likely to slay the king and the mayor in Smithfield' and how

all manner of good men of the king's party issued out of their houses and lodgings well armed, and so came all to Smithfield and to the field where the king was, and they were anon to the number of seven or eight thousand men well armed. And first thither came Sir Robert Knolles and Sir Perducas d'Albret, well accompanied, and divers of the aldermen of London, and with them a six hundred men in harness and a puissant man of the city, who was the king's draper, called Nicholas Bramber, and he brought with him a great company: and ever as they came, they ranged them afoot in order of battle: and on the other part these unhappy people were ready ranged, making semblance to give battle. . . .

Yet no blow was struck. The King persuaded them all to go away and they were warned that any who were found within the City walls by the following Sunday at dawn would be arrested as traitors and executed. John Ball and Jack Straw were later discovered hiding in an old house, betrayed by their own men, and duly executed, their heads being strung up on London Bridge along with Wat Tyler's.

The revolt of the peasants was over and the promise of their freedom was not kept, for Parliament declared that it had been extorted under duress, while the landowners and tenant farmers, bolder now that the immediate danger was passed, argued that the King had had no right to promise freedom to their personal serfs. The revolt gave little immediate benefit to the peasants, but this was the last stand of feudalism and in the years to come the peasants were gradually able to achieve their freedom by less violent means.

The same spirit of grievance and unrest was manifest in the towns, particularly amongst the craft guilds, and this applied particularly to London. The increasing volume of business, particularly in the cloth and wool trades, had necessitated the introduction of the entrepreneur and capitalist, which inevitably created great disparities in wealth. The capitalist merchant employing many people was taking the place of the old master craftsman who employed a few journeymen and apprentices, living and sleeping under his roof, all of them members of the same guild, which existed for their mutual benefit, fixing their hours of work and their wages and maintaining the standard of their work.

As the masters grew wealthier they employed more men, but it meant that fewer journeymen and apprentices could ever hope to become masters themselves. A social gulf between master and employee was created, as well as between the small manufacturer and the wealthy trading master.

Employees struck for higher wages. Yeoman guilds were formed amongst the journeymen, to which sometimes the smaller masters also belonged. They protested against the richer masters who were concerning themselves more and more with selling rather than craftsmanship and were gradually controlling their industry. The Statute of Labourers had been directed partly against this movement and the ordinary craftsmen were powerless against the new forces of industry and trade which were making the City as a whole so prosperous. The chartered Livery Companies were gradually established, although it was not until 1552 that the craft guilds were abolished by Act of Parliament and their estates bought in by the Companies.

The Companies were hierarchical, governed by a Warden and Court, who were usually rich merchants. The main body of the Companies were the prosperous shopkeepers and traders, who were entitled to wear the livery, and beneath them were the working craftsmen, who had served their apprenticeship and become freemen. Every craft had its own rules and no one could trade in the City or even make anything for sale who did not belong to a Company. Hours of work and wages were fixed and there was no appeal from the Warden's decision: strikes and attempts to form unions were strictly repressed.

The number of apprentices was limited and the boys, who entered service at about the age of fourteen, had to pay a premium and serve for at least seven years, and sometimes longer, during which time they were clothed and fed and taught their business. Some ran away. The indentures of the poorer boys were sometimes paid in instalments, and if the full amount were not forthcoming boys sometimes stayed on with their masters for years, as workmen or servants. In fact it has been estimated that little more than half the apprentices enrolled ever became freemen.

Only the Merchant Taylors and the Goldsmiths had halls of their own before 1400, but during the next century 26 more were built in London. Difficulties soon arose when several guilds had been engaged in branches of the same industry, for in 1423 there were no less than III guilds. The problem was solved by amalgamations. The leathersellers absorbed the glovers, pursers, curriers and pouchmakers, the armourers the bladesmiths and brasiers. The haberdashers incorporated the hatters, and the clothworkers the fullers and shearmen.

From very early days there was great disparity in wealth between the Companies, the 'Twelve Great Companies' being those of the Mercers, Grocers, Drapers, Fishmongers, Goldsmiths, Skinners, Merchant Taylors, Haberdashers, Salters, Ironmongers, Vintners and Clothworkers. During the fifteenth century, the Mayor and aldermen of London were nearly all elected from the Mercers, the Grocers or the Drapers, and to a lesser extent from the Fishmongers and Goldsmiths. Hardly any of these men practised the business of the Company they represented, but had acquired their wealth from foreign trade, mainly in wool, cloth and corn.

6

The Twelve Great Companies

The early history of the twelve great Companies reflects much of the story of the City in which, from the fourteenth century to the seventeenth, they wielded such great power. Their gradual loss of importance began then, as artisans began increasingly to resent the apprenticeship system and growing industrialisation made it, in many respects, obsolete, but it was not until late in the eighteenth century that most of the companies abandoned any assumption of controlling their industries, surviving mainly to administer the valuable bequests, charities and schools which had become their responsibility.

The Mercers received their charter from Richard II in 1393, but they had been in existence since the late twelfth century. Gilbert à Becket, father of St Thomas, had been a mercer, and some twenty years after Thomas's death his sister had built the chapel and hospital of St Thomas Acon close to Ironmonger Lane, off the north side of Cheapside, on the site of the house where he had been born, bestowing it on the Mercers: and Henry III gave them land between St Olave's church and Ironmonger Lane, which had belonged to two wealthy Jews, to add to their ground. Here they built their first hall and chapel. The chapel faced the street, standing in front of the 'great old chapel of St Thomas' and their hall was built above it.

In their earliest days the Mercers had been general dealers in all small wares, including wigs, haberdashery and even spices and drugs, which they carried round the fairs and markets, sitting on the ground to sell them, like pedlars. Their first London station, during the reign of Henry II, was on the north side of the Cheap, where their hall was later to be built, but then they moved to the south side, between Bow Church and Friday Street, a stretch of open ground which was to become known as the Mercery, and here, in a large meadow, they put up their first little stalls.

They prospered and in 1296 joined the merchant adventurers to establish a woollen manufacture in England, with a branch in Antwerp. Fifty years later the mercers were selling woollen clothing and becoming increasingly jealous of the Lombards: and in 1351 three of them were sent to the Tower for attacking two Lombards in Old Jewry. Whatever that provocation may have been, the wealthiest of the Mercers were already making charitable bequests for which hundreds of people were to be thankful.

Early in the fourteenth century William Elsing, a mercer, founded the hospital at Cripplegate for 100 blind paupers, perhaps becoming prior of his own hospital. The mercer John Barnes, who was Mayor in 1317, left a gift of a chest containing 1,000 marks, which was to be lent to young mercers in need of help at the beginning of their careeers, in return for which they were asked only to say a *Pater Noster*.

It was not until the time of Henry VI that the mercers became exclusively dealers in silks and velvets, leaving the haberdashers to deal with the smaller articles of dress in which they had earlier done business. They may have bought their silk from the Lombards in the first place, but later they probably imported it themselves, for many of their members were merchants with European connections, one of the most famous being William Caxton, who spent thirty years of his life in Bruges: and here, in 1462, Edward IV appointed him governor of the Company of Merchant Adventurers. In his later years he turned to literature, translating several books from French into English. Then he became interested in the new printing process which was being developed in Bruges and Cologne. In 1474 he printed the first two books to appear in the English language, one a romance, the other *The Game and Playe of Chesse*: and in 1476 he brought his printing press to London, setting it up at the sign of the Red Pale, close to Westminster Abbey.

Here not only did he translate twenty more books, but he printed nearly 100 others. The old laborious days of copying were over. While Edward IV and Richard III played out the last few years of medievalism and the Tudors claimed and won the throne of England, William Caxton, the Mercer, was bestowing on the country the gift of freely accessible literature, printing the best of English poetry, literature and 'joyous and pleasant histories of chivalry' – Chaucer, Gower, Lydgate and Malory.

Rhyme sheets which had become popular on the Continent now began to appear in London, including the cautionary tale of the schoolboy, Master John, who 'came to school late, jangled and japed, made game of his betters, played practical jokes, got up late and went reluctantly to bed, forgot to wash his hands before meals, and was always ready to say "don't care".'

Although Caxton's printing press was not within the walls of London he had business contacts with the City, for he was a considerable importer of foreign books. In 1488, for example, he imported 1,161 books as well as 'one container of books', all of which were treated as general merchandise and dutiable: and paper and binding materials for his own books were imported from Italy, France and the countries of the Rhine.

After Caxton's death his former apprentice, Wynkyn de Worde, moved his business into London, printing his books at his house in Fleet Street, at the sign of the Sun, and from this time London became the home of the book trade, its centre being in St Paul's churchyard.

The notorious Jane Shore, mistress of Edward IV, was the only child of a distinguished mercer of Cheapside. She had, it was said, been 'honestly brought up', and her father chose for her husband William Shore, goldsmith, of Lombard Street, 'a man of very fair character, both for religion and morals'. But Jane was very beautiful, and through her father, who had business at Court, she met the King. She became his mistress in about 1470 and exerted a great deal of influence over him,

for a proper wit had she, and could both rede well and write, mery in company, redy and quick of answers, neither mute nor ful of bable, sometimes taunting without displeasure, and not without disport.

It was after the King's death that Jane Shore's troubles soon began. Long since abandoned by her husband, William, she became the mistress of Lord Hastings and lived under his protection for a time at his home in London, Cold Harbour in Thames Street. However, Lord Hastings was executed for treason, and Jane was accused of the practice of sorcery against the new King, Richard III, being brought before the court of the Bishop of London charged as a harlot and a witch. She was condemned to do penance at St Paul's 'going before the crosse in procession upon a Sunday with a taper in her hand', and then imprisoned for a time in Ludgate.

Much to the mortification of King Richard, his own legal adviser, Thomas Lynom, fell in love with her and sought the King's permission to marry Jane. This Richard granted and they lived in great contentment for the next thirty years, Jane dying in 1527 in the reign of King Henry VIII.

Sir Richard Whittington, the most famous of all the City's Mayors, was a mercer, and the Mercers' Company were the trustees of the college and almshouses which he established on College Hill.

He and other mercers left large sums of money to Henry V and in 1513 Joan Bradbury, widow of a Mercer and Mayor of London, left the Conduit Mead, where now New Bond Street lies, to the Mercers' Company, to be used for various charitable purposes. About the same time they were granted other stretches of land, including 29 acres in Marylebone and 120 acres in Westminster and St Giles, which, with the passing years, were to become increasingly valuable.

The three Greshams, Sir John, Sir Richard and Sir Thomas, were all mercers. Sir Richard was Mayor in 1537 and his brother, Sir John, in 1547. Both lent money to the King and Sir Richard's second son, Sir Thomas, whose place of business was in Lombard Street, at the sign of the Grasshopper – his father's crest – was the organiser and builder of the Royal Exchange, which was opened in 1566.

During the years of the Reformation and the suppression of the monastic institutions, the Mercers had to surrender the chapel and hospital of St Thomas Acon, but on the payment of £969 by Sir Richard Gresham Henry VIII granted them back to the Company, together with the parsonage of St Mary Colechurch and a stretch of the surrounding land. The old church became the Mercers' Chapel. 'It is now called Mercers' Chappell,' wrote Stow, 'and therein is kept a free grammar school as of old time had been accustomed.' The grammar school was at first held here but later was moved to the Mercery. The new Mercers Hall was built, adjoining their new chapel, and with all the newly acquired land it stood in spacious grounds, with courtyards, cloisters and gardens stretching to east and west of Ironmonger Lane and Old Jewry.

The Mercers converted their old chapel, fronting the street, into shops, one of which was a bookseller's where Thomas Guy, the founder of Guy's Hospital, was apprenticed: and after the Fire of London he continued his trade of bookseller in a shop built on the same site.

Early in the reign of Queen Elizabeth the wardens of the Mercers' Company were summoned before the Queen's Council for selling their velvets, satins and damasks at too high a price, since English coin was no longer base and the old excuse for excessive charges was no longer valid.[1] The Mercers were an autocratic body of men, very conscious of their own importance and dignity. One of their idiosyncrasies at this time was a dislike of beards, and they were known to have expelled at least one member who refused to shave. On this occasion, however, they promised to reform, but rather basely begged her Majesty's Council to 'look to the Grocers'.

During the late sixteenth century, the chief sellers of Italian silks lived in Cheapside, St Lawrence Jewry and Old Jewry, and Strype speaks of the mercers' shops on the south side of Cheapside having been transformed from mere sheds into handsome buildings four or five storeys high.

As there were so many Italians living in this quarter sermons were preached at the Mercers' chapel in Italian, and in James I's time it became a fashionable

1 During the reign of Henry VIII and Edward VI the coinage had been grossly debased and Queen Elizabeth, on the advice of Sir Thomas Gresham, ordered the corrupt coin to be called into the Mint and melted down for re-casting. The face value of £638,000 was found to be intrinsically worth only £244,000. The first milled coinage was issued at this time .

place to hear the preaching of the learned Italian Archbishop of Spalato, who had been converted to Protestantism. Italian sermons were preached at the chapel for many years, the expenses being partly borne by English merchants who had lived abroad in Italy.

In 1640 Charles I forced a loan of £3,030 from the Mercers, and in 1642, when the City of London had declared against the King, Parliament borrowed £6,500 from the Mercers as well as arms from the Company's armoury. A year or two later the Mercers gave more arms to the Parliamentary forces and a further loan of £3,200, which proved a heavy burden on their resources. In 1698, in order to clear off their debts, the Mercers began an insurance scheme, in the first place granting annuities to clergymen's widows, graduated to the amounts which their husbands had paid in during their lifetimes. They pledged the rents of their lands as security for the fulfilment of their contracts with the moneylenders and thus became the first life-assurance agents. They limited the amount of the subscriptions to £100,000, but after some years they ran into trouble, finding that the annuities they were paying were too high. They lowered their rates but matters grew worse and in 1745 they had to petition Parliament for help. By this time they were paying out £7,620 a year in annuities. Subscriptions for future annuities amounted to £10,000 a year but their current income was only £4,100 a year. However, an Act of Parliament allowed them to issue new bonds and pay them off with a lottery, which restored their affairs to prosperity.

In Henry VIII's reign the Company consisted of 53 members, including freemen and livery, but by the beginning of the eighteenth century their numbers had increased four-fold, and they were paying out generous loans to members in need, on an approved security but interest free.

The Grocers of London were first known as the Pepperers, pepper being the principal commodity in which they dealt in the early days, and very important it was too, at a time when meat figured so largely in the diet and most of the time can have been none too fresh. The fraternity first appears in the records of Henry II, when they were fined for forming themselves into a guild without the royal assent, but it was not until 1376 that they were incorporated by charter as grocers, the word meaning a trader *en gros* or wholesaler.

After several temporary homes they built their hall, in 1428, in Old Jewry, on the site of a friary which had originally been the Jewish synagogue. The friars' beautiful garden remained, with its arbour and vines, its hedgerows and bowling alley, and members of the public were allowed to walk there freely. And here the Grocers built a row of seven almshouses for seven old people, several members of the Company, which now had 124 members, giving either money or land towards the maintenance of the old folk.

The Grocers came to deal in a variety of products, including drugs, whale oil and wool. They were also the first tobacco merchants and three of their members, who had become addicted to it, gave such offence when they smoked at a formal meeting of the Court, that they were fined for want of decorum.

The Grocers had a number of distinguished and generous members. Sir John Philpot, who was Mayor in 1378, fitted out a fleet at his own expense to capture a Scottish freebooter and fifteen Spanish ships, and later he transported an English army to Brittany to rescue a number of small English craft which had been impounded there.

John Churchman, who was a sheriff in 1385, acquired for the City the privilege of the custody of the 'King's Beam' at the wool wharf, which was used for weighing wool in the Port of London.

It was a grocer and former Mayor, Thomas Knowles, who in 1411, 'with his brethren and aldermen', began to build the Guildhall: and 'instead of an old little cottage in Aldermanberie Street, made a fair and goodly house, more near unto St Lawrence Church in the Jewrie', wrote Stow. Over the years many other Companies contributed to the building and it was Sir Richard Whittington who donated the money for the paving of the Great Hall with Purbeck stone.

Throughout the fourteenth and fifteenth centuries, the Grocers contributed to the rebuilding of St Antholin's in Watling Street, St Stephen, Walbrook, and the Guildhall Chapel, and they were responsible for repairing 'the muddy way leading to the Strand'.

Sir John Crosby, Sheriff in 1483, who lived in the beautiful Crosby Hall in Bishopsgate Street, gave many donations to the City for civic needs, including the repair of the wall, of London Bridge and Bishopsgate. Sir William Sevenoke founded the Grocers' school at Sevenoaks and Lawrence Sheriff, who was warden of the Company in 1561, founded Rugby School.

During the Civil War, the Grocers, like all the Companies, suffered badly. In 1654 Parliament exacted £50 a week from them, towards the maintenance of the troops, as well as money for the defence of the City and the care of the wounded soldiers. They had to sell some of their plate, and when Parliament demanded a further £4,500 most of the rest went too.

During the Commonwealth their Hall was used as a meeting place for Parliamentary Committees and it is interesting to read that in 1648 the Grocers were petitioning General Fairfax not to quarter his troops in the Hall of a 'charitable Company' like theirs.

The Hall, like that of the Mercers, was destroyed during the Great Fire of 1666 and the Grocers were by this time so impoverished that it was only through the generosity of one of their members, Sir John Cutler, that it was rebuilt.

In 1681, the year that Sir John More was Lord Mayor, he made further renovations to the Hall in order to make it fit for his residence there during his term
of office, for there was as yet no Mansion House.

The Drapers' first Hall was in Cornhill but in 1541 they came to Throgmorton
Street, where there were many beautiful houses. From Henry VIII they bought
the largest of them all, which Thomas Cromwell had built for himself, after
clearing away a number of small and half-ruined cottages. When this house,
almost windowless on the street side, and with three embattled towers, was
finished, Cromwell, deciding that the garden was not spacious enough, gave
orders that the palings of the garden adjoining it to the north should be removed and put back 22 feet. He then had a brick wall built round his enlarged
garden. Stow confirms this story, for he says:

> My father had a garden there, and an house standing close to his south pale:
> this house they loosed from the ground, and bore upon rollers into my
> father's garden, twenty-two feet, ere my father heard thereof. No warning
> was given him, nor other answere, when hee spoke to the surveyors of that
> worke, but that their master, Sir Thomas, commanded them so to doe; no
> man durst go to argue the matter but each man lost his land, and my father
> paid his whole rent, which was 6s.6d the year for that half which was left.

To this incredible high-handedness Stow merely comments that 'the sudden
rising of some men causeth them in some matters to forget themselves'.

The Drapers were originally makers as well as dealers in cloth. Before the
fourteenth century, when English wool was mainly exported to the Netherlands by the Staplers, manufactured cloth came back by way of the Steelyard,
the tolls being paid at Billingsgate. The drapers were soon flourishing in most
English provincial cities, selling mainly red, green and scarlet Flemish cloth.
However English weavers were increasing their output and in Stephen's reign
comes the first mention of English cloth made with Spanish wool. During the
reign of Edward I the cloth of Candlewick Street was already famous and when
Edward III forbade the import of foreign cloth and brought over the seventy
families of skilled weavers from the Netherlands, with their trade secrets, many
of them settled in Candlewick Street, so that by the reign of Henry VI nearly all
the London drapers were to be found there.

In 1521 Henry VIII ordered the Drapers to help fit out five ships for Sebastian
Cabot, whose father had discovered Newfoundland in 1497. They objected that
if was 'a sore adventure to jeopard ships with men and goods unto the said
island, upon the singular trust of one man, called, as they understood, Sebastian'. But protests were of no avail with King Henry and they had to pay up.

The sixteenth-century records of the Company describe a long list of ceremonial feasts and funerals, elections and pageants, as well as charitable bequests. Their feasts were gargantuan. In 1522, on the occasion of the election
of their new master, their dinner consisted of fowls, swans, geese, pike, half a
buck, pasties, conies, pigeons, tarts, pears and filberts, washed down with ale
and claret. Sometimes more than 200 people sat down to these banquets,
including guests and women members, the women occasionally dining with
the men but otherwise eating in a separate room.

At the Midsummer dinner of 1515 they ate six bucks, three boars, a sturgeon
and 24 dozen quails, and to the accompaniment of the music from the minstrels' gallery they drank three hogsheads of wine, 21 gallons of muscatel and
thirteen and a half barrels of ale.

The funerals of their important members were conducted in the same grand
manner and the Company maintained two priests at St Michael's, Cornhill,
to pray for their souls.

The London apprentices seem to have given a good deal of trouble, one way
and another. As feeling mounted against the Steelyard merchants towards
the end of the fifteenth century the apprentices, in one great riot, tried to sack
their warehouses, but the Drapers, armed with 'weapons, cressets and banners'
helped to guard them.

They treated their own apprentices firmly and the records describe the
punishment of one lad, called Needswell, who was flogged in the Company's
parlour by two tall men, disguised in canvas frocks, hoods and vizors, for
whom twopennyworth of birchen rods had been provided for the occasion.

During the reign of Henry IV the Drapers were granted a special duty to
visit the fairs held at St Bartholomew and Southwark, as well as Westminster
and Spitalfields, to inspect the quality of cloth being sold and check doubtful
measurements with their 'Draper's ell', on which occasions they were entertained with bread, wine and pears, a standard of refreshment well below that
of their customary fare.

They looked after their members who fell on hard times and awarded
them pensions, as well as dispensing a number of charities to the old and
needy.

The first Mayor of London, Henry FitzAilwin, was a Draper and Strype
calculated that between 1531 and 1714 53 of London's Mayors were drapers,
eight of them heads of noble families, 43 being knights or baronets; fifteen
were members of Parliament for the City and seven were founders of churches
and public institutions.

The Hall was lost in the Great Fire and rebuilt on the same site by Jerman,
round a large piazza surrounded by a colonnade, still set in its beautiful garden,

but it was badly damaged in another fire of 1774 and had to be largely rebuilt yet again.

By this time the Drapers had made their last public procession, which was in 1761, when the Master, Wardens and Court of Assistants walked in solemn procession to hear a sermon at St Peter's, Cornhill, carrying shoes, stockings and clothing, which were their annual legacy to the poor members of the Company.

The Fishmongers' Company, fourth in precedence and one of the wealthiest of the Livery Companies, received its first charter from Edward I. Henry III, in order to increase his customs' dues, had prohibited the landing of fish at any other spot than Queenhithe, the result being that a great fish-market grew up in Old Fish Street and the cook shops in Knightrider Street close by soon became famous for their fish dinners. Edward I, however, restored the fish-mongers' freedom to land their fish elsewhere in Thames Street and soon they were concentrated in Bridge Street, which became known as New Fish Street, and landing their fish at Billingsgate. The King fixed a tariff of prices, limiting the best sole to 3d a dozen, turbot to 6d each, mackerel, in Lent, to one penny, pickled herrings to 20 a penny, fresh oysters to 2d a gallon, eels to 25 for 2d and salmon to four for five shillings. He forbade partnerships with foreign fish-mongers and decreed that no fish, unless salted, was to be kept in London a second day. No one was to sell fish, except in the open market place, and no one was allowed to water fish more than twice, on pain of a fine and a spell in the stocks.

The Stocks Market, established in the heart of the City, on the site of the present Mansion House, round the punitive stocks, was also a fish market in the first place, before developing the sale of meat and general produce, and as late as 1545 there were 25 fishmongers in business there, compared with only eighteen butchers.

The first Fishmongers' Hall, on the site of the present one, at the corner of London Bridge and Upper Thames Street, was built in 1504, but they were established on this spot during the reign of Edward III, in a mansion which had belonged to Lord Fairhope, and like the other great companies they contributed to the French wars.

It was here that William Walworth was living during his term of office as Mayor of London at the time of the Peasants' Revolt, and to this day the dagger with which he killed Wat Tyler is preserved in the Hall.

It was at this time that the Fishmongers achieved their present rank as fourth in precedence amongst the Livery Companies and were returning six members to the Common Council, which was the maximum number sent by any Company: but there was a great deal of jealousy amongst the companies.

The worst quarrel had been 40 years earlier, between the Fishmongers and the Skinners, over a matter of precedence. They came to blows in Cheapside and then drew swords, and when the Mayor and Sheriffs and their serjeants intervened, the violence turned to bloodshed. Two Fishmongers were arrested, tried at the Guildhall and sentenced to be hanged in the Chepe, but in the end it was the Fishmongers who won, for they retained their fourth place, while the Skinners came fifth, but eventually lost to the Goldsmiths and were relegated to the sixth place.

Now there was more trouble. John de Northampton, who had been Mayor in 1380, declared that the Fishmongers' trade was no craft and was unsuitable to be ranked amongst the 'mysteries'. Enraged by the many frauds at Billingsgate, mainly in the selling of stale fish, he persuaded Parliament to decree that in future no Fishmonger should be admitted as Mayor of London. The prohibition lasted for only a year, for the Fishmongers pleaded successfully that they had been the victims of malice, but the quarrels went on for several more years, first with the Mercers and then with the Goldsmiths, mainly over the question of precedence.

They were neatly solved by the Court of Aldermen who ordered the over-sensitive Companies to take precedence over each other on alternate years, to dine together, exchange livery hoods and forget all about it.

The first Fishmongers' Hall was a building of great dignity. The Thames Street entrance opened on to a large paved courtyard, divided into two by the high-pitched, turreted dining-hall: and it had a splendid river frontage, with two wings, the recessed central part being surmounted by an octagonal tower and cupola. There was a balcony on the first floor and a small arched doorway on the ground floor led to the riverside terrace.

When the fire of 1666 broke out, this was one of the first buildings to be destroyed. It was rebuilt by Jerman, but again it was one of the first buildings to be damaged by fire during the air-raids of September, 1940. In 1951 the interior was beautifully restored by Austen Hall and amongst the treasures which were saved were Walworth's dagger and the Fishmongers' magnificent funeral pall of embroidered cloth of gold, one of the finest pieces of medieval needlework to be found in the country.

Among the many famous Fishmongers whose names are still remembered was Thomas Doggett, the Irish resident comedian of Drury Lane. He was a staunch Whig and with the accession of the Hanoverians he inaugurated the race from London Bridge to the Swan at Chelsea, for young Thames watermen just out of their apprenticeship. The prize was an orange coat and a silver badge with the Hanoverian horse. The race was first run on 1st August 1722, the year after Doggett's death, 1st August beingthe anniversary of George

I's accession, and the bargemaster of the Fishmongers' Company was the umpire. There was a golden guinea in each pocket of the prizewinner's coat and the Fishmongers provided prizes for the runners-up.

The race was run well into the nineteenth century, by which time the waterman's trade had become obsolete, but in recent years the race has been revived.

The Goldsmiths built their hall close to the Guildhall, in Foster Lane, which runs northwards from Cheapside to Gresham Street, the place where they had first practised their craft. The twelfth-century guild of goldsmiths was one of the eighteen fined by Henry II for functioning without the royal licence and their next piece of history seems to have been the thirteenth-century battle with the tailors, in which the clothworkers and shoemakers joined, until there were 500 combatants involved. There were several deaths before the Sheriffs and their men intervened and arrested the ring-leaders, thirteen of whom were condemned and executed, but no one seems to know what the quarrel was all about in the first place.

The Goldsmiths were incorporated by Edward III, the charter laying down that all members of Goldsmiths' Hall must have shops in the Chepe and sell no gold or silver vessels elsewhere, except in the King's Exchange. They were given the right to inspect and regulate all gold and silver ware in any part of the country, with the power to punish anyone found guilty of adulteration, for there were many complaints of fake jewellery at this time.

The Company was very small at first, with only fourteen apprentices, each of whom paid two shillings for admission. By 1343, however, there were 74 apprentices and the Company was also paying licences to employ foreign workmen and non-freemen.

Their early records describe their annual feast on the day of their patron saint, St Dunstan, and give accounts of the masses sung for them by their chaplain, payments for the ringing of the bells of St Paul's, candles and wine drunk at funerals and the chantries they maintained at their parish churches of St John Zachary, St Peter-le-Chepe, St Matthew Friday Street and St Vedast Foster Lane.

From the outset, the goldsmiths were watchful and tenacious of their integrity and in 1443 Henry VI was sending them a letter inviting them, as a craft which had at all times 'nobly acquitted themselves', to meet his queen, Margaret of Anjou, on her arrival from Paris. The Mayor, aldermen and representatives of the most important crafts were all present on this occasion, the Goldsmiths wearing 'bawderykes of gold, and short, jagged scarlet hoods'.

A few years later, John Chest, a goldsmith of Chepe who had slandered the Company, was condemned to come to Goldsmiths' Hall and on his bended knees ask the entire Company for forgiveness: and he was forbidden to wear the livery for a month. Another goldsmith, German Lyas, who had sold a tablet of adulterated gold, was also compelled to ask forgiveness of the Company on his bended knees and by way of a fine had to give them a gilt cup weighing 24 ounces.

By the reign of Edward IV there were 137 English goldsmiths in London and 41 foreigners, but the foreigners lived in mainly Westminster and Southwark.

In 1540 six goldsmiths were sent to fetch Anne of Cleves from Flanders, for her marriage to Henry VIII, all of them dressed in black velvet coats, with gold chains and velvet caps with gold brooches.

Sir Martin Bowes was the most famous goldsmith of this reign, leaving almshouses in Woolwich as well as two houses in Lombard Street for the Company.

The Goldsmiths were first governed by an alderman and later by four wardens – the prime warden, who was always an alderman of the City, a second warden and two renter wardens. Later a clerk-comptroller, four auditors and two porters were added to the government as well as the important office of assayer, whose function was to test the coinage issued from the Royal Mint. This test, known as the Trial of the Pyx, was taking place at least as early as the time of Edward I and is still held every March, when samples of coins are sent to the Goldsmiths' Hall for examination, each coin being in its own box or pyx. The first 'pyx' was kept in the Chamber of the Pyx at Westminster Abbey, an ancient, vaulted chamber, part of which dates back to the eleventh century. Here the hoard of money representing the treasury of England, was kept for a time, after its removal from Winchester, and also the pyx itself, the box containing the standard pieces of currency against which current gold and silver coins were tested each year.

By 1300 the Goldsmiths' Company had decreed that 'no vessel of gold or silver shall depart out of the hands of the workmen until it has been assayed by the Wardens of the Craft and stamped with the Leopard's Head'. And to this day, the Leopard's Head, the hall-mark of the Company, is a sufficient guarantee of value and workmanship anywhere in the world.

They had their full share of feasts, especially when they were entertaining royalty, and the usual troubles with over-exuberant apprentices, who were duly punished by flogging: and when they set out on their searches for bad workmanship and adulterated metal, they were very formal occasions. The Company's beadle led the procession, carrying his insignia of office. Then came the two chief wardens in livery and hoods, the colours of which were changed over the years, from red and black, decorated with silver and gold, to violet and scarlet like the Fishmongers. Then they took to violet gowns with black hoods but were soon back again in violet and scarlet. After them followed the clerk, and two renter wardens and the other officers, all in their liveries, and they proceeded down Cheapside and Lombard Street, giving, it would seem, ample warning to any goldsmith nursing a guilty conscience. They also visited the fairs at St Bartholomew's and Southwark and rode out to the great Stourbridge trade fair at Cambridge, set out in the fields between the Newmarket road and the river Cam. 'to see every hardware men show, for deceitful things, beads, gawds of beads and other stuff; and then they to drink when they have done, where they please'.

Little is known about the first small Goldsmiths' Hall. The second, built early in the fifteenth century, was also small but very elegant – a red brick building surrounding a small square courtyard, approached by an arched entrance from the street. During the Commonwealth it served as the Exchequer, for all the money sequestered from the Royalist estates was kept here. The third Hall, built after the Great Fire, was taken down in 1829 and the present building, designed by Philip Hardwick, and regarded as the finest of all the Company Halls, went up in 1835. Here in the beautiful Livery Hall and Court room, the magnificent drawing-room and Court dining-room, with their marble chimney-pieces and elaborately stuccoed ceilings, their chandeliers and great mirrors, are cherished the portraits and memories of past Goldsmiths and the treasures they have amassed over the centuries, including the gold cup, thought to have been made by Cellini, from which Queen Elizabeth drank at her coronation.

The Skinners had a Hall by the time of Henry III and it was in 1327, during the next reign, that they were incorporated, having their affray with the Fishmongers over the question of precedence a few years later. At this time they were very rich and during Edward III's French wars they contributed the sum of £40, which was double the sum paid by the Goldsmiths.

Furs had been traded in London for centuries. The Romans traded them for British wool and metals and then Norse traders brought them to Queenhythe from Scandinavia and Armenia. The Anglo-Saxons wore furs but it was during Norman times that they became highly prized and fashionable, and early in the twelfth century the first sumptuary laws were passed, restricting their wear. They were directed in the first place against the abbesses and nuns. In 1127 a Church Council at Westminster decreed that they were not to wear garments more precious than those of lamb's wool or of black cat's fur: and eleven years later the Papal Legate, presiding over another Council, declared that 'by papal authority we forbid that nuns wear furs of squirrel, sable, marten, ermine or beaver, put on gold rings, or twist or make up their hair. Any found to have broken this decree will be excommunicated'.

Members of the Court and the nobility wore furs in plenty. Their cloaks were lined with them and men's tunics and women's dresses were trimmed with sable and ermine. Richard I paid as much as £13 for four sable skins and a fur of ermine and another £12 to have two ermine linings sent to him from London, while he was away on his Crusade.

The Skinners were the importers and dressers of these rare and precious furs and grew wealthy in the process, but as England grew rich with her wool trade and merchants and their wives took to wearing furs, a sumptuary law of Edward III's reign decreed that only members of the royal family, prelates, earls, and barons, knights, rich priests and persons who gave at least £100 to the Church might wear ermine and sable. As for women, the wearing of costly furs should be restricted to those of 'blameless or at least noble birth', which seems a remarkably equivocal qualification. The wives of tradesmen must wear the furs of 'lambs, rabbits, cats and foxes'. These were handled by a different guild from the Skinners and the decree was a setback to the foreign fur trade, but the Skinners survived, concentrating now on rabbit and other English furs, which pedlars collected for them from the people of the country- side, and uniting with the fraternity which had formerly specialised in these skins.

Edward III, Richard II, Henry IV, Henry V, Henry VI and Edward IV were all brethren of the Skinners' Company and Stow describes the annual procession of the Skinners on the feast of Corpus Christi conducted with all the medieval pomp and splendour of the great companies. The procession, he says:

passed through the principal streets of the city, wherein was borne more than one hundred torches of wax (costly garnished) burning light, and above two hundred clerks and priests, in surplices and copes, singing. After the which were the sheriff's servants, the mayor's sergeants, the counsel of the city, the mayor and aldermen in scarlet, and then the Skinners in their best liveries. Thus much to stop the tongues of unthankful men, such as used to ask; Why have ye not noted this, or that? and give no thanks for what is done.

It was in the seventeenth century that the fortunes of the Skinners soared, for it was then that men took to wearing large hats made from beaver fur, which was first brought to Europe by French cod-fishermen from the Gulf of the St Lawrence. Early in the century Henry Hudson had followed John Cabot across the Atlantic to explore the river and shores of the bay which were to be named after him, and he returned to England with stories of the vast num- bers of wild animals he had seen, with pelts which would produce a great wealth of furs. He went back to North America, but died in an attempt to find the north-west passage to Asia.

The French had already established colonies along the St Lawrence river and were exploring south and west into the heart of North America, but a French traveller, Pierre Radisson, turned north, and he, too, reached the shores of Hudson Bay, where he began a flourishing trade in furs, but the French government intervened, declaring that he was trading without a licence. They confiscated most of his furs, whereupon Radisson left Canada, and after a consultation with the English Commissioner in Boston, arrived in London. He obtained an audience of Charles II and outlined a plan for developing the fur trade in Canada. The King was interested and an expedition was organised, financed by the King, the Duke of York, Prince Rupert and several wealthy London merchants. Two vessels set sail from Gravesend, one of which had to turn back, but the *Nonesuch* reached Hudson Bay and remained there for seven months, returning to London with a cargo of furs so valuable that the King granted a charter to a new fur-trading company. The Company of Adventurers of England Trading into Hudson Bay. The first company meetings were held in Prince Rupert's quarters in the Tower of London but they had soon accumulated so many furs that their disposal became a problem. Some were sold privately. Others were sent to the fur dealers of Leipzig, Amsterdam, Paris and Vienna: but the quality and quantity of the furs reaching London was so high that the European dealers were soon coming to London to buy and the City became the centre of the world fur market, a position which it held at least until 1939 and has been recovering during the post-war years.

The Skinners had met on Dowgate Hill since 1295 and the present hall was built after the Great Fire on the same site. It was given a new Classical façade in about 1790, which was destroyed by the bombs of the last war, but much of the main part of the beautiful building has survived, including the splendid staircase ascending to the seventeenth-century Court room and the restored livery hall, which is panelled with large paintings, commissioned from Sir Frank Brangwyn in 1902, depicting the work of the Skinners, while in the entrance hall still hangs the magnificent chandelier presented to the Company by the Empress Catherine of Russia.

The history of the Merchant Taylors is well recorded and shows, perhaps more clearly than any other documentation, the vital part that these companies played in the government and business of the City.

Their hall is in Threadneedle Street and they have been on their present site since 1331. Before that time, their hall was behind the Red Lion in Basing Lane, Cheapside, and it was near here, during the reign of Henry IV, that they built seven almshouses. The hall in Threadneedle Street, with its arched gateway, was built on the site of the house of Edmund Crepin and was composed of a ground floor with three storeys above and a steep roof surmounted by a lantern with a vane. In 1620 the hall was first wainscoted in place of the usual whitewash and later it was hung with a costly arras, but not until 1646 were red tiles laid on the floor in place of the rush-strewn beaten earth, which was found to be 'inconvenient and oftentimes noisome'.

As in all medieval dining halls, the tables were on trestles which could be easily moved, and on feast days they were covered with costly table linen and plate.

When Edward I gave the Merchant Taylors their first grant they were known as Linen Armourers. Their first master was their 'pilgrim', since he travelled for the whole company, and their wardens were described as 'purveyors of dress', for they were originally cutters and makers of clothes as well as dealers and importers of cloth. These London tailors made both men's and women's clothes, as well as soldiers' quilted surcoats, the padded lining of armour and the trappings of the war-horses.

Like the other Companies, they contributed to Edward III's war in France, and in 1377 they sent six members to the Common Council, which indicates that they were already one of the largest fraternities. Henry VI granted them the 'right of search and correction of abuses'. For testing the measuring of cloth the Company kept a silver yardstick, engraved with the Company's arms, which had been given them by Edward IV, and with this they visited Bartholomew Fair every year to check the lengths of cloth being sold there, the visit being followed by the inevitable feast, at which they wore their blue gowns and scarlet and puce hoods.

After their quarrel with the Skinners, the Mayor decreed that the two Companies should take precedence alternately and that they should dine in each other's halls twice a year, on the Vigil of Corpus Christi and the feast of St John the Baptist.

During the reign of Queen Elizabeth, he was ordering that ten Merchant Taylors and ten Vintners should guard each of the City gates every tenth day. The Merchant Taylors were required to provide and train 200 men for arms and in 1586 the master and wardens were reminded to make the provision of gun-powder which was required of all the London Companies, while in 1588 the Company was ordered to furnish 35 armed men, the quota demanded for service against the Armada.

They had founded their grammar school a few years earlier, in 1561, when their Master, Richard Hills, gave £500 towards buying the house in Candlewick Street where it was first held – the Duke of Buckingham's old house, the Manor of the Rose.

John Stow, like his father before him, was a tailor, but he developed his taste for historical research when he was still very young. He published several books but the only one by which he is known today is his immortal *Survey of London*. He impoverished himself in the writing of it and when he presented a copy to the Company, in 1592, they granted him an annuity of £4 a year, which was later raised to £10. He died in poverty and it was not until after his death, in 1603, that his work began to be appreciated. Then, in the first half of the seventeenth century, before the Great Fire, the Merchant Taylors erected his monument in the Church where he had always worshipped – St Andrew Undershaft in Leadenhall Street. Happily it has survived and shows him seated at a desk, with an open book before him and holding a quill pen; and now, every year about the time of his death, the Lord Mayor pays tribute to his memory by placing a fresh quill in his hand.

On the accession of James I the London Companies were asked to contribute £2,500 to the welcoming celebrations of the City, which included triumphal arches, pageants and masques, and of this amount the Merchant Taylors gave £234: and four years later the King and Prince Henry dined with them at the Company's hall. The feast cost £1,000 and they were diverted by a company of lute players and a masque especially written for the occasion by Ben Jonson. The children of the Chapel Royal sang grace and John Bull, one of the Chapel's organists, played on an organ which was especially installed. Added to all this, the Company presented King James with a purse containing £100, but the King was still nervous after the alarm of the Gunpowder plot, and not only was there a thorough search of the hall beforehand, but he and the Prince dined separately, in a chamber specially built for the occasion by cutting a hole in the wall of the hall and building a small room behind it. So this was very different from the occasion more than a century earlier when Henry VII had been enrolled as a member of the Company and 'sat openly among them in a gown of crimson velvet ... upon their solemn feast day, in the hall of the said Company.'[1]

The Company was given many gifts by wealthy members and in return donated scores of charities to needy people, as well as maintaining a number of chantry priests.

At the outset of the Civil War the Company was loyal to King Charles. As early as 1640 the Lord Mayor had ordered the Company to have ready stored in their garden 40 barrels of powder and three hundredweight of bullets, in addition to the 92 muskets, 70 pikes, 123 swords and 23 halberds already in their armoury. That same year they lent the King £5,000 towards the maintenance of his northern army and on his return from Scotland they took part in the procession that met him.

1. Strype.

Thirty-four of the gravest, tallest and most comely of the Company, apparelled in velvet plush or satin with chains of gold, each with a footman with two staff-torches, met the Lord Mayor and aldermen outside the City wall near Moorfields, and accompanied them to Guildhall, and afterwards escorted the king from Guildhall to his palace.

This was the last show of loyalty the City paid to Charles and later records are all concerned with loans to the Parliamentary armies and the Commonwealth demands, which became so heavy that the Company was forced to sell some of its property.

The hall was almost completely destroyed during the Great Fire and the precious plate was melted into a solid lump of metal, but when it was rebuilt it became the largest of all the London Livery Companies' halls. It was severely damaged during the 1940 air raids but was restored in 1959 by Sir Albert Richardson.

The Haberdashers were originally a branch of the Mercers and had their stalls next to them in the Chepe. When they were incorporated, during the reign of Henry VI, they divided into two fraternities, those of St Catherine being cappers or 'haberdashers' of hats, those of St Nicholas dealing in ribbons and laces as well as even smaller merchandise, including brooches, spurs, capes and pins, and it was these haberdashers in small articles and not the hat-makers who were first called milliners.

In the early part of Queen Elizabeth's reign more than £60,000 worth of pins were imported from Holland, which had the first market. This large consumption is not surprising when one considers the complicated dress of the Tudors, which was extremely expensive and had to last for years, and was none too strongly made in the first place. Before the advent of the pin, ladies we are told, used 'skewers', which must have wrecked many a kirtle or farthingale. However, by the end of the reign pins were made in England, the haberdashers made their fortunes and James I gave the pinmakers their charter.

By this time the St Catherine and St Nicholas fraternities were united again into one large Company, consisting of a master, four wardens, 45 assistants, 360 liverymen and a large company of freemen: and they were already dispensing large sums in charity, one of their members, Robert Aske, founding later in the century the almshouses and school at Hoxton. During the nineteenth century the almshouses were removed and the school developed into Aske's Haberdashers' School.

Like the other Livery Companies, the Haberdashers were severely taxed during the years of the civil war and the Commonwealth, when they lost some £50,000. Their hall, opposite the Goldsmiths, was destroyed during the

Great Fire. The second hall, built on the same site, was lost during the Second World War and today the Haberdashers Hall is to be found in the large modern block of offices, Garrard House, on the corner of Wood Street and Gresham Street, the entrance to the hall being in Staining Lane.

The Salters grew wealthy on the great amount of salt that was used for salting fish, large quantities of which were eaten on the numerous feast days imposed by the medieval Church. They were incorporated by Queen Elizabeth but received their first privileges from Edward III, in whose reign they were sending members to the Common Council. They built their first hall, with six almshouses adjoining, about the middle of the fifteenth century, in Bread Street, near their colleagues the Fishmongers of the old Fish Market in Knight-rider Street. This was burnt down in 1539 and its successor in Bread Street suffered the same fate in 1598. For their third hall they bought a mansion set in a beautiful old garden shaded by lime trees, near the eastern end of St Swithin's Church, by London Stone. It had once been the London house of a prior of Tortington in Sussex, and then of a wealthy alderman, and when the Salters bought it from Captain George Smith it was known as Oxford Place.

Two distinguished Salters who became Lord Mayors lived here during their terms of office, but the mansion was lost during the Great Fire. The fourth hall, built on the same site, was a charming brick building, quite small, with its entrance from a small courtyard under a little arcade of three arches. Adjoining it was the Salters Hall Meeting House, for many of the Salters were Nonconformists, and during the seventeenth century the Salters Hall was one of the centres of Nonconformity in the City.

The little hall in its large garden stood until 1821, when it was pulled down and the fifth hall built in Cannon Street.

Today the Ironmongers are the smallest of the Twelve Great Companies and their hall is at 35 Aldersgate Street, where it was built in 1925, but their history is long and for centuries they were established in Fenchurch Street, where three successive halls were built on the same site.

The raw material of their craft came from the iron workings of Sussex, Surrey and Kent, and their earliest records are of contributing to Edward III's French war and, a few years later, of sending four of their members to the Common Council.

At this time they were both merchants and traders, for from their large warehouses they exported raw iron in bars, but they also had shops, mainly in Ironmonger Lane, where they sold manufactured iron articles bought from craftsmen working throughout the country and in the provincial towns.

All through Queen Elizabeth's reign they were helping her. In 1562 they provided nineteen soldiers for her service, in 1566 three more. In 1575 they lent her £60. Two years later they provided 100 men as soldiers, the following year seven seamen and the year after 73 men for the defence of the kingdom. In 1591 they contributed £344 to help equip ten ships of war and a pinnace and five years later were lending the government £172, while in 1565 they contributed £75 towards the building of the Royal Exchange. But it was during the Commonwealth that the charges on the Company became a serious burden. In 1642 they paid Parliament £3,400 and the following year they record having paid Parliament £9.10s. every week for four months and having to sell their plate to meet a demand for a further £1,700.

Yet they survived and among the Ironmongers' bequests of the Restoration years are the almshouses in the Kingsland Road, near Shoreditch Church, which were donated by Sir Robert Geffrye, master of the Ironmongers' Company and Lord Mayor of London in 1685–6. The almshouses were built round a wide courtyard, situated at that time in open country, but as London spread they became surrounded by industrial development. In 1912 new almshouses were built at Mottingham in Kent and by 1914 those in the Kingland Road had been converted by the London County Council into the fascinating Geffrye Museum, which contains a collection of furniture and other house furnishings – panelling, staircases and doorways – taken from old London houses from Elizabethan times onwards.

The Vintners Hall is in Upper Thames Street, on the riverside near Queenhithe, and it has stood here since it was built in 1357, along with thirteen almshouses, on ground which Sir John Stodie, Vintner, had bestowed on the Company: and Geoffrey Chaucer, whose father was a Vintner, was born close by and must have watched it going up, although 1357 was the year he entered the household of Lady Elizabeth, wife of the Duke of Clarence, who made a note in her household accounts that year of the pair of red and black breeches, short cloak and shoes which she had provided for him.

Although the Hall was largely rebuilt after the Great Fire it had not been entirely destroyed and the Court room, built in 1446 and thought to be the oldest room in London, has survived. The seventeenth-century exterior of the Hall was rebuilt just before the First World War and it escaped damage in the last war.

The area round this part of Upper Thames Street was from earliest medieval times known as the Vintry, for it was here that the Bordeaux merchants unloaded their lighters and sold their wine.

Edward I granted the Vintners Botolph Wharf near Billingsgate. During Edward III's reign four of their members became Mayors: the Company paid £23.6s.8d towards the French war and by the end of the reign had become so important that they were sending six members to the Common Council.

Most of the medieval records were lost in the Great Fire but those which survived recount the entertainment of kings and princes by the Vintners, with splendid feasts, and, on a lower level, accounts of wine which had been adulterated, sold without a licence or at too high a price.

In 1428, while Orleans was being besieged and Joan of Arc was fighting for her life, the Mayor of London, furiously angry at discovering that the Lombard wine merchants had adulterated their sweet wines, ordered '150 vessels to be staved in, so that the liquor, running forth, passed through the cittie like a stream of rain-water in the sight of all the people, from whence there issued a most loathsome savour'. The Lombards were not the only culprits, for wines from Gascony and Guienne were also adulterated or sold in short measure at times.

Henry VI's charter forbade any but Vintners to trade in Gascony and four members of the Company, appointed annually, had the right of search in taverns and the regulation of prices: and all wine coming to London had to be unloaded above London Bridge, at the Vintry, so that the King's bottlers and gaugers could take their due custom.

The Vintners grew rich with their monopoly until the time of the Commonwealth, but after that the good days were over. On 5th February 1641, it was reported that

a bill was brought into the House of Commons concerning the wine business, by which it appeared that Alderman Abell and Mr. Kilvert had in their hands, which they deceived the King of, £57,000 upon the wine licence; the Vintners of London, £66,000; the wine merchants of Bristol, £1,051; all of which moneys were ordered to be immediately raised on their lands and estates, and to be employed to the public use.

Yet the Company survived and in their hall today possess some beautiful late medieval tapestries and valuable pictures, including a painting of St Martin of Tours attributed to Rubens, as well as a splendid collection of plate and eighteenth-century English wine glasses.

With the Dyers' Company, the Vintners enjoy the royal prerogative of owning swans on the Thames, from the City to Henley, and every first Monday in August the swan markers of the Crown, and of the Vintners' and Dyers' Companies, make a trip up-river, from Temple Stairs, just above Blackfriars Bridge, to count and mark the young birds.

The last in precedence of the Twelve Great Companies are the Clothworkers. They began as a branch of the Weavers' Guild, as did the Burrellers, who were inspectors and measurers of cloth, and the Fullers, fulling being a process of cleaning the cloth. In the time of Edward IV the shearmen, who were employed in a special method of clipping the nap during the process of cloth-making, were separated from the Drapers and Tailors and, by the time of Henry VIII had joined with the Weavers, the fraternity being known as the Clothworkers, but it was only after many arguments that they were designated one of the great twelve and the Dyers became the first of the lesser Companies.

The original Clothworkers' Hall in Mincing Lane, where the Minchins or Nuns of St Helen's, Bishopsgate, held property, had been bought by the Fullers in 1455, and more than two centuries later Pepys, who was a member of the Company and lived close by, described the night of the outbreak of the Great Fire.

'Between two and three in the morning, we were waked with the maids crying out "Fire, fire in Mark Lane!" So I rose and looked out, and it was dreadful.'

He hurried out to see where exactly it was 'and found it in a new-built house that stood alone in Minchin Lane, over against the Clothworkers' Hall, which burned furiously'.

The Hall which replaced it was as splendid as the medieval building which had been destroyed, but in 1860, when England was at the height of her prosperity and the cloth trade was bringing in large fortunes and dispensing generous charities, the Hall was rebuilt and greatly enlarged, for the Company bought the adjoining land, on which stood the Church and Churchyard of All Hallows Staining, which had derived its name from the fact that it was one of the earliest Churches in the City to have been built of stone. The Clothworkers demolished the Church but the Tower remains to this day and part of the little churchyard has been preserved as an open space.

But the new Victoria Hall, with its beautiful carving and abundance of handsome mirrors, its gold and white ceiling and all its treasures were lost in the bombing of 1941, and their fourth Hall, at the corner of Fenchurch Street and Mincing Lane, was not opened until 1958.

7

Tudor London — I

At the beginning of Tudor times the population of London, including its suburbs and the little villages of Charing and Westminster which were developing to the west, was approaching 100,000, and by the end of Queen Elizabeth's reign it had nearly doubled and was still increasing, despite the laws which were passed from time to time in an abortive effort to check its growth.

When Henry VII ascended the throne, the City had reached the peak of its medieval splendour. The Church, with its priories, abbeys and convents, set in their carefully tended gardens, the Cathedral of St Paul and the great conventual churches, the 120 little churches, with their chantries and graveyards, still covered a quarter of the area within the boundaries of the City. They were beautiful, with their stonework and fan vaulting, their glittering candles and brightly coloured walls, painted with scenes depicting the Bible stories and the lives of the Saints, their monuments and delicately carved woodwork: and their power over the lives of the people seemed absolute and eternal.

Yet already the first murmurs of resentment were being voiced at the enormous wealth and authority of the Church, the profligacy of a number of the wealthy clergy and the uselessness of many of the monasteries and friaries, whose members had long since abandoned their early ideals of chastity and poverty.

Along the river front, between the quays and warehouses, in the narrow lanes running up from the waterside to Watling Street, in Fenchurch Street and Bishopsgate, Aldersgate and Throgmorton Street stood the London palaces of the noblemen, all built to a similar pattern. They were approached by a gateway in the street wall which led into a large courtyard round which the house was built, its central feature being the great hall, with its high-pitched roof and oriel window: and sometimes, as in the colleges at Oxford and Cambridge, a second courtyard lay behind, approached by a covered way through the centre of the main building.

Baynard's Castle, which had been destroyed by fire in 1428, had been rebuilt by Humphrey, Duke of Gloucester, sited a little to the east of the old building. It became the London home of Richard, Duke of York, with his troop of 400 gentlemen and men-at-arms, and it was here that Edward IV assumed the title of king and that the Duke of Buckingham offered the crown to Richard III.

The mansion of Cold Harbour stood in Thames Street, by the church of All Hallows the Less, to the west of the Old Swan stairs. Sir John Poultney, four times mayor, was living there during the reign of Edward III and a few years after his death, when Richard II had dined there with his brother, the Earl of Huntingdon, Cold Harbour, still sometimes called Poultney's Inn, was described as a 'right fair and stately house'.

The Erber was a great old house in Dowgate, close to the river, first built by the founder of St Mary Overies. It had many illustrious owners and eventually passed into the hands of the Nevilles. When Warwick, the Kingmaker, inherited it, he lodged his father, the Earl of Salisbury, here, he himself living in a mansion in Newgate Street with his army of 500 retainers, and it was claimed that six oxen were eaten each day at breakfast alone, and that anyone who was allowed within the gates of Warwick House could take away as much roast meat as he could carry upon a long dagger.

The Erber passed to Warwick's son-in-law, the Duke of Clarence, who met his end in the Tower. Then Richard of Gloucester moved in, repaired the old place and called it the King's Palace, until he met his death on Bosworth Field.

On the site of the Heralds College in Queen Victoria Street stood Derby House, a mighty mansion approached by a doorway in the street wall built under an archway and surmounted by a tower. This was the London home of the Earl of Derby, who married Henry VII's mother, the Countess of Richmond.

In Watling Street survived the Tower Royal, a place half-palace, half-fortress, which, says Stow, 'was of old time the king's house, where King Stephen lodged' but afterwards it was called the Queen's Wardrobe: and it was here that Richard II's mother and her court fled for safety from the Tower of London, during Wat Tyler's rebellion. Richard III granted the old place to the Duke of Norfolk, but by Tudor times it was deserted. For a time it was used for stabling. Then it was divided into tenements, until it fell into an even more ruinous state and was demolished.

In Botolph Lane by Billingsgate the Earls of Arundel were living until the sixteenth century. The Earls of Northumberland were in Aldersgate Street, the Earls of Worcester in Worcester Lane by the riverside. The Duke of Buckingham lived on College Hill, the Beaumonts and Huntingdons by St Paul's

Wharf, the Lord of Berkeley near Blackfriars. Edward, the Black Prince, had a palace on Fish Street Hill, which later was to become a tavern. The Earls of Oxford lived at Oxford Court in St Swithin's Lane.

One of the medieval palaces which has in part survived is Crosby Hall, which once stood in Bishopsgate, nearly opposite Gresham House.

Crosby Hall, the home of the merchant prince John Crosby, was magnificent. He had inherited a large fortune but began work in the City as a silk mercer. By 1463 he had become a warden of the Grocers' Company and three years later was elected a member of Parliament for the City. He was a friend of many of the Florentine moneylenders, including the Frescobaldi and Bardi families, he represented the commercial interests of the German Hanse merchants in England and he became mayor of the Staple City of Calais.

There were only about twelve houses in Bishopsgate at this time, all of them owned by wealthy merchants. The original house into which Crosby moved was 'the great tenement' of a Genoese merchant called Pinello, and it was built on land belonging to the Prioress of St Helens', Bishopsgate. Church lands could not be sold but Crosby leased more land from the Prioress for his palace, although it is not certain whether he incorporated Pinello's mansion or demolished it and built afresh.

The main entrance of Crosby Hall was through a gateway in Bishopsgate Street into a courtyard, and there was an inner courtyard approached by the passage which ran through the middle of the house. The banqueting hall led off the passage to the left, the chapel, state apartments and servants' quarters to the right. Leading from the inner courtyard were the guests' apartments on the right, with gardens beyond them, and on the left the kitchens, bake-house, brewhouse and larders, with stables, sheds and outhouses at the back and another gateway which led to St Mary Axe.

The great hall, built of stone, was outstandingly beautiful, nearly 70 feet long, 27 feet wide and 40 feet high, with a minstrels' gallery, six windows and an oriel in the west wall and another six windows to the east, all carved in stone, a vaulted oak roof, marble floor and vast fireplace.

To the west of the great hall was another large hall with an even wider fireplace and an equally elegant oriel, and this room was later divided, the upper room being known as the throne room and the lower one as the Council Chamber.

In 1471 the 'bastard Falconbridge' marched upon London with his army of 17,000 men, to demand the release of Henry VI from the Tower. He stormed London Bridge and set fire to some of the houses on it, and it was Crosby, in command of London's citizen army, who repulsed him.

Edward IV knighted Crosby for his gallantry and during the next few years he undertook many diplomatic missions for the King, one of the most delicate being to treat with the Duke of Brittany that the young Prince Henry Tudor, last of the line of the House of Lancaster, who had taken refuge in Brittany, was kept in his charge, safely out of harm's way.

Yet Sir John derived little happiness from his gorgeous domain, for his first wife, whom he loved dearly, died before it was even finished, and he survived her for only nine years, dying in 1475. He had married again, but his second marriage had obviously been a failure, for although he had provided for the new wife in his will, he added that if she were not 'contented with my bequest, then I will ordain that all my said bequest to the said Anne, my wife, be utterly void, and that the said Anne have such part only as the law will then give her, without any other manner of favour to be showed her'. Lady Anne stayed on at Crosby Hall for a year or two and then it was let to Richard, Duke of Gloucester.

Edward IV died in 1483, leaving the young Prince Edward, only thirteen years old, in the care of Richard, who brought him to London from Ludlow Castle. The Mayor, aldermen, civic dignitaries and members of the Livery Companies rode out to Hornsey to welcome him to the City; and he was installed first in the Bishop's Palace in St Paul's Churchyard, and then in the royal apartments at the Tower of London, to await his coronation as Edward V. Richard meanwhile returned to Crosby Hall.

Accounts of the succeeding events are obscure and conflicting; but within a few days it was declared that Edward IV's marriage to Elizabeth Woodville was bigamous and the young Prince therefore illegitimate. The next in the Yorkist line to the throne was Richard himself. Prince Edward and his younger brother were never heard of again and Richard summoned the aldermen and a general assembly of citizens to Crosby Hall, asking them to accept him as their king. According to tradition, there was an obstinate silence, broken only by the assenting cries of a few of his followers who had been planted among the assembly, and Richard, disconcerted and fearing trouble, decided to transfer the ceremony to Baynard's Castle.

Richard did not return to Crosby Hall and by the time Henry VII was on the throne it was being used as the Mansion House for a succession of Lord Mayors. In 1501 the Crosby family sold the leasehold to Sir Bartholomew Reed, a member of the Grocers' Company who held his inaugural feast here when he became Mayor. He entertained Katharine of Aragon here when she arrived in England to marry Prince Arthur, and soon afterwards he was receiving the ambassadors of the Emperor Maximilian, who had come to condole with Henry VII on the Prince's death.

His successor at Crosby Hall was Sir John Rest, another Mayor and Grocer, who treated London to the finest Lord Mayor's Show it had ever seen, including 'four giants, one unicorn, one dromedary, one camel, one ass, one dragon six hobby horses and sixteen naked boys'.

But the most distinguished of all the residents of Crosby Hall was Sir Thomas More, who lived here from 1519 to 1524, before moving to his riverside home at Chelsea.

Another interesting old City mansion of late medieval times was Leaden Hall, built by Sir Hugh Neville early in the fourteenth century, which derived its name from the fact that the roof was lined with lead, but by about 1445 the old house was converted into a granary and Leadenhall market grew up within its precincts.

In addition to these mansions were the palatial episcopal residences, for as well as the Archbishop of Canterbury's palace at Lambeth and the Archbishop of York's in Whitehall, there were not only several bishops' residences in the Strand, including those of the Bishops of Durham, Bath, Chester, Lichfield Llandaff, Worcester, Exeter and Carlisle, but several in the City itself. The Bishop of Hereford lived in Fish Street Hill, the Bishop of Ely at Ely Place Holborn, the Bishop of Salisbury in Salisbury Square, the Bishop of St David's near the Bridewell and the Bishops of Winchester and Rochester in Southwark Matching these residences in splendour were the Guildhall, the halls of the Companies and some of the inns of the lawyers. Since early in the fifteenth century the Guildhall had been enriched and enlarged by the gifts of kings and merchant princes, and Henry VII, in gratitude to Sir John Shaw, the Mayor whom he had knighted on Bosworth Field, presented it with a magnificent kitchen, so that henceforth the City feasts which had formerly been held in the halls of the Merchant Taylors and the Grocers or in the Mayor's private mansions, were now given each year in the Guildhall, with the full panoply of gorgeous robes and insignia of office and the proud dignity of long established ritual.

Since the early thirteenth century, when Magna Carta had decreed that common pleas between subject and subject should be heard at a fixed court at Westminster, men of the law had sought quarters in London. Hostels appeared near the village of Holborn, in what was soon to be known as Chancery Lane, and when the Templars' estate by the riverside was expropriated the lawyers leased the land from the Knights of St John of Jerusalem and established their societies of the Inner and Middle Temple there. The Outer Temple was never more than a plot of land owned by the Templars. It had passed into the hands of the Bishops of Exeter, who had built Exeter House here as their London residence.

In the early fourteenth century Lincoln's Inn, once the London home of the Earls of Lincoln, had been taken over by the lawyers and become one of the Inns of Court, but it was rebuilt in Tudor times, about the same time that the lawyers leased Gray's Inn, the mansion of Lord Gray of Wilton, with its beautiful wainscoted hall.

Clifford's Inn in Fleet Street, Serjeant's Inn in Chancery Lane and Thavies Inn, Furnival's Inn, Barnard's Inn and Staple Inn in Holborn were all houses of Chancery in Tudor times, though they have not survived. At this time they were organised like the universities, with chambers, dining-halls, libraries and chapels, and the professional lawyers gave teaching in common law and the art of debate and disputation to boys from the grammar schools and universities. Most wealthy young men from Oxford or Cambridge passed on to one of the Inns for a year or two, whether they intended to practise or not, for they were regarded as finishing schools, and in an age of litigation a knowledge of the law was valuable to any man of property.

Fees were high but discipline was light and the living good. It has been estimated that during the sixteenth century there were some thousand students resident in the Inns of Chancery during term time and nearly as many at the four Inns of Court. Stow, writing at the end of the century, said:

> ... there is in and about this city a whole university, as it were, of students, practicers or pleaders, and judges of the law of this realm, not living of common stipends, as in other universities it is for the most part done, but of their own private maintenance, as being altogether fed either by their places or practice, or otherwise by their proper revenue, or exhibition of parents and friends; for that the younger sort are either gentlemen or the sons of gentlemen, or of other most wealthy persons. Of these houses there be at this day fourteen in all; whereof nine do stand within the liberties of this city, and five in the suburbs thereof. ...

Cheapside, the main shopping street of the City, was wider than it is today and there were gardens and orchards both within and without the City walls, but the side streets were narrow and tortuous and the timbered houses built above the shops were often three or four storeys high, each storey overhanging the one below, so that from the attic windows people could sometimes shake hands with each other across the street, while the inn signs which hung from every one, growing larger and more imposing with the passing years, were a considerable hazard in windy weather.

In between were the murky courts and alleys where the poor lived, in conditions which had improved very little from Anglo-Saxon times, and along the riverside, just outside the City wall, the grim Tower of London still

E

loomed threateningly, vastly increased in extent since the days when William I had built the White Tower. Henry III had built the water gate and wharf, on land reclaimed from the marshy river bank, and after one or two misadventures when, to the delight of the citizens of London, the whole embankment had collapsed, it stretched for nearly a quarter of a mile along the water front.

Until the end of the seventeenth century the usual approach to the Tower was by the river, which was still London's main highway, busy with wherries and river craft of all kinds, including, on festive occasions, the royal barge, flower-decked and gay with the music of minstrels, as it made its way from Greenwich to Westminster. But prisoners too were brought to the Tower, usually at dead of night and often manacled and fettered, to be landed at the sinister Traitors' Gate, with its grim portcullis and massive iron chains hanging over the worn steps and slowly lapping waters.

The inner ward of the Tower, where the royal family still sometimes stayed, was surrounded by a wall into which were built defensive towers – the Devereux, Flint, Bowyer, Brick and Martin towers along the north side, the Constable Broad Arrow and Salt towers in the eastern wall, the Beauchamp and Bell Towers in the western wall, and along the south side the Garden tower, which after the murder of the two Princes was called the Bloody Tower, the Wakefield and the Lantern tower, from which a lantern burned every night, as a guide to the river craft.

Within this ward were the original White Tower, the royal quarters, the Mint, which remained here until 1811, the Jewel-house, the Wardrobe, the Queen's garden, St Peter's Church, the Green, where the private executions took place – the less privileged meeting their end on Tower Hill – and, in later years, the house of the Lieutenant.

Most of the victims who had been executed on the Green were buried there but the more distinguished were moved to the crypt of the Chapel Royal, just to the north.

In the outer ward were several more towers and the whole grisly complex was protected along the river front by the Byward tower, St Thomas's tower over the Traitors' Gate, the Cradle tower, the Well tower and the Develin tower.

Until Tudor times every sovereign brought his personal bodyguard to the Tower when he was in residence, but Henry VII's Yeomen of the Guard, many of them Welshmen, were established there as a permanent body: and when someone noticed the large amount of meat allotted to them for their daily ration, they were dubbed Beefeaters.

There was also a fair-sized menagerie at the Tower. Henry I had kept some lions and leopards at Woodstock for the diversion of his courtiers and when the Emperor Frederick II sent Henry III three more leopards he decided to house them at the Tower, together with the animals at Woodstock which, in the natural order of things, were growing to an unmanageable number. But the City had to pay for them. In 1253 he ordered the sheriff to pay fourpence a day for the maintenance of his white bear and provide a muzzle and chain for him when he was fishing or washing himself in the river, and a few years later, when Louis IX of France sent him an elephant, it was the City that had to pay for building the elephant house. During the reigns of the first three Edwards the money spent on the maintenance of the lions and leopards at the Tower came to four times the wages of their keeper, but in later years the job became a fairly well-paid sinecure and the zoo remained here until 1834, when it was moved to Regent's Park.

The Bowyer tower in particular had some terrible cells. One was approached by a hole in the floor from which a trap-door led by a flight of steps to a dungeon of stark horror. In the Beauchamp tower there was a secret passage built into the wall, where spies could watch and listen to prisoners. The cell called Little Ease was so small that the prisoner could neither stand nor lie at full length. Others were full of rats which swarmed in from the river at high tide.

During the Wars of the Roses, London had favoured the Yorkists but had, for the most part, remained aloof from the struggle, lending money to one king after another, Henry VI, Edward IV and Richard III, all of whom courted the rich merchants, on whom they largely depended for the solvency of the Exchequer. The Staplers handled the export of the wool from the royal estates and the lands of the nobles, and in return their armies respected the precincts of the City.

The City's overseas trade was developing and the government within its precincts was in the hands of the great Merchant Companies, some of which were beginning to own their own ships for foreign trade. Many of the families of the old nobility had perished during the wars and of the remainder most had become impoverished. It was the end of feudalism and the days of the great City households were numbered. Apart from the fact that they could no longer afford to keep their large armies of retainers, Henry VII forbade them. Those mansions that were not immediately abandoned were occupied with a less arrogant display of power and wealth for a few years and then were divided into tenements, becoming increasingly derelict until they were demolished, while the great families of the new nobility which arose during the sixteenth century were to build their mansions outside the City to the west, along the Strand.

While these fundamental changes were taking place in England, events were happening in eastern Europe which were to mark the end of medievalism throughout the Continent – events in which England was to play her part and the City of London was to lay the foundations of her future international strength.

As during the early fifteenth century the Turks had advanced through the Balkans and Asia Minor towards Constantinople, the Greek scholars who, through the centuries, had kept alive the learning and tradition of the old Roman Empire, had taken the precaution of moving their libraries and schools to the Aegean islands and Italy: and Europe was re-introduced to a long-forgotten culture. In Rome and Florence began the Renaissance, a great revival of art and literature, inspired by the artists and writers of ancient Rome and Greece, which was to influence the culture of all Europe. In England, as on the Continent, scientists were able to gain access to the works of Ancient Greek philosophers and doctors. The clouds of ignorance and superstition were lifted and new horizons emerged. The Middle Ages faded before a great awakening of intellectual life, new thinking on science, philosophy, religion, art and architecture, literature and the drama, and adventurous journeys across uncharted seas, which were to be the prelude to the great sea voyages of late Tudor Times.

In the discovery of new lands the Portuguese led the way. They had freed themselves from the Islamic occupation of the Iberian peninsula a century or more before the Spaniards, and at the end of the fourteenth century King John of Portugal invaded Morocco. By 1415 he had captured Ceuta, of which his son, Prince Henry the Navigator, became governor. This was the limit of the Portuguese territorial conquest in North Africa, but Prince Henry and his brother began a systematic exploration of the West African Atlantic coast line.

The Arabs had traded the gold, salt and fine leather of the Sudan to Mediterranean Europe for many years, carrying it across the Sahara to North Africa, but they had barred the Sudan to all European travellers and Christians were forbidden to enter the Islamic cities of Timbuktu, Gao and Jenne, so that their only knowledge of inner Africa at this time had come from Arab tales which lost nothing in the telling – stories of the Niger river and the gold country, the Mountains of the Moon and a great Christian kingdom ruled by the mighty Prester John. Maps were few and for the most part wildly inaccurate, while some were deliberately faked, for geographical knowledge was eagerly sought and dearly bought. Venice, Genoa and the ports of Spain and Portugal all had their own collections of secret maps, drawn for the most part by Jewish cartographers.

There was a crusading spirit about Prince Henry's first journeys, a desire to find the Christian kingdom of Prester John, encircle the Infidels and drive them from the Continent: but in addition there was the purely commercial plan of making direct contact with the Sudanese and their products, so that they could be resold to Europe without the costly intervention of the Islamic middle-men.

The Portuguese were confident that Africa was surrounded by the 'all-encircling sea' and already – though they had no idea of its extent – they dreamt of the possibility of one day finding an easterly route round it to the Indian Ocean and the riches of the East.

Venice was at the height of her splendour and wealth, the great commercial distribution centre of Europe. She was on good terms with the Arabs and capturing ever more of the Eastern trade, to the discomfiture of Genoa and the Mediterranean ports to the west. Genoese merchants soon joined Prince Henry, therefore, in his explorations. The Mediterranean galleys proved too light for long sea voyages and with the help of Genoese sailors they built sturdy little three-masted caravels which were found capable of withstanding the hazards of the Atlantic.

They made voyage after voyage, each one extending a little further south, and during the 1430s they were able to make landings at the Rio de Oro, where they obtained small quantities of gold. They pressed on and finally entered the Gambia river to find Negroes, living in a country which the Portuguese called Guinea, the land of the Blacks. Here they were able to trade for much larger quantities of gold, which was in ever-increasing demand in Europe, for the quantity of goods and materials coming in from Asia was far greater than the amount sent back, and the balance had to be paid in bullion.

The Portuguese were determined to guard their West African finds from the predatory grasp of the rest of Europe and in 1454, the year after Constantinople fell to the Turks and the Venetian overland route to the Far East was blocked, Prince Henry obtained a Papal Bull from Pope Nicholas V declaring that the countries discovered by his seamen were to be unmolested by other nations, under penalty of excommunication. Thereby Portugal was given the Church's sanction to claim all the lands and islands which had been discovered south of Cape Bojador and to any which they might discover in the future.

By the early 1470s they had reached the Gold Coast, with its Arab gold mines. They captured the main trade from the Arabs with little difficulty and built fortresses along the coast to guard their first settlement.

They ventured eastwards into the terrible waters of the Bight of Benin where, as the old sailors' song had it, 'for one that comes out there are forty stay in', and the following year, in 1483, Diego Cão discovered the Congo.

Portugal now had control of the whole of West Africa south of the Sahara, and the envious longing of the rest of Europe was checked by the very real fear of excommunication.

By 1497 Vasco da Gama had landed at Table Bay, sailed round the Cape to Mombasa and across the Indian Ocean to reach the ultimate goal of India.

Within a few years they had occupied all the old Persian and Arab settlements along the east coast of Africa, from Mogadishu to Sofala, including the island of Zanzibar, and for the next two centuries Portugal was able to defend her new sea route to India. For Venice it was the beginning of the end of her prosperity and grandeur.

This opening up of direct trade with the East made the supply of West African gold even more important to the Portuguese, and by the beginning of the sixteenth century they were obtaining some £100,000 worth a year, which was probably about one-tenth of the entire world supply at this time.

While the Portuguese were exploring the west coast of Africa the Genoese sailor, Christopher Columbus, under the patronage of Isabella of Spain, sailed westwards across the Atlantic, hoping to land on the east coast of China. Instead he reached the island of San Salvador in the West Indies, of which he took possession for their Catholic Majesties of Spain, returning to them with specimens of the exotic cotton plant, strange birds and beasts and – most important of all – gold.

When Henry VII ascended the throne he made a shrewd appraisal of England's problems. He had an absorbing interest in foreign affairs and diplomacy and by maintaining English envoys abroad, as well as spies, knew most of what was going on in Europe. France was still the traditional enemy but Spain was growing in strength through the union of Castile and Aragon, and Ferdinand was consummating his power by the marriage of his daughter and heiress to the Archduke Philip, son of the Emperor Maximilian. Henry therefore arranged a marriage between his eldest son Prince Arthur and Ferdinand's daughter, Katharine of Aragon: and when Prince Arthur died, Katharine was married to his younger brother Henry. The validity of the marriage to a brother-in-law was questioned from the outset, but it was to continue for 22 years before the divorce proceedings were taken.

England's chief trade was still mainly along the coasts of northern Europe, but merchant adventurers were beginning to take her wool into the Mediterranean and by 1486 there was an English consul at Pisa, where English merchants were joining with the Florentines to capture the Venetians' diminishing trade, but England possessed very few ships suitable for such long journeys and the Hanseatic merchants of the Steelyard, increasingly resented by the London merchants, were still carrying a large amount of English merchandise.

Henry VII saw that England's security and future mercantile prosperity lay in the establishment of a navy. Hitherto the Royal Navy had consisted of only a few vessels, the property of the sovereign, which in time of peace were sometimes leased to merchants but were mostly used to patrol the Channel and the North Sea. In wartime they formed the nucleus of a fighting force, additional ships being supplied by the Cinque ports or commandeered from private merchants.

He added the *Regent* and the *Royal Sovereign* to his navy, both of which were larger and more heavily armed than any ships that English sailors had ever seen before: and he was the patron of John Cabot when he set sail in 1497 from Bristol with his three sons and a crew of only eighteen, on a new attempt to reach the East by way of the Atlantic. Cabot took a more northerly route than Columbus, which brought him to Cape Breton Island. Believing he had reached the shores of Asia, he took possession of the land in the name of King Henry VII. On the way home he touched the shores of Newfoundland and met shoals of codfish in such vast quantities that his sailors were able to catch them by the score, simply by lowering their baskets over the side of the boat.

The next year Cabot left Bristol once more, making first for Greenland. He then sailed up the north coast, hoping at last to touch the mainland of Asia. To his dismay he found no land of riches but an ever-increasing cold, with icebergs which each day loomed larger and more dangerous.

Finding no way through, he turned south, explored the coast of Greenland and then sailed southwards across the Davis Strait to Baffin Island and the coast of Labrador. He sought for warmth and splendour and found only the barren wilderness of snow and ice. At last, after sailing as far as the New England coast, he returned to Bristol, where shortly afterwards he died.

For the next few years no one attempted to settle in the lands that Cabot had discovered. A few sailors and adventurers still tried to find a way to the east by sailing across the Atlantic to the north-west, but they were always defeated by the ice. A few short-lived settlements were made in New England but in Canada and Newfoundland no Europeans settled yet, although Norman, Breton and English fishermen paid frequent visits to the rich fishing grounds of Labrador and the coasts of Newfoundland.

Henry VII was an intellectual and deeply interested in the new thinking of the Renaissance, but he remained all his life a devout Catholic, showing no sign of doubt of the omnipotence of the Catholic Church, despite the growing resentment of its power, expressed by an increasing number of English intellectuals, under the influence of Erasmus, who visited England early in the King's reign.

By the time Henry VIII came to the throne and married Katharine of Aragon, Spain's wealth and power were growing fast. England, through London, was still trading mainly with the coast of Europe, principally with the Netherlands and particularly with Antwerp, which was now the centre of European finance and business.

Henry brought about the Reformation for many reasons, not least being the fact that he was hard pressed for money after his war with France, during which he had expended nearly all his father's inheritance of £2 million. The City of London had led the criticism of the abuses which had taken place under Cardinal Wolsey's regime, when he had lived in a style more regal and extravagant than that of the King himself, and was for the most part ready for the Reformation, but it wrought great changes in the appearance of their ancient city.

With the dissolution of the monasteries and abbeys throughout the country during the 1530s, the Priory of the Holy Trinity at Aldgate, the wealthiest and most splendid in the City of London, with its magnificent church, its monuments and shrines, was granted to Sir Thomas Audley, who was to become Lord Chancellor. He ordered the complete demolition of the church and all its monuments and shrines, the material being sold for building or paving stones at sixpence the cartload, while the ring of nine bells he sold to Stepney Church and St Stephen's, Coleman Street. On the site he built a house which became known as Norfolk House after his son-in-law the Duke of Norfolk inherited it, but ultimately the family sold it back to the City and by the seventeenth century all trace of the house had disappeared, except the name of Duke's Place, where a colony of Jews settled who had been allowed back to England by Oliver Cromwell.

The Cistercian Abbey known as Eastminster was pulled 'clean down' and in its place were built naval storehouses and ovens for making ships' biscuits, while in the abbey grounds where the Mint now stands small tenements were built for people working at the docks.

The Minories – the convent of St Clare – close by, which had expended more than £400 a year on charity, went the same way and Stow says that 'in place of this house of nuns is now built divers fair and large storehouses for armour and habiliments of war, with divers workhouses, serving to the same purpose'.

The church of the Austin Friars, where scores of illustrious people had been buried, was granted to the Marquis of Winchester. He left the church standing but sold the monuments for £100 and on part of the estate built Winchester House, while on another part Thomas Cromwell built the house which was to become the Drapers' Hall.

Not all the surrendered buildings were entirely destroyed. Some were merely defaced, partially demolished or left to crumble into ruins.

The church of the Greyfriars was spared but its monuments and tombs were all destroyed, the marble being sold by Sir Martin Bowes for £50.

The Blackfriars church was partially destroyed and used, along with the refectory, as a storehouse for the 'properties of pageants' and a few years later the little Blackfriars theatre was to be built amongst the ruins.

The nunnery of St Helen's, Bishopsgate, was partially destroyed but the church became the parish church and the nuns' hall was taken over by the Leathersellers' Company. St Bartholomew's also survived in part, as we have seen, but the church of the Knights Hospitallers was blown up with gunpowder. The Charterhouse, which was at first granted to Sir Thomas Audley, eventually passed to Thomas Sutton who in 1611 endowed it as the Hospital of St James for decayed gentlemen and established here the boys' school which is now at Godalming.

The Abbey of Bermondsey was surrendered, the monks pensioned off and the monastery and manor granted to Sir Robert Southwell, Master of the Rolls. He sold them to Sir Thomas Pope, who pulled down the old priory church and built Bermondsey House on the site, which was later to become the home of the Earl of Sussex, Queen Elizabeth's Lord Chamberlain.

The holocaust included hospitals and colleges, all of which were religious foundations. The twelfth-century priory and hospital of St Mary Spital outside Bishopsgate, where there had been 180 beds for the poor and needy, was demolished and 'many fair houses built for receipt and lodging of worshipful persons' built on the site, but part of the large churchyard remained and also the famous Spital pulpit, where, for the next 300 years, a sermon was to be preached every Easter before the Lord Mayor and aldermen and attendant citizens. Elsing Spital, founded in 1332 for 100 blind people, was dissolved and part of the priory church pulled down, the rest being converted into the parish church of St Alphege, of which the porch is still preserved. The collegiate church of St Martin's-le-Grand was demolished as well as Whittington's college, attached to the church of St Michael's, Paternoster Royal on College Hill, but the almshouses adjoining it were preserved and later moved to Highgate. The College of Priests founded by Richard III and attached to All Hallows, Barking, came down and merchants' warehouses were later built on the site, while the church and college of St Thomas of Acon went to the Mercers.

In the churches that remained, the incense and candles disappeared, the painted walls were covered with whitewash, the altars were stripped of their ornaments and the gilded plaster saints were taken down from their niches, while the gorgeous robes of the priests gave place to the sober black dress of the Church of England clergymen.

The hospital of St Bartholomew survived as well as that of St Thomas, which had been founded for poor children in 1213, by the prior of Bermondsey, and was bought by the City of London as a hospital for the sick and poor. Another hospital which survived was St Mary of Bethlehem, close to St Botolph's church, a small but ancient foundation which Henry VIII gave to the City as a hospital for the insane. This was later moved to Moorfields, by which time it was known as Bedlam.

One of the greatest changes was at St Paul's Cathedral. The Chapel of the Holy Ghost was destroyed. In the beautiful Pardon churchyard, the cloisters with their frescoed walls depicting the Dance of Death, which had been donated by John Carpenter, the library and the chapel were all swept away and the churchyard became a garden. The charnel chapel, which had been endowed by Whittington, with its crypt full of bones and its chapel crowded with monuments, lasted a few more years, until Protector Somerset pulled it down, using some of the material for the building of the first Somerset House. The monuments were destroyed or dispersed and the bones carted off to Finsbury Fields, where they were dumped and left to decay.

Paul's Cross remained but inside the old Gothic cathedral only the choir was now used for worship. The chapels had been stripped and there was a public thoroughfare through the transepts, known as Paul's Walk, where hucksters sold their wares and clergymen congregated in the hope of picking up a curacy or a living, where scriveners plied their trade for those who were unable to read or write and young men paraded to hear the latest gossip of the day and display their finery.

So low did St Paul's sink that in 1554 the Common Council had to intervene to forbid the carrying of beer-casks or baskets of bread, fish, flesh or fruit through the Cathedral or the leading of mules and horses, under pain of a fine or imprisonment. Then there was a royal proclamation forbidding agreements for the payment of money to be made in the Cathedral or the causing of an affray by dagger, sword or hand gun. It made little difference and the central aisle degenerated into a meeting place of 'cheats, assassins, thieves and prostitutes'.

In 1561 the Cathedral was struck by lightning and the steeple burst into flames. The lead cover and the bells all melted and the roof fell in. By order of Queen Elizabeth, the roof was hastily rebuilt, but, to her annoyance, the steeple was never replaced.

Yet among the ruins more beautiful houses were being built in the City and Henry VIII built the last and shortest lived of the Royal Palaces – the Bridewell Palace. The site was an old Norman castle which had stood close to the Montfichet Tower, and in its precincts, which had become waste ground, remained the sacred well of St Bride, with the little church which had been built alongside it. Here, in 1522, King Henry built a 'stately and beautiful house' for the reception of the Emperor Charles V. Like St James's Palace, it was of red brick, with stone facings and out-of-date but impressive castellations. King Henry lodged his guest close by at his newly acquired monastery of the Black Friars and Stow says that a gallery was built 'out of the house over the water, and through the wall of the city, into the emperor's lodging at the Black Friars'.

With the Emperor's departure, after his expensive visit, King Henry often used the Bridewell Palace and it was here, only six years later, that he summoned the members of the Council, the peers of the realm, the mayor and aldermen and principal citizens of the Common Council, to hear him reveal his scruples of conscience at having married Queen Katharine and his intention to divorce her and marry Anne Boleyn. At the same time he warned that any who raised a voice against the proposal 'should answer with their heads for the presumption of their tongues'.

The divorce proceedings were held here, during which the Queen defended herself with great courage, and when it was all over she left the Court, never to return: and the King never lived again in his brave new palace.

He vowed that it had been his intention to spend some of the money from the disestablished monasteries, friaries, and chantries on the establishment of new schools and hospitals. This he never did, but he expended large sums on a thorough reorganisation of the navy and of the coastal defences. He created the Navy Office and built the royal dockyards at Woolwich and Deptford, as well as at Portsmouth. He established the Corporation of Trinity House and encouraged the planting and preservation of timber for ship-building, for the wooden ships in which the voyages of the following years were undertaken had to be built of the stoutest oak that was available.

Henry VII's *Regent* had been lost in 1512, during the French war, when Henry VIII unwisely attempted to retrieve his 'heritage of France', and for its replacement he ordered the magnificent *Henri Grace à Dieu*, known more familiarly as *Great Harry*, a four-masted ship of some 1,000 tons, carrying a complement of 700 men – 350 soldiers, 300 sailors and 50 gunners, equipped with brass cannon, iron guns, bows, arrows, darts and pikes.

The other ships of his navy were considerably smaller, the *Mary Rose*, for example, being only 600 tons. Her lower deck ports were only sixteen inches above the water line, so it is not surprising that she capsized off Spithead and sank with her captain and entire crew of 400 men. There was an appalling loss of life during these experimental days, but the urgency of competition to discover new countries and seek new trade inspired the shipwrights to new efforts of ingenuity. Throughout Henry's reign ships grew larger and more seaworthy and the Navy Office was efficiently run by the newly created office of the Lord High Admiral.

As the demand for English wool on the Continent increased, more farmers changed from arable farming to sheep rearing, for which they needed more land but less labour. With the dissolution of the monasteries, the Crown offered thousands of acres of farming land for sale, and much of this was bought by men who planned to use it for sheep pasture. In the process of conversion, many small arable farmers were evicted from monastic lands and in some places entire hamlets disappeared to make way for the sheep. It was the peasants who suffered most and when, with the beginning of the practice of enclosures, in order to bring about more efficient arable farming, they lost their common rights as well, many endured great hardship. The population was increasing, but the production of food declining. Prices rose sharply, particularly after King Henry, short of money again, debased the currency. Between 1500 and 1560 the price of food trebled and rents rose steeply. These rising prices tended to stimulate trade and the City of London did not suffer, but in the country districts there was ever more distress amongst the poor, for whom there were now no monasteries to give them charity.

Some, reduced to penury and vagrancy, drifted to the towns and many came to the City of London, but with the restrictive practices of the Merchant Companies there was little hope of their finding work and hundreds lived as best they could, in squalor and near starvation.

Shortly before his death King Henry, on the advice of Sir Thomas Gresham, agreed to grant the deserted house of the Grey Friars to the City corporation, for the relief of the poor, provided the citizens of London contributed to the funds for its maintenance. A month later the King was dead and nothing was done for a time, for the Regents of the young Edward VI were occupied with the enactment of the Chantries Act, which involved the dissolution of 2,000 chantries and chapels throughout the country, many with small grammar and song schools attached to them, and the sale of their estates to private buyers.

In the course of these transactions some 300 schools disappeared and others were endowed with a fixed stipend which rapidly declined in value. Edward VI's government promised, like the late King, to provide more schools, but all it achieved was a few dozen, and in the end it sacrificed more schools than it ever established.

In London the paupers and orphans, the sick and the disabled still haunted the narrow lanes and courts behind the thriving shops and taverns and houses of the merchants. The church and hospital of St Bartholomew admitted as many of the destitute as they could but complained that they were able to take less than one-tenth of those in dire need.

In 1552 Bishop Ridley, the Bishop of London, preached before the young King Edward at Westminster on the subject of mercy and charity, making an appeal for the plight of London's poor. The message went home and the King sent for the Bishop and asked him to make practical plans. A committee composed of the Lord Mayor, six aldermen, 24 members of the Common Council and the Bishop quickly set to work. They divided the poor into three categories, the poor by impotency, which included the orphans, sick, aged, blind and lame, the poor by casualty, such as wounded soldiers and people who, through no fault of their own, had fallen on hard times, and the wastrels, idlers and petty criminals.

For the sick and wounded St Thomas's hospital was restored to supplement the work of St Bartholomew's, and a separate lazar house was established for the lepers. For the orphans and children of the poor – both boys and girls – a school supplying food, clothing, lodging and education was to be established in the Grey Friars monastery, to be called Christ's Hospital and the friars' church, rededicated as Christ's Church, was to be opened for public worship.

The able-bodied unemployed were to be housed in the forsaken Bridewell Palace, there to be reformed, disciplined and given technical training in some useful employment.

In the autumn of 1552 St Thomas's hospital admitted 200 sick and aged people and plans for the reception of 400 children were well under way at Christ's Hospital.

Appeals for funds were sent to the clergy of every parish in the City as well as to every householder. Collecting boxes were given to the landlord of every inn and to the wardens of the companies. The response was generous and within six months the old monastery buildings had been renovated and made ready for the reception of the children. From the outset the boys were given a good grammar-school education, the girls the restricted education of the period, reading and needlework and, after some years, writing. They were treated with great humanity and when it was time to leave, work was found for them, the boys being provided with apprenticeships: and as, over the years, the school received bequests and endowments from generous citizens, many of the abler boys were able to pass on to the universities.

The inmates of the Bridewell did not fare so well during the early years. Useful work was the dominating theme of their existence. There were two treadmills, each worked by eighteen men, for grinding corn and there was a smithy where nails were made and offered for sale. The women baked bread and made cloth.

This idea of putting prisoners to work spread throughout the country and gaols for vagrants and vagabonds who were given useful employment became known as 'bridewells'.

Although Southwark was so closely connected with the story of the City, from the time of the first settlement at the southern end of London Bridge, it did not come fully under the City's jurisdiction until 1550. Before this time its status had been equivocal. It was referred to from time to time as a borough of Surrey but it had no mayor or aldermen and the land on which the little town developed was largely owned, until the Reformation, by the monks of Bermondsey Abbey and the friars of St Mary Overies, who had founded St Thomas's hospital.

The City's precise boundaries were often in dispute but had eventually been fixed at the stone posts at the Southwark end of the bridge: and beyond them anyone escaping from the authority of the City and its justice could hide himself in safety.

Southwark became the haunt of rogues and vagabonds and although it might have paid the medieval kings to allow London to have control over it, they hesitated to grant the City more privileges and power. Not until the time of Edward III was the first step taken, when the City was allowed to appoint the bailiff who collected the royal dues, although his other duties, particularly in the matter of keeping law and order, were never clearly defined. The principle on which the appointment of the bailiff worked was that once the annual sum – the fee farm – had been fixed, the office became one of profit, for the bailiff, on behalf of the City, was allowed to pocket any surplus revenues. However, as the fee farm was only £10 a year and the City had no other rights in the town, it was a hollow victory.

There were many famous inns in Southwark, for not only was it the place where travellers from the Continent approached London but the spot where the roads from Sussex, Surrey and Hampshire all met the Dover Road – the road of the medieval pilgrims to Canterbury. Most famous of all the inns was the Tabard, whose landlord in Chaucer's time had been his friend Harry Bailly. It was an ecclesiastical foundation built in 1307 by an Abbot of Hyde, part of the building being a town residence for himself and a guest house for brother clergy visiting London to attend the Bishop of Winchester, at his palace close by, on Bankside, built on land belonging to the Bermondsey Priory. And adjoining the Abbot's house was the pilgrims' inn, which was given the sign of the medieval herald's coat – the tabard.

Winchester House, with its courtyards, its gardens and fountains and fish-ponds, its great hall and state apartments overlooking the river, remained the London seat of the Bishops of Winchester, where they lived during the sitting of Parliament, until the Civil War, after which they moved to Chelsea, but the old palace survived until the nineteenth century, by which time part had become tenements and the rest was used for warehouses.

The Bishop of Rochester's house was close to Winchester House, also on land belonging to Bermondsey Abbey, the monks of which were the lords of the manor of the land to the west of the High Street, while the Archbishop of Canterbury was lord of the manor on the land to the east.

Along Southwark High Street many more inns were built – the Spurre, the Christopher, the Bull, the Queen's Head, the George, the Hart and the King's Head – for the accommodation not only of the pilgrims but travellers from the Continent, many of whom were fair game for the pickpockets, receivers of stolen goods, confidence men, card-sharpers and the like, for which Southwark became notorious, as well as the prostitutes who worked in the Bankside stews. These were a row of some twenty houses, each with its own sign painted on the wall – the Boar's Head, the Cross Keys, the Gun, the Castle, the Crane, the Cardinal's Hat, the Bell, the Swan – and they were leased from the Bishops of Winchester, one of the lessees during the reign of Richard II being the mayor who killed Wat Tyler, Sir William Walworth.

Brothels were forbidden in the City of London and from time to time attempts were made to close them on Bankside, but never with any notable success: and since unrepentant prostitutes were forbidden Christian burial the parish church allotted a special part of its cemetery to them, known as the Single Woman's churchyard, for even the keepers of the Southwark stews were not allowed to employ married women.

During early Tudor times the great attraction of Southwark was the bear gardens on Bankside. At the bear rings a place perched up on the scaffolding surrounding the arena cost a halfpenny, and they were particularly popular on Sundays, when people from all walks of life crowded in to watch the bear-baiting, in particular the performances of the two wily old favourites, Harry Huncks and Sackerson: and it was another century before the cruelty of the sport began to pall and people became, like John Evelyn, 'heartily weary of the rude and dirty pastime'.

Southwark had more than its fair share of prisons, despite the high proportion of disreputable inhabitants. The Clink, just to the west of Winchester House, was an ecclesiastical prison at first, where trouble-makers from the Stews were consigned. In later years it was moved to Deadman's Place, also on Bankside, but it was burned down during the riots of 1780 and never rebuilt. The Marshalsea prison was on the east side of the High Street, not far from the George Inn, the King's Bench prison and the White Lion prison a little farther south, close to the point where the High Street and the Dover Road met.

Many of the inhabitants of Southwark were, of course, honest tradesmen and with the passing years their numbers increased. They practised their crafts like the freemen of the City Companies, and being outside the City's precincts there were no means of preventing them. Although some of the Livery Companies, such as the Goldsmiths, had the right to search throughout the country, for others the rights were limited to the City and they complained that they had no means of judging the workmanship or controlling the prices and wages of the craftsmen.

It was in 1550 that matters came to a head. One particular quarrel was over the matter of inspecting and measuring the commodities brought to the port and landed on either bank, such as coal, grain and fruit. Another was over the sale of woollen cloth and also leather, for there was a flourishing community of leather workers in Southwark by this time. The exclusive sale of these commodities had been granted to the City within a seven-mile radius, and they insisted on their privilege.

The quarrels and disputes over these matters were endless and the situation was complicated by the fact that after the Dissolution, although the Crown held much of the land, many of the former tenants of Church lands in Southwark had bought the freeholds of their properties, either from the State or from speculators, including many City merchants, who had bought up large tracts of land for re-sale. This tangle of rights and privileges was solved when Edward VI sold his property in Southwark to the City for £647 2s. 1d., and despite protests from the Sheriff of Surrey, the neighbouring lords of the manors and the people of Southwark themselves, in a charter dated 23rd April 1550 Southwark became part of the City of London. It was called Bridge Ward Without, but to the consternation of the people of Southwark, unlike the other wards, their alderman was chosen by the City's Court of Aldermen and none of their own people sat on the Common Council. This arrangement did not change and although in the early years the alderman had manifold duties to perform, after 1635 the Justices of the Peace of Surrey took over much of his work and gradually the powers of the office of the alderman declined and it became a sinecure with little or no work to be done, usually granted to the senior alderman of the City.

The relationship between Southwark and the City was never particularly close after this but Southwark remained a City ward until the creation of the Metropolitan Boroughs of Southwark and Bermondsey in 1900, when they were finally separated.

The Bridge House and Yard which had begun as a storehouse for the stone and timber necessary for the maintenance of the bridge was, in Tudor times, being used as a warehouse for navy provisions as well as a storehouse for grain, and kitchens were attached where the Navy's biscuit was baked. It was also sometimes used as a banqueting hall, one notable occasion being at the inauguration of Southwark fair, granted by Henry VIII, when the Lord Mayor and sheriffs attended in full state, making a fine show as they rode over London Bridge.

It was only a few months after the opening of Christ's Hospital that King Edward died and the Catholic Mary Tudor ascended the throne. On the Continent there was a strong Catholic reaction. Charles V was now Emperor of Spain and the Netherlands, and when Mary announced her forthcoming marriage to the Emperor's son Philip the hearts of English Protestants turned cold with fear.

The desperate effort to place the Protestant Lady Jane Grey on the throne was aborted and Wyatt's rebellion failed. The Papal Legate arrived from Rome and sailed up the Thames to Westminster, to receive England back into the fold of the Mother Church. The City of London remained largely Protestant but elsewhere many returned to the Church into which they had been born: and the persecution of those who resisted was soon under way. Despite the warning of her husband and even of the Roman Church that her policy would do her cause no ultimate service, the killings began. Lady Jane Grey and her family were the first to be sacrificed and after them came the bishops – Bishop Ridley of London, Cranmer, the Archbishop of Canterbury, and Latimer. Then followed a melancholy procession of vicars and their parishioners. In a single day thirteen victims, two of them women, were burned at Stratford-le-Bow. Seventy-three Protestants of Colchester were dragged through the streets of London, tied to a single rope. In the course of three and a half years nearly 300 people were burnt at the stake in Smithfield.

It was the outspoken sympathy of Londoners for the victims of Smithfield and the protests of Parliament which at last stopped the persecutions. Mary was a sick woman and her marriage was a disaster. When no heir was forthcoming, Philip left her and returned to Spain. During the Spanish war with France which followed, Mary sent him unwilling help from England which brought nothing but fresh trouble, for it resulted in the loss of Calais, the Staple town, and our last foothold on the Continent.

Mary stubbornly pursued her policy of strengthening the Roman Church in England and refounded several abbeys which had been disestablished, but in 1558, after a reign of only five years, she died, and with deep relief the country welcomed the 24-year-old Princess Elizabeth to the throne.

England's fortunes were at a low ebb. The Exchequer was nearly empty. Henry VII's policy of placating Spain had been ruined, for although Spain was now the country's only ally and Philip supported Elizabeth for the first few years of her reign, he was a potential danger.

As early as 1543 Thomas Gresham, as a young merchant, was applying to Margaret, Regent of the Netherlands, for permission to export gunpowder to England, for the use of Henry VIII, when he was preparing for his war with France, but it was during the time of Edward VI that his work became so important. Although the City lent large sums to the Crown they had not yet enough resources for all its demands and Gresham was appointed the King's agent at Antwerp to raise private loans from merchants of the Netherlands.

The practice of lending money at interest had been employed in Christian countries for years, but in England it was still regarded as undesirable, and in 1552, just before the death of Edward VI, an Act of Parliament actually prohibited all taking of interest as 'a vice most odious and detestable'. This Act was in force all through Mary Tudor's reign and was not repealed until 1571, when Queen Elizabeth had been on the throne for more than twelve years.

8

Tudor London — II

One result of the Reformation was that English adventurers whose thoughts had long been turned towards the riches of West Africa had no longer anything to fear from excommunication, for the whole country was now excommunicated from Rome and they had the protection of their own new Church of England.

The first Englishman to visit West Africa was the father of Sir John Hawkins, 'old Mr Hawkins', as Hakluyt called him, 'a man who for his wisdom and experience in sea causes was much esteemed by King Henry VIII: he had made three voyages to the coast of Brazil, and in the course of these voyages he touched at the river Sestros, up the coast of Guinea, where he trafficked with the negroes and took of them elephants' teeth and other commodities which that place yieldeth'.

Shortly after this, in 1533, came the voyage described by Hakluyt as the 'First English Voyage to Guinea and Benin'. The vessels *Primrose* and *Lion*, financed by merchants of the City of London, manned by 140 men and commanded by Captain Thomas Windham, set off under the guidance of Antonio Pinteado, a Portuguese naval officer who had fallen from grace at the Portuguese Court and had offered to show the English where they could find gold and the Grains of Paradise, which we now call pepper.

Pinteado piloted them round the coast for the pepper cargo, but Windham, impatient for gold, refused to stop and insisted that they press on to the Gold Coast. Here they procured £150 worth of gold dust and then, despite Pinteado's warning that it was an unhealthy time of the year to visit Benin, made their way into the Bight.

Pinteado took a party of men ashore to visit the King of Benin, who understood Portuguese and received them graciously, but on board the waiting ships one man after another, including Windham, succumbed to malaria and died. When Pinteado returned the survivors insisted that they should leave at once, not waiting for the rest of the men still in Benin City. When Pinteado protested, they arrested him and sailed away. Pinteado died on board shortly afterwards and by the time they reached Plymouth there were only 40 survivors. No one ever knew the fate of the abandoned men in Benin nor how much of that £150 worth of gold dust ever reached the merchants of London, but the following year another expedition set out from the Port of London, under the command of Mr John Lok, which after seven weeks sailing reached the Ivory and Gold coasts. They obtained £400 worth of gold, 36 butts of Guinea pepper, and about 250 elephants' tusks, some of which were as thick as a man's thigh and weighed a hundred and twenty five pounds each' and arrived safely back in London, five months after leaving it.

The next year Master William Towerson set off with two ships, the *Hart* and the *Hind*, both of London, and did some equally successful trading, despite a brush with the outraged Portuguese and trouble with the natives, who complained that one of Mr Lok's captains had departed without paying for his gold and taken with him, into the bargain, four natives, one of whom was the son of a chief.

So Master Towerson made a second trip the following year, with the *Tyger* of London, the *Hart* and a pinnace, bringing back the natives and restoring them to their families. They fought off an attack from a Portuguese vessel, did some successful trading and made for home, encountering on the way a French merchantman which opened fire, but the English replied 'with cross bars, chain shot and arrows so thick that it made the upper work of their ship fly about their ears, and spoiled the captain with all his men. . . . There was aboard the *Tyger* a French trumpeter who, being sick in bed, yet on this occasion took the trumpet and sounded till he could sound no more and so died.'

The exploits of Towerson's third trip were even more hair-raising. His expedition consisted this time of four ships and a pinnace. On the way out they seized two Hamburg ships, took from them everything of value and let them go. They had a successful escape from an encounter with five Portuguese ships and then gave chase to four French merchantmen, capturing one and seizing its cargo of gold. On the return journey they had to abandon the *Tyger*, which was no longer seaworthy, and by the time they reached London again there were only 30 survivors to tell the tale, but they brought back enough gold for the merchants of London to prepare more expeditions, all of which the Portuguese regarded as piracy.

In 1553 Richard Chancellor, sailing from London, landed at Archangel, from where he was taken to Moscow and received by Ivan the Terrible. It was the first step towards the founding of the Muscovy Company, trading in furs, wax, tallow and valuable naval requisites such as ropes and masts.

It was during these exploits of the 1550s that Sir Thomas Gresham was in Antwerp, raising a private loan for the Crown, for wealthy as the merchants of London were becoming they could not produce between them more than about £10,000 in hard cash. Antwerp had now outstripped Venice as the commercial centre of Europe, and was exporting to England almost every article of luxury she required: precious stones, silver bullion, quicksilver, cloth of gold and silver, silks, gold and silver thread, drugs, sugar, cotton, linen, tapestry, glass, salt fish, arms of all kinds, ammunition, household furniture, as well as carpets, spices and perfumes from India, Persia and Turkey.

It was all carried into the dark warehouses and sheds attached to the houses close to the river, in Cannon Street (Candlewick Street), Thames Street, Lombard Street, Cheapside and Fenchurch Street, where the merchants lived, and here it was inspected and bought by the middle-men.

In return, England's woollen cloth and raw wool left London's quaysides as well as 'excellent saffron in small quantities, a great quantity of lead and tin, sheep and rabbit skins without number, with various other sorts of fine peltry, and leather, beer, cheese and other sorts of provisions', all of which were loaded into barges and lightered out to the mechantmen, lying at anchor in midstream.

The number of merchants who controlled all this trade was small. In the mid-sixteenth century there were only about 300 of them, but by the end of Queen Elizabeth's reign the number had risen to some 800.

Gresham borrowed from the Antwerp merchants in his own name and was soon able to raise the exchange rate in England's favour, from 16 Flemish shillings to the pound to 22, thereby saving £20,000 on the 14 per cent interest rate the Flemings had been charging and bringing it down to 10 per cent. At the same time, he was engaged with the Mercers' Company in shipping vast quantities of cloth to the Italian merchants in Antwerp in exchange for Italian silk, and at the peak of this trade the Mercers were sending a fleet of 50 or 60 ships laden with cloth twice a year to the Low Countries.

With the accession of Queen Elizabeth, Gresham was still royal agent and visited Flanders to procure loans and send over powder, armour and weapons. By this time Spain was overrunning the Netherlands and he was present at the funeral of Charles V and may perhaps have sensed the troubles that lay ahead.

For many years the merchants of London had felt the need of an exchange such as had been in existence for many years in Venice and Antwerp, where their commodities could be properly displayed for sale. Sir Thomas offered to build one from his own private fortune, made principally in the Antwerp trade, if the City provided the ground. The site of Leadenhall market had been discussed but in 1565 the City raised the funds to buy a plot of land in Cornhill, near the Stocks market. It was cleared of its 80-odd houses and the foundation stone of the first Royal Exchange was laid. It was the first Renaissance building of the City, a long, four-storeyed brick building, later stuccoed, built round a courtyard with covered walks supported by marble pillars and dominated by a bell-tower surmounted by the Gresham family crest of a grasshopper. The bell rang twice a day, at noon and six o'clock in the evening, summoning merchants to hear the news of the day and do business in its 100 shops. Above the arcades the shops were rented to milliners and haberdashers, who at first sold a miscellaneous assortment of goods, ranging from mousetraps to bird-cages, although within a few years the shops became fashionable and elegant: and on the floor above were the armourers, apothecaries, book sellers, gold-smiths and glass-sellers.

The Exchange was formally opened by Queen Elizabeth in 1570, by which time Gresham had ensured that all the shops were let and suitably equipped. 'Queen Elizabeth came from Somerset House through Fleet Street, past the north side of the Bourse to Sir Thomas Gresham's house in Bishopsgate Street and there dined. After the banquet she entered the Bourse on the south side, viewed every part; especially she caused the building, by herald's trumpet, to be proclaimed "the Royal Exchange", so to be called from henceforth,' wrote Stow.

The Exchange was a success, and soon with the waning glories of Antwerp, as the Spanish overran the Netherlands and intensified their persecution of the Protestants, it attracted the attention of merchants from all over Europe. Stow says it was 'crowded with merchants, grave and sober men, walking within in pairs or gathered in little groups. Amongst them were foreigners from Germany, France, Venice, Genoa, Antwerp and even Russia, conspicuous by their dress.'

There was another side to this picture, however, for like Paul's walk, the Royal Exchange began to attract the wrong people and there were complaints that on Sundays and holidays 'great numbers of boys, children and young rogues meet there, and shout and holloa, so that honest citizens cannot quietly walk there for their recreation'. In 1590 some women were prosecuted for selling apples and oranges at the Exchange gate in Cornhill, and

amusing themselves in cursing and swearing, to the great annoyance and grief of the inhabitants and passers-by: and a tavern keeper who had rented vaults under the Exchange – which had turned out to be too damp for the storage of other merchandise – was fined for allowing tippling and also for broiling herrings, sprats and bacon, to the vexation of worshipful merchants resorting to the Exchange.

Nevertheless, the Exchange prospered and when the law against usury was repealed, Gresham was able to transfer the business of the Royal loan from Antwerp to London, where by the end of the century merchants had grown so prosperous that they were able to advance loans of £60,000. Yet with all this money about, there were still no banks and merchants and goldsmiths kept their surplus cash at the Mint in the Tower of London for safe-keeping.

About the time of his knighthood, in 1563, Sir Thomas left his shop in Lombard Street for his apprentice to manage and moved to Bishopsgate, where he built the magnificent Gresham House, surrounding a large, square courtyard and set in gardens which stretched from Bishopsgate Street to Broad Street. He died in 1579 and in his will ordered that after the death of his wife the Exchange, with its valuable rents, should go jointly to the City of London and the Mercers' Company, while Gresham House was to become Gresham College, the endowments for which should come from the profits of the Exchange.

The race to capture foreign markets grew ever more competitive. While English merchants were being financed to make their piratical forays along the West African coast, others were making an increasing number of successful trading ventures through the Mediterranean to the Levant, and there were several gallant attempts to find a north-eastern passage to China and India, by way of northern Europe and the Arctic Ocean. Because of Queen Mary's marriage to Philip of Spain, London merchants had paid little attention to America during her reign, and for several years after the accession of Queen Elizabeth England remained on tolerably friendly terms with Spain.

The Portuguese had begun to trade in Negro slaves as early as the 1440s, transporting them first to Portugal and Spain to work on agricultural land redeemed from the Moors: and after the Moors were finally expelled and Spain planted her first colony in the New World, the Portuguese extended their slave trade to supply labour for the Spanish plantations and mines for their new empire in the Caribbean and later on the American mainland. The Portuguese also used them for their own plantations in Madeira, the Azores and the Cape Verde Islands, in the sugar plantations of the Gulf of Guinea, and later in the Portuguese colonies of Brazil.

These slaves came not from Guinea but from Senegal and Gambia, or from Benin and the region of the Niger delta, while those destined for Brazil were shipped from the Congo and Angola, for more convenient transport across the southern Atlantic. They were obtained from the Negroes themselves and most of them were prisoners of their own people, held for debt or other sundry misdemeanours.

The next notable journey of the English to Africa was undertaken in 1562 by Sir John Hawkins, who was the first Englishman to engage in the slave trade by carrying Negroes from West Africa to the New World for Spain: and for this the young Queen Elizabeth reprimanded him, saying that 'if any of the Negroes should be carried off without their free consent it would be detestable and call down the vengeance of Heaven upon the undertakers', but as at this time the wretched Negroes were mostly prisoners anyway, they had precious little say in the matter.

The loss of Calais had been a severe blow to the English wool exporters but they quickly followed the cloth merchants to Bruges and Antwerp. However, this channel of trade was soon to be closed. Spain had become the mightiest power in Europe. From Mexico and Peru her galleons returned to Cadiz laden with gold, silver and precious stones and Philip II was master of Naples and Milan, of the Low Countries and Flanders, with their immensely wealthy merchant cities of Antwerp, Bruges and Ghent; while the alliance of friendship he had made with Portugal, who had suffered a heavy defeat in Morocco and lost all her North African possessions, soon reduced her to little more than a vassal state.

Philip seemed invincible and the power of the Inquisition was at its most terrible. The Spanish governor of the Netherlands picked a quarrel with Queen Elizabeth and her privy council. He disliked them for their heretical Protestant-ism and their sympathy with the oppressed and tortured Protestants of the Netherlands and he now forbade them to sell their cloth in Antwerp, assum-ing that they would be forced to concentrate on the export of raw wool instead, which would have been of enormous benefit to the Netherlands cloth-manufacturing industry.

The English merchants did not fall into this trap and in 1567 moved their point of entry into Europe to Hamburg, but already the feeling against the Hanseatic merchants of the Steelyard was running high, for England now had shipping of her own and had no need of the transport they had provided. There was jealousy and rivalry between England and the Hanse towns and although the Steelyard was not finally closed until 1598, by the late 1570s the English were forbidden the use of Hamburg.

England was alone and the tension with Spain was mounting. For several years there was distress and unemployment in the wool trade, which was still largely a cottage industry, but now came England's reply. The merchants of the City of London financed new companies to trade further afield – in Russia, the Baltic, Turkey and the Levant – and English sailors followed Spain and Portugal across the Atlantic. Sir Francis Drake, defying the Spanish gal-leons, sailed into the Gulf of Mexico. He landed on the Isthmus of Panama and from the top of a tree caught his first glimpse of the Pacific and made his resolve that one day he would sail an English ship across it. In 1577, having gained an audience of the Queen and received her support, he set sail in the

Golden Hind, with only four other small ships and a total complement of 166 men. After nearly three years of incredible hardship, of storm and wreck, mutiny, sickness and near-starvation, he returned to Plymouth, having sailed right round the world, by way of the Cape Verde Islands and the southern Atlantic, the southern tip of South America, the Pacific, the Indian Ocean, the Cape of Good Hope, the coast of Guinea and the North Atlantic.

By 1583 Sir Humphrey Gilbert, half-brother of Sir Walter Raleigh, set sail with a patent for 'the planting of our people in America'. The largest ship of the expedition was only 40 tons but the equipment included 'music in good variety, for solace of our people, and allurement of the savages, not omitting the least toys, as Morris-dancers, hobby-horses, and May-like conceits to delight the savage people: and to that end, we were indifferently furnished of haberdashery wares to barter with these simple people'.

They reached Newfoundland and took possession of it, in the name of the Queen, thus establishing England's first colony, some 70 years or more after Cabot had discovered it for Henry VII. Then they sailed on towards Cape Breton but ran into a terrible storm and dense fog. The flagship ran aground and was lost. Sir Humphrey turned the expedition towards home, but off the Azores they met another storm and Sir Humphrey went down with his ship.

The following year Sir Walter Raleigh led a new expedition to North America where Drake, in attempting to find a more northerly route to the Pacific, had already staked a claim for England. This country Raleigh named Virginia and in 1585 the first body of settlers arrived, under the command of his cousin, Sir Richard Grenville. Although it was a failure – when Drake's fleet arrived the following year with supplies they begged to be taken home again – it was to be useful experience for future settlements.

That same year the Queen gave a group of merchants a patent for the West Africa trade and three years later a further patent to a company of merchant adventurers 'of Exeter and of the western parts and of London' for the Guinea trade between the Senegal and Gambia rivers. These voyages were not concerned with the slave trade but with commerce in gold, spices and ivory, and were made in defiance of the Portuguese, who still claimed a monopoly of the Africa trade, despite their growing preoccupation with their new American and Far Eastern empires.

Venice and the other merchant cities of Italy had fallen far behind in the commercial race, ruined by the increasing difficulties of the overland route to the East and by the use of the Cape route by the Portuguese, Dutch and English, with whom they did not enter into competition. The last Venetian argosy to visit Southampton, which was the Italian depot for English wool, was in 1587, but it was wrecked off the Needles. It marked the decline of Southampton as well, to the advantage of London, for after this time the Mediterranean and Far Eastern trade was diverted to the Port of London, and it was now carried in English ships.

Queen Elizabeth spent wisely and well on her navy and appointed Admiral John Hawkins to undertake its reconstruction. Although in number of ships it did not exceed that of Henry VII's navy, and by the end of her reign it was only 42, the design was different. They were of similar tonnage and complement as the older ships but were longer, and rode lower in the water. The old-fashioned, high-built castles which the Spanish galleys still carried almost disappeared on the English ships which were more easily manoeuvrable and carried half as much again in weight of guns. Richard Grenville's *Revenge* was of this type and also the *Ark Royal*, the flagship of the fleet, which had a tonnage of 8,000, a crew of 500 and cost Elizabeth £5,000.

These were the ships which proved England's naval supremacy over the Armada, when war between England and Spain was openly declared in 1588, and there was now little to stop her further advance in exploration and foreign trade. Venice was dying and the trade of Antwerp and the German and Baltic ports, already weakened by European wars and internal politics, gradually dwindled before the growing importance of London.

London still had its gardens and trees but during these years of prosperity many more houses and shops were built and dozens of taverns and ale-houses. The houses were built of brick and elaborately carved timber, with high-pitched gabled roofs, and were nearly all four or five storeys high, the third storey often being furnished with a balcony. The streets were filled with men of fashion, with city merchants and their wives, all followed by their attendant servants, with labourers, craftsmen and sailors and the ebullient apprentices, many of whom were the younger sons of country gentry who, knowing that their elder brothers would inherit the family properties, preferred to enter a life of commerce than one of the professions.

Paul Pindar's story belongs to the Stuart period, for he was a wealthy merchant in the Turkey trade who became James I's ambassador to Turkey, but his house in Bishopsgate was built in the sixteenth century and was typically Tudor, with its oriel windows and intricate carving. The main first-floor room had a magnificent plaster ceiling, an immense fireplace of oak and stone, surrounded with elaborate carving, and walls wainscoted in oak.

Crosby Hall was still occupied by rich merchants, several of whom became Lord Mayors. Sir Thomas More had sold the remaining 44 years of his lease to Antonio Bonvisi, a merchant from Lucca, and by 1542 his family had acquired the freehold of the property for £207. Almost opposite was Gresham House, described by Stow as 'the most spacious of all thereabouts; builded of brick and timber'.

In 1566 Alderman William Bond bought Crosby Hall for £1,600 and by 1594 the Bond family had sold it to Alderman Sir John Spencer, reckoned to be the wealthiest citizen of his time, for £2,500. Sir John enlarged Crosby Hall for the vast amount of entertaining he did there, which included the occasion when the gentlemen students of Gray's Inn and the Temple performed a masque in the Great Hall before Queen Elizabeth; but alongside the house Sir John built a large warehouse which was eventually to become the Jewish Synagogue in Great St Helen's.

Sir John spent a good deal of his time at his country mansion, Canonbury House in Islington, and while Crosby Hall was vacant it was let for the use of a number of distinguished foreign visitors and ambassadors, the last, during Queen Elizabeth's reign, being the Duc de Biron, with his company of 400 noblemen, a magnificent embassy from Henry IV of France, all of whom were accommodated in and around Crosby Hall. Such glory was ever short-lived. The Duc de Biron was executed for treason only a few months after his return to France and Sir John was committed to the Fleet prison in March 1599 for beating and ill-using his daughter and hiding her from Lord Compton, who wanted to marry her. Eventually Elizabeth escaped from Canonbury House in a baker's basket and married her lover, and when their first child was born it was Queen Elizabeth who brought about the reconciliation between father and daughter. All seemed set for a happy ending, but when Sir John died and Lord Compton inherited his vast wealth, it sent him off his head for a time.

Whether the Comptons ever lived at Crosby Hall is not certain but very soon after this the tenancy was granted to the Countess of Pembroke, mother of Shakespeare's friend William Herbert, and as Shakespeare himself was living in Bishopsgate at this time, it is a fair assumption that he was a visitor at the historic old house.

The City of London restored London Bridge to great splendour during Tudor times. At the Southwark end a new gate was built and a tower three storeys high, and a covered way below: and over the seventh and eighth arches, on the north side of the drawbridge, was built Nonesuch House, a huge, square building, four storeys high, with cupolas at each corner and a wealth of Tudor windows, with carved and gilded balconies. This house straddled the bridge, the traffic and foot passengers passing through the arched tunnel which ran through the middle of it. The entire structure had been brought from Holland and re-erected on the bridge, and at the same time a Dutch water-engineer established waterworks at the northern end of the bridge.

Yet amongst all this splendour the barbarous custom of exposing the heads of beheaded traitors and criminals on the bridge was to continue for many years to come.

By Elizabethan times London belonged entirely to its merchants and citizens, for there was no royal palace left within its precincts and the nobility had all left for their new mansions along the Strand, nearer to Westminster.

Until this time the Strand, the principal highway for wagons, horsemen and foot passengers from the City to Westminster, was 'full of pits and sloughs very perilous and noisome to the passers-by'. Three streams had crossed it, bridged by Ivy Bridge, Strand Bridge and a third just to the east of St Clement Danes, but now it was turned into a more practical highway.

There was a great deal of rebuilding at the Temple and the gardens were made with their lawns sloping down to the brick boundary wall alongside the river. Next to it was Essex House, on the site of the Outer Temple, which was rebuilt and occupied by the Earl of Leicester and then descended to his son-in-law the Earl of Essex, who met his end in the Tower. His son, the Parliamentary general of the Civil War, who took the precaution of taking his coffin with him into battle, was born here, and after the battle of Newbury received a deputation from the House of Commons and the citizens of London, headed by the Lord Mayor. The house lasted until the end of the seventeenth century, when it was demolished for the building of Essex Street, but we know little of what it was like, except that Pepys described it as 'large but ugly'.

Next to it the Norfolks built Norfolk House and adjoining its grounds were those of the first Somerset House, built in 1547 by the Lord Protector of Edward VI. It was probably the most splendid of all the Strand palaces. The Duke pulled down the adjoining houses of five bishops, as well as the old parish church of St Mary for the site, and for building material he ordered the demolition not only of the charnel house and chapel of St Paul's Cathedral and the buildings of the old Pardon Churchyard, but also part of the Church of the Priory of St John of Jerusalem at Clerkenwell. His glory was short-lived, for he was soon accused of corruption, and only five years later he was executed. The house survived as Crown property. Princess Elizabeth lived here for a time, before her accession. Then Queen Anne of Denmark held her court here and it was known as Denmark House. With the accession of Charles I it was made over to Henrietta Maria for her life. Cromwell lay in state here before his funeral, and at the Restoration Henrietta moved back again, while after her death Charles II's Catherine of Braganza held her court here during the years that Barbara Castlemaine was living at the Whitehall Palace.

Somerset House remained a royal palace, although little used, until 1775, when George III handed it over to the government. Then the old house was demolished and Sir William Chambers built the present Somerset House, which has never been used as a residence.

John of Gaunt's palace of the Savoy, ruined during the Peasants Revolt, had been rebuilt by Henry VII as the hospital of St John the Baptist, for 100 distressed people. It was suppressed at the Reformation but the beautiful old hall, said to have been similar to that of Crosby Hall, survived for a long time, although gradually sinking into decay. Part was used as a prison for a time, another part as the King's printing press, for the issue of royal proclamations. It came down early in the nineteenth century for the building of Waterloo Bridge, but its little chapel still stands in Savoy Street, for although it was grievously damaged by fire in 1860, Sydney Smirke restored it in its original style.

Durham House, just to the west of Ivy bridge, had been the home of the Bishops of Durham. It passed into the hands of the Crown and by 1553 the Duke of Northumberland was living there. The marriage of his son Lord Guildford Dudley to Lady Jane Grey took place at Durham House and it was from here, two months later, that she was conducted to the Tower, in readiness to be proclaimed Queen.

Queen Elizabeth gave Durham House to Sir Walter Raleigh, but after his downfall part of the house facing the Strand was demolished, together with the thatched stables, for the building of the New Exchange, a bourse with a public walk on the ground floor and all manner of shops above, which became very fashionable during the Restoration years. The old house behind survived into the eighteenth century, when it was pulled down for the building of the Adelphi terrace.

York House stood on the site of Buckingham Street and Villiers Street. It had once been the London home of the Bishops of Norwich but was taken over by the Archbishop of York for a short time, after the downfall of Wolsey and the loss of Whitehall Palace to the King. York House passed into the hands of the Crown and was bestowed on George Villiers, Duke of Buckingham, who rebuilt it in great magnificence. During the Commonwealth it was granted to General Fairfax, whose daughter married the second Duke, so that the Buckingham family were once more in possession, but he was an extravagant young man who ran into appalling debt, and he ordered the house to be demolished and the materials sold, to save him from bankruptcy: but part of the contract of the sale was that his name and titles should be preserved in the names of the streets built on the site: and at the bottom of Buckingham Street the great stone water gate, carved with the arms of the house of Villiers and the family motto, still stands, in solitary splendour, the only survival of all the grandeur that once was to be found here.

Farther west, where Northumberland Avenue now runs, stood until 1874, yet another of the great palaces of the Strand, Northumberland House, on the site of a religious foundation which had been suppressed. It passed into the hands of Henry Howard, Earl of Northampton and son of the poet Earl of Surrey. Here in 1605 he built a 'most sumptuous palace', designed round three sides of a great courtyard, which was open to the riverside garden. It passed to his nephew, Thomas Howard, the first Earl of Suffolk, and after two or three generations to Lady Elizabeth Howard, who married the Earl of Northumberland. The Earl instructed Inigo Jones to build a new frontage on to the Strand, and here Northumberland House remained, with its 150 rooms, its ballroom and wonderful marble staircase, its picture galleries and accumulated treasures, all through Stuart, Georgian and most of Victorian times, the scene of countless court intrigues and scandals.

One after another, the other grand mansions were demolished and the Strand filled up with shops and coffee houses and taverns. The old house saw the passing of the Thames watermen, the coming of the stage coach and its abrupt eclipse by the railway, and when it at last came down two vast Victorian hotels, the Grand and the Metropole, were built on the site, neither of which survived for more than 40 years.

The Abbots of Westminster had owned seven acres of 'fair spreading pastures' along the northern side of the Strand, half way between the Abbey and the City of London. Part they used as a burial ground and part as an orchard and vegetable garden for their daily needs: and they sold their surplus produce to the citizens of London.

In 1552 Edward VI granted this land of the Convent Garden and Long Acre to John Russell, Earl of Bedford. The Russells did little to develop it for several years, but their gardeners tended the monks' vegetable garden and Londoners still came to buy. Over the years, people from the neighbouring villages began bringing their produce to the Convent Garden to sell and created a convenient though as yet unauthorised market, which soon became known as Covent Garden. The rest of the seven acres the Russells let out to neighbouring members of the aristocracy, for the stabling and pasturage of their horses, and a few small cottages were built for the coachmen, ostlers and gardeners, but on the southern border, facing the Strand, they built Bedford House, 'with a great yard before it, for the reception of carriages; with a spacious garden, having a terraced walk adjoining the brick wall next to the garden, behind which were the coach houses and stables'.

Close by Lord Burleigh built Burleigh House during Queen Elizabeth's reign. Not far away, Sir William Drury had built the beautiful Drury House, standing back a little from the Strand, in the lane which was to become known as Drury Lane, and when the Earl of Craven, lovesick for the widowed Queen of Bohemia, later moved into it, he rebuilt it and called it Craven House, but it was not until the 1630s that the Russells were to engage Inigo Jones to lay out the Covent Garden piazza.

The western approaches to the walled City of London were, therefore, magnificent, but to the east it was a very different story, for as the houses of the traders and shopkeepers grew larger and more dignified, the poor retreated to their own suburbs. Eastward, beyond the bars of Aldgate, Stow writes that

> both sides of the street be pestered with cottages and alleys, even up to Whitechapel church, and almost half a mile beyond it, into the common field, I say, being sometime the beauty of the city on that part, is so encroached upon by building of filthy cottages, and with other purpressors, inclosures and laystalls (notwithstanding all proclamations and acts of parliament made to the contrary), that in some places it scarce remaineth sufficient highway for the meeting of carriages and droves of cattle: much less is there any fair, pleasant, or wholesome way for people to walk on foot, which is no small blemish to so famous a city to have so unsavoury and unseemly an entrance or passage thereunto.

Things were even worse by the riverside. 'From St Katherine to Wapping', he writes,

> the usual place of execution for hanging old pirates and sea rovers, at the low water mark, and there to remain, till three tides had overflowed them, and never a house standing within these forty years; but since the gallows being after removed farther off, a continual street, or filthy strait passage, with alleys of small tenements, or cottages, built, inhabited by sailors' victuallers, along by the river of Thames, almost to Radcliff, a good mile from the Tower.

The appalling lack of sanitation in Tudor times, and for two centuries after, bred widespread disease, and the death rate amongst all members of the population, but particularly amongst children and women in childbirth, was very high. Water was obtained from street pumps or wells and London's main-supply was from the Thames. There was no organised system of refuse clearance and household waste usually accumulated in the streets or ran into the open drains, from which it passed to the Fleet river or the Walbrook and so into the Thames. The civic authorities tried to make each householder responsible for the disposal of his own refuse, but this was no easy matter. The records of the Walbrook ward list dozens of occasions when attempts

were made to keep the Walbrook clear. In 1288 it was enacted 'that the water-
course of Wallbroke shall be kept clean and that no dung or filth be thrown
therein to the disturbance or annoyance of folk'. In 1301 there was an inquiry
as to who was liable for the cleansing of the stream and it was decided that
'the Parish of St Stephen's ought of right to scower the course of the brook'
and the sheriffs were ordered to compel the parishioners to do so. By 1415
someone had the idea of building a sluice in the stream by means of which
it could be periodically flooded and thus cleared of its debris and impurities
and by 1477 a Court of Common Council ordered that all the privies made over
the brook be 'utterly destroyed and taken down'.

There were several bridges over the stream, on many of which houses were
built, and the solution to the problem came when in 1473 it was ordered that
those 'who have ground on either side of the brook were to vault and pave
it over so far as his ground extended'. Charitable bequests provided for the
covering of the rest of the bridge and by the end of Tudor times the entire
stream had disappeared, but the Fleet remained an open and pestilential sewer
until the 1760s.

There were doctors practising in London but their fees were high, nor were
they a great deal of use, for medicine and surgery were in an exploratory stage.
The Italian scientists of the Renaissance had established the main principles
of anatomy but little was known of physiology and Harvey's discovery of the
process of the circulation of the blood was yet to come. Even less was known
about pathology, and medicine was very much a process of trial and error,
in which magic and astrology played a considerable part. Andrew Boorde, a
Tudor writer on medical matters, declared that 'above all things next to
grammar a physician must have surely his Astronomie, to know how, when
and at what time every medicine ought to be administered'.

Doctors did not associate themselves with social hygiene or any form of
preventive medicine, apart from urging isolation for plague victims. The Black
Death of the fourteenth century was followed by many more but less widespread outbreaks of the bubonic plague, carried by the rat-flea. The exact
nature of the contagion was not understood but most doctors held the theory
that its spread was due to a 'noxious miasma' in the air and advised all who
could to move to the purer air of the country.

Smallpox was also beginning to appear and both Henry VIII and Queen
Elizabeth suffered from it, but the sweating sickness was the scourge of Tudor
London, a mysterious disease about which little is known except that it was
often fatal: and after about fifty years it disappeared as suddenly as it had first
occurred.

Quarantine laws in time of plague epidemics were strict and the penalties for breaking them severe. Houses where a case had occurred, whether in London or the provinces, were marked with a red cross painted on a board and fixed to the street door, with the words 'Lord, have mercy upon us!' and the other members of the household, except in very exceptional circumstances, had to stay indoors for 40 days.

There was a particularly bad epidemic in 1513 and rules were made more stringent. Watchers guarded a house where a sufferer lay, to see that no one left it, and food, supplied from the City funds or from public appeal, was passed in without any contact being made with other members of the family. Funeral bearers swore an oath to have nothing to do with other people in the dead persons' house and carried a red or white rod as a warning sign, while the approach of the bier was heralded by the ringing of a bell.

Ineffective as they seem to have been, the physicians were a highly respected section of society and in 1518 Linacre founded the English College of Physicians at his house in Knightrider Street.

The barbers still performed such surgical operations as were deemed possible, such as trepanning a skull to release evil humours and the devil, amputating a limb for reducing a fracture, excising abscesses and extracting teeth, but surgeons themselves, a more highly educated body of men, though not yet considered the social equal of the physicians, were beginning to practise independently, and soon after the College of Physicians was founded the Barbers' Company and the Company of Surgeons united into the Company of Barber Surgeons, their hall being in Monkwell Street by Cripplegate.

The apothecaries were still associated with the grocers, for at this time drugs were mainly sold by grocers and pepperers or by the doctors. By the early seventeenth century the apothecaries and the doctors had formed a separate company, but the union lasted for only a few years and in 1617 Gideon Delaune, apothecary to James I and Queen Anne of Denmark, founded the Company of Apothecaries, to which, to the anger of the doctors, King James granted a charter.

The hall of the new livery company was in Blackfriars Lane, near Playhouse Yard, where the Blackfriars theatre once stood, and parts of the present building, with its seventeenth-century panelled court room and portraits of the Stuart Kings, date from 1670.

In 1673 Charles Cheyne leased a plot of land on the Chelsea riverfront to the Apothecaries for the creation of their Physic Garden, and when Sir Hans Sloane bought the manor of Chelsea he granted the society the freehold of the garden, on condition that it 'should at all times be continued as a Physic Garden'.

William Clowes was the most distinguished surgeon of Queen Elizabeth's

F

reign. He was surgeon to the Queen and was on the staff of St Bartholomew's hospital, to which three surgeons and a physician had been appointed, when the number of beds had been increased from 40 to 100 at the time of its re-organisation. Clowes had considerable success in the treatment of gun-shot wounds inflicted with the newly-invented cumbersome matchlock guns, and also with fractures and amputations, but he had no anaesthetics, apart from drugs which only partially dulled the pain. He recommended searing the wound with a hot iron, though he admitted that this cautery was 'offensive to the eye and bringeth the patient to great sorrowe and dread of the burning and the smart'.

Sickness and injury were times of terrible suffering, nameless terrors and deadly danger, yet with it all the London Elizabethans were living in one of the most romantic and colourful periods of English history. Most of them were prospering again after the troubles of the early part of the reign, and they spent lavishly. The furnishing of their homes was infinitely more comfortable, with chairs and settles, chests and cupboards. Floors were covered with carpets in place of the insanitary layers of straw, below which had often lain 'an ancient collection of beer and grease, fragments of fish and everything that is nasty'. Four-poster beds came into use, with sheets and blankets, mattresses of down and feathers, and pillows in place of the medieval logs of wood. In the homes of London merchants the first cushions and upholstered furniture appeared, although many bewailed the fact that Englishmen were growing soft.

Tableware became elaborate and valuable; spoons and plates as well as marvellously wrought salt cellars, candlesticks, bowls and dishes were of silver or even of imported Spanish gold. Plate was in fact an excellent invest-ment and an alternative to keeping spare cash in some secret hiding place.

They fed well and the home counties began to specialise in the production of the basic foods, such as wheat and rye, to supply the growing population of the City. Hops for the brewing of ale came from Kent, barley from East Anglia, for although the tables of the wealthy were loaded with more elaborate food, bread, beer and meat were the staple diet for thousands.

At the beginning of Tudor times, people were expected to dress according to their station. Citizens' wives had to wear white, knitted caps of woollen yarn, unless their husbands were gentlemen by descent, apprentices blue gowns in the winter and blue cloaks in summer, with breeches of white broadcloth and flat caps, and servants were not allowed gowns which reached below the calf of the leg. No man under the degree of knight might wear gold chains and bracelets or silk shirts 'upon peine of forfeiture thereof' and no one under the degree of gentleman any gold or silver decoration on his clothing. However, these laws were always being broken, giving cause for the complaint of the Puritan Philip Stubbes, in his *The Anatomie of Abuses,* published in 1583, that it had become difficult to tell 'who is noble, who is worshipful, who is a gentleman, who is not'.

It was early in the century, when Henry VIII was establishing friendly relations with France at the Field of the Cloth of Gold and England also had a close relationship with Italy, that dress began to grow elaborate and expensive. Men's dress became aggressively flamboyant and ostentatious. It still consisted of a doublet over a shirt, with trunks and an outer coat, but they were now all of velvet and heavy silk, the coat being lined and collared with fur and the sleeves grotesquely bolstered and puffed, making the shoulders far too wide for the rest of the body. Women's dress was not so elaborate at first, but with Queen Elizabeth's reign all restraint and grace disappeared and amongst the wealthy it was so formal and cumbersome that it was ungainly. Women's bodices were stiffened and boned and loaded with embroidery and jewels and the skirts became so full that they were eventually draped over farthingales. From Spain came the fashion, for women as well as men, of wearing highneck ruffs, which were at first wired, until a Dutch woman introduced the art of starching and goffering them with 'pokesticks'. As an alternative to the ruff, women sometimes wore large, fan-shaped collars of wire and stiffened lawn or lace, which grew in size until they reached as high as the top of the head.

Velvet and silks, damasks and grosgrains were arriving at the docks of the Port of London and women revelled in them. Stubbes complained bitterly of their extravagance, maintaining that they should be content with English wool, but nowadays, he said, 'if it comes not from beyond the seas, it is not worth a straw'.

In the country, fashions remained simple, but in London they grew ever more complicated, and when the Queen lost her hair and had to take to a red wig, false hair became the rage. Women's hair, declared Stubbes, was 'frizzled and crisped, laid out on wreaths and borders from ear to ear, propped with forks and wires', and 'on this bolstered hair, which standeth crested round about their frontiers, they apply gold wreaths, bugles and gew gaws'.

Some took to red wigs, to be like the Queen. They shaved their eyebrows and foreheads and powdered their skins to be 'of a pale, bleake colour' and the most enthusiastic even swallowed 'gravel, ashes and tallow' to acquire the fashionable pallor.

The men were as bad. They wore their doublets pointed in front, like the women's bodices, elaborately embroidered and padded. Gallants took to breeches for the first time, which were ballooned with padding to balance their broadened shoulders. This was the first break with the medieval hose, which

countrymen were to continue to wear for many more years. They were at
first called trunk hose or galligascons and they were so slashed and puffed that
they were far from easy to put on and even more difficult to wear. To make
sure that 'the long seams of their hose be set by a plumb-line, then we puff,
then we blow, and finally sweat till we drop,' declared William Harrison.
Stockings and shoes were lavished with ornaments and for both men and
women the Venetian high heel was introduced, so that they now trod 'on
corked stilts, a prisoner's pace'.

Men of fashion wore earrings and scent and their hats were remarkable and
varied, usually decorated with highly coloured feathers and jewelled brooches.
'Every article of wear is extravagantly fashioned,' wrote Stubbes.

> Hats are of all fantastic shapes and some people will have no kind of hat
> without a great bunch of feathers of divers and sundry colours, peaking on
> top of their heads, not unlike coxcombs. . . . Many get a good living by
> dyeing and selling them, and not a few prove themselves more than fools
> in the wearing of them. . . .

The habit of overdressing spread down the social scale to people who could
not afford it. Every penny they possessed went on their backs or the adornment
of their homes. Queen Elizabeth revived the sumptuary laws. Only the nobility
might wear imported woollen goods. Only those with an income of over £200
a year might wear 'velvet or embroidery, or pricking with gold, silver or silk'.
Only those with over £100 a year might wear satin, damask, silk camlet or
taffeta, which was just as well, for men were known to have paid £100 for just
a pair of breeches, which was about ten times the annual stipend of a parish
priest.

With the passing years and the increasing number of Puritans the craze was
to fade, but while the excitement of the new prosperity lasted, the pride in
dress was inordinate and, as Stubbes maintained, a poison in the country, for
amidst all the display of wealth the number of poor and destitute was increasing.

One of the first reforms of Elizabeth's reign was the issue of a new and stable
currency, but food prices had already risen and they remained high. And with
the fluctuating tastes of the new prosperity, with a new fashion coming into
vogue every year or two, merchants were accused of pandering to the taste
of the rich for foreign goods and neglecting to sell the work of English craftsmen, who were suffering long periods of unemployment.

Apart from those who were just poor, there was a growing number who had
no means of subsistence at all and were forced to beg. For the country as a

whole the number of beggars was estimated at 10,000, more than one in every 500 of the population. The problem was concentrated in the towns, where desperate people always went, hoping to find work of some sort, so it is probable that London had some 5,000 or 6,000.

The brutal laws of the earlier part of the century were ameliorated and with Elizabeth's first parliament, contributions to the parish relief of the poor were made compulsory in London and defaulters could be compelled by the magistrates to pay their share. An Act of 1563, the Statute of Artificers, gave magistrates the authority to fix the rate of wages in each county 'according to the plenty or scarcity of the time', thereby tending to make the control of apprenticeship, which hitherto had been in the hands of the craft guilds and companies, a national control: and anyone who refused to work at these rates could be treated as a vagrant.

It was after this Statute that the governors of the Bridewell were able to improve matters, for they introduced there a system of apprenticeship which was available not only to the homeless and destitute, but also to children of poor freemen of the City of London.

With the second and third of the Elizabethan Poor Laws the penalties for vagabondage were far less harsh and the responsibility for its own poor was laid on each parish government.

There are no records by which one can gauge the figures of deliberate crime, but punishments were so severe that they must have been, to a certain extent, a deterrent. Until 1472 there had been only one stocks in the City, at the Stocks market, but in that year the Lord Mayor ordered them to be set up in every ward, because of the large number of rogues and vagabonds haunting the City, and in 1543 the Common Council made a similar order, presumably because the earlier one had not been carried out, it being agreed that each of the Aldermen 'shall cause a payre of Stocks or a Cage to be made or sett up within his Warde at the costes of the Cytie with as much speede as it maye conveniently be done'.

A wilful murderer had his right hand cut off before he was put to death. During Henry VIII's reign a man caught trying to poison an enemy was taken to Smithfield and boiled in a cauldron 'let up and down divers times till he was dead'. Richard Ross, a cook, was also boiled to death at Smithfield for poisoning more than sixteen people, most of whom died. Perjurers were put in the pillory and then branded and deprived of their possessions. Anyone heard to be speaking sedition against the Crown or the government had his ears cut off.

Terms of imprisonment were not yet imposed as a form of punishment but prisons were used to house men awaiting trial, or their execution after conviction. They were terrible places, where men were 'lodged like hogs and fed like dogs'. Often they had to wait there for years before being tried and many died before their cases were heard, for there was a 'syckness of the prisons', which came of corruption of the air 'as many men be together in a little room, having but little air'.

Although medievalism had a long, hard death the sixteenth century in England, as well as marking the beginning of the City of London's rise to the most important commercial centre of the world, was a time of wonderful artistic and intellectual achievement.

Many more grammar schools, some of which were to become famous, were established throughout the country, to replace the cathedral, almonry, collegiate and chantry schools, numbering in all between 300 and 400, which had vanished with the Reformation. In London the ancient cathedral foundation of St Paul's had been replaced in 1512 by John Colet's new foundation, and other distinguished London schools in addition to Christ's Hospital were the Mercers', the Merchant Taylors', Charterhouse, St Olave's and St Saviour's, while the City of London school, which was not formed until 1836, was established with funds from a bequest for the education of four poor children, left by John Carpenter, town-clerk of London during the reign of Henry V: and Thomas Gresham endowed Gresham College.

The grammar schools were still under ecclesiastical supervision and masters had to be licensed by the Church, for the Roman Catholics were immensely strong still and there was a seminary at Rheims where Englishmen were given instruction for their conversion to the Roman Catholic priesthood and returned to England as secret missionaries. For its complete success, therefore, the English Church needed an informed laity to defend itself against the heretics. However, when Dean Colet refounded St Paul's school he had vested control in the Mercers' Company and stipulated that the headmaster should be a layman: and by Queen Elizabeth's time it was accepted that wealthy citizens and the State should take some of the responsibility for education, which had hitherto been left in the hands of the Church.

Schoolboys had to work. A boy entered a grammar school at the age of seven, by which time he was expected to be able to read and write, say his catechism in English or Latin and perhaps already know a little elementary Latin: and Dean Colet told the headmaster of St Paul's that when he was interviewing parents he was to say to them: 'If your child can read and write his own lessons, then he shall be admitted into the school as a scholar' but 'if your child, after reasonable season proved, be found here unapt and unable to learning, then ye, warned hereof, shall take him away, that he occupy not here room in vain'.

The play had come a long way since medieval times, when the clergy had enacted scenes from the Bible in their churches, for the instruction of an unlettered congregation. As these miracle plays became more elaborate they were performed at the Church doors and then they were mounted on carts or 'pageants' and paraded through the streets. The clergy began to write fresh. dramatic material and then the laity took a hand, both in writing and acting In the religious processions of the craft guilds their members would act a religious play of their own devising, and there were no inhibitions about portraying God, who was always seated on a throne, clad in a purple robe and with a golden face and prolific beard.

Then came the morality plays, written not only for moral instruction but also for entertainment, and by the fifteenth century they were being acted in the great halls of the nobility, to entertain their guests.

Plays on purely secular subjects were a natural development. Schools and universities and the Inns of Court all presented them and a few professional companies of actors were formed, each sponsored by a wealthy nobleman. At first they gave their performances in the courtyards of the inns, with the privileged spectators ranged in the surrounding galleries and the rest crowded below, round the improvised stage. With the Vagrancy Act of 1572 the position of the actors became difficult and the Puritans, of whom there were an increasing number in the City of London, disliked them, but two years later Queen Elizabeth gave licences to a few of the companies to act throughout the country and within the next few years there were six licensed companies based on London, who acted in the courtyards of London inns and from time to time, especially during times of plague, when they were prohibited, toured the country. The Belle Sauvage on Ludgate Hill, the Bull at Aldgate and the Cross Keys in Gracechurch Street all leased their wide galleries for the performance of plays, yet despite their wealthy patrons, the actors had a difficult time, for the inns took the money from the gallery spectators and the actors had to collect what they could from the courtyards.

In 1576 the actor James Burbage, whose patron was the Earl of Leicester, borrowed enough money from his brother-in-law, a prosperous grocer, to build the first London theatre. He chose a site in the suburbs, beyond the jurisdiction of the disapproving City fathers, calling it simply the Theatre. It was in Shoreditch, where the Holywell Priory had once stood. Close by, where Curtain Road now lies, was a second theatre, the Curtain, said to have been given its name because it was the first theatre to use a curtain. An illustrious group of Elizabethan playwrights came to live in Shoreditch – Robert Green, Tom Nashe, George Peele and Thomas Kyd – and then, in 1587, Christopher Marlowe, just down from Cambridge, arrived to offer his play *Tamburlaine, the Great* to the manager of the Curtain, Philip Henslowe.

It was accepted and Edward Alleyn was chosen for the lead. For the first performance the young Kit Marlowe sat in a box above the back of the stage over the green room. He saw the theatre flag hoisted and watched the audience arrive. As the latecomers hurried through the fields of Shoreditch, the theatre trumpeter blared forth a final warning that the play was about to begin. The Prologue appeared and as his majestic opening lines rang out from the stage the boisterous, exuberant Elizabethans were battered into an awed silence. Never before had they heard anything like this vivid, vital portrayal of the brutal Tamburlaine, who had ravaged all the lands from Syria to India. The play was a brilliant success and overnight Kit won fame.

That same year Philip Henslowe acquired the Rose theatre on Bankside, 'on that part of Surrey without the jurisdiction of the Lord Mayor', for the Mayor and Corporation still objected to the theatre. They said it was a waste of time, that the congregation of large numbers of people was highly dangerous in times of plague, that the play encouraged improper behaviour and for boys to be dressed as women for the women's parts was reprehensible. 'Will not a filthy play, with the blast of a trumpet, sooner call hither a thousand, than an hour's tolling of a bell bring to the sermon of a hundred?' thundered forth an irate preacher from Paul's Cross, while Philip Stubbes railed at the 'winking and glancing of wanton eyes' at the theatre.

Nevertheless, more theatres were built, though again outside the City's jurisdiction. Philip Henslowe was a typical entrepreneur of the sixteenth century. From humble beginnings as the employee of a bailiff named Woodward, in the service of Lord Montague, he married Woodward's widow, and with Woodward's savings bought land around his home in Southwark. Here he derived part of his income from the Bankside stews. He bought goatskins for the Southwark skinners and leathersellers and made money on the side as a dyer, pawnbroker and moneylender. His step-daughter, Joan Woodward, married Edward Alleyn, and together they bought a share in the Paris Garden, an ancient ecclesiastical manor which had come into the hands of the Crown. It had become a pleasure garden and was not regarded as part of Southwark until the nineteenth century. Here, amongst the bull and bear gardens, was the little Rose theatre, which Henslowe bought and rebuilt.

It was about 1588, the year of the Armada, that the young William Shakespeare reached London, and he had soon joined the company of actors under the protection of the Lord Chamberlain – the Chamberlain's men – and was giving performances at Court before Queen Elizabeth.

Some years earlier James Burbage had built a theatre in the precincts of the Black Friars where, although the house had been disestablished forty years earlier and the church demolished, the right of sanctuary still existed. Here, despite all attempts of the City to dislodge them, they prospered, and Shakespeare joined them for a time. In 1596 they were petitioning the Privy Council to allow them to repair and enlarge the theatre, which the Puritans of Blackfriars were still trying to close. The Council allowed them to make the repairs but forbade the enlargement of the theatre.

In 1599 Shakespeare's company were playing at Burbage's theatre at Shoreditch, but the ground landlord raised difficulties about the renewal of the lease. To solve the problem, the Burbage family, claiming that the building was theirs, promptly organised a band of workmen, headed by the carpenter Peter Street, to pull it down. 'In most forcible and riotous manner' they seized and carried the woodwork of the theatre away, ferried it across the Thames and dumped it on Bankside, near the Rose, and here Peter Street set about building the Globe theatre, just above the Bankside marshes. The Burbage family owned half the property and Shakespeare, with his four associates, who included William Kempe, the comedian, each received a tenth share. This was the scene of Shakespeare's greatest triumphs and the acting of his tragedian Richard Burbage, son of James, transcending the actor's earlier arbitrary rules of technique, and in contrast to the violently ranting performances of earlier actors in tragic roles, seemed to transport himself entirely into his parts, 'putting off himself with his clothes, as he never did (not so much as in the tiring house) assume himself again, until the play was done'.

Of the other Bankside theatres, the Swan, near the Globe, was successful for a time but fell into decay and was closed in 1613, and even less is known about the Hope. However, early in 1600 Henslowe, as an answer to the success of the Globe, built the Fortune theatre with Edward Alleyn, just outside Aldersgate, between Whitecross Street and Golding Lane, which was popular. It was burnt down in 1621 but rebuilt and lasted until 1649, when it was destroyed by some fanatical Puritans.

The Globe had been destroyed by fire in 1613 but was rebuilt. Shakespeare had retired to Stratford by this time but probably contributed towards the rebuilding of the theatre, and the Blackfriars theatre was still flourishing. In 1608 the Lord Mayor and aldermen had made a final attempt to close it but they were unable to prove to the Lord Chancellor that the City had ever exercised any authority within the Blackfriars precincts. Their petition failed and the theatre stood until the days of the Commonwealth, when all the London theatres were closed or demolished. It came down in 1655 and houses were built on the site.

Despite the gaiety and brilliance of the last years of Queen Elizabeth's reign, there were sinister undertones, the death throes of medievalism. Even before he left Cambridge Christopher Marlowe had paid secret visits to Rheims to report on the English Catholic seminary there for Sir Francis Walsingham's ruthlessly efficient espionage system, and with his success in the London theatre he became friendly with Sir Walter Raleigh, who invited him to his new home, Durham House, in the Strand, to join his circle of intimates who called themselves the School of Night. They were the free-thinkers of the time and included Thomas Harriot, the astronomer and mathematician, George Chapman, the translater of Homer, Matthew Royden, the poet, the eccentric Earl of Northumberland, the Earl of Derby, and Kit. Under the guidance of Thomas Harriot they met regularly to study and discuss the new problems of philosophy, theology, astronomy, geography and chemistry, which had arisen since the fallacies of the teaching on which they had all been brought up were now proven. The earth was not flat, nor was it, as the Church maintained still, the centre of the universe, but a planet moving round the sun. Blood did not receive the 'breath of the soul' when it reached the brain, as doctors had been taught for the last thousand years. They scorned the ancient theories of Aristotle and Galen and upheld those of Leonardo da Vinci, Vesalius and Copernicus.

London viewed with suspicion and horror the meetings of the School of Night. They were accused of practising black magic. One broadsheet described the gentle scholarly Tom Harriot as the devil incarnate, while another announced that

> The members of the School of Night indulge in the disgusting habit of tobacco smoking. A silver pipe is passed from man to man round the table, when they are in session. Their stomachs are therefore as black with soot as their hearts and minds with evil.

In 1593 Marlowe was 29. It was the year that Shakespeare published his first important poem *Venus and Adonis*, which was sold at the sign of the White Greyhound in St Paul's Churchyard. There was an outbreak of plague in London. The theatres were closed and the actors had departed for a long provincial tour. Marlowe was asked to attend an enquiry of the Privy Council, where he was questioned about his subversive views. He answered readily and the Council came to no decision but asked him to remain within easy reach of Westminster, so that he could be called for further meetings. A day or two later he received a message from one of the associates of his secret service days, asking him to meet him at a tavern on the Deptford water front. He was shown into a private room, where two other men joined them, and that was the last that was ever heard of Kit Marlowe, for he was found dead. At their trial for murder the men declared that they had quarrelled and Kit had accidentally fallen forward on a dagger. They were acquitted, but the evidence was suspiciously plausible and a doubt has lingered on ever since that some member of the Privy Council, afraid that Marlowe would be acquitted of the charge of heresy, paid them to kill him and silence his brilliant, questioning mind and disturbingly deadly logic.

The silent war against Catholicism and all forms of heresy continued, for Roman Catholics were regarded as a danger to the State, but trade and exploration, financed by the City of London, flourished, even although the seamen may have feared that each new landing might be on some enchanted spot, like Prospero's, inhabited by a malignant Caliban, to curse them with 'toads, beetles, and bats'.

In 1600 an English merchantman captured a Portuguese ship laden with Indian gold, pearls, spices, silks and ivory, which it brought back to London. It was the beginning of a more legitimate trade with India, for that year the Queen granted to a company of 215 London merchant adventurers a charter to trade with India for the next fifteen years and they called themselves the East India Company.

9

Stuart London

In early Stuart times the East India Company established small trading stations at Madras and Surat, to the north of Bombay, and by 1640 they had a third station in Bengal. They were too far away from England to expect protection by the Royal Navy and the company built its own East Indiamen, 'goodly ships of such burthen as never were formerly used in merchandise', which were equipped for both commerce and battle against their Portuguese and Dutch rivals, the Dutch East India Company having been formed in 1602.

The English company maintained friendly relations with the Indian Princes, for it had no territorial ambitions, and King James's ambassador to the Court of the Mogul Emperor was also the company's agent.

From Madras and Bombay the company traded with China and their ships also sailed into the Persian Gulf, where the Levant Company was already doing business with Persia by an overland route.

In 1609 King James renewed the Company's charter 'for ever', provided it might be recalled on three years' notice by the Crown, and it soon possessed 30 great vessels of over 1,000 tonnage, on which it had expended £300,000. Ships were sometimes wrecked. A few were captured by the Dutch or by pirates, but the seamen were preserved from the sailors' scourge of scurvy, for from the outset, the Company provided for them 'lemon water' and oranges.

They sold only a limited amount of woollen cloth in these warm countries but Queen Elizabeth had allowed them to export silver and gold coin, provided they returned with an equivalent amont of gold and silver bullion, and by 1621 the expenditure of £100,000 had realised £500,000 worth of oriental wares, of which only a quarter was consumed at home, the rest being resold abroad at a large profit. The main commodities arriving in London at this time were saltpetre, for the manufacture of gun-powder, raw silk and spices, particularly pepper, which was so greatly in demand at a time when fresh meat was scarce in winter.

The company prospered and in 1623, after its twelfth voyage, King James was demanding £20,000 before the fleet put to sea again.

During Elizabethan times the royal granting of monopolies and licences to trade in certain commodities to favoured individuals had been a cause of bitter resentment amongst London merchants, for it constricted both home and foreign trade and sent up the price to the consumer, and by the end of the Queen's reign she had suppressed every monopoly she had granted. However, the Stuart Kings, in order to raise money beyond that granted by Parliament, revived the custom, and in 1635 Charles I, disregarding the charter of the East India Company, granted to Captain Weddell, for a large but unspecified sum, the right to set up a second company for the Indian trade for five years – the Courteen Association. A few years later King Charles compelled the East India Company to sell him the entire stock of Indian pepper in their warehouses, offering bonds which were not honoured, and resold it at a lower price, thereby entailing a loss of £50,000. This calamity brought the East India Company to the verge of ruin and together with the mismanagement of the Courteen Association it nearly ended the English trade in the Far East for a time.

Moreover, towards the end of his reign, as the Civil War was brewing, the King, having been refused a loan by the City of London, seized the money which the goldsmiths had lodged for safe-keeping in the Mint, amounting by this time to £200,000, and compelled them to treat it as a loan. It was never repaid, and many goldsmiths were ruined.

In 1618 James I had granted a Royal Charter to a new English company for the 'Golden Trade'. This 'Company of Adventurers of London Trading into Africa' were given 'exclusive' rights in the Guinea trade, but this counted for little, for the French, Dutch and Portuguese were there already, and on the coast it was every man for himself. The Portuguese were offering 100 crowns for every Frenchman's head and the Dutch were prepared to fight all comers. However, the English managed to edge their way in and instead of doing business from their ships, as was the common practice, they built two settlements on shore, at the mouth of the Gambia river and on the Gold Coast.

George Thompson, a Captain of the Company, who arrived in the *Catherine* at the Gambia coast with nearly £2,000 worth of trade goods, made an expedition up the Gambia river with some of his men, but while he was away some 'vagrant Portingales' seized the *Catherine* and did to death the rest of the crew. Thompson, knowing nothing of this, sent some of his men down to the coast for fresh supplies, and when they learnt what had happened they fled for their lives, taking refuge with some sympathetic natives who took them to a safer part of the coast, whence they embarked for England, leaving Thompson and his eight companions stranded up river. The company in London, hearing of the disaster, sent a pinnace to rescue Thompson and found him, but he declared that he was not yet ready to return and in a small rowing-boat proceeded further up river, negotiating the falls of Barraconda, 250 miles inland, and pressing on to Tinda, where he had heard of a Negro merchant, Bucker Sano, who could put him in the way of much excellent business: but then the intrepid but unfortunate Thompson went mad and his men murdered him.

The company sent out another boat, thinking to bring back Thompson, under the command of Richard Jobson. Jobson and his men rowed up the Senegal river, reached Tinda and at last met Bucker Sano, the great merchant who had dealings with the Fula and Mandingoes of the Western Sudan and kept 300 horses to carry his salt trade alone. Bucker Sano offered slaves, but, said Mr Jobson, 'we were a people who did not deal in such commodities'. They came to terms with elephants' tusks, hides and cotton yarns, and Bucker Sano told Jobson of 'a town roofed with gold four moons away there and back to Tinda', the city of Timbuktu, which was just emerging from the power of the Sultan of Morocco.

The merchants of the Africa Company suffered terrible losses from malaria, and apart from the fierce rivalry of the Dutch, French and Portuguese their business was hampered by other English merchants outside the company who, disregarding the Royal monopoly, pirated the trade with their own private ventures, so that in the end the Company of Merchant Adventurers of London decided that they had become 'greatly tired of it' and withdrew their capital.

For the next few years the only Englishmen on the coast were unauthorised adventurers, and the Dutch seized the opportunity to make good their own position, founding a trading company under the patronage of the States General, while the French formed a company of merchants from Dieppe and Rouen.

Less than twenty years later, however, the merchants of London, watching the growing prosperity of Holland, decided to try their fortune on the Guinea coast once more and founded the Africa Company, under the patronage of Charles I, but shortly afterwards England became preoccupied with the Civil War and the company did not have sufficient support to match its rivals on the coast.

The Portuguese had missed their opportunity to establish a settlement at the Cape, being little interested in South Africa, and in 1620 two English captains took possession of it in the name of King James I, but at home London considered this remote part of the world of little account, for it seemed to offer no markets, and nothing further developed for many years.

While the East India Company was establishing its three small trading stations in India, which comprised little more than groups of warehouses, each protected by a fort manned by native sepoys, the Virginia Company was founded in London, and in April 1607 their three small ships sailed into Chesapeake Bay, to search for the remains of Raleigh's first settlement, made four years earlier, and establish here a new colony. There were only 105 Englishmen and the Indians they encountered in the sparsely inhabited regions of the Chesapeake Bay and the valleys of the Potomac and Susquehanna rivers were hostile. During the first few years they suffered appalling hardships and near-starvation but the tenacity of their leader John Smith held them together. They built houses and grew corn and tobacco. Fresh supplies of labour arrived from England and within fifteen years their numbers had risen to 5,000 and the Virginia tobacco trade was well established, soon to be centred on Bristol.

In 1614 one of their number, John Rolfe, married the little Indian princess Pocahontas and brought her back to London, where she met King James, Queen Anne and Sir Walter Raleigh, and was an object of great wonder and curiosity to the citizens. They stayed at the Savages' inn on Ludgate Hill – the Bell – but Pocahontas did not long survive the fog and damp of the City, and in March 1617 she died. She was buried at Gravesend and after that time the Bell became known as the Belle Sauvage and hung up a portrait of Pocahontas for its sign.

In 1620 the Pilgrim fathers, in search of religious freedom, set sail in the *Mayflower*, a barque of only 180 tons. The community comprised only 41 families and they landed on the coast of Massachusetts to face even greater hardships than the Virginians, in a more rigorous climate. By 1630 the colony was still only 500 strong but it was well established and able to pave the way for those who were to follow.

In 1634 Lord Baltimore, a convert to Rome, opened up the country north of Virginia, along the northern shores of the Potomac river, which he called Maryland, after Queen Henrietta Maria. He was determined that it should be a country where people of every shade of Christian belief should be free. 'No person within this province,' he declared, 'professing to believe in Jesus Christ, shall be in any ways troubled, molested or discountenanced for his or her religion, or in the free exercise thereof.'

King Charles I granted charters to the London companies which established the colonies of Virginia and Massachusetts, and with their financial backing the Puritan emigration began on a large scale. Within a year nearly 2,000 had sailed, landowners, clergymen, lawyers, University students and farmers, many coming from East Anglia.

The wealthy men who financed these companies had mixed motives. There was a large element of Puritanism amongst the London merchants, who sympathised sincerely with those who were emigrating for religious reasons, but at the same time they wanted to see a good return for their money and establish a new market for English goods in exchange for the products of the New World. By 1643 20,000 more emigrants had arrived in New England, at a cost to the company of £200,000, and 40,000 had landed in Virginia, New Hampshire, Connecticut and the West Indies, the interests of the newcomers being mainly the opportunities offered by the trading companies of free grants of land on which to grow the new and increasingly valuable crops of cotton, tobacco and sugar cane.

Many people in England deplored tobacco smoking. James I loathed it, calling it an 'ignoble habit, reducing a man to the level of a chimney, and rendering him liable to melancholia'. Various attempts were made to restrain the Virginian colonists from growing it and high import duties were imposed, but as the habit spread and the tax began to provide a handsome source of revenue there were second thoughts. By 1671 tobacco was providing an excise revenue of £100,000 a year and its virtues were now extolled. It was said to have medicinal value and to act as a disinfectant. It was now a cure for melancholy, rather than a cause, particularly when 'accompanied by psalm singing', and being a slight narcotic, was considered to make people less turbulent and inclined to sedition.

Very soon there was an acute shortage of labour in the American colonies. In West Africa the Dutch were prospering. They captured the Portuguese fort of São Jorge on the Gold Coast and a few years later attacked Angola, in order to secure slaves for Brazil. In 1642, by which time Portugal had recovered her independence from Spain, the Portuguese came to terms with the Dutch. Having found an alternative source of pepper in the Far East, they handed over all their possessions on the Gold Coast to Holland, in return for the withdrawal of Dutch claims in Brazil. Within a few years Portugal had fully recovered control of Angola and from that time on, until the early nineteenth century, they devastated the country by securing ever-increasing numbers of slaves for their Brazilian plantations.

In London the affairs of the Royal Adventurers were wound up and the Royal African Company formed, its concession being granted from the Port of Sally in South Barbary to the Cape of Good Hope, although in practice it operated the coast mainly below Sierra Leone, while the French and Dutch kept to the north, along the coast of Senegambia.

In the early days the new company prospered. From its forts at Cape Coast and on the Gambia and the coast of Sierra Leone it was able to develop and extend English trade and built many new ports, including Accra, Winneba and Sekondi. Into Africa it brought woollen and other manufactured goods to the value of £70,000 a year, sending back to London ivory, red wood and gold dust in quantities which coined 30,000 to 50,000 guineas at a time, recognizable by the company's sign of the elephant which was stamped on each one.

The Royal African Company also dealt in slaves, exporting large numbers to the Americas, albeit, as it claimed, 'at a moderate rate'. Spain, Portugal, Holland, France and England were all in dire need of labour for their new World colonies, many of which were virtually uninhabited, and one of the main reasons for their continued interest in Africa was its potential supply of slaves.

It has been estimated that by 1600 some 500,000 Negroes had been landed in the Americas and the West Indies, but with the development of the sugar plantations, which involved a large amount of labour, there came a great demand in Europe for sugar, and to supply it the need for Negro labour grew, so that within the next hundred years nearly three million Negroes were transported from Africa.

The Dutch first held the monopoly of the Slave-carrying trade from West Africa, the Portuguese continuing to run their own supply from Angola to Brazil, but the English and French were soon in competition, although English participation was not to gain a lead until early in the eighteenth century.

In London, to supplement the labour supply for the plantations, destitute youths were encouraged to emigrate. Through the agency of a ship's master or a London agent, they sold themselves in exchange for their passage money, and when they arrived they lived as slaves on their masters' estates and were driven to work with the Negroes, until, after some four years, the sum was worked off.

Ned Ward in his *London Spy* described them, during his walk from Thameside.

We peeped in at a gateway where we saw three or four well dressed blades with hawks' countenances, attended by half a dozen ragamuffinly fellows, showing poverty in their rags and despair in their faces, mixed with a parcel of young wild striplings like run-away 'prentices. I could not forbear enquiring of my friend about this ill-favoured multitude.

'That house,' says my friend, 'which they are entering, is an office where servants for the plantations bind themselves to be miserable as long as they live, without a special Providence prevents it. Those fine fellows, who look like footmen upon a holiday, are kidnappers, who walk the 'Change and other parts of the town, in order to seduce people who want employment and young fools crossed in love to go beyond seas. For every wretch they trapan into this misery they get so much a head from masters of ships, and merchants who go over. Those young rakes and tatterdemalions you see so lovingly herded are drawn, by their fair promises, to sell themselves into slavery, and the kidnappers are the rogues that run away with the money.'

During the Civil War there was little voluntary migration. For the most

part, the colonies were neutral, but in any case they were too far away to have
any active concern in the outcome of the struggle. The Commonwealth
government sent over some Royalist prisoners and also a few convicts, but
these men, together with the unfortunate boys who had been impressed,
ultimately worked out their freedom, and it was only the Negroes who remained in bondage for life.

In Europe, France was rising to the position of power which once had been
held by Spain, and Louis XIV's attempt at Catholic domination throughout
the whole continent provoked the War of the Spanish Succession, in which
Holland and England united against France. In West Africa the French defeated
the Dutch on the Senegambia coast and developed the settlements in Senegal
which were to be the foundation of their empire in French West Africa. Affairs
with the English Africa Company went badly and the whole coast was still
harassed by English pirating traders who 'by their sinister traffic . . . lowered
the price of European goods in Africa and rose the price of Africa goods'.

The Company appealed to the Government for protection and the sugges-
tion was made that for a period of thirteen years, which at the end of that time
was extended, the Guinea trade should be made free to all merchants whether
associated with the Company or not, in return for a duty of ten per cent to the
Company, levied with unjustified optimism, as it later transpired, for the upkeep of their ports and fortifications.

It opened the door to an even more sinister method of slaving. Before this
time most of the slaves transported by the Africa Company had been prisoners
who otherwise would have been put to death. They had been obtained by
native dealers from the chiefs, and they were carried in conditions which, by
seventeenth-century standards, were reasonably good. There was no kidnapping because, for purely practical reasons, the Company had to keep faith
with the natives in order to do business at all and to maintain their settlements
and stores.

With the admission of private adventurers to the trade, however, the old
order, though it had nothing to recommend it, deteriorated rapidly. The
newcomers had nothing to lose by kidnapping forays, for they could slip
away to sea before a just retribution overtook them. The competition for
slaves was so keen that, both in West Africa and Angola, traders went to the
length of promoting wars amongst the natives so that they could buy the
prisoners.

From the outset there were protests that Englishmen should be engaged in
the slave trade but the view of the English Parliament, which was supported
by most leading Churchmen, was that it was justified because it was a means
of bringing Africans in touch with Christianity: and it was supported by the

equally false but highly convenient argument that an all-wise God having decreed our lot in this world it was no one's business to question it.

Charles II established the Company of Royal Adventurers and while they were struggling to hold their own against the Dutch in West Africa the Dutch were developing their first settlement at the Cape, where Jan van Riebeck had arrived with his small band of colonists in 1651.

The commercial jealousy between the Dutch and English was still bitter despite temporary alliances and treaties. In 1662 Charles II married Catherine of Braganza and as part of her marriage dowry Portugal ceded the port of Bombay to England, providing a tremendous fillip to our India trade. It was a bitter pill for the Dutch and in 1665 the long succession of quarrels developed into open warfare.

In the City of London all this developing trade was bringing great wealth to her merchants and the city was spreading far beyond its ancient walls, as the population increased; but, as individual prosperity increased, the Corporation and the Companies which supported it grew poorer. An increasing number of craftsmen were moving out to the suburbs, where they could live and work free from Company control and the charges of membership. Even more serious was the fact that merchants, too, were moving away, to escape from the burden of sharing the government of the City, though at the same time making use of the port facilities which the Corporation maintained at its own expense.

The Companies complained and tried to enforce the rights granted to them by their charters. The City petitioned the Crown, saying that

the freedom of London which was heretofore of very great esteeme, is grown to be little worth, by reason of the extraordinary enlargement of the suburbs, where greate numbers of traders and handicraftsmen doe enjoy without charge, equally benefit with the freemen and citizens of London.

Both the City and the Crown attempted to check the tendency by prohibiting new building or the conversion of old houses into tenements within three miles of the City walls. James I and Charles I both issued proclamations which were disregarded and the Commonwealth government tried without success to forbid new building within ten miles of the City.

For the Corporation the solution would have been to incorporate the suburbs and create new wards, but this, for no very clear reason, it refused to do, despite several requests from Charles I and his advisers, who were anxious for the suburbs to come under a more orderly and efficient government than that provided by the new parishes.

However, the City Corporation took steps to ensure that the merchants who used its facilities, particularly those concerned with the new trading companies, took their full share of the responsibilities. By the first charter of Charles I, those living within ten miles of the City were compelled to take up their freedom if they wished to trade in the port. This helped things for a few years, but at a time of rapid expansion and development, the City was responsible for an increasing burden of vital services. It strove to maintain standards and prevent frauds in commodity dealings, as it had since medieval times, but it had no control over and received no dues from the new markets which had grown up in the suburbs. It was responsible for the conservancy of the Thames for the 60 miles from Staines to the estuary, which involved maintenance of the banks and continual scouring to preserve the passage for navigation, work which became more expensive every year, as the amount of shipping increased. In every direction, administration was growing more expensive and the burden of unpaid officials heavier.

During the years of the Commonwealth the Mayor and Corporation were able to retrench a little in such matters as elaborate entertainment, and since a good part of their income came from property in the City, their credit was good and they were able to borrow, paying interest out of income. By this time they had devised a valuable additional source of finance, too, from fines exacted from freemen who declined to take office as aldermen or Common Councillors because of the load of work it involved. The fine was on average £400 and many freemen paid it gladly, as the lesser of two evils.

As we have seen, during the Civil War, London, as well as most of the other seaports and manufacturing cities, was for Parliament, while the Royalist strongholds were in the rural and more conservative parts of the country, which had been least affected by the social and commercial changes of the previous hundred years.

Within the City, St Paul's was further desecrated when the soldiers of the Parliamentary armies used the ancient cathedral for the stabling of their horses. A few years earlier Crosby Hall had been used to accommodate two Russian ambassadors who had come to London to raise a loan of £60,000 from the merchants, but when war broke out the owner, the royalist second Earl of Northampton was in residence. He died for King Charles in 1642 but in his last letter to his wife, written only a few weeks earlier and sent to Crosby Hall, he wrote:

We hear of Mr Pym's motion for searching our houses. I hope you have taken care he shall not find much at Crosby Hall, and for the future we shall take such order that the searching of our country houses will be in little danger. Take care that your coach horses be not appointed for the militia.

Crosby Hall, like Gresham College and Lambeth Palace, became a temporary prison for 'malignants' who had remained loyal to King Charles and refused to lend money to Parliament. Amongst them was Sir John Langham, a Turkey merchant, who had taken a lease of Crosby Hall from the Northampton family and had become a sheriff of London. He was ultimately committed to Newgate and then to the Tower, but after some months the Commons, heeding the protests of the City and needing its money, released him, and a year or two later he was elected member of Parliament for the City, while at the Restoration he was one of the sixteen commissioners appointed to visit Charles at the Hague and invite him to 'take possession of his three kingdoms'.

Life in Commonwealth London was in many ways austere. Under the Puritan dictatorship the use of the prayer-book was forbidden. Soldiers had the right to enter people's houses to ensure that they were observing the Sabbath in the manner decreed by Parliament. The celebration of Christmas was banned. When John Evelyn was attending Christmas morning service at the chapel of Exeter House as 'the service was ended, and the Sacrament about to be administered, the chapel was surrounded by soldiers, and all the communicants and assembly surprised and kept prisoners'. They were detained for several hours and closely questioned. Evelyn was asked why 'contrary to an ordinance made, that no one should any longer observe the superstitious time of the Nativity, I durst offend. Finding no colour to detain me, they dismissed me with every pity of ignorance.'

All the London theatres were closed and most of them demolished; and everywhere Sunday games were banned. William Davenant, Shakespeare's godson, occasionally put on a play at the old Cockpit in Drury Lane, but on at least one occasion Puritan soldiers broke in, drove away the audience, broke up the seats and the stage, took away all the props and costumes and locked up the actors for a few days.

Yet Cromwell did a great deal for the education of boys and was strict in the licensing of schoolmasters and the administration of education endowments. There was a strong body of Puritan opinion which wanted to abolish the universities, but Cromwell not only defended them but established a new readership in Divinity at Oxford and tried to found new universities in London and in the north of England.

It was in the financial and commercial affairs of the City that real progress was made. In 1655 Cromwell's government, disliking monopolies, made the Indian trade free to all merchants and the East India Company suffered such severe loss that it was almost bankrupted, but only two years later the order was revoked and the Company given back all its former powers. It now became a joint-stock company. Until this time, money, on the joint stock principle, had been raised for each voyage. Sometimes it would produce a profit of as much as 30 per cent, but often it was far less, and if ships had been wrecked or captured the venture was, of course, a total loss, unless the Company had invested in the increasing practice of marine insurance. Now a permanent fund was created and this new general stock became highly profitable to the few who were fortunate enough to possess it, for by 1685 the market price of £100 stock was to reach £500.

During the Civil War nearly all the surplus money had found its way to the goldsmiths of Cheapside and Lombard Street and they in their turn lent it at the permitted rate of 6 per cent to men needing capital for fresh commercial enterprises. There was still a lingering prejudice against usury as an immoral practice but many years earlier a realist had observed that 'he who takes it goes to hell, and he who does not goes to the work house', and now that it had become legal the political economists argued successfully that there could be no moral rule beyond the letter of the law.

The number of London bankers increased, an important source of their finance being now the rents of the landed gentry. The bankers lent money to private individuals and the method of paying orders on bankers to the bearer on demand became common usage.

The records of the Russell family give an excellent example of the way the new method of handling large amounts of cash evolved. The family derived their income from the rents of their large estates in the West country, in East Anglia and Covent Garden. The money was collected by the various agents, brought to London in money bags and deposited in a large chest which was kept at Bedford House. There are no records of the messengers ever having been attacked by highwaymen, for they were well guarded, but it must have been a highly dangerous exercise and by the 1630s a safer and more convenient method was devised for the collection of the money from Devon and Cornwall. The bailiffs of the West country manors brought the money and their statements of accounts twice a year to the Russells' steward living at Russell House in Exeter. He then arranged a bill of exchange to be drawn on Thomas Viner, the London goldsmith of Lombard Street. When Viner had received it he informed the family's 'receiver general' at Bedford House, who then proceeded to Lombard Street, equipped with money bags and attended by two porters, to receive the cash, which was carried back to Bedford House and locked away in the chest.

From the accumulation of money in the chest the Earl made a certain number of small, short-term loans, at six per cent, and sometimes less, to private individuals and tradesmen, on the security of a mortgage or bond. These were repaid in cash and replaced in the chest, and not until the Restoration did the family take to the practice of depositing all its surplus coin with a goldsmith and dispensing with the chest.

When Charles II returned to England in 1660 he found the City of London little different from that of his boyhood. Houses in the main streets of Bishopsgate and Cheapside, Threadneedle Street and Lombard Street, where the rich merchants lived, were splendid in appearance but only a few were built of stone, the rest being timber-framed with a brick and plaster filling. Over the years, as additions had been made, many had extended in whichever direction there happened to be space, and this was most often in front of the original building. With no consideration for frontage lines, streets had inevitably become narrower, with bottle-necks where buildings had been brought forward to the limit of inconvenience. Threadneedle Street, for example, had dwindled to eleven feet in width and Thames Street was as narrow in places, where warehouses jutted out far into the roadway.

Church wardens increased their church revenues by letting the frontages of churchyards for buildings and also the space between the church and the street.

Behind the main streets the maze of side streets, narrow alleyways and courtyards grew denser and more complicated each year and the dwelling houses were sketchily built, often made from nothing but weather boarding nailed to timber frames.

With the large consumption of wood for house and ship building, timber had become in short supply, and since Elizabethan times coal for fuel had been shipped to London from Newcastle by sea. By the seventeenth century it was used by everyone, the smoke of thousands of chimneys in the small, congested area adding its quota of dirt and dust.

Markets still blocked the streets. The meat market and the butchers' stalls straddled Newgate Street. There were stalls in Cheapside and Leadenhall Street and the Stocks market blocked the corner of Cornhill and the Poultry.

Open gutters ran along the middle of many of the streets and the corners were often blocked by huge water conduits or by lay stalls, the contents of which were periodically collected and carried down river for disposal.

The Fleet river which had once been navigable as far inland as Holborn Bridge had become congested with refuse and silt and degenerated into an evil smelling sewer, 'very stinking and noisome' – not the least of the horrors for the inmates of the Fleet prison on its shores, just below the City wall.

Narrow cobbled streets had been sufficient for pack horses and porters but were totally inadequate for the wheeled traffic which, to the consternation of the Thames watermen, was being increasingly used in London and causing terrible congestion.

Carriers had been operating since Tudor times and by the seventeenth century there were regular services each week from most of the important towns to London. From Doncaster a carrier arrived on Fridays at the Belle Sauvage on Ludgate Hill, returning the next day or the following Monday to Yorkshire, the Northampton carrier arrived at Smithfield, the Cambridge carrier at the George in Holborn.

Both private and hired or 'hackneyed' coaches were coming increasingly into use, and as early as 1605 the Thames watermen had lodged a complaint that 'coaches have increased with a mischief, and have ruined the trade of the watermen by hackney coaches, and now multiply more than ever'.

They were extremely uncomfortable at first, with no springs and leather curtains in place of windows, and the Thames boats were often a good deal quicker, but they were dependent on the weather and the tide. It cost more to be rowed against the tide than with it, and in wintry conditions passengers had no protection.

The first hackney coach rank appeared in London in 1634, forming at the maypole in the Strand. These hackney 'Hell Carts' caused frightful traffic jams and when two met head on there was no room to give way, even if they had wanted to, which was very seldom. Wheels came off and coaches overturned, to the delight of the onlookers and the mortification of the passengers. Drivers haggled over fares and drove too fast. By 1635 there was an attempt to suppress them, but the coachmen had no intention of going out of business, and within a few weeks, after much argument and protest, 50 hackney coachmen were licensed again, being allowed twelve horses each. It was about this time that sedan chairs appeared in London, and while some people welcomed them, as a possible solution to London's traffic problem, it was a long time before they became fashionable, for there was at first a 'loathing that men should be brought to as servile condition as horses', and it was not until Queen Anne's time that there were some 300 licensed chairmen in London, as well as many privately owned sedan chairs, whereas by 1669 there were 800 hackney coachmen in London and Westminster, plying for hire.

The exact date of the beginning of a public coach service is not certain, but by 1637 two coaches were running each week between St Albans and the Bell Inn, Aldersgate, and there were also services to Hertford and Cambridge, which were probably made by coach during the summer and wagon in winter.

There was little development of the coaching services during the Civil War but by 1647 there was a regular service between Rochester and Gravesend, the place of embarkation for the Long Ferry to London. By 1656 there was a coach service from London to York and in 1657 a public coach to Chester, the port for Ireland, ran three days a week. Two or three years later coaches were running from London to Durham and Newcastle, Preston, Manchester and Kendal as well as to Exeter and Plymouth in the west, all of them established by the proprietors of the City of London inns, and as their coaching business increased so did the comfort and amenities of their inns. The first stage coaches had also come into use by this time and these, with the far cheaper stage wagons, all of them running from the London inns, added to the confusion and congestion of the City.

The bitter complaints as well as suggestions for solving the problem, by widening the roads, came in to the Guildhall in about equal numbers, but few people realised that by the time of the Restoration the City Corporation was on the verge of bankruptcy.

In 1664 the King and his cabal declared war on Holland. It was against the advice of Lord Clarendon and the Earl of Southampton but was thought to have been made under pressure from Henry Bennet, Lord Arlington, who had interests in the new Royal Africa Company and had much to gain by a quick victory over the Dutch, which would stop their trade rivalry in West Africa. Gilbert Burnet, in his *History of My Own Time*, said that the reasons 'were so slight that it was visible there was somewhat more at bottom than was openly owned. . . . The house of commons was so far from examining nicely into the grounds of the war, that without any difficulty they gave the King two million and a half for carrying it on'.

Early in May 1665 the English navy put to sea, and that same month the first case for 30 years of the bubonic plague occurred in St Giles. More people succumbed. Cases were reported from Holborn and the disease gradually moved eastwards. By the end of the month 43 cases were recorded.

On 6th June Pepys wrote in his diary: 'This day much against my will I did in Drury Lane see two or three houses marked with a red cross upon the door, and "Lord have mercy upon us" writ there; which was a sad sight to see, being the first of the kind that, to my remembrance, I ever saw.'

In June there were 590 cases. The Court moved first to Salisbury, where cases of the plague soon occurred, and then to Oxford, which remained immune, Barbara Castlemaine being given rooms at Merton College, about which she was soon complaining: but here they all remained for the next five months. The Judges moved to the edge of Hampstead Heath and today's Judges' Walk, once known as King's Bench Avenue, is the spot where they are said to have held their courts under the trees.

It was an exceptionally hot summer, with never a drop of rain or a cloud in the sky. In July there were 6,000 cases in the City. Half the population fled. Shops closed. Business came to a standstill. Craftsmen and labourers were thrown out of work and the quays were deserted, as shipping came to a stand-still. As the wealthier citizens fled, many of the doctors and Anglican clergy-men went with them. The pulpits were mainly left to the Nonconconformists, who declared to their terrified congregations that the plague was a punish-ment for their evil ways, but the gathering together of so many people only spread the infection and the meetings had to be discontinued.

The people were not altogether deserted, however, The Archbishop of Canterbury stayed at Lambeth Palace and the Lord Mayor ordered all the aldermen, sheriffs, common councillors and other officers to remain at their posts.

In August there were 18,000 plague victims, and in September 30,000. They were either taken to the pest houses or isolated in their own homes, from which no one was allowed to leave. Guards were posted outside the doors which bore the dreaded red cross and delivered supplies of food.

The quacks offered the wildest remedies but no one knew what to do. The doctors who stayed did their best. Some were put in charge of the pest houses and in July four were appointed to attempt to deal with the situation. Seven more doctors soon joined them, dividing the wards of the city between them and giving their services free. Recognizing that the plague was a disease of contact, they took precautions. Prophylactics were burned in the fireplaces of an infected household before they entered it. Some recommended tobacco. Public meetings and funerals were forbidden. Goods were not allowed to be removed from plague-infested areas and victims were not buried in the church-yards. Each night the death cart made its melancholy round of the streets, the carter's bell accompanied by the mournful cry, 'Bring out your dead'. The bodies were then taken to specially dug plague pits, where they were tipped in and destroyed by quicklime.

As the business of the City died the thousands who were without work or wages would have starved, but the King sent £1,000 a week to help, the City gave £600 a week and the merchants were equally generous, so that the Lord Mayor was able to arrange an efficient supply of food.

As ships arrived at the docks, to find the City stricken, some returned down-stream and others remained at anchor, afraid to land. Some families shut them-selves up in their houses and did not stir out of doors for weeks, for fear of contagion. One grocer in Wood Street, Cheapside, for example, shut himself up with his wife, five children and two maidservants for five months, allowing nothing into the house except necessary food, which was admitted through one upper window, after being fumigated with gun-powder, but he stationed his porter Abraham outside the door, to collect the news. The grocer's family survived, for theirs was the only house in the street to remain immune, but

Abraham caught the plague and died. His wife, before she herself died, sent another porter to replace Abraham, but in only a few days he also sickened and died.

Defoe in his *History of the Plague*, written 50 years later, gives an even more terrible picture of the awful silence and desolation in the City. He walked down to Blackwall, where he saw a poor man walking alone on the seawall. Keeping at a safe distance, he called out to him to ask him how people did thereabouts.

'Alas! Sir,' says he, 'almost desolate: all dead or sick. Here are very few families in this part, or in the village' (pointing at Poplar), 'where half of them are dead already, and the rest sick.' Then he, pointing to one house: 'There they are all dead,' said he. . . . Then he pointed to several other houses. 'There' says he 'they are all dead, the man and his wife and five children. There' says he, 'they are shut up; you see a watchman at the door; and so of other houses.'

He was a waterman and was maintaining his wife and two children by taking food each day to some ten ships lying at anchor in the river. 'All these ships have families on board, of their merchants and owners, and such like, who have locked themselves up, and live on board, close shut in, for fear of infection; and I tend on them to fetch things for them, carry letters, and do what is absolutely necessary, that they may not be obliged to come on shore,' he said, but he lived on his boat, making direct contact neither with his own family nor the merchant ships, for he left the money for his wife on the quayside, and the goods for the merchants in their small boats, moored alongside the merchantmen.

The plague 'broke the trade of the nation and swept away about a hundred thousand souls: the greatest havoc that any plague had ever made in England,' wrote Burnet. 'This did dishearten all people; and coming in the very time in which so unjust a war was begun, it had a dreadful appearance. All the king's enemies, and the enemies of the monarchy, said here was a manifest character of God's heavy displeasure upon the nation. . . .'

As autumn approached, the plague gradually spent itself and people began to return to the stricken city, but they came too soon, for there were more spasmodic outbreaks. On 1st October Pepys wrote:

I to Lombard Streete, but can get no money. So upon the Exchange, which is very empty, God knows! . . . Lord, how empty the streets are and melancholy, so many poor sick people in the streets full of sores: and so many sad stories overheard as I walk, everybody talking of this dead, and that man sick, and so many in this place, and so many in that.

Pepys had much to worry him, for the navy was not being paid. 'God knows what will become of all the King's matters in a little time,' he wrote, 'for he runs in debt every day, and nothing to pay them looked after'.

And through it all the Dutch war intensified. In June the battle of Lowestoft was a victory for the English, but the Dutch, undaunted, accepted help from the Danes and then from the French: and in the English Channel and the North Sea the Dutch admiral, De Ruyter, was pitting his wits against Prince Rupert, the Duke of York and the Duke of Albemarle.

By 22nd November Pepys was able to record that 'the plague is come very low . . . and great hope of a further decrease, because of this day's being a very exceeding hard frost, and continues freezing'. On Change it was 'pretty full again', but all the talk was of the calamity of the times, the lack of ready money, the king's extravagance and the rumours that the Dutch were preparing to land on the east coast. By the end of the month Pepys, with many misgivings, was venturing to use a hackney coach again. 'it being unsafe to go by water in the dark and frosty cold', but there were still 'few people in the streets, nor shops open'. He also reported that the goldsmiths 'do decry the new Act, for money to be all brought into the Exchequer, and paid out thence, saying they will not advance one farthing upon it . . .', a decree which in a year or two was to have disastrous consequences for some of the moneylenders, but they had been charging very heavy interest rates, far in excess of the accepted 6 per cent, doubtful, perhaps of the securities offered.

On 19th January 1663 Pepys had said that the Navy office was angry that the goldsmiths were charging them 15 to 20 per cent, 'which is a most horrid shame and that which must not be suffered', and a few months later he recorded how Sir John Hebden 'cries out against the King's dealing so much with the gold-smiths, and suffering himself to have his purse kept and commanded by them'.

The plague still lingered all through the winter of 1665-6 and as late as July 1666 there were still cases in London and it was raging in Colchester. On 6th August Pepys met Mr Battersby in Fenchurch Street. 'Do you see Dan Rawlin-son's door shut up?' he said. . . . 'After all the sickness and himself spending all last year in the country, one of his men is now dead of the plague, and his wife and one of his mayds sicke, and himself shut up.' Pepys, mightily troubled, returned home only to hear from Mrs Sarah Daniel that 'Greenwich is at this time worse than ever it was, and Deptford too' and that people from the infected areas were now coming to London.

Less than four weeks after this, during the night of 2nd September, a fire broke out in the most crowded part of the City, close to London Bridge and Billingsgate market. It occurred in a baker's house in the narrow Pudding Lane which joins Thames Street to Eastcheap. With buckets of water and a hand pump, the only fire-fighting apparatus at hand, the baker tried to put it out, but in vain. It spread in all directions. Three hours later the adjoining houses were ablaze and a strong east wind carried the sparks across to the inn yard opposite. A pile of hay caught and then the inn, and in a few moments the fire had spread to the warehouses of Thames Street, stocked full of tallow, oil, wine and spirits.

Driven by the wind, the flames spread westwards. By six o'clock on Sunday morning all Fish Street was ablaze and the fire was spreading so quickly that the panic-stricken people barely had time to run from their houses, salvaging what they could of their possessions. Some took them to the churches for safe-keeping. The booksellers of Paternoster Row carried their books into the crypt of St Paul's. Soon people were fleeing for their lives. Hundreds took to the river craft, others to the fields of Moorgate.

The Lord Mayor, summoned from his bed, would have pulled down the houses in front of the fire to make a fire-break but hesitated to do so before asking the consent of the owners: and he also wondered who would be expec-ted to foot the bill.

It was Pepys who took the news to Whitehall and when it had reached the King he at once sent orders that the Lord Mayor was to 'spare no houses, but to pull down before the fire every way' and sent soldiers to help. They found the City panic-stricken and the Mayor distraught. 'Lord! What can I do?' he cried. 'I am spent. People will not obey me. I have been pulling down houses, but the fire overtakes us faster than we can do it.'

All that day people were frantically moving their possessions from the roar-ing, driving fire. 'We stayed till, it being darkish, we saw the fire as only one entire arch of fire from this to the other side of the bridge and in a bow up the hill for an arch of above a mile long; it made me weep to see it,' wrote Pepys. 'The churches, houses, and all on fire, and flaming at once; and a horrid noise the flames made, and the crackling of houses at their ruin.'

The King and the Duke of York came down by barge, to find that it was too late. The wind still blew and the flames roared through the City. The following morning the King took control, putting the Duke of York in charge of estab-lishing stations in an arc round the fire, each manned by a member of the Privy Council, three Justices of the Peace, 30 soldiers, the parish constables and 100 men: and the Lord Lieutenants of the Counties were ordered to send all their militia, as well as workmen, tools and provisions. Yet by Monday night the Royal Exchange had gone, much of Cheapside, as well as Thames Street from east of Billingsgate to Puddle Dock, and the next day St Paul's and Christchurch, Newgate, died in the flames and the Guildhall was severely damaged.

The King and the Duke of York helped to make fire lanes, but as sparks leapt across them and made the work useless, they took to the desperate last measure of blowing up whole streets with gunpowder. This caused more panic than ever, as the terrified citizens were convinced for a time that it was an invasion by the Dutch or the French. Buildings in the Strand were blown up to save Somerset House and the alarm spread to Westminster, but late on the Tuesday evening the wind changed and died. Isolated fires still burned but it gave the fire-fighters a chance, and by this time there were many more of them. By nightfall the danger had passed, and although fires still smouldered in cellars and vaults, and were to do so for several days more, the sky was no longer 'all on a fire in the night'. But four-fifths of the city lay in ruins.

I walked into the town, and find Fenchurche-streete, Gracious-streete and Lumbard-streete all in dust. The Exchange a sad sight. . . . Walked into Moorfields (our feet ready to burn, walking through the towne among the hot coles) and find that full of people and poor wretches carrying their goods there. . . . Thence homeward, having passed through Cheapside and Newgate Market, all burned . . . all the towne burned and a miserable sight of St Paul's church with all the roof fallen, and the body of the quire fallen into St Fayth . . . .' wrote Pepys.

John Evelyn, describing the end of St Paul's, said that the stones 'flew like grenadoes, the melting lead running down the streets in a stream and the very pavements glowing with fiery redness, so as no horse, nor man was able to tread on them . . .', and on 7th September he wrote:

It was astonishing to see what immense stones the heat had in a manner calcined, and projectures of massy Portland stone flew off, even to the very roof, where a sheet of lead covering a great space . . . was totally melted. The ruins of the vaulted roof falling, broke into St Faith's, which being filled with the magazines of books belonging to the Stationers, and carried thither for safety, they were all consumed, burning for a week following.

That same day he wrote that 'Sir Th. Gresham's statue, tho' fallen from its nich at the Royal Exchange, remained intire, when all those of ye Kings since ye Conquest were broken to pieces.'

It was the most disastrous fire that Europe had ever known. A sober estimate of the damage was that 436 acres of the City, over 300 of them within the walls, had been destroyed, including 13,200 houses, the halls of 44 of the Companies,

89 parish churches, as well as St Paul's Cathedral, the Royal Exchange, the Customs House, part of the Guildhall and four of the City gates. The value of the commodities lost in the warehouses was estimated at about three and a half million pounds and the total loss, including buildings, furniture and personal possessions, at more than ten million, which at the current values was a calamitous figure which many could barely comprehend.

Louis XIV was shocked and even sympathetic, the Dutch grimly satisfied that Heaven had wreaked a terrible vengeance.

The most pressing need was to house the homeless. The King provided tents and also gave the City permission to put up rough temporary shelters in Moorfields. New markets were established and arrangements made for the care of the sick and destitute. Moreover, King Charles ordered all the corporate towns to set aside their labour restrictions and allow London refugees to practise their manual trades within their walls, in order that they could resume their livelihoods.

Within four days the Londoners had been housed, however inadequately, many of the artisans having put up little sheds on the smouldering ruins of their former dwellings. Some sought accommodation in the unburnt parts of the City and here, inevitably, rents soared. Others were soon acquiring leases of suburban properties, setting up shops in the Strand or moving down to Wapping and Deptford. A few, taking advantage of the fact that King Charles had opened the way for them, moved further afield. London merchants moved to Bristol, to engage in the tobacco trade, or to Liverpool, where opportunities were opening. Mr Smith, for example, 'a sugar baker of London', arrived in Liverpool, rented a piece of land and built the town's first sugar refinery for West Indian sugar, and from this time Liverpool became the most important centre for sugar refining in the country.

The Corporation of London was well aware of the danger of this exodus. London had to be rebuilt as quickly as possible and the population, with all its skills, trading connections and accumulated wealth, held together, or the whole organisation might disintegrate. The City government established itself in Gresham College, as did the Exchange, and the Custom House moved to Mark Lane. Within a week both John Evelyn and Christopher Wren had submitted plans to the King for a new city. There was general agreement that it must be less congested and built of less inflammable materials. King Charles was genuinely anxious that the new city should be more beautiful, with wide streets like those he had known in Holland, but his more urgent concern was that the City should begin functioning again as soon as possible. London was the principal port of the kingdom. Her stores, as well as her merchants and financiers were vital, while the Treasury was almost entirely maintained by the advances of her bankers, which were made on the security of customs and excise revenues.

Clarendon wrote that 'through Fire and Plague the two great Branches of the Revenue, the Customs and Excise, which was the great and almost inexhaustible Security to borrow Money upon, were now bankrupt, and would neither bring in Money nor supply Credit'.

A third source of revenue was 'chimney money' but there were now few chimneys left. The wharves were piled high with rubbish and the streets blocked with it. The landing stage and markets had gone. The water works on London Bridge had been destroyed and the supply pipes damaged.

By 13th September the King had issued a proclamation that rebuilding would be carried out in brick or stone with streets of a safe width. The City was asked to prepare a survey of the damage, showing the ownership of each plot and the conditions of occupation of the tenants. A preliminary plan was then to be made, with the new frontage lines, and citizens who might lose ground because of it were to be compensated.

But before the plan could be made, the city had to be cleared of rubbish. In places it was said to have been four feet deep and the task was not completed until December.

The King appointed Christopher Wren, Hugh May and Roger Pratt as Commissioners for Rebuilding, to work with the City surveyors Robert Hooke, Edward Jerman and Peter Mills, but the question of who was to pay for it all had not yet been considered.

The survey was complicated by many factors. Original building lines were not easy to establish and people who were to lose part of their ground, in order to conform to the new plan, demanded heavy compensation. Most of the citizens were living in leasehold properties and were therefore responsible for the rebuilding of their houses. The landlords were mainly people who had bought freehold properties or acquired long leases as an investment. It was a usual way of providing for widows and marriage portions. The City derived a quarter of its revenues from rents. Companies, hospitals and the churches were all drawing income from tenants and many charitable bequests and school endowments had been invested in this way.

The fire had therefore destroyed the savings of hundreds of people and there was little or no money available to help them. Parliament was too heavily involved in the Dutch war and already hard-pressed trying to repay money which had been advanced to them by citizens, on the security of Parliamentary taxes. The Exchequer could not help, for the King was already in debt and the yield from taxations had fallen short of expectations. The City was already spending in excess of income and facing an estimated £100,000 for the restora tion of its necessary public buildings, apart from the suggested improvements for the new City, which would entail about one and a half million pounds. A municipal or national loan was not feasible and the business of long-term borrowing had not yet been devised, most loans at this time being of less than £500 for terms of only three to six months.

In 1667 Parliament passed the first Rebuilding Act and from June of that year the City was granted for ten years a levy of one shilling per ton on all the coal coming into London. This enabled the Corporation to keep the course of affairs in its own hands but the grant was soon to prove totally inadequate, for it yielded an income of only £15,000 a year over the next three years.

The war with Holland was going badly and in June 1667 the country had suffered its worst ignominy. The greater part of the English fleet, including the proud flagships *Royal Charles* and *Royal James*, were laid up in Chatham docks, almost undefended. The Dutch sailed up the Medway, sending fireships ahead into the docks, which destroyed the *Royal Oak*, the *Royal London* and the *Royal James*, as well as many smaller vessels. The English were hopelessly unprepared and when the fireships had done their damage, the Dutch sailed away with the *Royal Charles* and the *Unity*. As Burnet said: 'The business of Chatham was a terrible blow; and though the loss was great, the infamy was greater.'

After this the Dutch took to raiding the trawlers from Newcastle bringing the precious coal to London. The Newcastle men hesitated to put to sea and on more than one occasion the City had to send its own protection vessels up to Newcastle, to escort the supplies down to London.

By 1670 the City was granted an additional two shillings per ton on coal for the next ten years. Three-quarters of the extra duty was to be spent on rebuilding the churches, a quarter of this sum to be set aside for St Paul's. The remaining quarter went to the City, but they had to render a strict account to Parliament of their expenditure.

At last the City was staked out with its revised plots and widened streets. Compensation was agreed for any loss of ground and a Fire Court was established in Clifford's Inn, where claims and disputes were heard quickly and efficiently.

The Rebuilding Act had decreed that conduits were to be removed from the main streets and the building line must be kept straight. The width of the streets was defined and they were to be paved. There were to be no spouting gutters from the rooftops, as in the old days, but pipes were to be fixed down the sides of houses. There was to be no wood on the outside of the houses and no jerry building.

The working of the Act was left to the City, who now took over control from the local authorities, insisting that the new houses were to be of a uniform

G

pattern, in the rigid convention first adopted by Inigo Jones and later by Wren, and in complete contrast to the old timbered houses with their casement windows and gables and high pitched roofs. The new brick houses were plain and square and comfortable, with hipped roofs, similar to those which were shortly to be built in Mayfair, and Wren's influence on house design was to last all through the eighteenth and early nineteenth centuries. Three types were allowed. The largest of them, intended for fronting the main streets of the City, comprised four storeys, built over a cellar, and a garret floor built into the roof. For other streets, the more important lanes and the riverside, houses of three storeys, with a garret and cellar, were to be built, and for the side streets and less important lanes two-storey houses, with garrets and cellars.

The cost of the largest of these homes was about £400, and for the next size only £300, so for people who had this amount of money stored away in their private chests, rebuilding was a feasible proposition. They had been guaranteed an extension of their leases, and with rents rising, they could recover their outlay, at 12 per cent, within a few years. For those who did not wish to rebuild or could not afford to, their leases were cancelled and the landlord was then free to rebuild himself or offer terms to another prospective tenant. If any sites were left unbuilt, those responsible were given nine months to begin the work or forfeit their rights, in which case the City valued them and sold them to anyone willing to buy.

Those who had no spare cash were therefore cast out and left to fend for themselves and there was inevitably a good deal of hardship. The City Companies were amongst the sufferers. Less than a quarter of the large sums of money they had lent King Charles and Parliament during the 1640s had been repaid and some Companies had received nothing at all. Their membership was dwindling and their grasp on industry weakening. Now many had lost not only their halls but property from which they had been receiving an income of rents.

The Drapers lost their hall and beautiful garden, on which they had recently spent £1,000, but much of their landed property was intact and they owned trust funds placed in loans whose security was not affected by the Fire. The Goldsmiths lost property worth £1,000 a year in rents and had many unpaid debts. The Grocers were already in debt but had been hoping for substantial funds from leases just due for renewal. They lost them all and were left with a debt of £20,000 and no assets. From 1672 to 1679 creditors occupied the roughly repaired ruins of their hall, and although they were able to move back in 1680, they were impoverished for many years.

The companies sold plate, borrowed on mortgage, collected contributions from members and appealed for a general increase of the livery. Of the 44 halls destroyed only three were never rebuilt. Many were re-established by 1672, although the court rooms and parlours had to be added later, as funds became available. By 1685 most were back in their old splendour, albeit on borrowed money, and it was not until the 1740s that they were really prosperous again. This was when the new building leases made after the Fire were due for renewal, by which time the value of their properties had greatly increased. These were the years of their greatest prosperity, although they came at a time when the Companies had outlived their original function in London's industry.

To speed the work of rebuilding the City, labourers and workmen were brought into London, with the inducement that if they worked there for seven years they would be allowed the same liberties as freemen for the rest of their lives, yet two years after the fire none of the churches had been restored, the City and the merchants were still using temporary accommodation and only 800 house sites had been claimed or bought for rebuilding.

The rebuilding of the churches began in 1670 and went on for the next 30 years, and the first stone of the new St Paul's was not laid until 1765. There was a general reorganisation of the parishes, and several were amalgamated, so that 35 fewer parish churches were needed.

The City spread its own rebuilding programme over seven years, beginning with the Guildhall and Sessions House, the Royal Exchange and the Customs House.

The Exchange, designed by Edward Jerman, was enlarged, and this entailed the buying of more land, but by September 1669 the merchants had moved into the new building and by 1671 the shops were ready and had all been let. However, Sir Thomas Gresham's trustees – the City and the Goldsmiths' Company – had had to borrow heavily and it was many years before the Exchange was making enough profit for their debt to be discharged.

By November 1671 the Guildhall had been sufficiently restored for the Lord Mayor's banquet to be held there again and the new Custom House, designed by Wren, was finished. The two Compters and Ludgate were almost finished and 7,359 sites for new houses had now been bought, with building proceeding quickly.

The City struggled on with its programme, by now paying heavy interest on loans made by the Goldsmiths, Grocers and Drapers. They rebuilt the cloth markets at Blackwell Hall and Welch Hall, where all the cloth made in England and brought to the City had to be passed for quality and for the duty to be charged. They built new markets at Honey Lane and south of Newgate Street. They bought the Stocks market from its owners and re-sited it. Leadenhall market had not been damaged by the Fire but the Corporation enlarged it by buying the ground of two adjacent gardens. They rebuilt Doctors' Commons, Sion College and the College of Arms. Christ's Hospital had had to pay for the rebuilding of the houses on its lands, but the City reimbursed them and the school itself was reinstated by private charity, the children, who had been sent to Hertfordshire, being back again in enlarged and more comfortable quarters by 1674.

The City monument, designed by Wren, was completed the following year, and at the western approach to the City, beyond the limits of the Fire, the widened Temple Bar was built to replace the old, much narrower gate.

Both Wren and Evelyn had included in their first plans a development of the Fleet river, which had once been navigable as far as Holborn bridge, but had degenerated into a narrow, evil-smelling sewer, choked with silt which had come down from the northern heights of London and an accumulation of household refuse, and fringed with a slum of decaying tenements, sheds and lay-stalls. They saw it as a neat canal, in the manner of the Dutch cities. Wren planned a canal 40 feet wide, running inland for half a mile and flanked by wharves 30 feet wide, with underground storehouses beneath them. Along each wharf were to be uniform houses of the second grade and the canal was to be arched with bridges high enough for the passage of lighters.

From May 1672 until October 1674 the contractor had 200 men working on the site, scouring the river, trying to check the silt and remove the refuse which was continually dumped in it, in their efforts to make a 40 foot channel. The City spent over £50,000 on the project, hoping to recover the cost from tolls and wharfage dues. The canal was cut and the wharves built, but the scheme was a failure. Few people wanted to rent the storehouses. Even fewer wanted to use the canal. Carts and coaches, parked on the wharves, broke the pavements and endangered the roofing of the vaults below.

It could have looked delightful but the truth was that road traffic was newer and on the increase, while water traffic was declining. The canal remained for a few years but in 1733 it was arched over from Holborn Bridge to Fleet Bridge to make a roadway, where the old Stocks market was established, and this ultimately became the Farringdon Road, while in 1766 the lower reach of the canal was covered, as an approach road to Blackfriars Bridge, which was built in 1769.

Another plan which greatly interested King Charles was the building of the Thames Quay from the Tower to the Temple, making a broad, paved quay flanked by houses, again in the Dutch style. Before the fire the water front had been a confusion of sheds, yards, landing places, lay-stalls and water steps approached by an inconvenient network of narrow, steep lanes. Orders were made for the clearing away of existing buildings but nothing more was done for a year or two, for other concerns were more pressing.

By the time the second Rebuilding Act was passed in April 1670, the stretch of riverside below the bridge, as far as the Tower, had already been rebuilt, according to the new building regulations, by the private owners of the wharves, for they were vital for the larger ships now using the port, and Billingsgate had grown into an important fish market.

Above the bridge the traffic was mainly lighters and barges, and Queenhithe was by now of less importance than Billingsgate, but on this stretch of the river arrived timber, building materials and coal, as well as a large quantity of fruit, all of which needed enclosed storage space on the wharves. Little had been done here and orders were re-issued for existing sheds and storehouses to be taken down, as well as the charred ruins of Baynard's Castle and other fire wreckage. After that nothing more was done, although piecemeal improvements were made as the money became available.

By 1672 King Charles was faced with bankruptcy, and at a meeting of the Privy Council, at which he was present, Sir Thomas Clifford proposed 'That as the King must have money to carry on the war against Holland, in which his honour was engaged, he knew of no other means at present than shutting up of the Exchequer.' The King, with many apologies, promised that 'it should only be for the space of one whole year, ending the last day of December next; that then no new orders shall intervene to break the course of such payments'. It confirmed the goldsmiths' worst fears, for it meant that the King had appropriated their money, amounting to £1,328,526, which he had insisted on being deposited at the Exchequer, and intended to treat it as a loan at 6 per cent. For a time there was no money available to make their payments to customers and many bankers and their customers were financially ruined.

The same year the City was also in dire straits and was forced to appropriate more of the coal dues, but the work of rebuilding went on.

By 1676 a vastly improved and restored City had come into existence, with neat brick or stone houses in orderly rows. Drains and sewers had been laid and water from the New River Company or the rival London Bridge Waterworks was already being supplied to many of the dwellings. Markets had been moved from the main streets, which were now provided with pedestrian tracks, protected by posts. Streets had been widened and even the least important were now the minimum fourteen feet, with gutters at the sides instead of running down the middle. In the south and west of the City, where the streets climbed up steeply from the Thames and the Fleet, gradients had been reduced. The approach roads and those running through the City had been made wide

and straight, while in its heart the new Royal Exchange, cleared of the clutter
of buildings which had surrounded the old one, was now the focal point of
the widened Poultry, Cornhill and Lombard Street as well as the new Prince
Street, and goldsmiths, bankers and important merchants all took houses
in this area, together with an increasing number of Jews, whom Cromwell
had readmitted, thereby creating a vitally important financial centre.

Yet as early as 1673 the City realised that many of the new houses were not
yet occupied. A census gave the number as 3,425, which represented a large
sum in unpaid rates. London, with its heavy rates and taxes, was becoming too
costly. Prosperous trade was moving westwards. The silk mercers, for example
were establishing themselves in the streets round Covent Garden, while the
poor were still crowding into the suburban slums to the north and east
beyond the City's jurisdiction, where the Fire had not reached and where the
living conditions were appalling and steadily deteriorating.

The City did not want them back. It needed solid tradesmen and merchants
Aldermen and Common Councillors living outside the City were ordered to
return. Then inducements were offered to others. First freemen of the Com
panies living outside London who were not freemen of the City were invited
to move in, being offered the freedom of the City without payment. A few
began to arrive. Then the price of freedom by purchase was reduced and
admission to even the most exclusive companies made easier.

The empty houses slowly filled but the whole system of selling or bestowing
the freedom of the City was breaking down, as the suburbs spread and the
population increased and the very walls were crumbling, never to be restored
The medieval privileges had become anachronisms and the freedom of little
value. In 1685 came the final humiliation. The interest the Corporation was
paying on its debts was far in excess of its income. The government of the City
of London had become bankrupt and had to declare a moratorium. But it was
allowed to live on. Its wealthy citizens supported it and it was to rise again
new splendour, still the ruler of the illustrious square mile.

The beautiful Wren churches were built: St Michael's, Cornhill; St Bride
Fleet Street; St Mary-le-Bow, Cheapside; St Stephen, Walbrook – one after
another they appeared, with large windows, galleries and simple altars, clea
lined and light, their tall stone spires soaring over the roof tops and markin
the parishes. Over the years more than 60 were built and Wren had a hand
many of them.

The building of St Paul's is a long, sad story. From the time the first stone was
laid in 1675 Wren seemed to be thwarted. His first plan for the new Cathedra
had been a Greek cross with a large central dome supported by eight pillar
This was rejected by the Commissioners appointed to supervise the building

and the new design adopted, with a long nave, in the Gothic tradition, and recesses along the side aisles which James II, confident that the country would soon be restored to Roman Catholicism, hoped would be used for side chapels.

For more than 40 years Wren laboured at the Cathedral, superintending every detail of the decoration. His Clerk of the Works was Nicholas Hawksmoor and amongst his team of superb craftsmen were Grinling Gibbons, Tijou, the French master ironworker, and a group of English master masons.

On 5th October 1695, John Evelyn recorded that he went to St Paul's

to see the choir, now finished as to the stone work and the scaffold struck both without and within, in that part. Some exceptions might perhaps be taken as to the placing of columns of pilasters at the East tribunal. As to the rest it is a piece of architecture without reproach. The pulling out the forms, like drawers, from under the stalls, is ingenious.

Celia Fiennes, another visitor about this time, during the reign of William and Mary, said that it was 'almost finished and very magnificent . . . with a sweet organ . . . but dome not yet in place.'

Some of the Commission became impatient at the time the Cathedral was taking to complete, and as members who had been life-long friends of Wren died off, those who remained became openly hostile.

The dilatoriness of the workmen became notorious. Ned Ward and his friend, during their visit to the Cathedral, observed 'ten men in a corner, very busy about two men's work' and the friend remarked that 'this is work carried on at a national charge, and ought not to be hastened on in a hurry, for the greatest reputation it will gain when it's finished will be that it was so many years building'. Yet even this sardonic couple were impressed with the beauty of the half-finished Cathedral and concerned about the 'parcel of wenches fit for husbands, playing at hoop and hide among the pillars'. 'This revelling of girls I thought was very indecent,' said Ned, 'and ought to be carefully prevented, lest the new church be polluted far worse than the old one, and instead of a stable, be defiled with beasts worse than horses.'

The last stone of the Cathedral was laid in 1710 and by this time the Commission was accusing Wren of unnecessary delays and corruption. He was able to refute the charges but his salary was withheld until the work was completed. He had wanted the interior to be decorated with mosaics but they decided that this would be too costly and gave Sir James Thornhill a separate commission to paint the cupola.

The placing of the dome was in itself a remarkable feat of engineering, which was not completed until the following year, and by this time Wren was an old man of 79.

For the next few years he remained as Surveyor of the Works, keeping in close touch with his masterpiece, but in 1718, when he was 86, he was summarily dismissed from office. By this time the Hanoverians were on the throne and it seems likely that they resented Wren's long association with the Stuarts. Wren retired to his house at Hampton Court, but once a year, recorded Horace Walpole, 'the good old man was carried to St Paul's to contemplate the glorious *chef-d'oeuvre* of his genius'. And here, when he died in 1723, at the age of 91, he was buried.

10

Banks and Coffee Houses

When Charles II closed the Exchequer in 1672 two of the heaviest sufferers amongst the goldsmiths were Sir Robert Vyner, who lost £146,724, and Alderman Edward Backwell, who lost £296,000. After much protest and litigation, the King agreed to begin paying interest on all the money. Vyner was paid £25,000 a year out of the Excise for a few years and his creditors were commanded not to sue him, which was not a great deal more helpful to Vyner than to the unfortunate creditors. Alderman Backwell was given a pension of £17,759. With his business ruined, he retired to Holland, where five years later he died, never having recovered from the shock of his treatment by the King whom he had served so well.

By 1699 an Act was passed which virtually deprived the goldsmiths of both the original sum which had been confiscated and the accumulation of 25 years' interest. This now amounted to well over £3 million, but by the terms of the Act it was decreed that 'after the 25th December, 1705, the hereditary revenues of the Excise should stand charged with the annual payment of three per cent of the principal sum contained in the letters patent, subject, however, to be redeemed upon the payment of a moiety thereof, or 664,263 l.'

This meant that the Government acknowledged only this amount of £664,263 as owing to the goldsmiths or their heirs and it became the first item of the national debt.

Backwell had given interest on money deposited as well as money at call, the money at call being paid 3½ to 4 per cent and money at twenty days' notice at 6 per cent. He had been banker to all the famous people of Charles's Court – Charles himself, his Queen, the Queen Mother, James, Duke of York, Prince Rupert, the Duke of Monmouth, the Duke of Richmond, the Duchess of Orleans, Barbara Castlemaine, Nell Gwynn and Lord Clarendon, as well as Henry Cromwell and Sir Josiah Child, the Chairman of the East India Company – and at the time of the seizure the East India Company held a balance with Backwell of nearly £160,000.

Both Samuel Pepys and Lord Sandwich banked with Backwell and Pepys mentions him often in his diary, which unfortunately ends before the ruin of the bank, but on 26th June 1660 he was going to 'Backwell, the goldsmith at the Unicorn in Lombard Street, to choose £100 worth of plate for my Lord (Sandwich) to give Secretary Nichols' and on 23rd November 1663 'Up and to Alderman Backwell's, where Sir W. Rider, by appointment, met us to consult about the insuring of our hempe ship from Archangell, in which we are all much concerned.'

On 6th July 1665 he says that Sir G. Carteret had told him in strictest confidence that Alderman Backwell 'is ordered abroad upon some private score with a great sum of money' and that 'the King and the kingdom must as good as fall with that man at this time'.

The financial problems of the King were a complicated tangle. On 11th July, while the plague was raging, Pepys, after spending an evening of dalliance with Mary, when, during a coach ride to Highgate and Hampstead, he 'had what pleasure almost I would with her', he dropped in to the evening' Change, to find every one discussing the news that 'Ostend is delivered to us, and that Alderman Backwell did go with £50,000 for that purpose. . . .'

A week or two later, on 8th August, the King was writing to the Lord General:

> Alderman Backwell being in great straits for the second payment he had to make for the service in Flanders, as much tin is to be transmitted to him as will raise the sum. Has [sic] authorized him and Sir George Carteret to treat with the tin farmers for 500 tons of tin to be speedily transported under good convoy; but if, on consulting with Alderman Backwell, this plan of the tin seems insufficient, then without further difficulty he is to dispose for that purpose of the £10,000 assigned for pay of the Guards, not doubting that before that comes due, other ways will be found for supplying it; the payment in Flanders is of such importance that some means must be found of providing for it.[1]

It was a haphazard way of running affairs and history does not relate whether or not the Guards were ever paid, but all these dealings were transacted by the London goldsmiths' device of the bill of exchange, which was simply 'an open letter of request from one man to another desiring him to pay a sum named therein to a third party on his account, either on demand or at a certain number of days after date or after signature'. This method of circulating money depended on mutual confidence, and every individual passing on a bill had to endorse it, thereby making himself responsible for its payment. It was in fact an exchange of credits.

1. *Calendar, Domestic* 1664–5, pp. 508, 9.

Bill brokers and foreign exchange brokers handled these bills, the bill broker being the agent between the lender and borrower and the foreign exchange broker procuring money for bills on foreign merchants and those who had payments to make, all this brokerage business taking place in the Royal Exchange every Tuesday and Friday.

The foreign exchange brokers fixed the exchange rate of every country in Europe, which was the standard for the day's negotiations.

As commerce developed and increasing amounts of capital were needed, banks became essential, and the earliest house in the City to concentrate purely on banking, instead of combining it with the goldsmith's trade and pawnbroking, was that of Child's, at the sign of the Marygold, later to be known as Number One Fleet Street, by Temple Bar.

The Marygold had been a tavern and 'public ordinary'. Next door was the old Devil tavern, which had been a favourite haunt of Ben Jonson, and behind it was another inn, with the odd name of 'The Sugar Loaf and Green Lettuce'. Early in the seventeenth century, William Wheeler took over the Marygold for his goldsmith's business, and to oblige his customers he kept 'running cashes'. One of his apprentices, Robert Blanchard, married Wheeler's widowed daughter, Mrs Child, the mother of Francis Child, who was also apprenticed to William Wheeler, his grandfather.

In the 1660s Francis Child joined forces with Blanchard and when Blanchard died, in 1681, Francis Child carried on the business, taking as partner his cousin John Rogers. The London bankers were a close-knit clan and one of Francis Child's grand-daughters, Elizabeth Child, married a son of Alderman Backwell, both of their sons ultimately coming into the business.

After the Great Fire Francis Child rebuilt the Marygold, to conform with the new building regulations, incorporating the old 'Sugar Loaf and Green Lettuce' at the back. The firm also rented rooms in Wren's new Temple Bar to store their ledgers, but the Devil tavern remained until 1787, when Child's bought it for demolition, building houses on the site.

Amongst the firm's earliest ledgers is the account of Nell Gwynn, who died in 1687 owing Francis Child and John Rogers £6,900. Sir Stephen Fox, on behalf of her son, the Duke of St Albans, paid off £2,300. The sale of her plate fetched another £3,791 and the remaining £800 was gradually paid off, the bank charging only 5 per cent on the debt.

Two years later there was a rumour that the bank was in a precarious state and that there was to be a run on it. The story goes that Sarah Churchill, later to be the Duchess of Marlborough, came to the rescue, collecting all the gold she could lay hands on from her friends and making a valiant dash down to Temple Bar in her coach, arriving just in time to enable the bank to meet its demands and re-establish confidence.

The firm was still engaged in the goldsmith and pawnbroking business and the early ledgers show a mixture of banking accounts, goldsmiths' accounts and 'Pawne' accounts, with sketches of pieces of jewellery which the bank was holding, but after 1690 they concentrated entirely on banking, issuing their own bank notes for the first few years. Pass books were first issued in 1715, and before that time customers used to call at the bank from time to time to check their accounts in the presence of one of the partners. If all was well and there were no queries, the customer signed his name in the ledger, stating 'I allow this account.'[1]

There were many schemes for establishing banks in London during late Stuart times. In 1680 Robert Murray suggested a national bank, to be based on land and other valuable securities, prefacing his scheme by saying that 'though it may be objected that banks are not safe under a monarchy, yet such objections hold only in countries under the dominion of an absolute and despotic prince, and not where the laws are clearly defined, and every man is preserved in his person and property'.

His idea came to nothing and in 1682 more proposals were made for the establishment of national banks 'whereby the profits in usury will supply his Majesty more plentifully than ever to carry on the war, exempt the nation from land tax, great customs, exceedingly promote trade and navigation, and give England many other advantages'.

The Corporation of the City also outlined their proposal for a bank of credit, 'made current by common consent in London, more useful and safe than money'. It was put forward by the aldermen and Council, anxious to restore their fortunes and honour after the moratorium. For many years they had been in charge of the large fund invested for the care, education and mainten-ance of orphans of freemen of the City, to which bequests were frequently added. This money had been let out at interest, much of it to Charles I and Charles II, or borrowed to defray the increasing expense of governing the City, and in 1672 the Corporation had had to admit that it was no longer able to discharge its duties to the orphans. However, early in the reign of William and Mary an Act was passed, imposing various levies and duties for the next 50 years, such as 2s 6d. for the binding of every apprentice, 5s. on the admission of every freemen to the City, 4s. a tun on all wine imported into the Port of London and 4d on every chaldron of coal, the proceeds of which enabled the City to discharge its debt to the Orphans' Fund and redeem its honour.

In 1691 England was at war with France and King William was in desperate need of funds. The government was borrowing heavily on the security of future public revenue, at 20 per cent and sometimes 40 per cent, and also

1 Child's Bank, now amalgamated with Glyn Mills, is still at No. 1 Fleet Street.

raising money from a land tax and State lotteries, but the National Debt had risen to £2 million and the government was in urgent need of another £1,200,000.

William Paterson, a Scottish merchant and a member of the Wednesday Club, suggested a public joint stock bank which would lend at 8 per cent, and he and his friend Michael Godfrey, as well as other members of the Club, put the proposal to the Privy Council, who were by no means enthusiastic at first. They were suspicious of the 8 per cent, saying that the Bank would never pay its way at such a low rate of interest, but when 40 merchants raised between them £500,000, offering it at 8 per cent if they were incorporated as a bank, the Chancellor of the Exchequer had second thoughts, as did many members of the Privy Council. Those in favour said it would be a national advantage and free the country from extortioners and usurers. It would lower interest rates, raise the value of land, revive and expand public credit, extend the circulation of money and thereby improve commerce. The opposition declared that it would 'become a monopoly and engross the whole money of the kingdom; that, as it must infallibly be subservient to the government views, it might be applied to the worst purposes of arbitrary power; that, instead of assisting, it would weaken commerce, by tempting people to withdraw their money from trade and employ it in stock jobbing; that it would produce a swarm of brokers and jobbers to prey upon their fellow-creatures, encourage fraud and gaming, and further corrupt the morals of the nation'.[1]

And amongst the opponents were, not unnaturally, the men who had been lending to the government at such high interest, disregarding Sir Josiah Child's observation, in his *Discourse on Trade*, that 'the lowering of interest enables merchants to increase foreign trade, whereby home manufacturers and artificers will be increased, as also our stock of other useful people; and the poor will be employed'.

However, the bill approving the establishment of the Bank was passed and commissioners were appointed. On 25th June 1694 the first Duke of Leeds was writing to Sir Francis Child:

Sir, I am informed that the subscription to the Bank do fill so fast that there is att this day neare £700,000 subscribed, so that it must now necessarily be a bank: I therefore desire that you will subscribe foure thousand pounds for mee, and pay in one thousand pounds on my account as the Act directs.

In July 1694 the *London Gazette* announced that the newly appointed Commissioners would meet at the Mercers' hall, Cheapside, to receive subscriptions of £500 or more for the Bank of England. Within ten days the whole of the

1 Macpherson, *History of Commerce*, Vol. III, p. 660.

£1,200,000 the Government needed had been subscribed, the subscribers becoming members of the Company of the Bank of England. From amongst
their number they elected a Governor, Deputy Governor and 24 directors.
They made their by-laws and decided that the bank should operate in the
Grocers' Hall in the Poultry.

The business of the bank was restricted to dealing in bills of exchange and in
gold and silver, and took no part in any mercantile concern, but it was authorised to make advances on the security of merchandise lodged with it and also
on pawns, but the pawnbroking side of the business very soon faded away.
Until 1759 the Bank issued nothing less than £20 notes and in the early years
they ran into trouble by issuing them in exchange for currency which had been
debased by clipping, whereupon the Government authorised the issue of a
new coinage. the cost, of well over £1 million, being met by the imposition of a
window tax.

The Bank recovered and with an increasing number of subscribers its wealth
and influence grew steadily. By early in the eighteenth century it was authorised 'to make dividends to their members of their principal or capital stock'
which was 'always to remain at least equal to all the debts they owe'.

Ever since the days of Raleigh and Drake, Englishmen had dreamed of the
untapped riches of South America and Mexico. In 1711, when the new Tory
government was faced with a National Debt which had by now risen to £10
million, Lord Harley, then Chancellor of the Exchequer, countenanced the
formation of the South Sea Company, the Company promising to reduce the
debt in exchange for the monopoly of trade with Spanish America. Lord
Harley promised them 6 per cent, this sum to be raised by an assured revenue
from permanent duties on wine, tobacco, silk and similar luxury imports,
and the Company was duly incorporated.

Business was booming at the time and there was a mania for speculation.
Investors quickly came forward for the new Company but the trade with
Spain never materialised, for Philip V of Spain would permit only one English
ship a year to trade with Spanish America, and the first vessel did not set sail
until 1717.

By 1720 the National Debt had risen to over £30 million and the South Sea
Company came forward again, offering, in return for certain privileges, to
take over the debt at 5 per cent for seven years and after that time at 4 per cent.
They offered £3,500,000. The Government approved the scheme but the Bank
of England opposed it, offering £5 million, whereupon the South Sea Company
raised the bid to £7,500,000 and the new Bill went through Parliament, only
Sir Robert Walpole opposing it, denouncing the 'dangerous practice of stock-
jobbing, and the general infatuation, which must end in general ruin'.

The naïve and gullible public poured money into the Company and in the frenzy of investment during the next few weeks the stock rose from 130 to 300 in a single day. By the end of May 1721 it was 530. When it tended to fall it was revived by rumours of free trade with Spain and the possibility of tapping sources of wealth which would yield 50 per cent profit to the investors. Then a story circulated that Gibraltar and Port Mahon were to be exchanged for Peruvian sea-ports, so that the Company could send out a whole fleet of trading ships.

Everyone who could raise money took to investment and dozens of small companies were launched, most of them ridiculous, such as the 'Insurance from Death by Drinking Geneva', 'Curing of Broken Winded Horses and Mares', 'Curing of Lunatic Persons', Briscoe's 'Transmutation of Animals' and 'South Sea Hops'. Then there was Puckle's Machine Company for discharging round and square cannon balls and bullets and making a total revolution in the art of war. The public was so touchingly convinced that the Joint Stock Company was the certain way to undreamed-of riches that a man had only to hire a room at some coffee house near the Exchange for a few hours, open a subscription book and the money flowed in. One hundred and eighty-five of these bubbles are listed in Lawson's *History of Banking*, perhaps the most outrageous being the one entered as 'Title Not Mentionable'. This was a company for carrying on an undertaking 'of great advantage, but nobody to know what it is'. The promoter opened an office in Cornhill one morning at 9 o'clock, offering 5,000 shares of £100 each and asking for £2 deposit on each share: and by the time he closed at 3 o'clock in the afternoon he had collected £2,000.

As the bubbles burst, hundreds of people found that they had lost their savings, but money still flowed into the South Sea Company. By 2nd June the stock had reached 890, but after a rumour that several members of the Court were beginning to sell, it slumped to 640, whereupon the directors ordered their agents to buy, and by August it was up to 1,000.

Then the rumour spread that Sir John Blount, chairman of the Company, had sold out, along with several directors. The stock tumbled to 400, and as it went on falling shareholders realised that they had been the victims of a vast swindle. Thousands of people lost everything and were ruined, and there were several suicides. Aislabie, the Chancellor of the Exchequer, resigned and the treasurer of the Company fled with all his records, while five of the directors were arrested.

The investigating committee which was quickly appointed discovered false entries in the accounts. Stock had been distributed amongst members of the government and the Court, but no money paid over, so that when stock fell they lost nothing, but when it rose they were paid as if they had been genuine shareholders. Among them was the King's mistress, the Duchess of Kendal, who made £10,000, which she prudently salted away in Hanover, but Aislabie was found to have profited by £800,000. He was sent to the Tower and the money confiscated to help those who had lost most heavily.

The Bank of England suffered from the exploits of the South Sea Company for it had lent money too freely, and, in August 1720, its loans were standing at £948,000 and it had only just over £1 million bullion in its vaults. But it survived, and as confidence was gradually restored, its business steadily increased, so that by the end of the century its balance was three and a half million.

In 1734 the Bank moved from the Grocers' hall to their new building in Threadneedle Street, on the site of the house and garden of Sir John Houblon, one of the Bank's first directors. The house was not visible from the street, being approached through an arched court, and it was closely surrounded by the Church of St Christopher le Stocks, three taverns and some twenty small private houses. All these were pulled down but the churchyard was preserved and became the central garden of the Bank, round which the offices were built, and one of the clerks, who was six foot six inches tall, was actually buried there, to save his body from being snatched by the Resurrectionists.

The original bank was designed by George Sampson and the east and west wings were added by Sir Robert Taylor between 1766 and 1786, while Sir John Soane was responsible for the final magnificent building, seven storeys high, which is enclosed between Threadneedle Street, Princes Street, Lothbury and Bartholomew Lane, although the building within the walls was largely reconstructed by Sir Herbert Baker between 1924 and 1939.

Throughout the eighteenth century many private banks came into existence, for whom the Bank of England acted as banker, often helping them through financial crises.

When Edmund Burke came to England from Ireland in 1750 he said that outside London there were not a dozen 'bankers' shops' in the whole of England. There was at least one, however, which had been running for more than a hundred years. This was the bank which Thomas Smith, mercer, opened in Nottingham. In 1658 he bought a house in Peck Lane, Nottingham, where he pursued his business of mercery, in the course of which he remitted cash to London. He then began to send money to London for the local merchants and landowners, who soon found it convenient to keep a balance or deposit funds with Smith, which could be withdrawn as required, either in cash or by means of a bill of exchange drawn on a goldsmith banker of London. As the business expanded, Smith kept increasingly substantial balances in London at interest. In 1672 he had, in fact, large balances with Alderman

Backwell at the Unicorn as well as another goldsmith, Gilbert Whitehall, who was similarly robbed. However, with his mercery business to help him out, Thomas Smith and his bank weathered the storm.

Smith's son and grandson continued in the business but in 1758 one of the grandsons, Abel Smith, came to London, joining with John Payne in a partnership to cover the Nottingham bank and a new bank to be opened in the City.

The Payne family had come from Northamptonshire to the City of London in 1696, prospering as merchants and linen drapers, and by the time of the partnership with Abel Smith John Payne was chairman of the East India Company and his brother Edward a director of the Bank of England and later to become governor.

The new bank of Smith and Payne opened at 9 Lothbury, where the Paynes had their counting house. John Payne died in 1764 and the bank moved to Number 18, Lombard Street; and until 1769 it still functioned only as 'a house to be drawn upon from Nottingham', so that it can claim to have been the first branch bank in English banking history.

During the Napoleonic Wars the Smiths subscribed large government loans which were mainly in the hands of Abel's second son Robert, who was friend and financial adviser to the younger Pitt and in 1796 was created Lord Carrington. By this time the bank, now known as Smith, Payne and Smith, had moved to George Street by the Mansion House, at the back of what is now Number One, Lombard Street, the site of which they bought in 1806.

In 1902 the last of the partners sold out and Smiths Bank amalgamated with the Union Bank of London Limited. In 1918 this union was merged with the National Provincial, but over the entrance of the National Provincial Bank at Number One, Lombard Street the inscription 'Smiths Bank' still remains and the partners' room is still much the same as it was a century ago, when Smith's was a private bank.

By the time of Queen Anne Martin's bank was established and also that of the Quaker family of Hoare, whose house ultimately amalgamated with Lloyd's, and by the 1760s there were some 40 banking houses in and around Lombard Street, including that of Robert Barclay, another Quaker. They no longer issued their own notes but made payments in Bank of England notes and gold.

In the early days each bank employed a 'walks clerk' whose duty it was to visit each bank in turn, presenting it with the cheques it had been instructed to pay and receiving in exchange the cash to return to his own bank. Soon the clerks were meeting each other half way, at the most convenient coffee house or tavern, but in 1775 the whole process was simplified and made safer by the establishment of the **Central Clearing House in Lombard Street**.

Coffee had become a popular beverage throughout the East towards the end of the sixteenth century and during the following years samples were brought to Europe, where it soon became a fashionable drink. The first coffee houses were opened in Constantinople and Venice. In England the earliest known was established in Oxford in 1650, when 'Jacob, a Jew, opened a Coffey house at the Angel, in the Parish of St Peter in the East, Oxon, and there it was by some who delighted in Noveltie, drank'.

Four years later another Jew, Cirques Jobson, had taken over this house and Jacob seems to have moved to London. In the meantime, in 1665, an apothecary named Arthur Tillyard was induced to sell 'coffee publickly in his House against all Soules College' and the students who frequented it formed themselves into an informal club. Anthony à Wood, who complained that the students were wasting too much time, says that 'about 1655, a club was erected at Tillyard's where many pretended wits would meet and deride at others'. One of them was the brilliant young Christopher Wren and it was probably here that the Royal Society was born.

In 1652 an English merchant home in London from Smyrna with his Greek servant, Pasqua Rosee, served coffee to his friends and acquaintances. They liked it and he found that they were calling so often and taking up so much of his time that he told Pasqua Rosee to open a coffee-house where they could drink all they wanted, without wasting any more of his time. Accordingly a public announcement was issued that coffee was 'made and sold in St Michael's Alley in Cornhill, by Pasque Rosee at the signe of his own Head'. The new coffee house was immensely popular, to the consternation of the ale-house keepers, who saw a threat to their livelihood. They petitioned the Lord Mayor, complaining that Pasqua Rosee was a stranger and no freeman and therefore had no right to carry on his business, but he was allowed to continue, and Alderman Hodges, whose daughter had in the meantime married the Smyrna merchant, Mr Edwards, now sent his coachman Bowman to join Pasqua Rosee. But Bowman was no friend to Pasqua Rosee. He took the precaution of becoming a freeman and soon separated from the Greek and set up a rival establishment in a booth in St Michael's churchyard just opposite. Pasqua Rosee was not very bright and soon disappears from the story, but Bowman prospered and his customers were soon contributing sixpence each to enable him to build a proper house and take an apprentice.

The fashion for coffee drinking soon spread and despite the vilification of the brewers and vintners who described the new drink as a syrup of soot and old shoes which made men unfruitful, more coffee houses soon appeared. The government made several attempts to suppress them, complaining that they were breeding grounds of sedition. Beer, they said, was preferable, because coffee was a stimulant which kept people awake and made them inclined to argument and rebellion, while somnolent beer kept them loyal.

James Farre, a barber, opened the Rainbow Coffee House by Inner Temple Gate in Fleet Street in 1656, selling his drink 'of a soote colour dryed in a furnace, and that they drink as hote as can be endured', but the following year his neighbours, several of whom were booksellers, prosecuted him

for making and selling of a drink called coffee, whereby in makeing the same, he annoyeth his neighbrs. by evil smells, and for keeping of ffire for the most part night and day, whereby his chimney and chambr. hath been sett on ffire, to the great danger and affrightment of his neighbrs.

However, Farre repaired his smoking chimney and was allowed to continue his business.

Chocolate also became fashionable as a drink about this time, having been brought by Cortes from Mexico to Spain. According to one recipe, its preparation was no light task, for the cocoa nibs were to be lightly crushed and boiled for hours with white sugar, cinnamon, Mexican pepper, cloves, almonds, orange-flower water and vanilla straws and then 'enriched with milk and beaten eggs'.

As early as 1610 the Dutch East India Company imported a small consignment of China tea, grown on the small Japanese island of Hirado, as a gift to the Dutch Royal family. They liked it. The Company imported increasing quantities and tea-drinking became fashionable amongst the Dutch aristocracy. Apart from being a pleasant drink it was considered to have medicinal properties and the Dutch physician Cornelius Bontekee advocated at least ten cups a day.

The Dutch East India Company introduced tea to London, where it became equally popular amongst the few who could afford it, but it cost anything up to £10 a pound. However, the English Company were soon bringing in their own supplies and in 1657 Thomas Garraway, who ran a coffee house in Exchange Alley, was announcing that he had acquired supplies of tea which he could sell from 16s. to 50s. a pound.

The following year another advertisement for tea appeared in a London news-sheet.

That excellent and by all Physicians approved China drink called by the Chinese Tcha, by other nations Tay, alias Tea, is sold at the Sultanese Head, a cophee house in Sweeting's Rent, by the Royal Exchange, London.

Tea, chocolate and sherbert were now served in the coffee houses as well as coffee, all drawn from large barrels. In 1660 Pepys recorded that 'I did send for a cup of tea, a China drink of which I never had drunk before', but at 16s. a pound it was still very expensive.

Women were not allowed in the coffee houses so took to tea-drinking in their own homes, keeping the precious leaves carefully locked in beautiful tea-caddies. Yet some of the early brews must have been strange for the mystique of tea-making was still in an experimental stage. A Jesuit returning from China said that 'the hot water should not stay upon the tea-leaves any longer than you can say the Miserere Psalm very leisurely' but in 1688, when the Duchess of Monmouth sent some tea as a gift to friends in Scotland, they boiled the leaves, threw away the liquid and tried to eat what was left as a vegetable.

The British East India Company at first imported China and Japanese tea by way of Java but in 1684 the Chinese allowed them to build a small trading station at Canton, after which tea was brought to London in increasing quantities, but the government now imposed an import duty of 5s. a pound, so that the price remained too high for most people. On the Continent it was selling at less than 1s. a pound and it was now that the smuggler came into his own.

Business men would supply the money for large purchases of tea, as well as tobacco and brandy, which was bought at low prices in Europe. The contraband was brought over the Channel and the North Sea to points off the south and east coasts, where English fishing boats, on moonless nights, sailed out to meet it. It was transferred to the smacks of the English smugglers and landed secretly along the lonely stretches of shore, where willing hands helped to store it in barns, cellars and churches. Even Parson Woodforde accepted smuggling, recording the payments to Moonshine Buck, the smuggler, for cognac, tea and wine.

From the hiding places, the night riders set out on the long journey to London, their saddle bags stuffed with illicit packages and kegs. The penalty for smuggling was hanging, but compared with the hundreds who were actually involved, only a relatively small number were caught.

Pitt brought smuggling almost to an end in 1784 by drastically reducing the import duties, thereby putting the smuggler out of business, but up until this time it was estimated that of the 12,500,000 pounds of tea consumed each year, duty had been paid on only 5 million pounds, the rest having been smuggled; and it was during this period that tea became a popular drink of the poor as well as the prosperous.

With the Restoration the number of coffee houses in London increased very quickly, particularly round the Royal Exchange, where there were dozens, and by Queen Anne's time there were said to have been nearly 500: 144 within the City walls and the others scattered throughout Westminster. As in Oxford, they soon became informal clubs where men with similar interests met to discuss their affairs and the news of the day.

The Puritans regarded them as a welcome alternative to the taverns, where drinking was becoming as excessive as at Court and amongst the nobility, who 'with wines and spirits habitually heated or stupefied their brains morning, noon and night'. And in a pamphlet published in 1665 the writer says that 'Coffee and Commonwealth came in together for a Reformation to make us a free and sober nation'. He urges that liberty of speech should be allowed 'where men of differing judgements crowded; and that's a coffee house, for where should we discourse so free as there?'

White's Chocolate House in St James's Street, Piccadilly, was probably the most exclusive. Tories met at the Cocoa Tree and Whigs at the St James's Coffee House. At Will's in Covent Garden Dryden held court and the company of listeners became so distinguished that, although it had neither rules nor subscription, it became in effect one of London's first literary clubs, but after Dryden's death its prestige faded before the rise of Button's, made famous by the patronage of Steele and Addison.

The members of the Royal Society, which had moved to London at the Restoration, meeting every Wednesday afternoon at Gresham College, favoured the Grecian Coffee House in the Strand, which was also the favourite haunt of lawyers and students of the Temple, as well as men of letters. Ralph Thoresby mentions an occasion when, after a meeting of the Royal Society, he came back to the Grecian and spent the rest of the evening with Sir Isaac Newton.

Within the City walls many of the coffee houses became meeting places for men of business where deals were discussed and bargains sealed. For some years after the second Royal Exchange had opened, merchants met there and traded their wares by sample, the bulk of their goods being stored in the riverside warehouses, but as the coffee houses grew in popularity merchants deserted the Exchange and before long individual coffee houses were associated with groups of merchants with common interests, often providing sale rooms where their commodities could be auctioned.

The merchants in the West India trade, which included sugar, rum and coffee, met at the Jerusalem and Garraway's, both in Exchange Alley off Cornhill. The Virginia and Maryland coffee house in Threadneedle Street was the meeting place for merchants interested in the tobacco, sugar and cotton of the southern states of America, and close by was the Baltic, where men dealing in the Russian and Baltic trade in timber, oil, tallow, hemp and seeds did business. In 1744 the Virginia and Maryland joined forces with the Baltic and re-opened as the Virginia and Baltic. By now their customers were as interested in the ships as their cargoes and met the owners and captains. They were able to check their movements and the amount of cargo space they had available at any given time. For example, a merchant wishing to send tea and coffee he had bought from the East India Company to customers in America might arrange with a Captain bringing tallow and grain from the Baltic to reload his ship in London with the tea and coffee and advise his American customers to have ready a cargo of sugar and tobacco, which the ship could carry on the return journey to Europe, thereby saving both time and money. In this way the shipping market was established, which soon became as important as the commodity market.

In 1810 the Virginia and Baltic moved to the Antwerp Coffee House in Threadneedle Street and was renamed the Baltic: and a few years later the members formed themselves into a club and established a sale room. Tallow was still the most important commodity, but at the end of the century they began dealing in imported wheat. This side of the business almost ceased during the Napoleonic wars and within the next few decades gas-lighting spelt doom to the tallow trade, but by then the repeal of the Corn Laws made for greatly increased imports of wheat and the Baltic became the largest market in the country for foreign grain as well as the centre of the world's shipping market.

West Indian merchandise was auctioned by sample at the Jerusalem and Garraway's, and before long Garraway's became the most important auction room for many foreign commodities. Bidding in the early days was 'by candle'. The auctioneer lit an inch of candle as a sign for bidding to begin and it continued until the candle had burnt out.

It was here that the Hudson's Bay Company held their first auction of beaver skins, the committee having ordered that 'Mr. Rastell take care to putt up public bills upon the Exchange tomorrow morning for Sale of the 3000 lbs weight of beaver coates and skins at Mr. Garraway's Coffee house upon Tuesday 5 December, 1671 at two a clocke afternoon. . . .', and when the Company outgrew Garraway's it moved to a sale-room in Fenchurch Street, where it remained until 1865.

Most of the East India Company's imports were sold at their sales at East India House in Fenchurch Street, which they built in 1726, but before this time they had had premises on the same site. Pepper was particularly profitable, costing 3d a pound in India and selling in London for 3s. a pound. They also traded in snuff, saltpetre, small pieces of furniture, such as tables and screens, made from exotic woods, cotton cloth, embroidered hangings, ivory, silk, brocades, arrack, spices, cloves, nutmegs, mangoes, carpets and rugs: and the

Indiamen who went on to China and Japan for tea also brought back porcelain and, in the second half of the century, beautiful hand-painted Chinese wallpaper.

The custom of marine insurance was practised in the City very early and was probably begun by the Lombards. In a letter of 1560 Sir Thomas Gresham was referring to a ship 'I have caused to be assured upon the Bourse at Antwerp'. Until the Great Fire, marine insurers had met in the Royal Exchange, 'for the sole making and registering of all manners of assurances, intimations, and enunciations made upon any ship or ship's goods or merchandise in the Royal Exchange, or any other place within the City of London'. Then they moved to a room in Cornhill, and when Edward Lloyd opened his coffee house in Lombard Street, in 1691, the assurers became his most important customers and Lloyd's the centre of shipping news. Lloyd himself collected much of the information, passing it on in the form of a news sheet – *Lloyd's News* – which first appeared in 1696.

In October of the following year *The London Gazette* was advertising:

On Tuesday the 8th November next, Bennet's Coffeehouse in Plimouth will be exposed to Sale by Inch of Candle, 3 Ships with all their furniture: the Names whereof are the Teresa, the St. Thomas, and the Palmo, two of 400 Tuns and the other 100. The Inventories thereof to be seen at Lloyd's Coffee-house in Lombard Street, London. The said Ships are entered out for Barbados and Virginia.

Lloyd's news sheet was mainly concerned with shipping news but he also indulged in retailing general gossip, and when one particular item offended the House of Lords the publication had to be abandoned. However, in 1734 appeared *Lloyd's List and Shipping Gazette*, which can claim to be the oldest London newspaper with a continuous existence to the present day.

Merchants with overseas interests and the ship-owners themselves all met at Lloyds and the assurers willing to insure ships and cargoes on the high seas formed themselves into the Lloyd's Society. The system begun at Lloyd's 300 years ago has not changed. It is not an ordinary insurance company but a society of individuals who, having been admitted as members, are prepared to contribute, with other members, compensation for a loss. The person seeking assurance contacts a broker who submits the proposition to members, who nowadays act in syndicates, each syndicate employing an agent. The broker's proposition passes round the agents, each initialling and 'underwriting' it with the amount his syndicate is prepared to risk, until the whole amount has been underwritten.

In 1774 Lloyd's moved back to the Royal Exchange. The second Exchange
was destroyed by fire in 1838, and with it went most of Lloyd's records, but in
1884 they were back in the third Exchange, where they remained until in 1928
they moved to their new building in Leadenhall Street.

Until 1698 dealers in stocks and shares in the trading companies used to meet
each day in the Royal Exchange but then, the Exchange having become
'vexatiously thronged', they moved to Jonathan's Coffee house in Change
Alley, and it was here that the London Stock Exchange came into being.
World events were soon affecting the price of money and stocks and the dealers
in Change Alley soon learned that early information was the key to success.
Sir Henry Furnese paid for special dispatches to be sent to him from the battle-
fields of Holland, Flanders and France, while a Jew called Medina is said to have
paid the Duke of Marlborough handsomely for the privilege of being actually
present during his campaigns, so that he could judge for himself the result
their outcome was likely to have on the London stock market. There were
even secret despatches to Change Alley at the time of the first Jacobite rebellion,
the outcome bringing profit to a few astute speculators.

The stockbrokers stayed in Change Alley until early in the nineteenth
century, when they moved to the building in Capel Court, a small Georgian
courtyard hidden away by the side of the Bank of England and here the Stock
Exchange remained until 1970, when it was demolished to make way for the
present building, with its 26-storey tower block, half as high again as the City
Monument.

The beginning of the eighteenth century saw the dawn of the age of the daily
newspaper, the first being the *Daily Courant*, which appeared in London in 1702.
The Evening Post was published in 1706, the *London Journal* in 1725 and *The Craftsman*
in 1727. Within the next 40 years *The Daily Advertiser, The Westminster Journal, Lloyd's
Evening Post, The St. James's Chronicle, The Middlesex Journal* and *The Morning Chronicle*
had all been launched.

In 1771, after the editors and printers of eight London newspapers had been
called to the bar of the House of Commons, the London Press, supported by
the City, won its right to publish Parliamentary proceedings and debates, and
after this time *The Morning Post* appeared in 1780, *The Times* in 1785 and *The Sunday
Observer* in 1791.

These newspapers were available and avidly read in the coffee houses. The
Chapter Coffee House in Paternoster Row, hidden away at the corner of
Chapter House Court and the meeting place for the booksellers, was famous
for 'its punch, its pamphlets and its newspapers', and they were read in dozens
of less famous and distinguished coffee houses. When the twenty-year-old

César de Saussure visited London in the 1720s from his home in Lausanne he wrote of the great number of coffee houses 'which to tell the truth, are not over clean or well furnished, owing to the quantity of people who resort to these places and because of the smoke, which quickly destroys good furniture'.

The attraction was mainly the newspapers. 'Workmen,' he said, 'habitually begin the day by going to coffee-rooms to read the latest news. Shoe blacks and other persons club together to purchase a farthing newspaper' and as early as 2nd August 1712 *The British Mercury* was saying that 'About 1695 the press was again set to work, and such a furious itch of novelty has ever since been the epidemical distemper, that it has proved fatal to many families, the meanest of shopkeepers and handicrafts spending whole days in coffee houses to hear news and talk politics.'

In some of the coffee houses Saussure said that 'men will sit smoking and reading newspapers . . . talking so little you can hear a fly buzz' and much later in the century, by which time many were selling wine, punch or ale as well as chocolate, coffee and tea, C. P. Moritz, the German pastor visiting London, said: 'Near the Change is a shop where for a penny or even an half-penny only you may read as many newspapers as you will. There are always a number of people about these shops, who run over the papers as they stand, pay their halfpenny and then go on.'

Some of the coffee houses in the City advertised themselves as letter-receiving houses for Murray and Dockwra. A post office known as the Letter Office had been set up during the reign of Charles I, the headquarters being on Dowgate Hill, and Charles II had settled the revenue from it on the Duke of York. In 1681 Robert Murray and William Dockwra founded their company for a penny post in London. They operated from Lime Street, and with the cooperation of the coffee houses were very successful. Letters were franked for the first time and delivery was quick and efficient. However, the company was soon repressed by the Government for infringing their monopoly, and shortly afterwards the Government's London Penny Post was established, although the charge very soon rose to twopence.

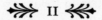

II

Georgian London

London was becoming a vast metropolis, extending far beyond the old City boundaries, which by the end of the eighteenth century contained only one-sixth of the million people who were now regarded as Londoners.

To the west the building development had been gracious and well planned. The mansions of the Strand were now disappearing but Inigo Jones's Covent Garden Square was begun in the 1630s. Leicester Square was built about the same time and Soho Square a few years later. Bloomsbury Square was laid out in 1665, Lincoln's Inn Fields and Red Lion Square in 1684 and they all remained fashionable until after the development of Westminster and Mayfair.

The first mansion of Piccadilly was the Earl of Clarendon's ill-fated Clarendon House, which was hardly completed before his downfall and was demolished less than twenty years later, but St James's Square was completed in 1684. Hanover Square was built between 1716 and 1720, Grosvenor Square at about the same time and the first houses of Berkeley Square were ready by 1738. Fashion and wealth moved westwards from Covent Garden into these new squares, leaving the piazza and the arcades to the theatre people, the artists and the market, but Leicester Square remained fashionable for a few years longer, while Frederick, Prince of Wales, the father of the future George III, held court at Leicester House.

Kensington had developed after William III bought Nottingham House and converted it into Kensington Palace and the riverside village of Chelsea grew round the five mansions which had stood there since Tudor times, including Sir Thomas More's house and Henry VIII's palace which, at the Restoration, had been bought by the Cheyne family.

North-west of the City, Portman Square, Manchester Square and the squares and streets of Bloomsbury were all being built during the 1770s and 1780s, the northern limit of London at this time being the New Road from Paddington to Islington, built in 1756, which today is represented by the Marylebone, Euston and Pentonville Roads. Hampstead and Highgate, on the hills beyond it, were still separated by the royal park and the fields and farms of Chalk Farm and Belsize.

In between these aristocratic developments there were nevertheless islands of squalor. In old Westminster and Tothill fields, which were soon to join up with Chelsea, grew up evil little streets and alleys – Cabbage Lane, Rogue's Acre, Dirty Lane, Long Ditch, Pick Pocket Alley and Bandy Leg Walk – which were to linger on until Victoria Street was cut through it all in the nineteenth century, while to the west of Charing Cross, where Trafalgar Square was to be built, was a rookery of ramshackle buildings and hovels, murky alleys and dingy courts – strange, sinister places with exotic names like the Caribee Islands and the Bermudas, with Porridge Island in the middle famous for its dubious cookshops. This patch of human desolation on the fringe of Pall Mall and St James's Square was no better than the terrible rookeries of St Giles just to the north.

The eastern spread of London was sadly different from the western development. Partly because of the manner of land tenure which enabled copyhold tenants to let on short leases, Stepney, Spitalfields, Ratcliffe, Limehouse, Wapping, St George in the East, Mile End and Bethnal Green filled out in a straggling, muddled way, while the south bank was given over to industry, including the tanneries of Bermondsey and the timber yards of Lambeth.

J. W. Archenholtz, writing of London in 1780, in his *View of the British Consitution*, said:

> The east end, especially along the shores of the Thames, consists of old houses, the streets there are narrow, dark and ill-paved; inhabited by sailors and other workmen who are employed in the construction of ships and by a great part of the Jews. The contrast between this and the West end is astonishing: the houses here are mostly new and elegant; the squares are superb, the streets straight and open. . . .'

Wealthy merchants tended now to move out of the City, many of them favouring Essex or the rural parts of Middlesex, while the richest of all established themselves in the West End.

Yet London, now twelve times the size of any other city in the kingdom, was still the place that adventurous young men hoping to make a fortune were moving to from the country. If they were poor and could not afford to become freemen of the City, which would have enabled them to trade or practice one of the City crafts, they drifted to the eastern slums – St Katherine's by the Tower, the liberty of East Smithfield, the waterside hamlets east of the Tower or parts of Southwark – finding work in the port or the shipbuilding yards, where by 1700 a quarter of London's population was engaged.

Scots, Welsh and Irish all came to London as well as Huguenots and Polish and German Jews, escaping from religious persecution. While the wealthier Jews took up residence in the City, the rest settled mainly in Whitechapel, Houndsditch, Mile End and Petticoat Lane, many of them as tailors, others as retailers or hawkers, and by 1800 there were 20,000 of them.

Towards the end of the century there were also a number of negroes living on the East End waterfront, who had come mainly from the West Indies and the southern states of North America, as well as Indian lascar seamen who had been recuited by the East India Company.

As the population of the outer reaches of London steadily increased, the resident population of the City declined. In 1700 it was 208,300 and by 1801 it was only 134,000, but the City's importance as a centre of finance and international trade was steadily growing.

The administration of the large area which now comprised the capital, containing so many different elements, was complicated, for each part had evolved its own form of local government.

Westminster, the home of government and Parliament, of the Courts of Justice, the Royal Court and fashionable society, was governed jointly by its Court of Burgesses, the vestries of its nine parishes and the Middlesex justices, while outlying parishes were ruled by their own separate vestries.

Southwark was still administered by the City ward of Bridge Without, although its surrounding parishes were controlled by Surrey, which, like Middlesex, was administered by its justices of the peace. Its assizes were held with those of London and its Members of Parliament were returned by the City of London Sheriffs.

The City of London retained its own clear identity and form of government. The Lord Mayor and the two Sheriffs of London and Middlesex were still elected by the Livery Companies, who also chose the City's four members of Parliament. The Livery met in the Court of Common Hall, which was open to all freemen of the City's Livery Companies who were entitled to wear the livery.

Both the Sheriffs and the Mayor were selected from among the senior aldermen, the Mayor having first served as a Sheriff, and the members of Parliament were also mainly chosen from amongst the aldermen.

The 25 aldermen were elected for life from the freemen ratepayers of the wards, each of which they represented. They had to be the sons of Englishmen, but they were not now required to live within the City precincts, although they served as magistrates within their wards. They were mostly wealthy men – bankers, directors of the large companies or holders of large blocks of Government stock – and many of them lived in the prosperous new districts of west and north-west London.

They conducted the courts of law and amongst their duties were the appointment of the Recorder and other City officers, the government of the prisons, the issuing of licences for ale-houses and control of the City's accounts.

The Court of Common Council, over which the Lord Mayor and the Aldermen presided, was composed of some 200 freemen ratepayers who were elected annually from the wards, but they had to be resident within the wards which elected them and they had the right to appoint certain of the City officers, such as the Town Clerk and the Common Serjeant. These Common Councillors were mainly retail shop-keepers and master craftsmen – haberdashers and linen drapers, apothecaries, bakers, carpenters, cabinet-makers and vintners – with only a small minority of bankers and merchants in a relatively small way of business, and by the middle of the century they had been powerful enough to insist, despite protests from the Livery Companies, that they should be allowed to employ non-freemen craftsmen if they wished.

The work of the Common Council was increasing all the time, as the trade of the port increased. The matter of bridges had to be considered, for rickety old London Bridge was becoming dangerous. Markets and prisons had to be enlarged, sewers maintained, streets kept clean and paved, all of which entailed the formation of new committees and the appointment of salaried staffs.

The wardmote still played a part in the running of the individual wards, the meeting, conducted by the alderman, being open to all ward ratepayers, whether freemen or not. The wardmote elected the ward officers and nominated its Common Councilmen, but the various duties which they had undertaken since medieval times, such as supervising the cleaning and the lighting of the streets, licensing ale-houses, suppressing gaming houses and brothels and appointing watchmen were gradually taken over by the Court of Common Council and the Court of Aldermen, and by the end of the century the authority of the wardmotes had declined.

The care of the poor was an unsolved problem for it still depended on the Elizabethan Poor Law which had, in its time, been adequate enough, entrusting the care of the poor to the Church wardens and the Overseers of the Parish, who had been authorised to levy a Poor Rate. But during the eighteenth century, as the population increased, so did the numbers of the poor and destitute. In the City, the wards levied and collected the poor rate and the parish dispensed it, but all too often the rate was quite inadequate for the number of people needing help.

An act of 1662 had laid down that any destitute person who had not been apprenticed in the Parish or was not occupying a £10 tenement within it could be made chargeable to the parish of his birth and removed there. The result was that unfortunate vagrants, while they had breath in their bodies, were

often hustled over the boundaries of the parish where they had ended up.
These extracts from the parish accounts for St Swithin's, London Stone, in
the very heart of the City, show how the system worked.

1661	For getting severall poore people out of ye Parish	8d
1679	Pd for clearing the Parish of a woman bigg with child	1/-
1682	Pd for clearing the Parish of two women bigg with child	4/-
1683	Given to James Edwards for clearing of the Parish of Children and a greate Bellyed women.	2/-
1692	Pd for clearing ye Parish of a woman and two children, ye came after father who was pressed	3/-
1702	To Coach Hire to carry a poor woman to prevent her dying in ye Parish	2/-
1710	Given Mrs. Ajar a big belly'd woman to go into ye country	5/-
1712	Paid to a woman in Labor to goo out of ye Parish	3/6
	To a big bellyed woman to goo out of ye Parish into Lombard St	1/-
1719	To gett rid of a poor Black Woman with a bigg Belly	2/6
1727	Pd to severall Algiers slaves permitted to begg with a pass	3/6
1769	Cash paid at East India house for the discharge of Wm Fletcher a parishioner for having entered himself as a Common soldier intending to leave his wife and child (Bigg with another) for the P'sh to maintain in his absence	£4-4-11

And the only light relief in this tale of human misery is the payment in
1785 to Eliza Jones of 14s. 6d. to take her clothes out of pawn.

London in the eighteenth century was still a manufacturing city as well as
a centre of international trade and shipping, and although Amsterdam was
still the world's money market, London was increasingly a serious rival.

London had also become a vast consumer's market and as Defoe said in
his *Tour Through the Whole Island of Great Britain*,

the whole Kingdom, as well as the people, as the land, and even the sea, in
every part of it, are employ'd to furnish something, and I may add the best
of everything, to supply the city of London with provisions; I mean by
provisions, corn, flesh, fish, butter, cheese, salt, fewel, timber etc., and cloths
also; with every thing necessary for building, and furniture for their own
use, or for trades.

Meat came to Smithfield. During the time of Charles I the City had finally
taken full control of Smithfield and organised it as a market for live cattle,

paved and enclosed with railings. Cattle from Scotland, Wales and Kent and sheep from Lincoln and Leicester were driven down to London by the drovers. Monday was the day for fat cattle and sheep. Tuesday, Thursday and Saturday morning were for the sale of hay and straw and the afternoons for horses and donkeys, while on Fridays cattle, sheep and milch cows were sold.

Much of the slaughtering was done in West Smithfield and the meat was sold by the butchers of Newgate market, and this arrangement lasted until the middle of the nineteenth century, conditions growing more appalling, both for the animals and the market people, each year.

C. P. Moritz in 1782 wrote that 'Nothing in London makes so disgusting an appearance to a Foreigner as the butchers' shops; especially in the environs of the Tower. Guts and all the nastiness are thrown into the middle of the street, and cause an insupportable stench.'

Covent Garden, well outside the City's boundaries, was the most popular market for fruit and vegetables, much of which came from the market gardens of Chelsea, Kensington and Battersea, but there were also the Stocks market in the heart of the City and the Borough market, while in 1682 John Balch, a silk spinner, applied for a permit to hold a market in Spital Square twice a week. Spitalfields was already associated with the silk-weaving industry and when, in 1685, Louis XIV revoked the Edict of Nantes and the Huguenots fled, many came to London, those with weaving skills settling in Spitalfields, where the market rapidly developed. Elegant little cottages were built for the weavers with large windows on the first floors for their looms. Their skill was incomparable and they produced the most beautiful silks and velvets, which were soon to be exported all over the world. As the population of Spitalfields grew there was soon a network of lanes and alleys covering the fields which once surrounded the Spital, and of the 35 French churches in London during the eighteenth century, eleven were in Spitalfields and Bethnal Green, in addition to Nicholas Hawksmoor's beautiful Christ Church; and as it increased so Spitalfields became a general market for fruit, vegetables and poultry. A family called Goldschmidt took over from John Balch, but early in the eighteenth century the market building was burnt down and the market continued in open stalls and sheds until 1876, when a new leaseholder, Robert Horner, put up new market buildings.

In medieval times the bakers supplying London were concentrated in the eastern suburb of Stratford, obtaining their flour from the farmers of Essex and Kent, and they brought their bread into the City each morning. Their principal markets were in Cheapside and Cornhill and later in Bread Street. As the population and demand increased, the bakers had to go further afield, to Norfolk, Sussex and Suffolk, for their corn, and additional supplies of foreign corn were landed at Billingsgate and Queenhithe, although the bakers always preferred English grain when it was in good supply.

There were various corn markets in the City but they gradually concentrated in two main areas. The first was in Whitechapel, where Essex farmers bringing their corn to London used to meet. As business increased they would leave samples of their crops with the landlord, who took orders from the bakers and brewers who came to inspect them. The landlord would pass the orders back to the farmers and receive a commission on the sale, thus establishing an early Corn Exchange.

Down in Thames Street, where the grain ships from the Baltic continued to discharge their cargoes long after the Steelyard had been closed, was Jack's Coffee House, which in the same way became a market for imported corn. Corn merchants who acted as brokers would buy cargoes in bulk and resell them to the bakers and brewers.

In 1747 the market was reorganised when a large Corn Exchange was built in Mark Lane to house the growing business of Whitechapel and Jack's Coffee House.

Leadenhall market, where at one time wool and woollen cloth, hides and skins and metal ware were sold, came to specialise in poultry, game and eggs. Broadcloth still went to Blackwell Hall, meal and malt to Queenhithe, while hay, much of which came from the fields of Hampstead, was delivered to the Haymarket and Smithfield, Whitechapel and the Borough being supplied from the eastern and southern counties.

Billingsgate was the fish market, for the Thames abounded in fish. 'What should I speak of the fat and sweet salmons daily taken in this stream, and that in such plenty (after the time of the smelt is past) as no river in Europe is able to exceed it?' wrote Stow. 'But what store also of barbels, trouts, chevens, perches, smelts, breams, roaches, daces, gudgeons, flounders, shrimps, eels etc., are commonly to be had therein.' The river supplied at least half of London's consumption and fish caught in the Thames estuary and the North Sea was also brought to Billingsgate.

Until the end of the eighteenth century there was an important salmon fishery up-river at Putney and even at the beginning of the nineteenth century, before pollution killed off all the fish, fishermen were catching salmon, roach, plaice, smelts, flounders, eels, dace and dab in the Thames in large enough quantities to make a living from their sale at Billingsgate.

It had begun as a general market but as fish became an increasingly important item of food so did the importance of Billingsgate as a fish market, until by the end of the seventeenth century it was almost entirely devoted to fish. In 1699 an Act of Parliament made Billingsgate 'a free and open market for all sorts

(*Above left*) 'The manner of shutting up the Houses, with a Watch-man, a Red Cross, and Lord Have Mercy on Us on the Door, and Searchers with white Sticks in their Hands, the Dog Killers killing the Dogs, also the Fires that were made in the streets and the Sedan carying the sick to the Pesthouse.' (*Above right*) 'How multitudes did fly from London by Water in Boates and Barges, and Lighters laden with Goods ' (*Below left*) 'Their flying by land on Horsebacks in Coaches, and in Waggons with their Goods, the Country people stopping them, to shew their Certificates ' (*Below right*) 'The manner of carrying the Corps to the Ground by the Bearers, with red Staves in their hands, so that people might shun them, some being carried with a Bell before them.'

Plague bell

Diseases and Casualties for the Week, 15–22 August 1665

The Great Fire of London, 1666 A detail – showing St Paul's – of the only extant contemporary painti

Seventeenth-century fire-fighting equipment

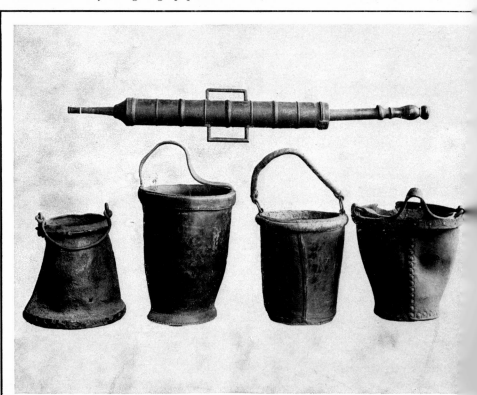

Wren's second model design for St Paul's Cathedral, rejected in 1675

The old Custom House, 1753, from a view by Maurer

Temple Bar in Dr Johnson's time

Dividend Day at the Bank, 1770

Garraway's Coffee House shortly before it was demolished

The Fleet ditch

Crosby Hall

Cheapside on Lord Mayor's Day, 1761

The Swan with Two Necks

The inner court of the Belle Sauvage

The Docks 1872, by Gustave Doré

(*Left above*) The Corn Exchange, completed in 1828
(*Left below*) The Mint, c. 1800

South aisle, All Hallows
Barking, 1910

St Paul's: the high altar in
ruins, 1940

Farringdon Street Market
where 380 people were killed
by a bomb, 1945

Middle Temple Hall, bombed
in 1940

The Parish Church of
St Olave

St Bartholomew's,
Smithfield, 1975

of fish whatsoever, six days of the week, and on Sundays (before Divine service) for mackerel'.

Roads were appallingly bad throughout England and until the building of the canals in the second half of the eighteenth century sea and river transport were used wherever possible, particularly for the bulky commodities such as coal, which still arrived in London from Newcastle by coastwise shipping and river barge.

Although London now drew so much on the provinces, she still had many trades and crafts, a large number of which were by now far beyond the province of the 60 trades represented by the City companies and were no longer organised on the medieval pattern of the old craft guilds, the number of workpeople employed being by this time controlled merely by supply and demand.

The old master-craftsmen complained, but in vain, for there was by now little means of checking employers, records were not always kept and the problem had grown too big.

By 1749 395 trades and occupations were listed in the Westminster poll book and by 1791 *The London Directory* mentions 492. They included the trades connected with the life of the port, the ship and barge builders, the coopers, brewers, distillers and sugar refiners, porters and watermen. Scores of people were employed in the coffee houses and victualling trades. There were peruke makers and barbers, shoemakers and stocking knitters, tailors, mantua makers and milliners, booksellers, stationers, surgeons and apothecaries.

There were also the craftsmen making the luxury goods for which London already had a high reputation, their trades including clock and watch-making, cutlery, surgical instruments, plate, jewellery, furniture, saddlery and coach building.

The silk weavers, as we have seen, settled in Spitalfields. The watchmakers concentrated in Clerkenwell and by 1798 120,000 watches were being made there, each year, of which 70,000 were exported. Some of these highly skilled craftsmen were descended from Huguenot refugees. Etienne de Tessier, for example, was a Huguenot refugee who after several years in Switzerland arrived in England in 1712, where his son Lewis became a merchant in the City. Two generations later the family was buying jewellery from refugees from the French Revolution, but by the beginning of the nineteenth century they had left the City to open their first jeweller's shop in South Audley Street.

The Aspreys were another Huguenot family who had fled from France at the end of the seventeenth century. They were skilled watchmakers, silversmiths, weavers and leather workers, the descendants ultimately opening their first Bond Street business during the 1830s, all their beautiful dressing-cases

H

and writing-cases, jewellery and gold, silver and leather work being made and designed in the workrooms above the shop, as they are to this day.

The first English factory for the manufacture of stoneware, a form of hard-baked earthenware, had been opened in 1671 by John Dwight at Fulham and about the same time two Dutchmen had established a pottery at Lambeth. By the middle of the eighteenth century two more potteries had been built here and Doulton's, beginning with the manufacture of chimney pots, drain pipes, ink and blacking bottles, was, by the nineteenth century, producing German and Flemish stoneware and beautifully decorated faience and terra-cotta.

During the 1740s the little English porcelain factories were opened at Bow and Chelsea, inspired by the Chinese porcelain that the East India Company was bringing over from China and which had first been copied at the Meissen factory near Dresden.

The coachmakers were in Long Acre and also the furniture makers. It was in the 1750s that mahogany began to arrive in England in large quantities from the West Indies, having first been carried as ballast. In the country districts furniture was still made of solid oak but the luxury furniture of Queen Anne's time and the early Georges had been of walnut veneer on beech or some similar relatively inexpensive wood. Now mahogany became more popular and for many years was used almost exclusively.

Chippendale opened his workshops in Long Acre about 1745 and later moved to St Martin's Lane. A few years later Hepplewhite opened his business in Cripplegate. Robert Adam was purely a designer, who passed his drawings on to the practical cabinet-makers and Thomas Sheraton did not arrive in London until 1790, but there were dozens of other cabinet makers in London at this time, many of them using the designs published in the catalogues of the great masters. Although many were in the West End there were also a large number in the City, in Lombard Street, Fenchurch Street, Mark Lane, the Barbican, St Paul's Churchyard and St John Street, Smithfield.

Seddon, the cabinet maker of Aldersgate, was famous in his day, and Sophie v. La Roche, visiting London in 1786, describes a visit to his workshops.

He employs four hundred apprentices on any work connected with the making of household furniture, joiners, carvers, gilders, mirror-workers, upholsterers, girdlers – who mould the bronze into graceful patterns – and locksmiths. All these are housed in a building with six wings. In the basement mirrors are cast and cut. Some other department contains nothing but chairs, sofas and stools of every description, some quite simple, others exquisitely carved and made of all varieties of wood, and one large room is full up with all the finished articles in this line, while others are occupied by writing tables, cupboards, chests of drawers, charmingly fashioned desks, chests, both large and small, work- and toilet tables in all manner of wood and patterns, from the simplest and cheapest to the most elegant, and expensive. . . .

Charming dressing-tables are also to be seen, with vase-shaped mirrors, occupying very little space, and yet containing all that is necessary to the toilet of any reasonable person. Close-stools, too, made like a tiny chest of drawers, with a couple of drawers in, decorative enough for any room.

She wrote of 'chintz, silk and wool materials for curtains and bed-covers; hangings in every possible material; carpet and stair-carpets to order; in short, anything, one might desire to furnish a house. . . .'

However, it was during the eighteenth century that many of London's industries began to move to the country districts and the Midlands, where food, rents and labour were all cheaper and craft regulations less strict. Shoe-making, for example, had begun to move to Northampton in the 1730s and by 1750 nearly all London's shoes were made there. In 1660 most of the country's stocking knitters were living and working in London, but they gradually migrated to Nottingham, Leicester or Derbyshire, and by 1782, by which time there were 20,000 knitting frames throughout the country, London had only 500.

In 1769 Sprimont, the proprietor of the Chelsea porcelain factory, sold out to William Duesbury of Derby, which was about the time that Josiah Wedgwood was transferring his potteries at Burslem to the new factory and village for his workmen which he called Etruria.

Trade rather than industry was the source of the City of London's increasing greatness and wealth, for by 1700 she was handling 80 per cent of England's imports, 69 per cent of her exports, and 86 per cent of her re-exports. She owned 140,000 tonnage of ships, compared with the total of 103,000 tons of all the other ports, and eight times that of Bristol. César de Saussure, writing in the 1720s, was enchanted with the Thames. He described the hundreds of galleys, barges and small craft of every sort above the bridge, while below, the river was almost hidden by

merchant vessels from every country. All these ships are anchored in rows, forming streets with open passages between. The French vessels form one line, the Dutch another, those that transport coal from Newcastle a third, and so on. In this way you can easily discover any ship you desire to look for, and the arrangement as viewed from the bridge is charming.

Defoe was writing at this time and he noted in the Pool three wet dock 22 dry docks and 33 yards for laying-up, repairing and building merchant ship apart from the boat-builders, wherry-builders and barge builders. By this tim the East India Company's Howland dock at Rotherhithe had been built by th Russell family.

In 1696 the first Duke of Bedford had arranged a marriage between his fou teen-year-old grandson, Wriothesley Russell, who was to become the secon Duke, with the thirteen-year-old Elizabeth Howland, the daughter of Joh and Elizabeth Howland and granddaughter of Sir Josiah Child. The Howland had been drapers of Cheapside in the time of James I and the Childs had bee London clothiers, having come from Worcestershire, where, like the Chil of the banking family who came from Wiltshire, they had prospered in th wool and cloth trade.

When John Howland married Elizabeth Child he was Sheriff of Surre and had bought the ancient manor of Streatham and Tooting Bec, whi Elizabeth's father, Sir Josiah, was governor of the East India Company i Bombay.

Wriothesley's father had been executed for his alleged conspiracy in th Rye House plot and his grandfather, during his wardship of the boy, saw a goo deal of Elizabeth Howland, who had a great deal of money invested in th East India Company and also in its ships, as well as possessing property alon the Thamesside at Rotherhithe. The Duke took up shares in the East Indi Company and with Elizabeth Howland and his daughter-in-law, the mothe of Wriothesley, planned and built a dry dock and then a wet dock at Rothe hithe. The dry dock was leased to the Wells Brothers, and Wells' Yard was soo busy with shipbuilding, while the wet dock, named the Howland dock, wa used by the East India Company. The Russells also had an interest in sever of their ships by now, the *Streatham*, the *Bedford*, the *Tavistock*, the *Russell* and th *Howland* all being built at the Wells' shipyard by the beginning of the eighteent century.

In 1725 the South Sea Company undertook to try to revive the flaggin fortunes of the Greenland Company, which had been formed a hundred yea earlier, by members of the Russia Company, for the whale-fishing trade. Th South Sea Company agreed to lease part of the Howland dock, at a rental £550 a year, and the Russells bought an interest in two of the ships and the cargoes, the *Bedford* and the *Henrietta*. However, the Greenland venture was no successful. The journey was hazardous and difficult, the sailors suffered appa ling hardships and they failed to catch many whales. The fourth Duke's on sixteenth share in the profit of the *Henrietta*, after she had caught a whal was only £77s.2d. and a one-eighth profit from the *Duke of Bedford* in the follow

g year, 1761, was £125.9s.6d., after which the Russell interest ended and the
ips were sold.

The East India investments were far more profitable, however, despite the
mpany's troubles at the beginning of the century. William III had granted
e Company a new charter for 21 years, but Parliament, disputing the King's
ght to grant trade charters and jealous of the Company's wealth, made some
ose investigations and discovered that the Company had been distributing
ibes amounting to £90,000 in order to maintain its monopoly. In 1698 the old
ompany was dissolved and a new one formed, but the original Company
gained some of its old powers and for several years the two operated in deadly
valry. However, by 1708 the two companies were amalgamated under the
me of 'The United Company of Merchants of England Trading to the East
dies' and throughout the century acquired enormous power and wealth.

At the peak of their prosperity they were employing nearly 4,000 men in
e vast warehouses which they built in Cutler Street and four hundred clerks
the magnificent East India House, with its beautiful Court room, Committee
oms, Directors' rooms and the large sale room, where 200,000 pounds of
a were sometimes sold in a single day at the annual tea sales.

There was a military department for superintending the recruiting of the
dian army and the buying office governed the warehouses and organised
e home market.

The Company grew rich yet the journeys to the East were very slow and
vestors had to wait a long time for a return on their money. The Bedford
mily would invest as much as £2,000 in a voyage and take a proportionate
are of the profits. Gladys Thomson, in her book *The Russells in Bloomsbury*,
otes a letter received by the Duke's agent at Bedford House, Bloomsbury
uare, in September 1750, from an East India Company representative.

Sir,

You are desired to meet the owners of the *Streatham* on Friday, the 28th
instant, at the Jerusalem Coffee House at one o'clock in the afternoon, to
receive a dividend for His Grace the Duke of Bedford.

Please bring the Bill of Sale with you.

I am,
Your most humble servant,

John Hallett

The *Streatham* had left Rotherhithe on 30th January 1747 and had lain off
ptford to receive stores and then sailed on to Gravesend, to receive more
rgo, including bales of cloth, as well as taking on board some of the Company's

soldiers bound for India. It was not until the third week in April that, in the company of seven other Indiamen, they eventually set sail. While they were still in the Channel the *Streatham* had lost her long-boat and with it the third mate: and at the same time another disaster was recorded. They discovered that the beer on board was sour and off Spithead it all had to be thrown overboard.

It was not until March 1748, fifteen months later, that they rounded the Cape and by the following October they had reached Bombay, to begin the business of sending goods ashore and receiving their return loads, which included saltpetre, pepper and cotton yarn. They reached London again in September 1749, but it was not until September 1750 that the accounts had been settled and John Hallett could invite the Duke's agent to the Jersualem Coffee House to settle his share of the profits.

Sometimes the Bedfords would send their own bales of cloth, which had come up from the cloth merchants on their Devon estates, out in the Indiamen, but Devon weavers also dealt directly with the East India Company. Lacking capital, and not being able to afford to wait until the goods were sold, perhaps two years later, they would borrow from the Duke, but sometimes he would buy from them speculatively, paying them at the time of the sale.

The East India Company held its monopoly until 1784, when the Government stepped in and took over a measure of control, allowing private merchants to export goods in the Company's ships. By 1833 the value of this private trading had grown larger than that of the Company's. Their China monopoly was abolished and their power declined. In 1858, after the India mutiny, when the government of India was transferred to the Crown, the Company was wound up and in 1862 the Old East India House was demolished.

After the Restoration London trade with the Baltic had increased, particularly in timber for shipbuilding and for the rebuilding of London: and there was also a rapid increase in the colonial trade with America and the West Indies, in return for which she increased her exports of woollen cloth, leather, metals, fish and corn, and the re-export of colonial products to Europe.

Our stake in North America and the West Indies was growing, for in 166 English settlers had founded the colonies of North and South Carolina, and Henry Morgan, the Welsh buccaneer, was making the West Indies safe from Spanish aggression from the mainland of South America, for the English government had granted him the status of a privateer, which meant that his piratical adventures had their blessing, provided he attacked only ships which were enemies of the realm.

At the Treaty of Utrecht in 1713 Britain had won from France the monopol of the slave trade to the Spanish American colonies and the Africa Company undertook to deliver them a minimum of 4,800 slaves a year, a quarter of the profits to go to the King of Spain and another quarter to Queen Anne. In addition to this, between 1680 and 1780, Britain imported well over two million slaves to her own colonies in the West Indies and America.

London merchants had been first in the field with this slave trade, which was mostly from the Guinea coast and West Africa, but after the collapse of the South Sea Company many London merchants found themselves without capital to continue and the trade fell into the hands of the Bristol men, who now travelled from Bristol to West Africa for slaves, carried them across the Atlantic and returned with cargoes of tobacco.

There was nevertheless a certain amount of trafficking in the City of London and in the middle years of the eighteenth century some 20,000 Negro slaves were sought and sold at the Royal Exchange, each one branded and wearing a padlock engraved with the name or the coat of arms of his owner.

As early as 1678, after Crosby Hall had ceased to be a private residence, had been badly damaged in a fire of 1673 and had then become first a Presbyterian meeting house and then a warehouse and auction room, a sale was announced there of 'tapestry, a good chariot and a black girl about fifteen' and in 1769, 100 years later, *The Public Advertiser* was announcing:

To be sold, a Black Girl, 11 years of age; extremely handy; works at her needle tolerably, and speaks English well. Inquire of Mr Owen, at the 'Angel' Inn, behind St. Clement's Church, in the Strand.

However, only three years later, as a result of protests from Granville Sharp, a test case was brought concerning one of these slaves, and the Lord Chief Justice decided that once a slave set foot on British territory he was free and could not be taken back into slavery. Yet abolition was a long way off, and as the Bristol slavers grew rich the Liverpool men watched them enviously.

During the seventeenth century Liverpool had been carrying Irish linen and dairy produce to the West Indies, returning with sugar and tobacco, but when the English government decided to forbid the Irish trade with the West Indies, Liverpool lost her carrying business and Manchester the supplies of flax, with which she was establishing a weaving industry. The manufacturers were already receiving small quantities of cotton from London, which was imported by the Levant Company and bought mainly for making candlewicks. A Manchester weaver now had the idea of weaving this 'cotton wool' into cloth, but the cotton still had to come from London and the importers could supply it only after they had met the demands of the candle-makers. Moreover the

East India Company began to raise objections, fearing for the future of their imports of Indian woven cotton.

About this time, West Indies colonists found the cotton plant growing wild. They began to experiment with its cultivation and occasionally, in the cargoes of rum, sugar and tobacco, they despatched to Bristol, Liverpool and London a few bags of cotton, in the hope of finding a market for it. Merchants from Manchester and south Lancashire were soon making the long journey south, by pack-horse, in order to pick up any consignments of West Indies cotton that were available. The damp climate of Lancashire was found to be particularly well suited to the handling of cotton and soon the West Indian supplies were being directed to Liverpool.

By 1709 Bristol had 57 slavers in service. Liverpool men were prepared to enter into competition with them by carrying Manchester cotton to Africa, African slaves to the West Indies and West Indian cotton back to Manchester, but they lacked the capital to equip their ships, buy the cargoes of Manchester goods and wait for the return of their money until the twelve-month trip had been completed. They therefore worked their way into the business by the illegal but simple method of carrying Manchester cottons direct to the West Indies and selling them to Spanish traders from Cuba and the mainland, who sailed to Jamaica in small schooners and smuggled them back into the Spanish colonies free of the 300 per cent duty imposed by Spain.

Spain protested in no uncertain terms but it was no easy matter to stop either her own smugglers or the Liverpool pirates. At the height of the smuggling the Liverpool men's annual profits were over a quarter of a million pounds and they soon accumulated the capital for their first slave ships. It was not until 1747 that an Act of Parliament forbade foreign vessels to visit British West Indian ports. This made it more difficult for Spanish smugglers to call at Jamaica but it no longer mattered to the Liverpool merchants, for they now had the money they needed, As early as 1730 they had sent fifteen slave ships to Africa. By 1737 the fleet had increased to 33 and by 1752 it was 58. Bristol and London were still engaged in the trade, but by 1771 only 23 slavers sailed from Bristol and 58 from London, while 107 went from Liverpool.

The passage across the Atlantic took seven or eight weeks and the slaves were confined in such appalling conditions that many did not survive, while others deliberately starved themselves to death.

One of the most scandalous affairs was the trip of the slave ship 'Zong', which sailed from West Africa to Jamaica in 1781 with a cargo of 440 slaves. Through bad seamanship on the part of the master, Captain Collingwood, they missed Jamaica and were two months at sea. Food and water ran short and fever and dysentery broke out. Sixty slaves died and many more were dying. Collingwood called his crew together and suggested that the slaves who could obviously not recover should be thrown overboard, for, he said: 'If the slaves die on board, the owners will lose, but if we maintain that the slaves were thrown overboard for the preservation of the ship, the underwriters will have to bear the loss.' And in the course of the next two days 78 slaves, shackled and manacled, were tossed overboard to drown.

This was, of course, an exceptionally bad case and it was the preaching of Dr John Newton, who had been captain of a slaver himself in his early days, which helped to bring about the abolition of the Liverpool slave trade in 1807, and it was from the pulpit of St Mary Woolnoth in Lombard Street, where he was vicar for 30 years, that he proclaimed his anti-slavery movement, gaining the ear of people of influence, including the newly-elected Member of Parliament, William Wilberforce.

When César de Saussure arrived in London in 1725, the first thing that impressed him was the strict customs search, the officers, he said, being 'extraordinarily clever at discovering anything contraband, a share going into their own pockets'. They noticed that the breeches of one of his travelling companions, a French refugee Captain, were rather bulky in the seat and found a packet of Flanders lace hidden there. Then they turned their attention to the Captain's mother and sister, and 'being impudent enough to search beneath these French ladies' petticoats, found several more packets of lace'.

He complained that he had to wait several days before recovering his boxes from the Customs House, although he carried no sort of contraband, and it cost him four or five half-crowns. 'It seems to me that making strangers pay for bringing work clothes into a country is not creditable to the English nation, and I have heard it said that it is the custom in no other country', he wrote. He was impressed with Wren's new Custom House although 'the hall on the first floor was so crowded with merchants, captains of vessels and other applicants that you have difficulty in making your way in' and the bargemen 'use singular and even quite extraordinary terms, and generally very coarse and dirty ones, and I cannot explain them to you'.

He saw the sights of London, the Tower and the menagerie, 'a small and rather dirty place', St Bartholomew's Fair, for which he cared nothing, for the noise and uproar was continuous and overwhelming, and there was a perpetual risk of being crushed to death and also of being robbed, 'for I think that no cleverer pickpockets exist than in this country, and in every crowd you must beware, else your pockets will soon be picked and emptied'.

He visited the Bethlehem Hospital, which had been rebuilt in 1675. It was a magnificent building, he said, and one of the largest and handsomest in

London, the frontage being modelled on that of the Louvre: and here, for the payment of a penny to the porter, you could see the poor lunatics in their little cells ranged on either side of a wide gallery. The harmless ones were on the ground floor but the dangerous maniacs, 'chained and terrible to behold', were consigned to the floor above.

He saw the Lord Mayor's procession, which at this time and until 1856 went by river to Westminster to give the oath of loyalty to the Tribunal of the Exchequer. They returned to the Fleet canal, where they landed and mounted their horses to ride in procession to the Guildhall for their feast. It was a general holiday in the City, when 'the vulgar populace, the most cursed brood in existence . . .' was 'particularly insolent and rowdy, turning into lawless freedom the great liberty it enjoys'.

At one of the six-weekly hangings at Tyburn, he saw thirteen criminals all hanged at the same time, amongst them the notorious Jonathan Wild, who lived for many years in the large and elegant house in the Old Bailey – 'the second door south of Ship Court'. Here he had carried on a highly profitable business in restoring stolen property, for a handsome reward, to people who had been robbed by the disreputable crowd of thieves, living mainly in Alsatia, the liberty where the White Friars monastery had once stood, and whom Wild organised with great skill, blackmailing them into bringing their goods to his office on his own terms.

De Saussure wrote of the Fleet marriages which were performed by rundown clergymen imprisoned in the Fleet for debt. They were often allowed out on bail, provided they kept within a mile and a half of the prison and had the money to pay a licence of 8d. a day, as well as a shilling a day to the tipstaff who had to accompany them all the time. At one time there were at least 40 'marrying houses' in the cellars along the canal or in the surrounding pubs, where people could be married quickly and secretly, for the price of a drink or a few pence, and it was not until the marriage act of 1753, when marriages became civil as well as religious contracts, that Fleet marriages became illegal.

He admired Ludgate Hill with its beautiful mercers' shops and thought that the Strand, Fleet Street, Cheapside and Cornhill were the finest streets in all Europe. He was impressed with the Royal Exchange, the crowds of foreign merchants and the rich merchandise of the shops. He admired the convenience of the penny post, with the large number of small offices in every quarter of the town, and was impressed by the fact that 'every person has the facility of insuring his house against fire', the insurance companies employing their own firemen and all insured houses bearing the insurance company's sign.

These fire insurance companies had been established at the same time as

Lloyd's shipping insurance. London Assurance and the Royal Exchange covered fire as well as marine insurance. The Sun Fire Office had been established
in 1710 and the Westminster in 1717: and by the end of the century there were
several more, including the Union, Phoenix, Equitable and Amicable Insurance
offices.

De Saussure was also impressed by the City's water supply, describing how
in every street there was a large oak pipe with little leaden pipes carrying water
to people's houses, from the New River reservoir at Islington, the York Buildings machinery near the Strand or the Bridge water works. By paying yearly
every house could have one or two taps, the water being available for three
hours each day: and there were also street pumps and wells.

The amount of water English people employ is inconceivable, he said,
especially for the cleaning of their houses. They were not slaves to cleanliness
like the Dutch, but still 'remarkable for this virtue, and not a week passes but
well-kept houses are washed twice in the seven days, and that from top to
bottom; and even every morning most kitchens, staircase, and entrance are
scrubbed. All furniture, and especially all kitchen utensils are kept with
greatest cleanliness.'

In another letter he returns to this business of cleanliness, saying that
'English women and men are very clean: not a day passes by without their
washing their hands, arms, faces, backs and throats in cold water, and that in
winter as well as in summer.'

But he adds 'Would you believe it, though water is to be had in abundance in
London, and of fairly good quality, absolutely none is drunk?' Beer, porter,
ale and gin were the drinks of the working classes and quantities of port and
Bordeaux claret were consumed in the better class taverns, despite the heavy
tax. He ventured a hazard that three times as much smuggled wine was drunk
as was ever imported, though much of it was diluted by the inn-keepers or
laced with spirits. Gin was distilled from English corn and its manufacture
was encouraged for a time. Defoe said this was because it consumed such large
quantities of corn that the farmers and large landowners reaped handsome
profits. After the heavy import duties were imposed on wine and brandy, gin
was made in England in such vast amounts that it was cheaper than beer,
and during the 1730s and 40s there were said to be between 6,000 and 7,000 gin
shops in London alone. The poor drank so much of it that they died in their
thousands, and by 1751 the situation was so grave that gin was taxed and people
were not allowed to sell it without a licence. By this time more tea was being
smuggled into the country than was arriving by the orthodox routes and it
was during these years that the poor, no longer able to afford the heavily taxed
gin, managed to get hold of supplies of illicit tea and learnt to like it.

On the whole, de Saussure enjoyed his years in England. He disliked the lower orders, whom he regarded as brutal, insolent and quarrelsome, but the ordinary run of Englishmen he found sincere, brave and honourable and possessed of solid good sense, though greatly prejudiced in their own favour and disliking foreigners.

He considered that people were 'esteemed for their wealth more than anything else' and that 'commerce was not looked down upon as being derogatory as it is in France and Germany. Here men of good family and even of rank may become merchants without losing caste', and he noticed, as so many had before him, that 'English merchants after obtaining wealth often retire to live the quiet life of an English gentleman'. It was not until the nineteenth century that the snobbish attitude to commerce, trade and industry developed: and it was often strongest amongst the people whose families had acquired their wealth and landed properties from them only a few generations earlier.

De Saussure did not, like Ned Ward, who was writing at the same time, visit the museum of the Royal Society at Gresham College. Sir Thomas Gresham had planned for seven professors to lecture each week on divinity, astronomy, music, geometry, law, medicine and rhetoric, the salaries of £50 a year to be defrayed from the profits of the Royal Exchange. The Duke of Norfolk had presented 2,000 books from his own library and the lectures began in 1597 and were read every day, except Sunday, in Latin at 9 a.m. and in English at 2 p.m. By 1663 the Royal Society was meeting there but in 1710 they moved to Crane Court, Fleet Street, where they remained until 1780, when they moved to the new Somerset House, and later to Carlton House Terrace. The lectures at Gresham College were poorly attended and in 1768 the house was demolished. The lectures were read for a time in a room above the Royal Exchange and met with little more success, but after the new Gresham College was built in Gresham Street, in 1843, there was a revival of interest in the lectures delivered in English, although the Latin ones were discontinued through the lack of an audience. The college was rebuilt in 1913 and is now the Graduate Business Centre of the City University, in Northampton Square, St John Street, Clerkenwell, which was founded in 1891 as the Northampton Institute and later became a college of advanced technology, being created one of the new technological universities in 1966.

Before the building of the Mansion House the Lord Mayor had resided in his own house in the City, but as early as 1728 the Court of Aldermen were considering the idea of building a Mansion House. It took them a very long time to make up their minds. By 1730 the Court of Common Council had decided that

This Court doth receive and Order that all moneys which shall hereafter be paid into the Chamber of London as a fine for not holding the office of Sheriff shall be appropriated for the Building a Mansion House for the Lord Mayor of this City under the directions of this Court,

but not until 1734 was a committee appointed to consider a suitable site. It was finally decided that 'the Stocks Market is the most free from Building, and contains Ground sufficient of the City's own Estate for the Erecting of a Mansion House suitable to the Honour of the City and the Dignity of its Chief Magistrate'.

By 1737 the Sheriffs had obtained permission from the House of Commons to build the Mansion House and remove the market to the Fleet ditch. The site was cleared and enclosed and plans for the new building were considered.

Lord Burlington submitted a design by Palladio but

the first question in Court was not whether this plan was a suitable one or not, but whether this same Palladio was a Freeman of the City or not. On this great debate ensued, and it is hard to say how it might have gone, had not a worthy deputy risen up and observed gravely that it was of little consequence to discuss this point, when it was notorious that Palladio was a Papist, and incapable of course. Lord Burlington's proposal was then rejected *nem con*, and the plan of a Freeman and Protestant adopted in its place.[1]

Four architects were then asked to submit designs and estimates. That of George Dance the Elder was accepted and work began. When a carpenter member of the Common Council tried to corner the contract for the piling and planking of the foundations, he was at once reprimanded. Moreover, a Bill was prepared to prevent any member being concerned in the future in any works belonging to the City and the Bridge House: and in a tract published soon afterwards the author commended the Court for shutting its doors against corruption, thereby establishing in the eyes of the world a confidence in the integrity of the City, a quality which, despite the cynics and a few backsliders, it has always cherished.

In the end, the building cost £71,000, compared with Dance's estimate of £26,000, for the builders ran into serious difficulties when they began to dig the foundations, owing to the number of springs and underground streams running into the course of the old Walbrook which they encountered. The Mansion House had to be built on piles, but in 1753 it was finished. The Court of

1 *Ralph's Review of Public Buildings*, (1756) quoted in J. G. White, *A History of the Ward of Walbrook* 1904 (Private Circulation).

Common Council voted £4,000 for its furniture and the Lord Mayor of that year, Sir Crisp Gascoigne, moved in, celebrating with an enormous feast, 'becoming the grandeur of so opulent a City'.

The nobility and gentry who honoured it by their presence were the most numerous that ever attended on the like occasion. The first course at dinner consisted of 600 covered dishes from the kitchen alone, exclusive of other eatables, and in the whole the number of dishes sent up is said to have exceeded upwards of 1,000.

On the next Lord Mayor all this traditional fare was lamentably wasted for the poor man died of 'gout in the stomach' only three weeks after taking office.

The Mansion House was by no means comfortable as a residence and extremely damp. There were so many complaints that in 1793 the Common Council seriously considered building a new house on an alternative site. George Dance was dead but his son suggested that the central courtyard should be covered in, 'thus furnishing a noble and convenient access to the Egyptian Hall as well as rendering the House free from the dampness which now exists'.

This was done and proved effective. The unsightly attic floor above the ball-room, irreverently dubbed the Noah's Ark, was removed in 1842, and after the Great Exhibition the Corporation bought £10,000 worth of statuary, most of which was placed in the Egyptian Hall, the stained glass windows being added a few years later.

The ancient walls of the City came down between 1760 and 1766 and the gates were demolished, the Ludgate prisoners being moved temporarily to the workhouse in Bishopsgate Street, until, in 1794, they were re-housed in a building adjoining the compter in Giltspur Street. In the meantime London Bridge had become ruinous. Until 1749 it was still London's only bridge. A project for a second bridge, between Westminster and Lambeth, had been proposed two years before the Great Fire, but the City had opposed it, anxious that the traffic and trade which passed through London should remain concentrated on London Bridge and the City.

It was not until 1738 that work began on the first Westminster Bridge, the City again protesting, as well as some of the taverners of Southwark and the Thames watermen, but this time they were overridden by the Archbishop of Canterbury, who was tired of the old ferry service between Lambeth and Westminster. With some sympathetic peers, he procured the passage of an Act of Parliament for the building of the new bridge, which took eleven years, the money being supplied by Parliamentary grants and public lotteries. It was an elegant and attractive bridge, designed by the Swiss architect, Charles Labelye, but before long some of the piers became unsafe and by the mid-nineteenth century it had to come down for the building of Sir Charles Barry's bridge.

Blackfriars Bridge was begun in 1760, while England was in the throes of the Seven Years War, and was opened in 1770, being first called Pitt Bridge, in honour of the man who had 'recovered, augmented and secured the British Empire in Asia, Africa and America, and restored the ancient reputation and influence of his country amongst the nations of Europe'. By 1863 it was found to be too narrow for the increasing size and volume of the traffic it had to carry and was replaced by the present bridge, which was opened by Queen Victoria in 1869.

Vauxhall Bridge had been built in 1816, Rennie's Waterloo Bridge in 1817 and Southwark Bridge, also by Rennie, in 1819, and at this time old London Bridge was still standing. By the end of the seventeenth century the roadway had been widened. Houses at the northern end which had been lost during the Great Fire had been replaced in the style of the new City houses and by 1710 most of the old timber houses had been rebuilt, but by the middle of the century they were in a poor condition and the shops were run down. The fashionable mercers and drapers had gone, leaving only little haberdashery shops where 'economical ladies were accustomed to drive . . . from the west end of the town to make cheap purchases'.

A committee appointed to report on the bridge decided that the houses had become 'a public nuisance, long felt and universally censured and complained of' and in 1757 they were all demolished. Sir Robert Taylor and George Dance then set about repairing the bridge, cutting it in two and building a new, wide central arch, but the join became so insecure that people hesitated to venture over it. The stone from the old City gates was used to strengthen the foundations of the new arch, but within a few years they were loose again, through the scouring of the current. The repairs of the Bridge were costing £2,500 a year, yet it was not until 1823 that the City decided that a new bridge must be built. A site was chosen a hundred feet to the west and Rennie set to work. He died before the first stone was laid, but his two sons continued the work as he had designed it and the bridge was opened in 1831, being widened in 1902–4.

12

Prelude to Victoria

By the end of the Seven Years War in 1763 Britain had turned her trade rivals, the French, from both India and Canada, and a few years later Captain Cook had claimed for Britain all the lands he touched during his South Sea voyages, including Australia and New Zealand. It was the birth of the British Empire, but with no imperial policy as yet, Britain lost her American colonies in 1776, through trying to govern them from London.

After that defeat, many members of the government argued that colonies were costly and unrewarding enterprises for which Britain had little use and could well do without. In Canada, at this time, Manitoba, British Columbia and the North West were unknown. Australia was an unexplored continent with a fringe of coastal settlements used mainly as a convenient dumping ground for convicts. West Africa meant nothing to most people but a chain of widely separated coastal stations, with an appalling climate which few Englishmen were able to survive for more than a year or two. In India, territories which Clive had won had been brought under some measure of order by Warren Hastings of the East India Company, but there were constant costly disturbances amongst the Gurkhas and Mahrattas, who bitterly resented the intrusion of the foreigners.

Colonies, far from being an asset, were a liability, said the politicians, and trading stations at strategic points throughout the world were all that was needed for the maintenance of Britain's rapidly developing commerce. The City of London prospered, despite the rift that was growing deeper each year between the wealthy and the poor. In 1780 broke out the worst riots the City was ever to see, which, although sparked off by a fear and hatred of Roman Catholics, developed into a social protest of unprecedented and appalling violence.

During the early years of the Restoration Nonconformists had been persecuted as assiduously as the Roman Catholics, but their problem gradually solved itself, for their numbers were so large, particularly in the City of London, where they included many wealthy merchants and skilled artisans, and their work was so important to the economy of the country, that persecution became impractical. A compromise evolved. Some worshipped at their parish church and like the Catholics, who were estimated to represent one-eighth of the population at this time, held their own religious services in private. Others, including the Congregationalists, the Baptists, and the Friends, refused to conform, and by the eighteenth century were able to conduct their own services freely in their own churches and meeting places.

The position of the Roman Catholics was very different, and after the Jacobite rebellions of 1715 and 1745 their persecution was intensified. With the Catholic Relief Act of 1778 there were loud protests from the anti-Catholics, supported by many members of the Whig element in the Common Council and other middle-class Radical merchants and shopkeepers, for whom Roman Catholicism represented the old enemies, France and Spain, and the despotism of a wealthy and aristocratic ruling class.

The Protestant Association was formed and at a meeting held in the Coachmakers' Hall in Noble Street, Foster Lane, they passed their resolution to march with Lord George Gordon, a fanatical anti-Papist, at 10 o'clock on the following morning, 2nd June 1780, from St George's Fields to the House of Commons, to demand its repeal, Lord George Gordon warning them that 'if less than 20,000 of his fellow-citizens attended him on that day, he would not present the petition'.

The deputation, composed of the 'better sort of tradesmen', duly arrived in Parliament Square, but while they waited they were joined by a rioting mob, described as 'upwards of 50,000 true Protestants', and with yells of 'No Popery' the six days of terror began.

For the first two days they concentrated on burning the private chapels and houses of Roman Catholic gentry in Westminster and the City. On the Thursday morning, 8th June, Justice Hyde read the Riot Act and ordered the Horse Guard to disperse them, but before the Guards were in action one contingent of the rioters swarmed to Newgate Gaol, set fire to the gaoler's house, tore open the prison gate, set all the prisoners free and then burnt the prison. Another crowd raced to Lord Mansfield's house in Bloomsbury Square. As the Lord Chief Justice, he had incited their wrath by proclaiming his views on religious toleration, when he had directed a jury to return a verdict of 'Not Guilty' against a Roman Catholic priest informed against for celebrating Mass. They burnt down his house, including his valuable library and private papers accumulated over 50 years, which he had been planning to publish, and he and Lady Mansfield escaped only just in time, by way of the back door.

Some then made for the Mansfields' country house at Ken Wood, Highgate, but were diverted by the landlord of the Spaniards Inn, who invited them in

for free drinks. It was a very hot day and they had come a long way. The copi-
ous supplies of beer, supplemented by barrels hurriedly sent over by the
steward of Ken House, changed their mood, and by the time they had slept it
off they were prepared to drift away, but in the City the destruction and violence intensified. At one time 36 separate fires were raging, the worst being when
they attacked the business of a Roman Catholic distiller with premises which
lay between Holborn and the Fleet. They fired the cellars, where an estimated
120,000 gallons of gin were stored, and the blaze spread so quickly that 21 neighbouring houses caught fire. Then they attacked the Fleet prison, releasing the
prisoners, and joined another group on the south bank, to set fire to the King's
Bench prison, the New Gaol, the Surrey House of Correction and the Marshalsea. Resenting the halfpenny toll which had been imposed for the crossing of
Blackfriars Bridge, they attacked and burnt the toll gates, stole the money and
burnt the account books.

Their last attack was on the Bank of England, but the Bank was ready for
them. Armed clerks and volunteers of the London Military Association were
stationed on the roofs and in the courtyards and detachments of horse and
foot guards waited outside and in front of the Royal Exchange. The rioters'
first rush was greeted with a volley. They re-formed but the second attack was
weaker and the defenders, who included Wilkes, were able to take several
prisoners. The rest fled, leaving behind their dead and wounded.

The next day there was still some skirmishing in the City but by this time the
military were in control and the riot petered out. Of the 450 prisoners taken,
160 were brought to trial, 25 being hanged and 12 imprisoned, while nearly 300
were killed in the fighting. After this a detachment of Guards used to march
to the Bank of England every evening to protect it.

When two years after the Gordon riots Pastor Moritz visited London he
landed below Deptford and continued his journey to the City by post-chaise,
explaining that 'because of the astonishing number of ships which are always
more crowded together the nearer you approach the city, it frequently re-
quires many days before a ship can finish a passage'.

He caught his first view of London from Greenwich 'enveloped in thick
smoke or fog. St Paul's arose, like some huge mountain, above the enormous
mass of buildings' and he said that 'there was hardly less stir and bustle on
the river than in some of London's crowded streets, with the great ships below
the Bridge and the countless swarms of little boats passing and re-passing,
many with one mast and one sail, and many with none, in which persons of
all ranks were carried over'.

Most visitors complained of London's smoke and fog. P. Grosley in 1772
had said that the new London was as much buried in dirt as the old, because

of the burning of sea coal during eight months of the year and the glass manufacturers, potteries, blacksmiths and dyers' yards, all of which trades and
crafts were established in the very heart of London and on both sides of the
river.

Moritz had the same trouble with the customs as de Saussure had had more
than half a century earlier, having to tip one officer after another in order to
get through. He wrote of the coffee houses where 'there generally prevails
a very decorous stillness and silence. Every one speaks softly to those only
who sit next to him. The greater part read the newspapers, and no one ever
disturbs them.' And like de Saussure he commented on the English cleanliness. 'The English,' he said 'are certainly distinguished for cleanliness, rich
and poor', and in another part of his account of his visit he says that 'no people
are so cleanly as the English; nor so particular about neat and clean linen'
but when he was on his way home, waiting for a favourable wind for Hamburg,
he stayed at a lodging house in St Katharine's and described it as 'one of the
most execrable holes in all this great City', a narrow, dirty street and a mass of
ill-built, old and ruinous houses.

He spoke of the Navy press gangs, which were at the height of their activities
in these years. On 4–6th May 1790, for example, the *St James's Chronicle* reported
that 1,500 men had been taken at Wapping, others in Southwark and 'in all
upwards of 2,100 men' . . . 'Four tenders went down the river yesterday morning
crowded with impressed men to be shipped on board a vessel of war lying in
Long-Reach ready to receive them. The same tenders were expected up again
with the return of the tide, upon the same errand.'

In 1793 France declared war on England. The red coats and pipe clay of the
British army, the old-fashioned cannon and cumbersome flintlocks went into
action again, but now the flintlocks were equipped with bayonets.

On land the war went badly for the English at first and by 1795 the Dutch
Republic, with its vast financial resources, still greater than those of London,
was affiliated to France. There was a sharp financial crisis and an economic
recession. The ship-building industry was one of the worst to suffer, the
Thames-side shipyards being particularly hard hit. Several country banks
closed and there was an alarming increase in bankruptcies. There was a brief
recovery but by 1797 an even greater recession and a further slump in foreign
trade. Because of heavy loans, the Bank of England's stocks of bullion fell to a
dangerously low level and the number of bankruptcies increased. Food prices
rose and as the price of wheat soared the poor suffered grievously. In 1793 it had
been 50s. a quarter and by 1812 it was 126s. a quarter, by which time America
had declared war against England and her exports suffered a further setback.

At sea things went better. Howe won a great victory in 1794. The English captured Ceylon and the Cape of Good Hope from the Dutch, and when Spain and Holland joined with France in an attempted invasion of Ireland, their fleets were scattered. In 1797 Jervis scored a victory over the Spanish fleet at Cape St Vincent and Duncan over the Dutch at Camperdown, but Austria signed a separate peace and England was left to wage the war alone. Mutiny in the Navy against the appalling conditions below decks added to her troubles. Only about one-third of the crews were regular sailors, many of them recruited from the peacetime merchant navy. Of the rest many were impressed by the barbarous press gangs. Others were transferred from debtors' prisons and workhouses. Criminals were allowed to volunteer and were brought from their prison cells, but there were hardly any volunteers from the free civilian population. Wages were low and irregularly paid. Food was usually nothing but ship's biscuit and salted beef and discipline was enforced by flogging. However, after this time conditions slowly improved.

The City had in the main supported the war, being mostly Tory and in sympathy with the younger Pitt, although there was a strong Whig element amongst the freemen of the Livery companies who, like the Holland House circle, had been sympathetic towards the French revolutionaries. But they voted money for the campaigns of 1793 and 1794, and after the naval mutiny at the Nore and the dread of Jacobinism, they raised companies of volunteers. By July 1803, when Napoleon was preparing to invade England and was about to proclaim himself Emperor of the French, eleven regiments of infantry and a corps of cavalry had volunteered in the City and received their colours, while the employees of the Bank of England and the East India Company had formed separate corps, as well as the watermen and lightermen.

Yet these were the years of the agrarian and industrial revolution in England and despite the war, the temporary setbacks and the increasingly bitter divisions of class and wealth, England's economy and industries expanded dramatically as the inventions of Arkwright and Hargreaves, Samuel Crompton, Cartwright and James Watt provided the cotton mills of Lancashire and the woollen mills of Bradford and Leeds with power-driven machinery, the initial capital for which was provided by the money market of London.

Coal and iron became vitally important industries, by means of which Britain was able to capture the cotton and woollen trade and become the most important manufacturing country in the world and the first in the field with industrialisation.

Coal production in 1770 was some 6 million tons a year but by 1830 it had risen to 23 million tons. Iron production was only about 250,000 tons in 1800 but by 1835 it had risen to one million tons, the capital for all this development again coming from the City of London. At the beginning of the nineteenth century Great Britain had the lead in the world metal trade, for most of the tin and copper in use throughout the world came from Cornwall and large quantities of lead were mined in the Pennines, the present great metal-producing regions of the world not having yet been developed.

Russia, Austria, Sweden and Naples had allied themselves with England against France after 1804 and the total value of England's foreign trade with Europe, America and the expanding Colonies rose from £41,500,000 in 1792 to £68 million in 1815, by which time the Bank of England was paying 10 per cent on a capital of £11,642,000.

The ship-building industry revived with the peace but the new shipyards were built at Newcastle, Sunderland and Leith, while the old London shipyards declined in importance, although the amount of shipping using London's harbours and wharves was increasing rapidly and the London docks had been rebuilt to accommodate it.

The West India dock was opened in 1800 and before Waterloo the London, East India and Surrey Commercial docks were all in use, while the St Katharine dock was built and completed in 1828.

Towards the end of the eighteenth century European investors and creditors were increasingly subscribing in bonds and stocks of the Bank of England and the great London companies, as well as Government bonds and short-term loans: and London was closely rivalling Amsterdam in offering long-term capital at low interest.

During the Napoleonic wars Holland had suffered a series of financial disasters. In 1796 the Dutch East India Company was dissolved. In 1815 Cape Colony was ceded to Great Britain, on the payment of an indemnity of £6 million to Holland. Four years later the Bank of Amsterdam failed and by the time it had recovered it was too late to regain its former power and prestige. The City of London was becoming the world's banking and financial centre, as well as the largest and most important port in the world and the centre of shipping insurance.

The City was also England's banker, the chief centre of her overseas trade and the largest consumer of the country's agricultural and industrial products.

It was during the Napoleonic wars that the English mail coach supplanted the stage coach, in speed if not in comfort. In 1782 John Palmer planned a service of mail coaches which by means of changing horses every seven to ten miles would increase the speed of the post to eight or nine miles an hour: and he argued that by allowing passengers to ride in the mail coaches the extra cost of the shortened posts would be offset and the postage of mails need cost no more.

Palmer won his concession and the first mail coach ran from Bristol to

London in 1784, the coachman armed with two pistols and the guard with two guns and a blunderbuss. Five innkeepers had been engaged on the route to horse the coach and the London terminus was the Swan With Two Necks in Lad Lane. By 1785 the Norwich Mail was on the road and the first cross posts established, and within a few months there was a network of routes all over the country.

John Palmer was appointed Comptroller General of the Post Office. The ordinary stage coaches were as numerous as ever, for many long-distance travellers preferred travelling by day and enjoying a comfortable bed at an inn each night of their journey, but the mail coaches gained a prestige. Their turn-out was extremely smart and their time-keeping astonishingly accurate, while nervous travellers felt that the security of the armed guard outweighed the dangers of the ever-increasing speed at which they travelled.

By 1795 Thomas Hasker had succeeded Palmer at the Post Office, an extremely efficient man who insisted on the mail coaches maintaining their speed and keeping to schedule, so that travellers had to snatch their meals in the shortest possible time. After many complaints, Hasker wrote to his guards:

Stick to your bill and never mind what the passengers say. Is it not the fault of the landlord to keep them so long? Some day when you have waited a considerable time, suppose 5 or 8 minutes longer than is allowed by the Bill, drive away and leave them behind, only take care that you have a witness that you called them out two or three times – then let them go forward how they can.

The craze for speed caused some terrible accidents, many of them fatal, when coaches overturned, and it is small wonder that by the turn of the century stage coaches had become as popular again as the mail coaches. The principal City coaching inns were the Bull and Mouth, St Martin's-le-Grand, the Belle Sauvage on Ludgate Hill, the Swan With Two Necks Lad Lane, the Spread Eagle in Gracechurch Street, the White Horse in Fetter Lane, the Blossom Inn Lawrence Lane Cheapside, the Bolt-in-Turn Fleet Street, the Cross Keys Wood Street Cheapside, the Golden Cross Charing Cross, the George and Blue Boar in Holborn, the Bell and Crown Holborn, the Bull Inn and the Three Nuns in Aldgate and the Saracen's Head and the King's Arms both in Snow Hill.

All these inns had stabling for bringing horses in late at night and taking them out early in the morning, as well as stables for the night coach and mail horses which stayed all day in London; and the London end of the coaching business was mainly in the hands of six competitors, William Chaplin, Edward Sherman,

Benjamin Horne, Robert Nelson, Mrs Ann Nelson of the Bull Inn, Aldgate and Mrs Mountain of the Saracen's Head, Snow Hill.

William Chaplin succeeded William Waterhouse at the Swan With Two Necks in about 1825 and then acquired the White Horse, Fetter Lane, the Spread Eagle in Gracechurch Street and the Cross Keys. His coaches went to all parts of the country and he owned stables at Purley, on the Brighton Road, at Hounslow, on the road to the west, and at Whetstone, at the beginning of the Great North Road. Lad Lane no longer exists, for it has been merged into Gresham Street, but in Chaplin's day the inn yard was in a narrow lane approached by a low arch and extremely difficult of access. The courtyard was surrounded on three sides by three tiers of galleries, approached by outside staircases, and so it remained until it was demolished in 1856, but as his business expanded Chaplin had underground stables built for 200 horses, and in the 1830s he was employing 2,000 people and owned or part-owned 68 coaches and 1,800 horses. Of the 27 mails which left the City every night, he horsed fourteen on the first stage out of London and the last stage in, and his annual returns were estimated at half a million pounds.

From the General Post Office in Lombard Street, or the new building in St Martin's-le-Grand, to which it moved in 1829, all the mail coaches, except those bound for the west, departed every evening at 8 o'clock, having first loaded up their passengers and luggage from the inns. To avoid congestion, the west-bound passengers assembled at booking offices and inns in Oxford Street or Piccadilly, or were taken there in coaches or omnibuses from their City inns, while the guards collected their mail-boxes from the Post Office and drove down to the West End departure points to join the mail coaches.

Edward Sherman, who established himself at the Bull and Mouth, St Martin's-le-Grand, in 1823, was second only to Chaplin in the coaching business. He was the pioneer of the long-distance day coaches to Carlisle, Glasgow, Liverpool, Manchester, Holyhead and other places in North Wales, and after marrying three elderly, rich women in quick succession he was able to rebuild his seventeenth-century galleried inn, with a courtyard large enough to accommodate 30 coaches. Every Monday 21 coaches left his yard and 21 arrived, and his pride was the Manchester Telegraph, which first ran in 1833, and by starting from London at 5 o'clock in the morning reached Manchester the same day, at 11 p.m., covering 186 miles in 18 hours, although it was closely rivalled by Chaplin's Defiance.

The Bull and Mouth, which became the Queen's Hotel after the rebuilding, in 1830, was the stopping place for Manchester men, and long after the coaches were off the road it remained their favourite London inn.

William Horne became proprietor of the Golden Cross early in the century and soon acquired the Cross Keys in Wood Street and the George and Blue Boar in Holborn, as well as West End offices; and by the time he died in 1828 he and his son Benjamin were working 700 horses.

There were several coaching inns in East London but the most important, and considered one of London's best, was the Bull Inn in Aldgate, owned by Mrs Ann Nelson. She ran nearly all the coaches on the eastern routes, and also the Exeter Defiance, which was driven by her son George. At the Bull, Mrs Nelson kept a room especially for her coachmen and guards, where they

> dined with as much circumspection as the coffee-room guests, drank wine with the appreciation of connoisseurs, and tipped the waiters as freely as any travellers down the road. A round dozen daily gathered round the table of this sanctum. . . . Everything at the Bull was solid and substantial, from the great mahogany chairs that required the strength of a strong man to move, to the rich old English fare, and the full-bodied port its guests were sure of obtaining.[1]

When Mrs Nelson retired, her son John carried on the business and saw the dawn of the railway age and the end of the coaches. In 1807 her third son, Robert, took over the Belle Sauvage from Robert Gray, who moved to the Bolt-in-Tun in Fleet Street. The Belle Sauvage was a magnificent place in Robert Nelson's day, its galleried courtyard busy with his fast day and night coaches, running to Bath, Cheltenham, Brighton, Cambridge and Manchester and the Newmarket–Norwich Mail. He kept 400 horses in his stable and the inn was famous for its comfort and good food. To rival Sherman, Nelson established a new service with his Beehive, announcing that it would leave the Belle Sauvage at eight o'clock every morning and arrive in Manchester the following morning, in time for the coaches leaving for Carlisle, Edinburgh and Glasgow.

The sixth important coaching proprietor in the City was Mrs Ann Mountain of the Saracen's Head. In 1823 she put the Tally-Ho coach on the road to Birmingham which, to the fury of William Horne, travelled 109 miles in eleven hours. He quickly established his Independent Tally-Ho on the same road, arranging for it to set out an hour and a quarter before Mrs Mountain's coach, in order to attract her customers, but her Tally-Ho was only one of 30 coaches which left the Saracen's Head each day and at the back of the inn she had a coach factory, where her own coaches were built: and other coaches built here were leased to her partners at the rate of 3½d. a mile.

During the halcyon days of the coaches few people realised the significance

1 Charles Harper, *London Coaching Inns*, Chapman and Hall, 1906.

of the age of steam which had already arrived. In the year of Waterloo the first steamboat had been seen in the Mersey and in 1819 an American steamboat, the *Savannah*, crossed the Atlantic from New York, calling at Liverpool on its way to St Petersburg. By 1823 the General Steam Navigation Company of Britain had fifteen small steamers plying between London and Europe and in the same year the first goods railway was opened, to make the short run between Stockton and Darlington, at a maximum of sixteen miles an hour. Then Stephenson produced his *Rocket*, which reached a speed of 35 miles an hour, and the railway age was fairly launched, despite the protests that steam engines were against all the laws of Providence, that hunting would be ruined, cows would not graze within sight of the locomotives, women would miscarry through sheer fright, farm houses would be burnt from flying sparks and horses would become extinct through disuse.

The London and Birmingham railway was opened in 1838 and a network soon spread over the country. By 1845, at the height of the railway mania, 357 new railway companies were advertising in the newspapers, inviting investment, and nearly everyone who had any spare cash bought railway shares. In some cases the companies were operating stretches of line too short to make a profit and their investors lost every penny of their money, but the big companies flourished. By 1848 most of the main line railways had been established and by 1850 there were 6,000 miles of railroad in Great Britain.

It marked a steady decline in the use of the canals which had been built during the 1760s and 1770s and had developed into a vitally necessary system of inland water communication for the industrial north and Midlands, but the coaches disappeared from the roads within a matter of months and scores of grand old coaching inns were suddenly faced with disaster, which all too often was irretrievable.

'Steam, James Watt and George Stephenson have a great deal to answer for,' declared *The Times* as early as 1839. 'They will ruin the breed of horses, as they have already ruined the inn-keepers and the coachmen, many of whom have already been obliged to seek relief at the poor-house, or have died in penury and want.'

In the City, the inn and coach proprietors came to terms with the railways. Chaplin sold all his coaches to buyers on the Continent and invested the proceeds in Pickford's, the carriers, and in the London and South Western railway, of which he eventually became Chairman. Benjamin Horne joined him in the carrying business of Chaplin and Horne, but the Swan With Two Necks, where Chaplin had made his fortune, was pulled down in 1856. The great yard of Sherman's Queen's Hotel became a railway goods' yard, although the hotel remained until 1887. Mrs Nelson's Bull at Aldgate came down in

1868. The Bell and Crown became Ridler's Hotel and survived for a few more years, but Mrs Mountain's splendid Saracen's Head in Snow Hill degenerated into a public house before the end. The historic Belle Sauvage went in 1850, to make way for Cassell's publishing house, and the Golden Cross, like the White Hart in the Borough, began a slow descent into what David Copperfield described as a 'mouldy sort of establishment', but although the archway in the Strand was demolished in 1851, the inn continued into the present century.

In the City of London the advent of the railways meant that a steadily increasing number of residents took the opportunity to move out to the suburbs, and as the importance of London as a financial and trading centre increased and more and more office space was needed, the dwelling houses disappeared. Work on the London and South Eastern Railway, with its terminus at London Bridge station, began in 1838. Charing Cross Station was built in 1863 and Cannon Street Station in 1866, while Liverpool Street Station, the terminus of the Great Eastern Railway, was built in 1875.

While early in the century the coaches were accelerating their rate of travel each year, the lumbering old tea wagons of the East India Company were still taking five or six months on their round trip to China, often sailing off course for a time to avoid both the typhoons and the pirates of the China seas.

Their first challenge came in 1812, when war had broken out with America. American mercantile shipping was badly outnumbered by English warships but they developed a small, three-masted, fully rigged privateer, carrying an unprecedented amount of sail, which was fast enough to outstrip the British warships. Then they designed the Baltimore Clipper, which was first used on the opium run and then to carry tea from China to America. She was fast, but too small to be profitable, and in 1845 a clipper of 750 tons, designed especially for the tea-carrying trade, was launched from New York and was back from China within seven months, having recovered her cost and earned a profit.

In 1849 the British navigation laws were repealed and English ports were opened to foreign shipping. The following year the American clipper *Oriental* sailed into the West India docks with a cargo of 1,000 tons of new season's tea aboard, only 97 days out from Canton river, while the British tea ships were still rounding the Cape.

Britain took note and acted quickly. That same year the first British clipper was launched from Aberdeen and the race was on to be first in London. However, in 1859, when gold was discovered in California, the American clippers were diverted to take miners from the East Coast, round Cape Horn to the west. They never returned to the China seas, leaving the race to be run between the British clippers themselves. By 1868 a hundred were on the China run, racing to be first in London with the new season's tea and a bonus reward. When they arrived in the Downs off Deal they often had to wait for a favourable wind to bring them up river, but once they had been sighted in the Channel the tea merchants knew approximately when they were due. In order to be first down at the docks they installed wind-clocks in their City offices, marked with the points of the compass, a single hand being connected with a weather vane on the roof. A night clerk kept watch and when the hand moved to the south-west he reported to a messenger who rode off to awaken his employer: and the merchant thereupon galloped down to the docks to buy the new season's crop.

One of the last of the Clippers was the *Cutty Sark*, built in 1872, nearly 50 years after the launching of the first steamboat, to race against the *Thermopylae*. Through a series of misadventures, the *Cutty Sark* did not win and it was the end of the China run. Nevertheless, the *Cutty Sark* was transferred to the Australia run with cargoes of wool for a time, but the days of the Clippers were now numbered, for the cutting of the Suez Canal in 1869 had shortened the journey for the steamboats and the Clippers were no longer practical.

Today the *Cutty Sark* lies in dry dock at Greenwich, for all to see and admire.

13

The City Food Markets

By the middle of the nineteenth century the Little Englanders, both Conservatives and Liberals, who had advocated the dismemberment of the Empire, were defeated. Sir John Macdonald had spoken for the conception of the Empire and Disraeli inspired not only his own party but the whole country with the principle of imperialism. In Australia the pioneers on the south-east coast, around Sydney, had crossed the Blue Mountains and made the first inland settlement at Bathurst. By 1839 the transportation of convicts to New South Wales had ceased, and as more free colonists arrived each year the industry of sheep-rearing grew steadily. In 1851 gold was discovered in New South Wales and Victoria, giving a sudden impetus to immigration, and at the peak of the gold rush people were arriving at the rate of 2,000 a week: and in 1901 the various colonies in Australia had joined in an independent federation of states, with a governor-general who represented the British government.

By 1840 the first 2,000 colonists had arrived in New Zealand and twenty years later, by which time their numbers had risen to 100,000, most of whom were engaged in the sheep-rearing and woollen industry, they received the right of self-government within the Empire.

The Empire Loyalists who had fled to Canada at the time of the American War of Independence had settled in Nova Scotia, New Brunswick and Ontario. During the war of 1812 America had invaded Canada, but with no success, and after 1815 the Loyalists were joined by thousands of English and Scottish immigrants. Later the French Canadians attempted to establish a French republic on the St Lawrence, but Lord Durham, sent out to report on the situation, advised a union of British and French Canada, with ultimate self-government. The Act of Union was passed in 1840 and Lord Sydenham became the first governor of a united Canada, subsequent settlements in the west being included in the Dominion.

In India, after the subjugation of the Mahrattas, Britain assumed direct rule in a number of inland states, moved towards a defensible frontier in the north-west and conquered Burma. After the Indian mutiny and the dissolution of the East India Company, Queen Victoria was declared sovereign of India, twenty years later being proclaimed Empress.

In South Africa the first consignment of British immigrants had arrived in 1820 and the Boers moved northwards into the interior, resenting both the British and their championship of the Bantu, to whom in 1828 the British had granted the same rights to which the English were entitled, although these rights were later eroded.

The British Empire covered half the world, much of it still to be explored, developed and populated. It required vast sums of money, all of which were provided by the City of London in sterling capital. From a country which had been predominantly agricultural and self-sufficient in essential commodities, England became a great manufacturing centre. The industrial towns of the North and the Midlands developed and England was the workshop of the world, the markets for her products being assured by the growing needs of the pioneers of her Empire.

The population of England was increasing rapidly, mainly because of improved medical knowledge and skills and a sharp decline in the death rate. It rose from nine million in 1800 to 20 million in 1861 and 32 million in 1900, and to feed them all food was imported cheaply from the Empire, while wool, which had been the principal source of her wealth for centuries, was now imported from Australia and New Zealand to the woollen factories of Yorkshire.

England turned her back on the land and the farming industry suffered. Half a million agricultural workers were forced to leave their farms and go into industry, but it made no difference to the overall economy of the country, for British manufacturers were in universal demand not only in the rapidly developing countries of the Empire but in every corner of the world.

The London docks, already the largest in the world, had to be rebuilt to accommodate the vast flow of traffic which now passed through them: wool, mutton, lamb, cheese and butter from New Zealand and Australia, beef from the Argentine, coffee from Brazil, wheat and timber from Canada, wheat and tobacco from America, sugar, bananas and rum from the West Indies, tea from India and Ceylon, wines and fruit from southern Europe, mahogany from West Africa, ivory, tortoise-shell, ostrich feathers and fruit from South Africa, carpets from India, Persia, Turkey and China; while from London and the other ports of Great Britain went manufactured goods of all kinds, machinery, hardware and cotton and woollen cloth.

And the financial centre of this vast trade, doing business throughout the whole world, was the City of London. It provided the great merchant vessels, first under sail and then under steam. Lloyd's provided the insurance cover, the Baltic Exchange arranged the shipping. The City provided the commodity markets. Within the Empire trade and money exchanged freely. London capital invested in Sydney, Johannesburg, Ottawa or Singapore brought more profits and business to the heart of the Empire.

The London bullion market fixed the price of gold and every country in the world found that British sterling was the most convenient currency in which to do its business. The merchant bankers of London, Baring, Schroeder, Lazard and Rothschild, through skilful dealings on the London Stock Exchange, grew enormously rich and provided money for the floating of new companies and commercial enterprises in whatever part of the world they were needed. It was London money which financed the building of the Trans-Caucasian railway for Russia and supplied the capital for industrial development in South America, China and many parts of Europe. As the world awakened to the dawning of the industrial age, it was to the City of London it turned for financial help and the initial loans.

The City made Britain the wealthiest and most powerful country in the world, supreme and impregnable. Apart from a few trade agreements, she had no foreign alliance and was able to pursue an international policy of proud isolationism.

To feed her rapidly growing industrial population, the ancient City food markets had to be reorganised. By the early nineteenth century Smithfield market was a terrible place. Dickens gave a grim description of it in *Oliver Twist*.

> . . . the ground was covered nearly ankle-deep with filth and mire and a thick steam perpetually rising from the reeking bodies of the cattle and mingling with the fog which seemed to rest upon the chimneytops, hung heavily about it. All the pens in the centre of the large area, and as many temporary ones as could be crowded into the vacant space, were filled with sheep; and tied up to the posts by the gutter-side were long lines of oxen, three or four deep, . . . The whistling of drovers, the barking of dogs, the bellowing and plunging of beasts, the bleating of sheep, and grunting and squeaking of pigs; the cries of hawkers, the shouts, oaths and quarrelling on all sides, the ringing of bells, and the roar of voices that issued from every public house, the crowding, pushing, driving, beating, whooping and yelling . . . rendered it a stunning and bewildering scene, which quite confused the senses.

Newgate market, where the meat was sold, was no better, as it was both a retail market and also the place where meat arrived from all over the country. All this business was crowded into far too small an area.

Through the filthy lanes and alleys no one could pass without being butted with the dripping end of a quarter of beef, or smeared by the greasy carcase of a newly-slain sheep. In many of the narrow lanes there was hardly room for two persons to pass abreast.

In 1855 the City of London decided to move the cattle market to Islington, where proper slaughter houses were built. In the 1860s the Central Meat Market was built on the Smithfield site and the traders from Newgate moved in, with an impressive ceremony by the Lord Mayor, followed by a traditional banquet for 1,200 people.

St Bartholomew's Fair moved with the cattle to Islington and became known as the Caledonian market, where at one time many a bargain could be found. The market closed on the outbreak of war in 1939 and never re-opened, but the slaughterers remained there until 1967, since when there has been no public abattoir in Inner London.

The Central Meat Market was designed by Sir Horace Jones, who was influenced by Paxton's Crystal Palace. The building, covering an area of three and a half acres, is a gigantic shed, the arched entrance giving on to a wide arcade supported by slender iron columns and roof girders. Crossing the Grand Avenue at right-angles is the Central Avenue from which further avenues lead off, row after row, each lined with butchers' shops displaying thousands of carcases of lambs and sheep, calves, cattle and pigs, which hang from enormous meat hooks, as well as vast quantities of meat in boxes, which have been prepared at abattoirs.

To the west of the Central Meat Market is the Poultry Market and beyond it, at the corner of Charterhouse Street and Farringdon Street, the General Market for eggs, poultry, game, bacon and cheese, as well as meat.

After 1876, when the first consignment of frozen meat arrived at Smithfield from the Argentine, cold stores were built under the market and surrounding streets, and the whole complex at Smithfield, including the storage warehouses, covers ten acres.

In 1937, just before the Second World War, four out of five carcases of mutton and lamb exported to England from Australia and New Zealand and half the exports of South American mutton and lamb, as well as two-thirds of the total quantity of chilled beef exported to England from South America and nearly two-thirds of Australian and New Zealand frozen beef exports, came to Smithfield and it was the principal centre for the sale and distribution of the surplus meat and poultry supplies of Great Britain and Ireland, the Dominions, South America, France and other countries of Europe.

Throughout the 1930s the amount of imported meat was beginning to decline and today the trading pattern has changed drastically, but Smithfield remains the wholesale market for at least eight million Londoners, and 90 per cent of the meat passing through is sold in London and the home counties. Meat comes from all over the world, notably from New Zealand, the Argentine, Eire, Australia and South Africa, but two-thirds are from Great Britain and Ireland.

It is a free market owned by the City Corporation and goods and produce are bought on the spot and carried away to the buyers' retail shops, hotels and restaurants. The Corporation charges rent for the shops on the basis of the number of square feet occupied, and there is also a toll for every ton of meat passing through the market.

Smithfield market pays for itself and most of the money goes to its upkeep and administration, which includes the Market police force. Any surplus goes into the City's cash account, which is used to maintain the open spaces it possesses, notably Epping forest, and to entertain distinguished foreign visitors to the City.

Smithfield is also a food processing plant. Eighty per cent of the meat is cut up there into primary joints, which are bought by the retail butchers, who then cut them into smaller, handier joints for their customers, and the rest of the meat is bought by the manufacturing firms for meat pies and sausages.

All sales in the market are by private treaty, which means that no prices are displayed and each transaction is separately negotiated. Once the salesman and buyer have agreed on a price they will abide by their word. It is the tradition of integrity which has persisted among all City merchants and is particularly strong at Smithfield.

The market is open at midnight for the delivery of produce and the lorries arrive in a continual stream all through the night. The 'pullers back' take the meat from the inside of the vans to the tail boards. Then the pitchers take over, humping the meat to the shops. Their work is finished by about 4 a.m., when the cutters, helped by the 'humpers', set to work cutting the carcases into primary joints, after which they are weighed. The salesmen arrive about half-past four and the first buyers are there by five o'clock, their purchases being carried away to their lorries by the market 'bummarees' or one of the firms associated with the market. Throughout all this time that the market is in operation environmental health inspectors, employed by the City Corporation, are in attendance.

At noon trading stops. The prices obtained are sent to the Superintendent's office, where a range of prices is prepared, and by 1.30 p.m. each day these are shown on the notice board in the market entrance, together with the amount of tonnage which was sold on the previous day, the figures being also reported to the Press: and by 2 p.m. the market is empty and ready for the cleaning gangs to move in who make ready for the next day's marketing.

In 1876 the present fish market, also designed by Sir Horace Jones, was built at Billingsgate, the third building on the site. Although much smaller than Smithfield, it is similar in style, with a glass roof supported by iron pillars. It has a floor space of nearly an acre and below are cold-storage chambers and workshops. Billingsgate Buildings, another subsidiary market for fish, with a floor space of about 5,000 square feet, was built opposite the main market in 1888, but this was demolished in 1972, when the roadway was widened.

The main fish market is surrounded by shops and the floor of Billingsgate is divided into 'stands', which are nothing more than a 60 square foot patch of red tiled floor space, the rest of the floor being of black tiles. There are more than 200 of these stands, which are leased from the market authorities, the superintendent collecting the rents and a toll on every hundredweight of fish sold.

Until 1936 deliveries of fish were landed at Billingsgate by trawler, but today it all comes either by rail or long-distance lorry.

When fishermen land their catch at British ports it is sold by auction at the quayside. The buyers are coastal wholesalers who sell to inland wholesalers, arranging the despatch of the fish by train or road. Although there are large fish markets throughout the country, notably at Grimsby, Hull and Lowestoft, a large proportion of the catches come to Billingsgate, which is still the most important inland wholesale distribution market, handling most of the fish during three hectic hours in the morning, from 6 until 9 o'clock.

The amount of fish eaten in England was declining throughout the 1930s and the trend continues, but at the end of the nineteen-sixties the market was handling between 350 and 400 tons each day, representing about an eighth of the total amount of fish landed each day in Britain.

There are three methods of business. Port merchants may send their fish direct to Billingsgate, to be sold by their agents. Stall holders may order direct from the port merchants for re-sale. Or London merchants may buy direct from the trawlers through their agents at the ports.

Billingsgate traders sell only complete packages of fish, which remain intact from the coast, where they are packed, to their final destination. Speed is essential in the marketing of fish, and so efficient is the organisation at Billingsgate that it is more practical for fish to be sent to London and then redistributed to the home counties than to send it direct from the ports to its ultimate destination. The extra time taken is slight, for fish leaving port on Monday is through Billingsgate and on sale in retail shops by Tuesday morning, and the advantages are many. A retailer buying at the port has a

I

more limited choice and must pay the price asked. At Billingsgate he can see what he is buying, for fish is offered by sample on the stands: he has a wider range from which to choose and he can bargain for the price. All the fish at Billingsgate is inspected by the Fish Meters of the Fishmongers' Company, who will seize any fish they consider unfit for sale.

The buyers make their purchases by private treaty from the samples on view, confident that the bulk will be of the same quality, and it is the fish porter's job to pick up the supplies from the salesman's van and transfer it to the buyer's van.

The work has to be done as quickly as possible and they sometimes have to carry loads of up to one and a half hundredweight, for distances of anything up to three hundred yards. They are all licensed and renowned for their speed and efficiency, and as in other City markets, there is a strong family tradition, many porters' families having been in the service of Billingsgate for several generations.

By 8.30 or 9 o'clock in the morning the selling for the day is over and the cleansing squads move in.

The superintendent of Billingsgate market is also in charge of Leadenhall market. This too was designed by Sir Horace Jones and opened in 1881 as a wholesale poultry and game market, but the bulk of the wholesale poultry trade has now gone to Smithfield, so that Leadenhall has become mainly a retail market for general produce, as well as a variety of other goods. It is a glass-roofed arcade of some 70 shops, each occupying a floor space of about 30 square yards, lying east of Gracechurch Street and running between Fenchurch Street and Leadenhall Street, in the very heart of the City. About a quarter of the tenants now deal in poultry and game but there are also butchers, greengrocers and provision marchants, with fishmongers on the Gracechurch Street side of the market, who buy their supplies each day from Billingsgate.

With the City offices pressing close round it, Leadenhall comes as a pleasant surprise, especially at Christmas time when it is crowded with turkeys from all parts of the country: and during the grouse and pheasant shooting seasons the forlorn rows of birds bring a breath of the moorlands and highlands. But the market is always busy, for the shops supply the restaurants, clubs and canteens of the City and several specialise in provisioning liners for their luxury cruises.

All these shopkeepers pay rent to the Corporation of London, through the market superintendent of Billingsgate.

Covent Garden, which has recently moved to Nine Elms, was never a City market, the City's fruit and vegetable market being at Spitalfields, hidden away behind Bishopsgate, which Robert Horner had built in 1876. It flourished and by the beginning of the present century the market had far outstripped the facilities of the buildings. In 1920 the Corporation of the City of London, which owned the freehold of the land, acquired the leasehold of the market, realising its importance for home-grown produce as well as the supplies of imported fruit and vegetables which in these years were steadily increasing.

An extensive plan of expansion and reorganisation began. Horner's market had covered three acres but the new main building extended over five acres. It is surrounded by wide roads and has 13 broad crossroads inside: and every stand in the market has at least one side fronting an internal road, so that produce can be directly loaded on to it, thus saving an enormous amount of time, handling and porterage.

The perimeter warehouses have upper floors and basements, so that altogether there are nearly 10½ acres of floor space for display and storage. Just before the Second World War the flower market was opened and in 1965 the Corporation bought another building in Spital Square – now called Eden House – which has been converted into three large warehouses for the sale of fruit and vegetables.

In 1929 the London Fruit Exchange was opened, opposite the main market, in Brushfield Street. Until that time, and for a hundred years earlier, a large proportion of London's fruit had been auctioned at the City Sale Rooms, the business being in the hands of four fruit brokers who handled much of London's fruit throughout the nineteenth century, but by the beginning of the twentieth century not only were people eating more fruit but there were better and quicker communications with the fruit-growing countries of the world.

London then became a distribution point for fruit from the Continent as well as the United Kingdom. By the 1920s the City Sale Rooms were not large enough for the increased volume of business and the four fruit brokers joined forces with two others to form a central fruit exchange for buyers and sellers. In conjunction with the Central Markets Committee of the City Corporation these six firms organised and brought about the building of the London Fruit Exchange, where the fruit was auctioned by sample. However, these sales are no longer held and the Fruit Exchange is now mainly used to house the offices of firms connected with the wholesale fruit and vegetable trade.

Today home-grown produce is delivered to the market from farms throughout the British Isles and large quantities of imported produce arrive each day. Some growers operate their own stands but more often a market merchant sells for the grower on commission, while imported produce is either sold on commission or bought and resold by the merchant on his own account.

Of the Spitalfield weavers no trace remains. By 1832 there were 50,000 people in Spitalfields dependent on the silk-weaving industry, with 14,000 to 15,000 looms at work. They suffered from the competition of power looms but refused to give up their handlooms and struggled on for many more years. By the end of the century there were still a few left, ill-paid and desperately poor. They loved singing birds and amused themselves with singing matches between their pet birds, which were timed by the burning of an inch of candle, and they eked out their meagre earnings by catching linnets, woodlarks, goldfinches and greenfinches, which they sold in the Victorian street markets.

In his book *London's Markets*, written nearly 40 years ago, W. J. Passingham describes coming by chance across a few elderly Flemish weavers, who must have been the last of these highly skilled people. They were living around Cranbrook Street in Bethnal Green, a little to the north of Spitalfields, still working at their handlooms, making silk cloth for Jewish prayer shawls and neckties: and nostalgically they recalled their childhood days, when thousands of yards of beautiful velvet and silk were being sent from Spitalfields all over the world and 500 master weavers were living in Spital Square.

14

The Commodity Markets

s with foodstuffs imported commodities have their special markets. In large-cale buying, purchases are usually made by a broker, and if the commodity aries with each consignment that arrives at the docks, as, for example, with uch things as tea, wool and furs, then the sales must be made after the exami-ation of samples. Tea must be tasted, wool inspected in the warehouse, furs xamined in the fur-brokers' offices.

There are certain commodities, however, which do not vary a great deal nd which, as in the case of metals, can be identified by standardised descrip-ions, and here buying and selling becomes simpler, being little more than matter of exchanging documents.

With goods such as these, it is possible to buy in advance, for periods which an be as long as eighteen months. In this way the buyer is protected from uctuating prices, and if they should suddenly drop he has a means of com-ensating himself, which will be explained later in the chapter. This buying 1 advance is obviously convenient for manufacturers planning a production rogramme of a year or more ahead, in which they must know what the cost f individual items is going to be.

The seller is also protected from changing prices, for very few of these ad-ance contracts end with the sale and delivery of one consignment of goods. he contract is usually liquidated by making a further contract so that, on alance, neither side loses or gains unduly from price variations, which may e due to a number of causes, either physical, such as drought, or economic.

Markets where this forward buying is practised are known as 'futures' and ne of the great advantages of the system is that it helps to keep trade moving egularly and smoothly through the shipping lines and in and out of the ort. This is how it works.

Supposing a London merchant has agreed to supply a customer with 100 ons of a certain commodity from Australia. The customer has agreed to buy : at the price it will be when it reaches London a month later. The merchant ays £80 a ton for it to the Australian company, but by the time it reaches

London the market price has fallen to £78 a ton. This is the price at which he has agreed to supply his customer, so he loses £200 on the deal, at £2 a ton. But as a member of the relevant London Commodity Exchange he can negotiate a hedge transaction to compensate for this. As soon as he has placed his order in Australia for 100 tons at £80 a ton he sells on his London Exchange 100 tons for delivery in a month's time at £80 a ton. When the commodity from Australia is sold to his London customer at £78 a ton he then buys in on the Exchange 100 tons at £78 a ton, in order to fulfil his earlier hedge sale. The merchant has now completed two transactions: he has bought in Australia at £80 a ton and sold it direct to his customer in London at £78 a ton and also sold forward 100 tons on the Exchange at £80 a ton and bought from the Exchange at £78 a ton, making a loss of £200 on the first transaction but a profit of £200 on the second.

This hedging device is as good as an insurance policy to the dealer and helps to keep manufacturers' prices stable.

In London there are futures markets in such commodities as rubber, cocoa, shellac, jute, sugar and wool tops; in copper, tin, lead and zinc; and in maize and barley.

The London Commodity markets are nearly all situated in the small area between the Bank of England and the north bank of the river, which is the traditional trading district of the City. The British consume prodigious amounts of tea, estimated at almost a quarter of the world's production. In 1833, when the East India Company lost the monopoly of the tea trade with China, they considered the possibility of growing tea in India. It was then discovered that the tea tree grew wild in the Assam jungle of North-east India. Experiments in the cultivation of China tea in India failed, but Charles Bruce, acting for the British government, now paid particular attention to the indigenous tea tree of Assam. He transplanted young tea bushes into nursery beds and with the help of Chinese coolies who knew the tricks of the trade and had been smuggled out of China to help him, Bruce prepared a small sample of Assam tea, which was tested in Calcutta and approved.

By 1839, 95 chests of Assam tea arrived in London and were auctioned. It was liked and the government invited private merchants to take over the Assam tea gardens and produce tea for the British market. People gradually came to prefer Assam tea, which was treated differently from China tea, the leaves being fermented to produce 'black tea', as opposed to the unfermented 'green tea' of China. By 1850 the Assam company was making a profit. Tea was planted elsewhere in India, particularly in Darjeeling, the Himalayan foothills and Madras, and gradually India became the greatest tea-growing and exporting country in the world, producing in 1974 nearly 1,000 million pounds of tea from 7,000 tea gardens, about half of which was exported, but within the last few years Sri Lanka's exports of tea have equalled this, for she has nearly 600,000 acres under tea cultivation, and of the annual crop of about 450 million pounds, 410 million pounds, worth about £89 million, were exported, representing about 40 per cent of her entire exports. Imports to the United Kingdom are far less than they were a few years ago and many British firms now buy directly from the sources of supply. However, not including China tea, which is sold in only small quantities in London and by different methods, nearly 2,000 varieties of tea are despatched from the tea gardens of northern and southern India, Sri Lanka, Indonesia and Africa for sale in Britain.

The old London tea warehouses are no longer in use and although some comes to London most of the tea arrives at Avonmouth, Hull or Liverpool, where it is stored in tea warehouses round the docks or in the modern warehouses which have been built in the Midlands, particularly at Banbury and Birmingham, points from which it can be easily distributed to all parts of the country.

The tea destined for London is addressed to one or other of the merchant firms, most of whom have offices in Sir John Lyon House, Upper Thames Street, who instruct their brokers to sell the tea for them, at the same time sending the necessary orders to inspect the tea at the warehouses and extract samples for tasting.

The firms who are planning to buy the tea send similar instructions to their brokers, who obtain samples for tasting, most of which are nowadays collected at the Tea Clearing House which adjoins Sir John Lyon House.

The inspectors of the merchants' brokers first of all examine the packages to see that they are in good order, and then extract a small sample from each to judge the quality and condition of the leaves and also to ensure that the standard of the consignment is the same throughout. From the whole break they take a quantity of tea – about a kilogramme, but varying according to the size of the consignment – back to the tasting rooms.

Here begins the ritual of tea-tasting. Into a row of small pots are placed quantities of tea equal in weight to the old sixpence, or, in some cases, as with the tasters at Brooke Bond's (who within the last few years have moved from Cannon Street to Leon House, Croydon), to the old shilling. Half a pint of water which is just boiling is poured on to the leaves. If it is over-boiled the sensitive palates of the tea-tasters will know at once and the sample will be rejected. After six minutes' infusion, the tea is poured into small cups and tasted both with and without milk. It is not swallowed but spat out again into spittoons. Beside each cup is a sample of infused tea and also a canister of dried leaves, the remains of the sample.

From these tests the taster can judge what he considers to be the right price for the tea. He arranges the cups in the order of his preference and the price he gives for each sample is entered on the catalogue by the attendant clerk.

These reports are made not only to establish a reserve price for the forthcoming auction but also for the benefit of the tea-planter, who relies on the tea-tasters for advice on changes of quality which may have come about on the plantations through varying weather or soil conditions and altered its value and also on changing tastes and preferences amongst the buyers.

At the same time, the buyers themselves are tasting the tea, in the offices of the buying brokers, and fixing their own prices, which may differ considerably from those of the sellers. The tasters are extremely skilled and may taste between five and six hundred different teas in a day.

As soon as the catalogues are ready the auctions take place at the new Tea Trade Centre in Sir John Lyon House. They are held every Monday, tea from North India, Bangladesh, Malawi, Kenya, Uganda, Tanzania, Mozambique, Mauritius, Rwanda, New Guinea, Burundi and Brazil being auctioned first, and from Sri Lanka and Southern India last, in the afternoons.

The consumption of tea in the United Kingdom has been declining for some years, although the decline is now thought to have halted, but world consumption is increasing as the peoples of the Middle East and of India and Sri-Lanka have taken to tea-drinking.

Wool is another commodity which must be bought by sample. Today most of Britain's wool comes from Australia, New Zealand and South Africa, with additional smaller supplies from the Falkland Islands and Chile, but there are also special auctions of English wool.

London was once the world market for wool, but even before 1939 large consignments of Australian wool were going direct to the wool manufacturers of Japan and America, without passing through London, thereby saving on freight charges. During the Second World War there were no wool sales in London and today more wool than ever is being shipped direct to the manufacturing countries, in particular Japan and America. Before 1939 an average of 500,000 bales would be sold each year at the Wool Exchange in Coleman Street but by 1958 it was down to about 340,000 bales, Bradford manufacturers buying direct from abroad and large amounts also going direct to Hull and Liverpool.

After the Second World War and until 1959 the wool auctions in London were run by the Committee of London Wool Brokers, who represented the six firms of brokers engaged in selling wool. Then a private company, London Wool Brokers, Ltd, took over.

The wool, already classified and graded, arrived at the London docks in huge bales, each weighing three hundredweights and bearing the mark of the grower, and were lightered up to the dockside warehouses. The warehouse of the London Wool Brokers was at Machonochie's Wharf on the Isle of Dogs, and on the first floor was the huge sample room, with a glass roof admitting the necessary north light, so that buyers could make a proper examination

After the demolition of the Coleman Street Exchange, wool was auctioned at the Spitalfields Exchange, but now, like the fruit auctions, the London wool auctions are no longer held.

In 1939 the London fur market was the largest in the world. During the Second World War it was closed and the international trade moved to New York, but by the 1950s the London fur trade, with its traditional skills, had regained its old pre-eminence.

From the day when Garraway sold its first beaver skins, the business of the Hudson's Bay Company increased steadily. Apart from all the other furs they had to offer, they held the monopoly of beaver, and men continued to wear large beaver hats until about the time of Waterloo, when they took to the tall silk hat. In the early years there was strong opposition from the French fur-trading companies in Canada, but after 1763, when the French territories in Canada were ceded to Britain, the Hudson's Bay Company's fur market in London was the world headquarters of the trade.

In Canada a rival company of Scottish Canadian traders of Montreal began challenging their charter and ignoring their trading rights, forming in 1784 the North West Company, but in 1821 the two companies amalgamated, the governor of the Hudson's Bay Company continuing to administer the vast area of Rupertsland, which had been allotted to it in the seventeenth century.

In 1870, however, the Company relinquished its rights to the land, which was transferred to the Canadian Government, and operated as an ordinary commercial trading company. Over the years they became not only the largest fur company in the world but developed many other commercial concerns in Canada, but the auction house in London remained the sole distributor for their furs. The business had declined after 1870 but revived during the early years of the present century. After 1865 they had moved to the old silk warehouse of the East India Company in Wine Street but in 1928 they established themselves at Beaver House in Little Trinity Lane, in the heart of the City's fur quarter. Here on College Hill, Queen Street, Garlick Hill and all the other narrow lanes running down steeply from Queen Victoria Street to the western end of Upper Thames Street, and in Upper Thames Street itself, are the City's fur warehouses and the offices of fur-trading companies and fur-brokers, close to ancient Queenhithe, where the first foreign furs were landed in Anglo-Saxon times, and to the beautiful hall of the Company of Skinners on Dowgate Hill.

In 1940 the Hudson's Bay Company absorbed the long-established Lampson, Fraser and Huth Company, with their American connexion, and established a second auction house in New York, while in 1949 they opened a third auction house in Montreal.

In 1957 the London end of the Company was reorganised to become a subsidiary, known as Hudson's Bay Fur Sales Ltd, and in 1972 the headquarters of the parent company, which was still in London, was transferred to Canada. At the same time, Hudson's Bay Fur Sales amalgamated with another old-established London fur auction company, which during the course of more than a century of re-formations had become Anning, Chadwick and Kiver. The new firm, Hudson's Bay and Anning, is now the largest fur auction company in the world, handling Canadian, American and Russian furs.

The other important London fur auction company is Eastwood and Holt Ltd, which has been established for over a hundred years, and these are the two firms which hold their auctions all through the year at the London Fur Auction Room – Beaver Hall – in Beaver House.

Furs arrive in London's fur quarter from all over the world. When they reach the warehouses the skins are sorted and graded, the London graders being famous for their reliability. The graded skins are made up into bundles of usually 200 skins, and bundles of similar quality are grouped together as 'strings'. Once this work is finished a catalogue is prepared for the auction, listing the type of skin, the number of skins in the bundle and the letter and number indicating the type, grade and region from which the skins come.

A few days before the sale sample bundles are set out in the warehouse display rooms, the grading having been done so skilfully that buyers can be confident that the sample shown is an absolutely fair example of the bulk of the lot it represents.

The buyers are both London and international authorised dealers who buy on commission for British manufacturers or overseas buyers, although most buy directly for re-sale, for the home trade represents little more than five per cent of the buying, the rest being for re-export.

Of the London Exchanges where buying has no need to be by sample but is mainly concerned with 'futures' the Metal Exchange is the most important. At the beginning of the nineteenth century Great Britain led the world in the production of tin, copper and lead but within half a century, as her industrialisation absorbed ever increasing quantities, and as other countries industrialised and produced their own supplies, she became the world's largest importer. Since most of the overseas mining development had been promoted with British money, London became the general clearing house and exchange for the world's surpluses of metals.

Merchants and their brokers began to meet at the Jerusalem Coffee House to discuss information about the amounts of metal which were being moved across the world and also the amounts which manufacturers were needing. By the 1850s they had taken to meeting each day at the Royal Exchange to do business in the buying and selling of copper, lead and tin, although the actual metals were rarely seen, except by the assayers, who visited the warehouses and ports to inspect the metals and certify that the weights and quality were correct.

At the end of the 1860s they were meeting on the ground floor of the newly opened Lombard Exchange, and by 1877 business was so prosperous that a small group of leading metal dealers formed the London Metal Exchange Company, establishing themselves, in 1882, at their present home in Whittington Avenue, hidden away off Leadenhall Street and adjoining the market: and although the building was largely reconstructed in 1961 it still has an air of quiet, Victorian dignity.

By 1900 the United States was the main world producer of copper, and since then the vast resources of central Africa have been developed. Malaya was the leading producer of tin, the United States of lead, and Germany of zinc, but the London Metal Exchange was the largest market in the world for these four metals. During the Second World War the exchange was closed, for the government undertook the buying of all such commodities, but it was reopened in 1949 and they now also deal in silver.

The Metal Market and Exchange Company are the proprietors of the Exchange and its shareholders are the members. Membership can be by an individual subscriber or a representative subscriber from a firm or company who may be granted the privilege of dealing in the Ring if considered to be of sufficient financial standing. Today no individual deals in the Ring on his own account and trading on behalf of any company in the Ring organisation must be represented by a duly elected subscriber with Ring privileges.

The Ring dealing community consists of about 30 companies and the Exchange has become a meeting place for buyers and sellers from all over the world, an international terminal market providing a service to industry on a world-wide basis, establishing world market prices and reflecting trends in world economy.

Business is conducted by direct contact as well as by Ring dealing and 'open outcry'. The Ring sessions are from 12 noon until 1.05 p.m. and from 3.35 until 4.35 p.m., with two separate five-minute periods of dealing for each metal in both sessions, the Ring itself being formed by four curved benches facing inwards, each with ten seats.

The Corn Exchange in Mark Lane is mainly a merchants' market and com-plementary to the Baltic Exchange, which in addition to being a freight market is a wholesale grain market. Many members belong to both Exchanges, but the Corn Exchange is largely a market for home-grown grain, the Baltic dealing only in imported supplies.

The first Corn Exchange in Mark Lane was built in 1751 and in 1827 another exchange was built next door, specialising in the sale of oats, but in 1929 the two Exchanges amalgamated. In 1941 the Corn Exchange was destroyed in an air raid and in 1953 the present Exchange, built on the same site, was opened. It is the biggest distribution point in the country for cereals and cereal products, including fertilisers and animal feeding stuffs, and is also the central market for vegetable and agricultural seeds, which are of extremely high quality and a valuable export commodity.

The Corn Exchange Company acts as landlord, renting stands and office accommodation to dealers and others. It serves as a meeting place for traders in grain and all the commodities associated with agriculture, as well as for shipowners and brokers, insurance brokers who insure goods in transit, and representatives of the lightermen who transfer cargoes from the ships to the wharves, and the men who take charge of it in the riverside warehouses.

Seven hundred firms are represented on the Exchange and there are 1,200 individual members.

The large market hall leads from the members' club room. Many of the members have stands in the hall, where samples are laid out on display, while others have offices in the building where they can always be found quickly for business.

There are no windows in the hall but it is lit by a domed glass roof, giving the north light upon which buyers insist. Here in small dishes are laid out every conceivable kind of grain, feed and fertiliser, from ground oyster shells for chickens to the finest malting barley, from locust beans to guano. The sale room is open five days a week but Monday mornings are usually the busiest and trading is naturally heaviest during the harvest weeks of late summer. Brewers and maltsters, millers, bakers and farmers all come to Mark Lane to examine the samples, often taking them out into the street to study them more minutely.

Like the Baltic, the Corn Exchange is a wholesale market, but it deals in smaller quantities. While a member of the Baltic might buy an entire shipload of grain, sales at the Corn Exchange can be as small as 50 tons and are usually not more than 1,000 tons, except for the large manufacturers buying in bulk for compounding.

There are no auctions at this Exchange. Sales are by private treaty and contracts and delivery arrangements are made not by the Exchange Company but by one or other of the trade associations which have offices close by, such as the British Association of Grain, Seed, Feed and Agricultural Merchants Ltd, the Grain and Feed Trade Association, Limited and the Compound and Animal Feedingstuffs Manufacturers National Association, Ltd.

In 1973 there was a great deal of reconstruction and reorganisation at the Corn Exchange. A new floor was established for the members of the Corn Trade, to include facilities for the reception of overseas traders from countries in the European Community, and trading areas were opened for the affiliated member markets of the London Commodity Exchange Company, comprising the Coffee Terminal Market Association of London, the London Cocoa Terminal Market Association, the London Vegetable Oil Terminal Market Association, the United Terminal Sugar Market Association, with facilities for the Federation of Oils, Seeds and Fats Association Ltd (including the London Copra Association), the London Jute Association, the Rubber Trade Association of London, the London Shellac Trade Association, the General Produce Brokers Association of London and the London Produce Clearing House Ltd.

Many of these commodities had been traded in Mincing Lane for centuries. During the eighteenth century the merchants of London had sent their ships across the seven seas to seek new merchandise for sale in London and they established a tradition of prompt payment and good trading. The East India Company sorted and held their sales on their own premises, but the produce of the West Indies, including sugar, rum and coffee, was auctioned at the Jerusalem and Garraway's, the cotton going direct to Liverpool. Both these coffee houses were burned down in 1748. It was the end of the Jerusalem but Garraway's was rebuilt. Then, in 1811, the London Commercial Sale Rooms were opened in Mincing Lane, and in 1863 Garraway's closed. The new Sale Rooms formed a central market exchange for the marketing of produce which had no special market exchange of its own, the most valuable commodity in the early days being sugar, large amounts of which, like the eight million gallons of rum which came in every year, was for re-export. When the East

India Company's monopoly came to an end and the trade was free for all, the tea sales were also held here and other commodities handled included tallow, wine, spices and shellacs.

The Sale Rooms were completely destroyed during an air raid in 1941 and members were invited to the home of the London Rubber Exchange in Plantation House, which had been opened in Mincing Lane in 1936. Here they remained until 1954 when the London Commodity Exchange was formed, still in Plantation House: but by the 1970s it was needing more room and has therefore moved into the Corn Exchange building.

The repeal of the Corn laws in 1846 resulted in a great increase in the import of foreign corn, and the business of the Baltic Exchange expanded rapidly, first with Russia and then with Canada, the Argentine, the United States and Australia. In 1857 the Baltic moved to South Sea House in Threadneedle Street, which had once been the home of the Merchant Adventurers, and it became the world's information centre concerning the new steam shipping. A similar exchange, specialising in the movements of the world's cargo steamers, the London Shipping Exchange, had opened at the Old Jerusalem Coffee House and since the activities of the two exchanges overlapped in many ways, when they both needed larger premises they amalgamated, the present Baltic Exchange in St Mary Axe being opened in 1903.

The principal feature of the Exchange is its vast floor, on to which only members are allowed. With its marble pillars, solid mahogany doors and large central dome, it covers 20,000 square feet, and the only remaining evidence of its coffee house origins is that the attendants, in their nineteenth-century liveries, are still called waiters, although their main function today is to summon members to the telephone or deliver messages.

The floor is divided informally into markets, with the freight market in the middle, the air freight market to one side and the rest of the space occupied by the commodity markets in grain, oil and oil seeds, which include ground nuts, linseed and linseed oil, castor seeds and castor oil and soya beans.

Today the freight market is the most important and it is concerned mainly, although not entirely, with tramp ships as opposed to cargo liners. Owners lease tramp ships to trade in any part of the world where cargo needs to be carried and it is usually a cargo of only one commodity at a time, while cargo liners run at regular times on regular routes, carrying whatever cargoes are available at the time that they are making their journeys.

Shipping, particularly tramp shipping, is international. There are thousands of deep sea tramp ships of all nations ready to be chartered by any country of the world to carry cargoes, and the freight market, operated by members of the

Baltic, plays a vital part in organising this complicated business by centralising all the information about the demand for, and the supply of ships world-wide.

On the freight market the broker representing the owner of the cargo ship negotiates with the broker acting for the charterer who has cargo. The charterer's broker will aim at the lowest rate, the owner's broker at the highest, and depending on circumstances, negotiations may be speedy or protracted. Here as in other City markets and exchanges, the Baltic member's word is as binding as a written agreement. The formal contract, the charterparty, is eventually prepared and signed and a copy sent to the captain of the ship, in whatever part of the world he may happen to be, giving him the details of his next voyage.

The air freight charter market at the Baltic, begun soon after the end of the Second World War, is growing in importance every year, having developed for both passenger transport and cargoes. The process has some similarities with the shipping operation, but obviously there is less time for negotiating to avoid flights by empty aircraft.

Aircraft are particularly useful to shipping, and shipping companies use the market for the quick transport of crews or the delivery of replacements of machinery which may suddenly become necessary.

During the Second World War the Government took over the buying of grain and the other commodities formerly marketed on the Baltic, and it has never regained its former importance as a grain exchange. As, during the last few years, the size of carrying vessels increased, the United Kingdom docks became too small to handle them. Grain transit elevators were built both at the docks of the exporting countries and also in Europe: and in the United Kingdom vast grain elevators have been built at Tilbury and Liverpool, from where the grain is transhipped around the coast or transported inland by lorry or rail.

In 1973 the London Corn Trade Association and the London Cattle Food Trade Association amalgamated to form the Grain and Feed Trade Association, comprising shippers, manufacturers and brokers, and the main standard forms of contract issued by this organisation are used for the transport of goods in Great Britain and also for the transport of grain and its derivatives the world over, involving some 80 million tons of grain business. Any disputes that may arise are dealt with by arbitration in London, which as a world business centre offers its expertise in banking and insurance and is the principal world freight market.

Since the United Kingdom joined the European Economic Community in January, 1973, it has been subject to the extremely complicated regulations of the Common Agricultural Policy, which lays down minimum prices of many agricultural products, particularly of grain, including minimum prices to Common Market grain producers and minimum prices at which grain may be imported into the Community.

The Grains Futures Ring at the Baltic, first established in 1933, was reopened in 1954 for imported coarse grains, extending by 1965 to home-grown barley and wheat. This is an octagonal wooden rail, rather like an outsize umbrella stand, about ten feet across and waist high. It would appear to be nothing more than a convenient bar against which to lean, but in practice, by gathering round in a circle, members, who make their bids by 'open outcry', have a clear view of each other's faces and expressions, which at times can be useful to a shrewd buyer.

Trading begins as a gong strikes and is carried on from 11.30 a.m. until 1 p.m. and from 2.45 until 4.15 p.m. As prices are fixed across the Ring, they are recorded on a board and broadcast to the world by brokers and press agencies. Futures contracts must always be made at the price which has been fixed across the Ring and the difference between this price and that at which the contract for a future delivery has been made must be paid up on the same day.

In 1974 women were admitted to membership of the Exchange and in 1976 foreigners who had lived in the United Kingdom for three years were allowed entry as representatives.

As Hugh Barty-King says in his history of the Baltic, 'The existence at the Baltic of a deep-rooted and strictly enforced tradition of commercial probity and financial reliability without parallel in any other city in the world was a major contribution to the continuing strength of the London freight market. . . . The Baltic remains unique and has earned its position by its unbroken tradition of service and efficiency.'

Lloyd's describes itself as an

insurance market where, with few exceptions, any insurable risk can be placed with Lloyd's Underwriters through Lloyd's Brokers: it is also a society incorporated by Act of Parliament in 1871, and the world centre of marine intelligence. At Lloyd's insurance is accepted by individuals with personal and unlimited liability, in a competitive spirit, and yet as members of a society in which they share a common loyalty.

Lloyd's remained at the Royal Exchange until 1928, when it moved to Leadenhall Street, to what is now the old building, standing on the site of

East India House. The members still use this building but in 1957 they moved to the huge building opposite on the corner of Lime Street. Here between 2,000 and 3,000 underwriters and brokers meet each day. The market is under the control of a committee of sixteen, elected from among the Underwriting members of Lloyd's. They serve four-yearly periods, before retiring by rotation, and elect their own Chairman and two Deputy Chairmen annually.

It is not the Corporation which accepts insurances, but the individual members, and it is they who are directly responsible for the liabilities which they incur. This means that the rules of membership are strict. An applicant must prove himself to be a man of integrity and solid financial standing. He must be nominated by a member and the nomination must be supported by other members of Lloyd's. He must deposit a large sum of money with the Committee as security for the risks he will shoulder, pay an entrance fee and an annual subscription. The premiums he receives from the insured are placed in a trust fund, from which liabilities and expenses are paid, and from which only ascertained profits may be removed. He must also contribute to a central fund, to meet the needs of any member whose underwriting liabilities should exceed his security or his private fortune, and submit his accounts to a strict annual audit.

Since 1890 Lloyd's have accepted other forms of risk as well as marine insurance and today marine, motor and aviation insurances are transacted on the ground floor of the underwriting room, and in the gallery, fire and almost every other form of non-marine insurance except long-term life and financial guarantee.

In 1969 foreign underwriters were admitted as members for the first time, and in 1970 women underwriters.

The underwriting members are formed into syndicates which vary in size from a few to several hundred names, each syndicate being represented by its agent, who accepts business from brokers representing clients wishing to place risks in the market. All business brought to Lloyd's must be placed through a Lloyd's broker.

The details of the risk are entered on a slip prepared in the broker's office and then shown to an underwriter who is known to specialise in the particular type of risk involved. He will suggest a justifiable premium. If the broker does not approve the figure he can approach another underwriter, but if he does, the underwriter, known as a leader, will enter on the slip the agreed rate and the percentage of the risk which his syndicate is willing to accept, which he initials. Personal integrity is unquestioned and a member's initials are accepted as a final word. Having acquired his lead, the broker continues round the Room, approaching other underwriters for their acceptances of portions of the risk, who will now judge it not only for itself but for the name of the leader who has made the first signature.

When the complete amount of the risk is underwritten a policy is prepared and sent to the Corporation's policy signing office, through which two million policies pass each year. It is checked, signed on behalf of the underwriters concerned and the seal of the Corporation is affixed.

There are many precious traditions at Lloyd's. The underwriters' desks in the vast, pillared underwriting room are pew-like boxes, like the tables of the old Lloyd's coffee house. The members' dining-room is still known as the Captain's Room, a survival from the days when one of the Society's rooms at the Royal Exchange was set aside for the use of ships' captains. In the Nelson room are relics which include the log book of the Euryalus, Nelson's signal frigate at Trafalgar, with the record of his famous last message. The liveried attendants are called waiters and on the central rostrum the Caller sits in his long, full-skirted, scarlet coat to summon members to the telephone, his voice being carried above the decorous but insistent hum of conversation by means of a pencil microphone.

Behind his rostrum hangs the Lutine bell. *La Lutine* was a French man-of-war surrendered to the British at Toulon in 1793. In 1799, as the frigate *Lutine*, she was attached to the North Sea fleet but was wrecked on a sandbank off the coast of Holland, with a cargo of gold coin and bar insured at Lloyd's for £1,400,000, which had been destined for the credit of English merchants in Hamburg. Many attempts were made to salvage the fortune but it was not until 1859 that £45,000 was raised as well as the cannon, the rudder and the ship's bell, the bell being brought back to the Underwriting Room, where it is now used when special announcements are to be made, ringing once for bad news, such as the discovery of the wreck of an overdue vessel, and twice for good news.

In the centre of the room is the casualty book in which, with the traditional quill pen, are entered the names of all ships, from liners to the shabbiest of small tramps, which have become total losses; and on the casualty board are announced all sea and air casualties, fires, floods, robberies and similar catastrophes, which are reported to Lloyd's Intelligence Department from one or other of the 1,500 Lloyd's agents posted throughout the world. These agents also settle claims which have been made payable abroad and survey damage to cargoes and ships.

The vast amount of shipping information which comes to Lloyd's, including general shipping news and details of arrivals and departures of ships throughout the ports of the world, is printed each day in *Lloyd's List. Lloyd's Shipping Index*, another daily publication, lists alphabetically some 13,000 ocean-going vessels and gives their whereabouts and their journeys.

Lloyd's Register of Shipping is a society which classifies shipping, and although it has its origins in Lloyd's coffee house it is a separate society from Lloyd's with offices in Fenchurch Street. The Register is a complete list of all ships in the world of over 100 tons. The society has established world standards of shipbuilding which are maintained by the regular inspections of over 500 of the society's surveyors, who work in the chief ports of the world: and if the surveyor of Lloyd's Register of Shipping is satisfied with the condition of a ship it is registered A1 at Lloyd's, a standard which has universal respect and trust.

The Corporation of Lloyd's has close affiliations with the Register of Shipping and is represented on its Committee, as are all those concerned with shipping and insurance.

The Port of London Authority was created in 1909 to administer the port. The City thereby lost its control of the river, the Authority taking over the 70-mile stretch from the Nore to Teddington and reorganising the port into the largest and most efficient in the world. By 1939 the five great dock systems were the London and St Katharine docks, on the promontory bounded by the Upper and Lower Pools of the river, to which came mainly fruit and wine from the Continent: the Surrey Commercial docks, consisting of eleven great timber docks, each surrounded by warehouses: down river again, three or four miles beyond the City's boundary, the India and Millwall docks: farther east again the three huge, rectangular basins of the Royal docks, the Royal Albert, the Royal Victoria and the King George V docks, between them providing 53 deep water berths and covering nearly a square mile, with 230 acres of water and eleven miles of quays: and 26 miles from London Bridge, the Tilbury docks.

The docks were badly damaged during the Second World War. Most of the warehouses round the eastern dock of St Katherine went and no one who saw the terrible red glow of the blazing timber sheds of the Surrey docks lighting up the darkening sky on that September night of 1940 will ever forget it.

They were all repaired in due course but today the Port of London Authority is gradually moving the docks further down river, to concentrate on Tilbury, with its deep water berths and modern developments to accommodate the growing size of tankers and other bulk containers. The St Katharine docks have already gone and this corner of London has been redeveloped with the Tower Hotel and the World Trade Centre, as well as blocks of riverside flats, while the vast Cutler Street warehouses, covering five acres, which were built

by the old East India Dock Company in the eighteenth century, and for years
had been crammed with Jamaica and Havana cigars, vintage wines, dangerous
drugs, including opium, and thousands of lovely and precious Oriental rugs
and carpets, imported and marketed by the Armenian carpet mechants of this
quarter, are at last coming down.

15

The Stock Exchange and the Money Market

The London Stock Exchange, in its mighty new tower, is a market in stocks and shares, which represents money lent by members of the public to Government and business enterprises. Stocks are generally accepted to be money lent at a fixed rate of interest and shares to be money invested in some commercial enterprise, the value of which varies with the fortunes of the business concerned.

Business is transacted in the tradition of the other London Exchanges. The messengers are known as waiters and a distinctive ritual surrounds the dealings. Only members and certain clerks of the Exchange may take part in the buying and selling and membership is an expensive business, with a heavy entrance fee and an annual subscription. A nomination must be purchased and substantial securities deposited.

Members are in two categories: the brokers, with whom the public has contact, and the jobbers who do the actual buying and selling. The Exchange is governed by a council of 36 members, of whom a third retire each year, although they may be re-elected, and the work of the council includes ensuring that the rules are maintained and correctly interpreted. They decide what stocks and shares may be bought and sold on the Exchange, and settle any disputes.

Some 9,000 securities are quoted on the Exchange[1] and it has been estimated that four-fifths of all Britain's industry and commerce is carried on by companies whose shares are bought and sold here, nine-tenths of the shareholding in industrial companies being represented by small amounts of a few hundred pounds.

When the broker has received his instructions from the investor he will contact the jobber, and jobbers always specialise in particular markets, each market having its own place on the Floor of the Exchange.

The price of shares is not decided by the Stock Exchange but fluctuates with supply and demand, so it is the buying and selling by the jobber which ultimately makes the price. Prices are also influenced by general trading conditions

1 At the end of March, 1976 these had a total market value of £250,000 million.

throughout the country and the political situation both at home and abroad. Even the weather is said to influence business on the Exchange.

When the broker approaches the jobber, the jobber does not know whether the broker wishes to buy or sell. When therefore the broker asks the price, the jobber gives two prices – say 145p to 149p – the lower being his buying price and the higher his selling price, the difference being known as the jobber's turn.

If the broker is not satisfied, he may approach another jobber dealing in the same commodity, who offers 146p and 148p. The broker makes a snap decision and buys at 148p. He states the number of shares he wants and he and the jobber make a note of the deal. The business is transacted and the shares bought in a matter of seconds. The verbal exchange is all that is necessary at this stage, but the following morning the broker's clerk will check the deal at the Exchange Clearing House and the necessary transfer deeds will be prepared. By settlement day, which is usually only a fortnight ahead, the broker must pay for the shares, and when he receives the deed they are signed and paid for by the customer and lodged at the office of the relevant company for registration.

The charge for their services varies with the price of the shares but in the price range of 148p it would probably be between two and three pence a share.

The margin between the buying and selling price of a share is influenced by its popularity. If it is constantly changing hands the jobber can afford to risk making only a small profit, knowing that he can easily get rid of it again, but if it is a commodity in which normally very little business is done he runs the risk, when he buys it, of having it on his hands for a very long time, thereby tying up his capital or credit, and he must therefore give himself a good initial profit.

The broker is bound to secrecy in regard to his customers' dealings and, like the jobber, is responsible to every other member of the Exchange for each piece of business which is transacted. Jobbers and brokers must pay up on settlement day, even if the customers fail them.

By way of a safeguard, there is a Stock Exchange Compensation Fund, from which, at the discretion of the governing body, money can be drawn to cover such a contingency.

Money itself is something which can be bought and sold, with profit to the dealer. The money market of London, apart from the bullion market, which is a different matter, deals in the abstract commodity of credit: and credit may be defined as permission given to a customer to take goods and defer payment.

It is the mainspring of the City's life, for it is only by lending and borrowing and giving credit that international trade can be transacted. It could never have reached its present stage of speed and efficiency if every process of production, from the growing or producing of the raw material to its transporting marketing, manufacture and resale had to be paid for as a separate piece of business, accompanied by the passing of hard cash.

Through London's money market these payments may be made without the actual handling of money, and if its services were withdrawn the result would be long and tedious delays and disastrous stoppages in the general flow of business.

The institutions which comprise the London money market are the English Scottish and Dominion banks, banks of foreign countries which have offices in the City, the private merchant bankers and acceptance houses, the discount companies, the bullion brokers, the head offices of the large insurance companies and, presiding over them all, the Bank of England.

The domestic banks which we all use, Barclay's, Lloyd's, the Midland and the National Westminster, together with Coutts, the District, Glyn Mills, the National and William Deacon's, all belong to the London Banker's Clearing House in Post Office Court off Lombard Street, where it has been since 1775, having been rebuilt in 1951: and the Institute of Banking, founded in 1879, is housed in the same building.

The cheques are sent from the branches of the banks all over the country to the London Clearing House, where they are sorted and cleared every day, each of the banks calculating what it owes to the others and the amounts being settled by a cheque on the Bank of England.

A large proportion of current account money as well as money on deposit is put to work by the banks to earn the interest paid on deposit accounts and to pay for the general expenses of running the bank. About eight per cent is held available in loose cash and a further ten per cent put into their Bank of England accounts, from where it can be drawn on demand, for immediate use. A further sum, of about one-fifth, is spent on treasury bills and discounted bills of exchange, which will mature in a few weeks, and the rest is lent to customers needing loans for business and commercial enterprises.

It was the private merchant banks of London who first began business in bills of exchange. There are eighteen of these merchant banks in the City today, including such famous names as Rothschild, Lazard and Baring. In their capacity as acceptors of bills of exchange they are known as Acceptance Houses and are all members of the Acceptance House Committee. Once the Acceptance Houses have accepted the bills of exchange they are saleable. To quote from the Radcliffe Report on the Working of the Monetary System: 'An accepting house ... when accepting a bill, confers on the drawer of the bill the certainty of being able to get sterling in exchange for it from a bank....'[1]

To unload their stock of bills, the accepting houses sell them to discount houses, which buy the bills at slightly less than their face value, at a rate of interest which is the 'discount'.

There are eleven main discount houses in London, five money traders and two discount brokers, which form the London Discount market. They buy the bills, borrowing money from the banks in order to do so, and make their profit by charging a slightly higher rate of discount than they have to pay to the banks for borrowing.

The Government and not only commercial firms has recourse to bills of exchange to meet its commitments. These are called treasury bills. Each week the Government announces through the Bank of England the number of treasury bills it has for sale, which is another way of saying how much money it wants.

The Bank of England issues millions of pounds worth of these treasury bills each week, some of which are offered to the discount houses, and like commercial bills of exchange, they can be marketed on the money market, the profit or loss to the discount house being measured by the difference between the price at which they are sold and their value at the time when they are redeemable, the discount houses agreeing amongst themselves each week the price they will offer for them.

Other buyers in the open market are overseas organisations which hold sterling, industrial companies and banks which are not associated with the big group of London clearing banks.

The Bank of England also offers treasury bills at a fixed price to the clearing banks, which can choose bills which will mature at dates when they know they will be needing money, and to government departments, such as the Post Office Savings Bank and the National Insurance Fund.

The Bank of England was nationalised in 1946, and after compensation was arranged for the stockholders, its vast amount of stock was transferred to the State, so that the Treasury is now the owner of the Bank. Its governing body, the Court, which meets each Thursday morning, now consists of a governor, a deputy-governor and sixteen directors, all appointed by the Crown.

The Bank of England is the centre not only of London's finance but of the money transactions of the whole country. It is the Government's bank, holding the account of the Exchequer, which is treated like any other account. The Bank borrows for the Exchequer on the money market, through the issue of treasury bills. It deals with treasury bills which have matured and are presented or repayment. It manages the issue of Government stock and pays out the

1 *Radcliffe Report on the Working of the Monetary System*, H. M. Stationery Office, 1959.

dividends to stockholders. It manages the Exchange Equalisation Account, administers foreign exchange control, cooperates with the financial administrators of other sterling area countries and takes part in the work of the international financial institutions.

Long before the Bank was nationalised, its instructions to the printers to print banknotes and to the Royal Mint on Tower Hill to manufacture silver and copper coins were made only on Government orders. Until 1939, although Britain had already gone off the gold standard, the amount of gold bullion in the Bank vaults was still equivalent to one-third of the value of the currency issued. There is not, at today's valuation of gold, enough of it in the world to balance the enormous sums of money which are now involved in international finance. Notes have taken its place and the number of notes issued must still be related to the amount of money in the Bank, even though that money is now in the form of securities.

Money is sometimes cheap, sometimes dear. These fluctuations are levelled out by the monetary control which regulates the flow of money through the numerous channels of commerce, from the producers to the buyers, distributors and retail customers. It must be kept at a regular rhythm and prices must be at a level at which all are receiving sufficient reward to enable them to carry on their businesses.

If people are spending according to this rhythm the wheels of the financial machine work smoothly. If a firm finds that its customers are not buying at the usual rate, either through shortage of money or a feeling of uncertainty about the future of the markets, it must contract its business, sell too cheaply, perhaps dismiss some of its staff, and the downward spiral of a slump begins.

The Government can check this tendency and put a greater amount of money into circulation by allowing the banks to lend more and to buy securities from customers. This has the double effect of giving customers more money in their pockets and raising the level of the amount of money in the banks, so that they become willing lenders and buyers of securities and bills of exchange. Raising money from the bank becomes easier, money is cheap and trade booms.

If on the other hand money is flowing too freely it produces the condition of inflation. It leads to too much speculation, and foreigners, taking advantage of a low interest rate of borrowing, sell their English money and the value of the pound falls in the foreign exchange market. The remedy is to reverse the process. Loans are called in and money becomes more difficult and expensive to borrow.

The other method of controlling the flow of money is to raise or lower the Bank rate, which is the rate charged by the Bank of England for discounting bills, and is defined in the *Radcliffe Report* as the 'rate of interest payable on loans or rediscounts by the Discount Office . . . which may be more strictly defined as the minimum rate at which the Bank of England stands ready to lend at last resort to a discount house which has the privileges of access to the Discount Office of the Bank, either by rediscounting bills of approved quality or by lending against security of such bills of short-dated Government securities'.

Changes in the bank rate are decided by the Treasury and the Court of Directors of the Bank, and they affect the rates of interest in many other spheres, including that of interest on bank deposits, the interest on loans to customers and the rate at which one can borrow from a building society.

Of the great merchant bankers of the nineteenth century, the name of Nathan Rothschild is almost legendary. He came to England from Frankfurt in 1789, with a capital of £20,000, setting up business first in Manchester and then in the City of London: and by buying and selling on the stock exchange on a vast scale he was able to exercise a profound influence on the stock markets. His transactions were always surrounded by great secrecy, and with family connexions throughout Europe and brothers in Frankfurt, Naples, Vienna and Paris, he usually had the advantage of possessing news of important events likely to affect the stock markets a day or two before other financiers, and could buy or sell ahead of them.

As well as accepting bills of exchange, the merchant bankers did important business in raising loans for foreign governments, arranging through their international contacts for customers to produce the money, by buying bonds at specified rates of interest, the money being realisable after a defined number of years.

Baring's, who specialised in business with America, raised vast loans for the American and Canadian developments during the industrialisation years, as well as building the Trans-Caucasian railway for Russia and providing funds for commercial and industrial developments in China, South America, France, Germany, Belgium, Austria, Hungary, India, Iraq, Egypt, Italy, Japan, Portugal, South Africa and Turkey. Rothschild's raised the loan to the Government of £21 million to reimburse the slave owners in the British dominions when slavery was abolished. They floated the £16 million loan for Great Britain to enter the Crimean War.

Today the merchant bankers of the City are formed into an Acceptance House Committee and the bills they accept become such valuable items of financial exchange that each acceptance house has to satisfy the Bank of England, at frequent intervals, that its capital is adequate for the enormous responsibilities that it undertakes.

Just as the joint stock banks have to retain liquid assets, so must the acceptance houses, for they bear the ultimate responsibility for honouring the bills they accept. Though it is unlikely they would be called upon to do so in hard cash, the possibility is always there, and if they did not provide for it they would not be allowed to do business, any more than a Lloyd's underwriter might, until he had satisfied the committee that he was in a position to take his share of any liability.

The acceptance houses no longer handle all the bills of exchange which pass through London, as they once did, for the joint stock banks have entered the business themselves, but they handle a substantial proportion of them: and since the business of foreign loans has now almost ceased, although not entirely, they manage many of the loans floated in Britain to launch new companies and enterprises or to substantiate some take-over bid. In this role they are known as Issuing Houses, their function being to bring together those who need capital for a long period and those who are prepared to provide it as an investment. The issuing house will partly underwrite these loans, in collaboration with one of the insurance companies.

A gold-market is held every morning at Rothschild's bank, New Court, in St Swithin's Lane, where much of the vast South African output is offered: but the sale of gold is restricted because of the complications of international currency regulations, brought about by the fact that so many European countries, including Great Britain, have only a small proportion of their treasury funds matched by actual bullion. To steady the market, the value of British sterling has been pegged to that of the American dollar.

The bullion market is in the hands of four bullion brokers and two firms of refiners, one of which is Rothschild's. The Rothschild representative also acts on behalf of the Bank of England, being the intermediary between the Banks and the supplier, which is mainly the Reserve Bank of South Africa.

Bearing in mind how much they want, how much is available, and the limit between which the price of gold may rise and fall, the members of the market make their bids and suggest a figure, which has to be agreed by telephone with the Bank of England. Since 1968 there has also been an afternoon price-fix in American dollars.

Gold is a commodity which is actually handled in the market and the bullion merchants store it in vaults which would defy the ingenuity of the most dedicated safe-cracker. The main buyers today are Continental banks and Eastern merchants, who are notorious hoarders of gold, believing it to be still the best and safest investment.

The silver market is transacted at offices in Great Winchester Street by the same bullion brokers who handle the gold, the silver coming largely from Australia: and since 1885 there have been vast silver vaults in Chancery Lane.

The foreign exchange market is the most complicated of all the London financial markets, although there is no tangible market place, all the business being done by telephone. People from foreign countries may need sterling to pay for goods either here or in some other country willing to accept payment in sterling. London may need foreign currency to pay for goods either immediately or in three months' time, when the currency may be cheaper or dearer, due to political crises, trading conditions, floods, tempests, droughts and the usual marketing laws of supply and demand.

Nearly all the banks in the City deal in foreign exchange and are members of the foreign exchange market, as well as the foreign banks, whose main purpose for existence in the City is to finance the trade of their own countries through London.

Foreign exchange dealings were strictly controlled during the Second World War and are still controlled in Britain, the buying of foreign exchange being limited, in the main, to people needing it for trading purposes.

In the past, variations in the amount of trade between countries caused wide and disturbing fluctuations in currency values, and in order to steady the market governments had to step in and make large-scale sales or purchases of foreign currency, in order to adjust the exchange values. In 1932 the British government set up its Exchange Equalisation Account, to provide a fund, supplied from the Exchequer, to buy and sell foreign currencies, so that these excessive variations could be prevented, and many other countries have similar institutions. There is also the International Monetary Fund, to which most countries belong, each country having agreed not to alter the value of its currency without consulting the other members.

The insurance companies are able to circulate vast sums of money in the City. The British Insurance Association has 250 members, but by far the greatest amount of insurance business is in the hands of about 100 companies, the most important of which nearly all have their head offices or branch offices in the financial quarter of the City, near the banks, the issuing houses and the Stock Exchange.

They invest about one-third of their funds in Government guaranteed securities and about one-fifth in ordinary stocks and shares. They figure largely in the underwriting of large loans arranged by the issuing houses and a substantial part of their funds is lent on mortgage to companies constructing and owning large blocks of offices, shops and flats, as well as to local councils.

The growth of the building societies during this century has been extraordinarily rapid. In order to exist they must obviously attract as much money in savings deposits as they pay out in loans, and the interest on loans must be slightly more than the interest on deposits, for the margin represents the money from which running expenses are paid and reserves accumulated.

The interest payable on a loan for a house tends to follow the bank rate, and when it rises the society may raise its interest rates, even within an existing contract.

The societies provide funds for two-thirds of the private building in the country and more than a quarter of the deposits of their investors are in small amounts of £2,000 or less.

The building societies originated in the Midlands and even today few of their offices are in London, but the vast sums which pass through their hands are put to work in the City, and the constant movement of their millions of funds, like those of the insurance companies and the Hire Purchase Finance House Association, have an important effect on the City markets.

16

The Century of Change

It was mainly to protect her interests in India that Great Britain allowed herself to be involved in the tragic and futile Crimean War, which achieved nothing, although it indicated the direction in which the alignment of the great powers might fall in future struggles to maintain the balance of power in Europe.

For the remaining years of the nineteenth century the City of London seemed to be at the peak of its prosperity. The country was exporting and importing more than ever before, the population was increasing rapidly, wages were low, but food was cheap and good, particularly in the City. There was terrible squalor and poverty behind the scenes, to which the country's social conscience was being slowly awakened, but the overall economy seemed to be working, and superficially times were good.

These were the days when you could feed well in the City for eightpence: and for those who could afford something better there was turtle soup to be had at the Ship and Turtle in Leadenhall Street, Joe's off Cornhill specialised in steaks and Williams' in the Old Bailey in boiled beef. Dolly's, off Paternoster Row, was a quiet and excellent chophouse. The Salutation in Newgate Street served a three-course ordinary every day at 5 o'clock for 1s. 6d., which included beer, although you were expected to order other drinks as well.

The Three Tuns tavern at Billingsgate offered their fish ordinary at 1 p.m. and 4 p.m., which consisted of four different kinds of fish, besides meat and cheese, for 2s., with beer at 6d a pint and claret at 1s. 6d. a bottle, but this was 'for gentlemen only'.

In and around Fleet Street were the Rainbow, which was noted for its good wines, Dick's, the Mitre, the Cock, specialising in steaks and chops, and the Cheshire Cheese, the steak and chop-house which served its famous beefsteak pudding on Saturdays. The Lord Mayor's Pantry, opposite Bow Church in Cheapside, and the European Coffee House, facing the Mansion House, were reliable for good food and service.

The Cock, which had been on the north side of Fleet Street for over 300 years, where Number 201 now stands, was pulled down in 1886 and the old sign moved to the other side of the Street. The Rainbow became an Espresso bar, but the Cheshire Cheese survives, nursing its tradition that Dr Johnson used to dine there, when he was living close by in Gough Square.

Crosby Hall in Bishopsgate had also become a restaurant. Before this time the beautiful medieval hall, which was all that was left of the great palace, had suffered a long period of decline, the final indignity coming when the ancient banqueting hall, still with its carved roof, its tall arched windows and oriel, and its marble floor, became a packer's warehouse: and when the packer's lease expired, it fell empty and became even more ruinous. By 1832 there were plans to demolish it, but at the last minute money was raised for its restoration. The City contributed and in 1836 the hall, with the original Bishopsgate Street entrance, was opened by the Lord Mayor, with a mayoral banquet, although the purpose for which the hall had been restored was not yet clearly defined. By 1842 it had been equipped as a Literary and Scientific Institute, with a library and reading room, where lectures were arranged for the young men of the City. For a time it was immensely popular, but the Institute did not pay its way and by 1860 the hall had become a wine merchant's storehouse. However, in 1867 another effort was made to save the hall. Again it was restored and this time it became a restaurant, well appointed, very comfortable and elegant and immensely popular for many years, and the headquarters of the Bishopsgate Ward Club.

It lasted until 1907, when the Bank of India having acquired the land on which it stood, it was at last decided, after much debate and protest, to move the hall to Chelsea, where it was rebuilt on the site of Sir Thomas More's old garden on the Embankment: and there it stands to this day, by now incorporated in the headquarters and hostel of the British Federation of University Women and forming the east side of their quadrangle.

With the disappearance of the coaching inns in the mid-century new hotels were established in the City, including the London Tavern in Bishopsgate and the Albion in Aldersgate Street, both of which were famous for their public dinners. Gerard's Hall Inn in Bread Street and the Bull and Mouth and the Castle and Falcon in St Martin's-le-Grand were still in business and there were a number of hotels near St Paul's Cathedral. The Cathedral Hotel offered dinner for 2s. and the Grand Café Restaurant de Paris on Ludgate Hill gave a table d'hôte dinner, with half a bottle of claret included, for 3s. 6d.

In 1874 De Keyser's Royal Hotel opened in New Bridge Street, Blackfriars. Sir Polydore de Keyser was a Belgian who had come to London as a waiter and became Lord Mayor: and his hotel, with 400 bedrooms, was very popular with foreign visitors. The *Baedeker* for 1879 says it was 'conducted in continental fashion, was well situated but somewhat expensive'; and here, as at hardly any other London hotel, foreign newspapers were provided. It was exclusive and, as at many of the West End hotels at this time, people had to have a personal introduction before they were given accommodation. It lasted until 1914, when it was taken over by the Royal Flying Corps and then by Lever Brothers, who later built Unilever House on the site.

Anderton's Hotel in Fleet Street was another popular City hotel in Victorian times, famous for its dinners and smoking concerts, and it survived until 1936, when it was demolished.

There were also the City clubs, including the City of London Club in Old Broad Street, the City Carlton Club at 24 St Swithin's Lane, the City Liberal Club in Walbrook and the Gresham Club in Gresham Place.

As early as 1851 *Murray's Handbook* says of the City that

> . . . this spot, teeming with its hundreds of thousands by day, its streets gorged to impassability by carriages, cabs and carts, presents at night, and still more on a Sunday, the spectacle of a deserted City. . . .
> The banks closed and the post gone, the railway carriage, the omnibus and the steam boat disperse like some centrifugal force those busy throngs of men – the clerks to the outskirts, the merchants and principals to their villas and mansions at the West End. . . .

There was in fact still quite a considerable resident population in the City at this time, with people living over their shops and businesses, although the decline was steady and travelling was made easier by the opening of the 'two-penny tube' from Shepherd's Bush to the Bank in 1900. By 1901 the number of residents was 27,000 and by 1931 it was down to 11,000, while today it is less than 4,250, the daytime population being about half a million.

As the resident population moved out to the suburbs, the City became a man's world until the last quarter of the nineteenth century, when women were first employed there. A report of the Headmistresses' Association read at Oxford in 1886 said that 'women bookkeepers were being employed in houses of business and there was an increasing demand for cashiers and clerks, while there was already a disposition on the part of bankers, accountants and stock-brokers to give preference to women clerks, many being already employed by the Prudential Assurance Company'.

The first typewriter appeared in 1873 and young women, with their new machines, began to take over from the copying clerks. Five years later the first public telephone exchange opened in London, and although as late as 1900 there were still only 10,000 telephones in the whole country, women were employed in the exchanges as well as at the post offices.

The first tea-shop had been opened in the Strand by the Aerated Bread Company in 1861 and had proved a boon to young women who were just beginning to enter the world of business: and in the following years, with the stream of typists, clerks and telephone girls increasing every year, dozens more tea-shops were opened in the City, where they could take their midday meal in modest seclusion, while the men continued to frequent the chophouses, clubs and pubs. And now the tea shops have given place to the coffee shops and snack bars.

The face of the City was changing. There is little left today of the sombre grey brick of the nineteenth-century City and even less of the warm red brick of Wren's London, after the Great Fire, but two splendid examples are Wren's Deanery in Dean's Court, to the south west of St Paul's, and the Chapter House in St Paul's Churchyard, to the north of the Cathedral. It was built by Wren in 1714, altered by the Victorians and badly damaged by bombs in 1941, but it has now been beautifully restored to Wren's original design.

The Temple precincts are not within the jurisdiction of the City but farther east, behind the modern façade of Fleet Street, there are dozens of little court-yards, alleys and passages which have survived from the eighteenth century and earlier, and Dr Johnson's house in Gough Square, off the north side of the street, still stands, a delightful seventeenth-century house, where, with the help of six assistants working in the attic, he compiled his dictionary.

It is particularly in the narrow winding lanes and passages which run down from Queen Victoria Street, Cannon Street and East Cheap to Upper and Lower Thames Street that Dickens' London lingers on – in Bull Wharf Lane, Vintners Place, St Botolph Lane and the tortuous little Lovat Lane where, hidden away but very much a living, active church, is the outstandingly beautiful St Mary-at-Hill, still with its box pews and sword rests, where Thomas à Becket is thought to have been curate and parts of which survived the Great Fire and were incorporated in Wren's rebuilding.

The Guildhall has become a strange mixture of architectural styles, for in 1789 George Dance the Younger gave it a new Gothic frontage which ill-matched the Classical wings. Between 1864 and 1884 Sir Horace Jones, the City architect, did a good deal of rebuilding and restoration and in 1909 the east wing was rebuilt, while after the bomb damage of the Second World War Sir Giles Gilbert Scott restored it yet again: but through all the changes the medieval porch of the gatehouse, with its fifteenth-century vaulting, a part of the Great Hall, which enshrines so much of the City's history, and the magnificent crypt have survived, and over the porch is the City coat-of-arms, the red cross of St George on a white field, with the sword of St Paul in the upper dexter quarter, the motto being *Domine dirige nos*.

K

The Royal Courts of Justice were moved from Westminster and established in the new Law Courts in the Strand, just outside the City boundary, built by Sir George Street in 1874, and four years later Wren's Temple Bar, replacing the old wooden gateway which had marked the boundary, was taken to Theobald's Park.

The building of Holborn Viaduct, to connect Holborn Circus with Newgate Street, high above Farringdon Street, the old valley of the Fleet river, was completed in 1869, and the same year Queen Victoria Street was cut through from Blackfriars Bridge to the Mansion House.

Tower Bridge, begun in 1885, was opened in 1894, the first bridge to be built below London Bridge and the river's only movable one. It was designed by Sir Horace Jones and Sir John Wolfe, the central span of the carriageway being composed of two drawbridges, each weighing about 1,000 tons, which are raised hydraulically to allow the passage of large vessels. The towers at either end of the bridge are also linked, near their summits, by a footway, high above the river and approached by lifts.

While the Tower Bridge was being built, Cecil Rhodes' envoys were negotiating with Lobengula, King of the Matabele, at his kraal at Bulawayo, to buy the mineral rights of the country between the Zambezi and Limpopo rivers. Hardly anything was known of the country by Europeans but traces of gold had been found and many thought this was the land of Ophir from which the Queen of Sheba had obtained her gold for Solomon.

There were many rivals in the field, including Boers, Germans and Portuguese, and when they learnt that Rhodes had been successful and the Chartered Company was being formed, they tried to persuade Lobengula not only that Rhodes did not represent Queen Victoria, the Great White Queen Over the Water, but that she did not even exist.

Lobengula thereupon sent two of his warriors to London to find out for themselves. The Queen received them and they were shown the sights of London and the City, which included a visit to the bullion vaults of the Bank of England. All doubts dispersed, the British pioneers set out from Kimberley in 1890 on the perilous and difficult six-month trek northwards, to stake their claims, and the country of Rhodesia was born, but they never found the land of Ophir and its fabulous gold.

At the end of the century, when the Boer War broke out, the City Imperial Volunteers were amongst the volunteers who achieved glory for their gallantry. The war went on far longer than anyone had expected and when the news of the relief of Mafeking reached London there was wild rejoicing in the City. Bankers and merchants, jobbers and brokers and their clerks flung away their Victorian top hats, linked arms and danced in the streets, and when the C.I.V.

were home again the Lord Mayor bestowed on all of them – 1,750 officers and men – the Freedom of the City.

During the last years of the nineteenth century and the early years of the twentieth, the famous London schools, St Paul's, Charterhouse, Christ's Hospital and the Merchant Taylors', were moved away from the City to the suburbs or the country, while the City of London School for Boys, established in 1835 in Milk Street, Cheapside, partly from the income derived from John Carpenter's bequest of the fifteenth century, was moved to the Embankment in 1885, where the girls' school was opened in 1894.

The terrible old Bridewell, which had begun as a refuge for destitute children, where they were to be trained for an apprenticeship, and had degenerated into a house of correction for prostitutes and criminals, was at last demolished and by 1855 the revenue from the Bridewell property was used for its original purpose, a general education for boys and girls. Their first school was opened at St George's Fields, and the name of Bridewell, with its horrible associations of public floggings, solitary confinement and the treadmill, which went on until the very end, was dropped. The boys were re-established at St George's School, Witley, Surrey in 1867 and the girls joined them there in 1952.

The Sheriffs' two debtors' prisons, the Compters of Wood Street and the Poultry, had gone by the beginning of the nineteenth century. The Fleet prison, rebuilt after the Gordon riots, was demolished in 1846 and the Memorial Hall of the Congregationalists built on the site, but Newgate prison, also rebuilt after the riots, was still standing at the end of the century, although public hangings were no longer held outside the prison after 1867. The prison came down in 1902, when the Central Criminal Court of Old Bailey was built on the site.

There were 74 parish churches in the City of London after the rebuilding of the seventeenth century, but as the resident population of the City decreased several disappeared and parishes were amalgamated. St Christopher-le-Stocks was pulled down in 1781, St Martin Ongar in 1824, St Michael, Crooked Lane, in 1830 and St Bartholomew-by-the-Exchange in 1841. By the 1920s 21 had been demolished, leaving only 53: and to the dismay of the City Corporation, the Bishop of London's Commission, with no reference to the Common Council, recommended the demolition of a further nineteen, and the sale of the freeholds, for they were regarded as the absolute property of the Church. But the Corporation argued that they were the gifts of wealthy citizens to the City. The matter was brought to the House of Commons and in 1926 the Corporation won its point. The plan for their demolition was condemned as nothing more than confiscation and they were saved.

The 1920s were difficult years for the City as well as for the whole country, the climax of 50 years of slow economic decline in relation to her world competitors. In late Victorian times Britain, with her great empire, seemed all-powerful. In every field of industry she appeared to be expanding. She was using more wool and cotton in her mills, producing more coal and pig-iron. By 1911 there were more miners in England than agricultural labourers and the merchant fleet was expanding. As wages rose, under justifiable pressure from the trade unions, more consumer goods were being sold and the retail trades were all prospering.

Nevertheless, after 1873, the overall commercial position began to show signs of a depression, as the value of exports slowly declined in relation to the imports, through foreign competition. It was no sudden collapse but a slow, insidious trend of which many people were not aware. America's output of coal gradually outpaced Great Britain's. Germany, after 1870, surpassed Great Britain's steel production and so did America, while Belgium, Bohemia, Silesia and France all became active competitors. America's cotton spinning was becoming more efficient and Germany was well ahead in the light chemical and dyeing industries.

At the turn of the century few people saw anything significant when Lancashire began exporting second-hand textile machinery to Japan, India, China and Europe, but by 1906 several million pounds' worth was being sent to the new manufacturing countries from Great Britain and students from India and Japan were arriving in the technical colleges, universities and night schools of the textile towns to study all aspects of the textile business.

By 1914 the inevitable competition was accepted in Britain but the general feeling was that she was more than holding her own. The serious economic troubles began after the Armistice. The Versailles Treaty had demanded enormous reparation from Germany, which she could pay only in manufacture and export at the expense of the Allies' own markets, and by borrowing heavily from the Allies in order to reorganise her industries. The Allies seized £100 million of German assets, but within a few years Germany was borrowing back £50 million, mainly from the United States and Great Britain.

Great Britain had lent millions of pounds to the Allies during the war and borrowed heavily from America. Now came the time for repayment to America and Great Britain and France began to press Germany for reparations. After the first payment, in 1921, the mark declined in value. The German economy almost collapsed and the French occupied the Ruhr, by way of compensation for no more payments. Germany was saved by a loan from America. The French withdrew from the Ruhr and by 1925 Germany was well on the way to recovery, but at the expense of British trade and commerce.

William Dibelius[1] was writing in 1930 of the 'post-war ascendancy of the

United States. It is the great gainer by the war, financially, industrially and politically. It has gathered in Europe's gold in payment for war supplies; it is the creditor of the States of Europe and takes ruthless political advantage of its financial superiority. . . . Financial power has further immensely increased American commerce; while British exports to all parts of the world have fallen, American have gone up. Where Germany has been driven from the field it has been to the advantage, not of Britain, but of America – and Japan. While American industry expands, British industry, in its vital sections (coal, cotton) contracts. America has become the greatest financial magnate in the world.'

During these post-war years British industrial and commercial concerns struggled to reassert themselves in the world markets and all too often found that others were there before them. By July 1921, there were more than two and a half million unemployed in Great Britain. In May 1926, the year that saw the end of the British Empire and the formation of the British Common-wealth of Nations, came the general strike, but it lasted for only nine days and settled nothing.

The depression in Britain deepened, as her markets were threatened by the expanding industries of America, Germany, Italy, Japan and the Dominions, and then came the world slump. It began in the United States, with the collapse of the money market on Wall Street. The effect was quickly felt in Europe. In Germany five million men were thrown out of work and in Britain the unemployment figure rose to nearly three million.

By 1931 Great Britain was off the gold standard and the pound was devalued, and then, in 1939 came the Second World War, with Japan an enemy this time instead of an ally. And as in the First World War, although technically the enemy lost, in practice and in the long term, they won in the economic field.

During the first ten years or so of the peace it was not apparent to many people in England. Prices were rising but so were wages and 1954 saw the begin-ning of the short-lived new prosperity. Trade boomed and Britain seemed to be establishing her overseas markets again. The shops were filled with things people had not seen for years. During the 'fifties the number of cars on the road doubled and there was an orgy of spending such as the country had never before known, helped by the facilities of the Hire Purchase firms. The national bill for hire purchase mounted from 725 million pounds in 1959 to 1,000 million pounds in 1964. Everywhere there was change – modernisation, rebuilding, reorganisation.

The City had suffered grievously from bomb damage. Nearly all its re-maining churches had been damaged and some were totally destroyed. Eleven

¹ William Dibelius, *England*, (Translated by M. A. Hamilton), Cape, 1930.

of them, of which seven were built by Wren, have never been rebuilt, but 39 remain, now beautifully restored and maintained, and the towers of ten others have been preserved.

St Paul's was carefully guarded by a voluntary team of fire-watchers all through the war. Nevertheless, it received a direct hit in 1941 which shattered the high altar and the north transept and broke much of the stained glass. The damage was repaired and the glass replaced by clear glass.

The greatest devastation was in the northern part of the City, a stretch of 62 acres between Aldersgate Street in the west and Moorgate in the east and from Gresham Street in the south to Fann Street in the north, near the City boundary, the area where the textile quarter of the City had been concentrated. Hardly anything was left after the fire of 29th December 1940 and the whole area had to be entirely rebuilt, as the Barbican development. Today it consists of multi-storey blocks of flats and offices, elevated pedestrian walks, warehouses, shops and restaurants. It has been planned with a commercial zone to the south and a residential and cultural area to the north. At a first glance it seems to be nothing but massed blocks of sombre grey concrete built into a vast and imposing three-dimensional maze, harsh and uncompromising, but it is relieved by unexpected courtyards at unpredictable levels, furnished with tubs of flowers and shrubs to give a measure of relief, as well as cafeterias and a pub, graced by the name of the Podium.

This area was once crossed by the street known as London Wall and today London Wall passes through eighteen-storey blocks of offices connected by elevated walks and over the remains of the Roman Cripplegate fort. It crosses Wood Street, where the tower of St Alban's church has been preserved: and Wood Street follows approximately the line of the Roman street which ran north to Fore Street, the site of the fortress. In the churchyard of St Alphage church, which is now a public garden, a section of the wall is preserved, showing the Roman foundations, with medieval foundations above it: and opposite the garden, in the midst of the towering office blocks, still stand the fourteenth-century tower and porch and the crypt of the chapel of Elsing Spital.

The Cripplegate itself seems to have been at the junction of Fore Street and Wood Street and close by, in Fore Street, is the only church in the Barbican, St Giles, Cripplegate, where John Milton was buried. The church was rebuilt in 1545, largely restored in the nineteenth century, and again after the German bombing of 1940.

In the south-west corner of its churchyard is a large bastion of the City wall and to the south two more bastions were revealed by the bombing, the wall connecting them, and that skirting St Alphage's churchyard, being part of the boundary of the Roman fort.

To the north-west is the new building of the City of London School for Girls, which was completed in 1969, surrounded by new blocks of flats, and close by, in Aldersgate Street, is the splendid new Museum of London, housing all the collections from the Guildhall and the London Museums. Here only a quarter of a mile from St Paul's Cathedral the long story of London and its people is unfolded in dioramas, printed records, books, pictures, prints, models and exhibits, from prehistoric times to modern, a magnificent display, ranging from sculptures from the Temple of Mithras, Roman pottery and glass, bronze and terracotta figurines, toilet articles, leather sandals and gloves, to Saxon and medieval finds, including pilgrim signs and badges, jewellery, pottery and weapons. Later London exhibits include pottery and glass, glazed tiles, pipes, articles of dress, with some woollen Tudor caps, and eighteenth-century manacles from Newgate prison.

Within the last twenty years the face of the City has been transformed. The Rennies' London Bridge came down in 1968 and the new concrete London Bridge, designed by Harold King and Charles Brown, has taken its place. At Puddle Dock, to the east of Blackfriars Bridge, the Mermaid Theatre was opened in 1959, the first theatre the City has seen since the seventeenth century.

Little is left of the old days, apart from the Churches and the halls of the Livery Companies, the Guildhall, the Mansion House, the Royal Exchange and the Bank of England, and the new tower blocks of offices which are rising look brash and uncomely among the older mellowed buildings.

In 1954 the number of parishes in the City was reduced from 108 to 24 and fifteen churches were designated Guild Churches, with specific functions, St Lawrence Jewry becoming the official church of the City Corporation and here the Spital Sermon is now given each year on the second Wednesday after Easter, before the Lord Mayor and Aldermen. Despite all the alteration and rebuilding, the churches remain full of memories, and although they are not all open for worship on Sundays, some are and many have weekday services and are active, living communities, doing invaluable work. St Ethelburga's in Bishopsgate, probably a Saxon foundation, is where Henry Hudson made his Communion before setting out in 1607 to search for the North-West Passage. St Giles, Cripplegate, is where Oliver Cromwell was married and many illustrious men, besides John Milton, were buried, including Sir Martin Frobisher. In St Helen's, Bishopsgate, are the table-tombs of Sir John Crosby and his first wife and of Sir Thomas Gresham. St James' Garlickhythe, on Garlick Hill, close to where garlick was sold at the riverside market, and now in the midst of the fur quarter, still has its hat racks and sword rests and much of the seventeenth-century woodwork, including the panelling, the communion table, the churchwardens' seats and the font cover, has survived. St Katherine

Creechurch in Leadenhall Street has its early sixteenth-century tower and it
seventeenth-century plaster ceiling, embossed with the arms of the Chie
Livery Companies, as well as its monument to Sir Nicholas Throckmortor
after whom Throgmorton Street was named. Before the Great Fire and th
rebuilding by Wren, Miles Coverdale was rector of St Magnus the Martyr, i
Lower Thames Street, and was buried here. St Margaret Lothbury has mag
nificently carved woodwork, some of which is attributed to Grinling Gibbon.
St Margaret Pattens, in East Cheap, with its two canopied pews and its alabaste
font, was once the patten-maker's church. The west wall of St Martin-withir
Ludgate is part of the old City wall. St Mary Abchurch in Cannon Street ha
a Grinling Gibbons reredos and panelled box pews. St Mary Aldermary, i
Queen Victoria Street, is one of the few churches which Wren rebuilt in th
original Gothic style, in accordance with the terms of the bequest made b
Henry Rogers for its rebuilding after the Great Fire. At St Mary-le-Bow i
Cheapside, with its beautiful campanile and spire, surmounted by the griffi
weathervane, and its early Norman crypt, the Court of Arches is still hel
for hearing cases of ecclesiastical law and confirming the election o
bishops.

St Mary-at-Hill, hidden away in Lovat Lane off Cheapside, still with it
seventeenth-century box pews, has some outstandingly fine wood carving
St Mary Woolnoth in Lombard Street, where John Newton preached to h
fashionable congregation against the evils of the slave trade, is a Nichola
Hawksmoor church: and in the south wall is a memorial to Edward Lloyc
St Michael's, Cornhill, is a Wren church to which Hawksmoor added a Goth
tower, and it was largely restored by Sir George Gilbert Scott in the mid-nine
teenth century. Close by is St Peter's, Cornhill, another Wren church with
brick tower and some splendid panelling and carved woodwork. St Micha
Paternoster Royal in College Street, derives part of its name from the pate
nosters and rosaries which were once made in this corner of the City and th
last part from the fact that the market for Bordeaux wines from the distri
of La Réole was on the wharf close by. Sir Richard Whittington was buried i
the old church which stood here before the Great Fire, for he lived close b
on College Hill. St Nicholas, Cole Abbey, in Queen Victoria Street, near th
College of Arms, still has some of its seventeenth-century woodwork, despi
all the war damage. The original name was Cold Abbey, probably derived fror
Cold Harbour, meaning a shelter for travellers. St Olave, Hart Street, off Fer
church Street, with its twelfth-century crypt, was terribly damaged in 19
but has been restored. This was the church where Samuel Pepys and his wi
worshipped and were buried: and the bust of Elizabeth, which Pepys placed i
the church after her death, is still there.

The Holy Sepulchre Church at the eastern end of Holborn Viaduct, opposite the Old Bailey, is one of the largest of the City churches, a Crusader foundation, rebuilt and restored a great deal throughout the centuries, although the tower and the three-storeyed, fan-vaulted porch have survived.

Early in the seventeenth century John Dowe, citizen and merchant taylor of London, gave £50 to the church on condition that 'after the several sessions of London, on the night before the execution of such as were condemned to death, the clerk of the church was to go in the night-time, and also early in the morning, to the window of the prison in which they were lying'. He was there to ring 'certain tolls with a handbell appointed for the purpose, and afterwards, in a most Christian manner, to put them in mind of their present condition and approaching end, and to exhort them to be prepared, as they ought to be, to die'.

The bell is still preserved in the Church. As the death cart passed it the following morning, on its way to Tyburn, the clerk stood waiting to ring it again and offer prayers, and each criminal was presented with a nosegay, one of the last being Sixteen-String Jack, the highwayman, who stuck it in the buttonhole of his pea-green jacket.

Roger Ascham, the Elizabethan schoolmaster, was buried here and also Captain John Smith, the Governor of Virginia whom Pocahontas rescued after his capture by her fellow Indians.

It is also the burial place of Sir Henry Wood, and in 1955 the north chapel was dedicated as the musicians' memorial chapel, a special service being held here on St Cecilia's day.

St Stephen, Walbrook, just behind the Mansion House, where Sir John Vanbrugh was buried, is one of Wren's most beautiful churches. The circular dome was destroyed by German bombing but has been finely restored and much of the seventeenth-century woodwork, including the font cover, pulpit and altar rails have survived.

St Vedast, Foster Lane, Cheapside, looking very small amongst the modern buildings which surround it, but wearing an air of venerable distinction, was rebuilt by Wren, mutilated in 1940, but is now restored, and still has its steeple, its Renatus Harris organ and its seventeenth-century pulpit, attributed to Grinling Gibbons.

St Swithin's church in Cannon Street, a medieval church rebuilt by Wren, was so badly damaged during the Second World War that in 1962 it was demolished and the Bank of China built on the site. In the outer southern wall of the church had been set the London Stone, which had originally stood on the south side of the street, firmly fixed into the ground. Strype, writing in the seventeenth century, said:

This stone, before the Fire of London, was much worn away, and, as it were, but a stump remaining. But it is now, for the preservation of it, cased over with a new stone, handsomely wrought, cut hollow underneath, so as the old stone may be seen, the new one being over it, to shelter and defend the old venerable one.

And the ancient stone has been placed in the wall of the new Bank of China.

Today there are 84 Livery Companies in the City, representing in all some 10,000 liverymen, the Apothecaries – still an examining body in medicine and surgery – having the most, with more than 650, the Ironmongers the least, with less than 30. By 1939 only 35 Companies had City Halls, 17 were destroyed and 15 severely damaged by bombing. Today after rebuilding or restoration, there are 28, and, of these, the Apothecaries', the Fishmongers', the Goldsmiths', the Stationers' (which in 1933 became the Stationers' and Newspaper Makers' Company), the Skinners' and the Vintners' Halls are of outstanding distinction.

Several of the Companies are still very wealthy, using their money to maintain schools and further education. They devote large sums to charities, while some help the trades with which their names are associated.

In 1965 the new administrative district of Greater London was created, divided into 32 new London boroughs, each with its own mayor and council, and the old London County Council was superseded by the Greater London Council.

The City of London continues to be administered separately, by its own Lord Mayor and Corporation, at the same time enjoying the powers held by the other boroughs and having, like Westminster, two seats on the Greater London Council.

Within the square mile of the City the Lord Mayor still gives precedence to none except the sovereign of the realm. He is the chief magistrate of the City and his Court is held in the Mansion House. At the time of his election he is handed the City Purse, symbol of the City's treasury, and the Sceptre, which is the oldest and most important item of the City's regalia. It is a small mace, only eighteen inches long, with an engraved crystal shaft which is thought to be Anglo-Saxon, and a head and fillets of gold, set with pearls, sapphires and large, uncut rubies. The silver-gilt Great Mace, which he carries during the procession on Lord Mayor's Day, in his gorgeous coach, is early eighteenth century, and the Sword of State, which is laid across the Mace during the meetings of the Common Council, is late seventeenth century, while the Pearl Sword, with its pearl embroidered scabbard, and his chain of office, with its brilliants and rose diamonds, are Tudor.

His household comprises the Swordbearer, the Macebearer, the City Marshal and the principal clerk to the Mansion House justice room, the City Marshal being the man who was once, with his assistant marshals, responsible for keeping order in the City streets, but since 1829 the City has had its own police force. The City police are a separate body from the Metropolitan police. Their headquarters are in Jewry Street, off Poultry, and they are distinguished from them by their crested helmets and red and white armbands.

The chief officers of the Corporation are the Recorder, who is the Senior Law Officer and a Judge of the Central Criminal Court, and who presents the Lord Mayor to the Judges of the High Court on Lord Mayor's Day; the City Chamberlain, elected by the Livery, who is the treasurer in charge of the City's cash and also the keeper of the Roll of Freemen of the City; the Town or Common Clerk, versed in corporate law and procedure, who attends the Court of Aldermen and the Court of Common Council, advising, conducting and recording the business, and who is also the City's archivist; the Common Serjeant, junior judge to the Recorder, who also shares the work of the Mayor's and the City of London Court, whose appointment is in the hands of the Crown; the Comptroller and Vice-Chamberlain, a law officer and conveyancing solicitor in charge of the title deeds of the City's properties and of the rentals of the City and Bridge House estates; the Remembrancer, a law officer of the City Corporation who attends the Houses of Parliament when they are in session on behalf of the City, to guard its interests, whose ceremonial duties include the invitation and reception of officers of State and other distinguished guests at the annual Guildhall banquet and similar official occasions, and the organisation of the Lord Mayor's procession; the City Solicitor, who drafts the City's by-laws and prosecutes any who infringe them; the Secondary, who works for the Sheriffs, performing many of their duties for them, apart from the ceremonial functions; and the City Surveyor.

The Lord Mayor and the two Sheriffs preside over the Common Council, which still comprises 25 other aldermen, who are elected each year by the rate-payers, and the Common Councilmen, also elected annually, whose numbers were reduced in 1959 from 206 to 159; and the City is still divided into its 26 wards, each of which is under an alderman who is also a Justice of the Peace.

After the sovereign, it is mainly the Lord Mayor and Corporation who dispense hospitality to distinguished foreign guests, as well as Commonwealth and British guests especially deserving of honour, meeting the cost from their own estates and resources, for the City is still wealthy, owning, like the Livery Companies, a great deal of property, much of it within the square mile, which has greatly increased in value over the years.

On all ceremonial occasions the Lord Mayor's bodyguard is provided by a company of pike men and musketeers of the Honourable Artillery Company of the City of London, which is the oldest military body in Britain. The origins of the company, which served so well in both World Wars, is not certain, but it was incorporated by Henry VIII as the Guild and Fraternity of St George, and the officers of the City Train Bands were chosen from it. Milton, Wren and Pepys were all members of the HAC and it is now the senior regiment of the Army Volunteer Reserve, taking precedence after the regular army and enjoying the privilege of marching through the City with 'bayonets fixed, drums beating, and colours flying'.

The City today looks spruce and prosperous, with its new shopping precincts, its old taverns modernised, its beautifully maintained churches and civic buildings and the towering blocks of new offices overshadowing them all, but the rents of the new offices are high and many are empty, the firms who were formerly established here having moved out to the provinces, where rents are far less and offices less cramped.

After the false dawn of a new age of prosperity, during the 1950s, has come the grim reality of the present depression. The value of the pound has fallen disastrously and the country has become a heavy borrower from the International Monetary Fund.

The continuity of tradition in Britain has been disrupted and her people have been bombarded with propaganda of every shade of opinion from extreme Left to extreme Right, but in the City of London the traditions hold firm and it is still regarded as the money centre of the world.

Books consulted

ASHLEY, MAURICE, *Life in Stuart England*, London, Batsford, 1964

BAGLEY, J. J., *Life in Medieval England*, London, Batsford, 1960

BANKS, F. R., *Penguin Guide to London*, Harmondsworth, Penguin Books, 1971

BENHAM AND WELCH, *Medieval London*, London, Seeley & Co, 1901

BENN, JOHN, *Something in the City*, London, Allen & Unwin 1950

BESANT, WALTER, *London*, London, Chatto & Windus, 1910

BIRLEY, ANTHONY, *Life in Roman Britain*, London, Batsford, 1964

BRIGGS, ASA, *How They Lived Vol. III*, Oxford, Blackwell, 1969

BROOKE, CHRISTOPHER and KEIR, GILLIAN, *London 800–1216 – The Shaping of a City*, London, Secker & Warburg 1975

BRYANT, ARTHUR, *Makers of the Realm*, London, Collins, 1953

COLLINGWOOD, R. G. and RICHMOND, I., *The Archaeology of Roman Britain*, London, Methuen, 1969

DIBELIUS, WILHELM, *England*, London, Cape, 1930

FERRIS, PAUL, *The City*, London, Gollancz, 1960

GOSS, CHARLES, *Crosby Hall*, London, Crowther & Goodman, 1908

GREEN, J. R., *A Short History of the English People*, London, Macmillan, 1921

HARPER, C. G., *Old Inns of Old England*, London, Chapman & Hall, 1906

HARPER, C. G., *The City of London Guide*, London, E. J. Burrow & Co., 1938

HOBSON, OSCAR, *How the City Works*, News Chronicle, 1959

JOHNSON, DAVID, *Southwark and the City*, London, O.U.P., 1969

LAWSON, W. J., *History of Banking*, London, Bentley, 1850

LEYN, HENRY, *The Norman Conquest*, London, Hutchinson, 1965

LOFTIE, W. J., *London City*, London, Leadenhall Press, 1891

MARÉ, ERIC DE, *London's Riverside*, London, Max Reinhardt, 1958

MERRIFIELD, RALPH, *The Roman City of London*, London, Benn, 1965

MERRIFIELD, RALPH, *Roman London*, London, Cassell, 1969

MITCHELL, R. J., and LEYS, M. D. R., *A History of London Life*, London, Longmans, 1958

MORITZ, C. P., *Travels in England in 1782*, London, Humphrey Milford, 1924

MURRAY'S HANDBOOK, *Modern London, 1851*, London, John Murray, 1851

PAGE, R. L., *Life in Anglo-Saxon England*, London, Batsford, 1970

PASSINGHAM, W. J., *London's Markets*, London, Sampson Low, 1935

PEPYS, SAMUEL, *Diary*

POOLEY, ERNEST, *The Guilds of the City of London*, London, Collins, 1945

POWER, EILEEN, *The Wool Trade in Medieval History*, London, O.U.P. 1941

POWICKE, MAURICE, *Medieval England*, London, Oxford Paperbacks, 1969

PRICE, F. G. HILTON, *Handbook of London Bankers*, London, Chatto & Windus, 1876

PRICE, F. G. HILTON, *Temple Bar*, London and Midland Archaeological Soc., 1875

REDDAWAY, T. F., *The Rebuilding of London after the Great Fire*, London, Cape, 1940

ROBINSON, E. F., *Early History of Coffee Houses in England*, London, Kegan Paul, 1893

RUDÉ, GEORGE, *Hanoverian London*, London, Secker & Warburg, 1971

SAUSSURE, CÉSAR DE, *A Foreign View of England in the Reigns of George I and George II*, London, John Murray, 1902

STENTON, D. M., *English Society in the Early Middle Ages – 1066–1307*, Harmondsworth, Penguin, 1962

STOW, JOHN, *Survey of London*, London, 1603

THOMSON, G. SCOTT, *Wool Merchants of the 15th Century*, London, Longmans, 1958

THOMSON, G. SCOTT, *Life in a Noble Household*, London, Cape, 1937

THOMSON, G. SCOTT, *The Russells in Bloomsbury*, London, Cape, 1940

TREVELYAN, G. M., *English Social History*, London, Longmans, 1942

WALFORD, EDWARD, *Old and New London*, London, Cassell, 1890

WARD, NED, *The London Spy*, London, Cassell, 1927

WHITE, J. G., *History of Walbrook Ward*, London, 1904 (private circulation)

Index

D*